T0250718

Lecture Notes in Artificial Intelligence (LNAI)

Vol. 345: R.T. Nossum (Ed.), Advanced Topics in Artificial Intelligence. VII, 233 pages. 1988.

Vol. 346: M. Reinfrank, J. de Kleer, M.L. Ginsberg, E. Sandewall (Eds.), Non-Monotonic Reasoning. Proceedings, 1988. XIV, 237 pages. 1989.

Vol. 347: K. Morik (Ed.), Knowledge Representation and Organization in Machine Learning. XV, 319 pages. 1989.

Other volumes of the Lecture Notes in Computer Science relevant to Artificial Intelligence:

Vol. 203: B. Buchberger (Ed.), EUROCAL '85. Proceedings Vol. 1, 1985. V, 233 pages. 1985.

Vol. 204: B.F. Caviness (Ed.), EUROCAL '85. Proceedings Vol. 2, 1985. XVI, 650 pages. 1985.

Vol. 221: E. Wada (Ed.), Logic Programming '85. Proceedings, 1985. IX, 311 pages. 1986.

Vol. 225: E. Shapiro (Ed.), Third International Conference on Logic Programming. Proceedings, 1986. IX, 720 pages. 1986.

Vol. 230: J.H. Siekmann (Ed.), 8th International Conference on Automated Deduction. Proceedings, 1986. X, 708 pages. 1986.

Vol. 231: R. Hausser, NEWCAT: Parsing Natural Language Using Left-Associative Grammar. II, 540 pages. 1986.

Vol. 238: L. Naish, Negation and Control in Prolog. IX, 119 pages. 1986.

Vol. 256: P. Lescanne (Ed.), Rewriting Techniques and Applications. Proceedings, 1987. VI, 285 pages. 1987.

Vol. 264: E. Wada (Ed.), Logic Programming '86. Proceedings, 1986. VI, 179 pages. 1987.

Vol. 271: D. Snyers, A. Thayse, From Logic Design to Logic Programming. IV, 125 pages. 1987.

Vol. 286: B. Bouchon, R.R. Yager (Eds.), Uncertainty in Knowledge-Based Systems. Proceedings, 1986. VII, 405 pages. 1987.

Vol. 301: J. Kittler (Ed.), Pattern Recognition. Proceedings, 1988. VII, 668 pages. 1988.

Vol. 306: M. Boscarol, L. Carlucci Aiello, G. Levi (Eds.), Foundations of Logic and Functional Programming. Proceedings, 1986. V, 218 pages. 1988.

Vol. 308: S. Kaplan, J.-P. Jouannaud (Eds.), Conditional Term Rewriting Systems. Proceedings, 1987. VI, 278 pages. 1988.

Vol. 310: E. Lusk, R. Overbeek (Eds.), 9th International Conference on Automated Deduction. Proceedings, 1988. X, 775 pages. 1988.

Vol. 313: B. Bouchon, L. Saitta, R.R. Yager (Eds.), Uncertainty and Intelligent Systems. IPMU '88. Proceedings, 1988. VIII, 408 pages. 1988.

Vol. 315: K. Furukawa, H. Tanaka, T. Fujisaki (Eds.), Logic Programming '87. Proceedings, 1987. VI, 327 pages. 1988.

Vol. 320: A. Blaser (Ed.), Natural Language at the Computer. Proceedings, 1988. III, 176 pages. 1988.

Lecture Notes in Artificial Intelligence

Subseries of Lecture Notes in Computer Science
Edited by J. Siekmann

Lecture Notes in Computer Science

Edited by G. Goos and J. Hartmanis

Editorial

Artificial Intelligence has become a major discipline under the roof of Computer Science. This is also reflected by a growing number of titles devoted to this fast developing field to be published in our Lecture Notes in Computer Science. To make these volumes immediately visible we have decided to distinguish them by a special cover as Lecture Notes in Artificial Intelligence, constituting a subseries of the Lecture Notes in Computer Science. This subseries is edited by an Editorial Board of experts from all areas of AI, chaired by Jörg Siekmann, who are looking forward to consider further AI monographs and proceedings of high scientific quality for publication.

We hope that the constitution of this subseries will be well accepted by the audience of the Lecture Notes in Computer Science, and we feel confident that the subseries will be recognized as an outstanding opportunity for publication by authors and editors of the AI community.

Editors and publisher

Lecture Notes in Artificial Intelligence

Subseries of Lecture Notes in Computer Science

Edited by J. Siekmann

345

Rolf T. Nossum (Ed.)

Advanced Topics in Artificial Intelligence

2nd Advanced Course, ACAI '87
Oslo, Norway, July 28 – August 7, 1987

Springer-Verlag
Berlin Heidelberg New York London Paris Tokyo

Editor

Rolf T. Nossum
Oslo College of Engineering
Cort Adelers gate 30, N-0254 Oslo 2, Norway

2nd Advanced Course in Artificial Intelligence, ACAI '87

Organizer

European Coordinating Committee for AI (ECCAI)

CR Subject Classification (1987): I.2.1, I.2.3–4, I.2.6–7

ISBN 3-540-50676-4 Springer-Verlag Berlin Heidelberg New York
ISBN 0-387-50676-4 Springer-Verlag New York Berlin Heidelberg

Printing and binding: Druckhaus Beltz, Hemsbach/Bergstr.
2145/3140-543210

PREFACE

Artificial Intelligence being a rapidly developing scientific field, there continually exists a need for rapidly disseminating its latest advances to students and practitioners.

Conferences and conference proceedings are a relatively rapid communication channel, but often the quality of the material presented in them is variable, and the style of presentation quite demanding.

The biennial Advanced Courses in Artifical Intelligence, organized under the auspices of ECCAI, the European Coordinating Committee for Artificial Intelligence, provide a forum for communicating the latest results of the field. World-class AI scientists are invited to lecture, and are asked to provide written accounts of their lectures for publication. The present volume draws on the material presented at the second Advanced Course, which was held in Oslo, Norway, in July 1987.

In contrast to the first Advanced Course, reported as Springer Lecture Notes in Computer Science vol. 232, which covered the foundations of AI extensively, the second Advanced Course emphasized in-depth treatment of a selection of special topics in AI. Inevitably, the course also contained reports on advances in some of the same areas as were covered in the first course.

Philippe Jorrand's chapter gives a unified view of computational mechanisms based on syntactic manipulation of algebraic terms. Dis- and anti-unification are introduced, and their significance explained by way of examples. Term rewriting systems, functional programming systems, and logic programming systems arise as instances of a common computational foundation.

The chapter by Wolfgang Bibel contains new material on enhancements of matrix-based automated deduction, and tells of recent research on how it extends to non-standard logics. A case is made that matrix-based deduction is particularly amenable to this kind of extension.

In the chapter on Qualitative Reasoning, Tony Cohn surveys the state of the art of this important and rapidly developing field as it appears in the summer of 1987.

The chapter on Knowledge Acquisition, by Bob Wielinga and his co-workers, focuses on a major bottleneck in the practical deployment of AI in the form of Expert Systems. It contains a comprehensive overview of elicitation techniques in use today, and stresses those that result in formal specification of knowledge bases.

Alan Biermann's chapter on Learning Systems presents a unified framework for classifying such systems. The reader may wish to refer to his chapter in vol. 232 of the Springer Lecture Notes in Computer Science for background material.

Sam Steel gives an up-to-date and in-depth treatment of the essential Topics in Planning, in the chapter so named.

The chapter on Natural Language Systems by Jens Erik Fenstad gives insight into the situational semantics approach. The reader will appreciate the relationship with other branches of AI, for instance, with AI planning, and the plan-based theory of action, both of which, like situational semantics, appear to owe much to a logical framework laid in the 60s by McCarthy.

Springer-Verlag deserve a special word of acknowledgement for recognizing the value of the material contained in this volume, and offering their very efficient publishing services. This adds to the feeling of satisfaction that comes from organizing an event like the Advanced Course in Artificial Intelligence.

Rolf Nossum, Oslo.

CONTENTS

FUNDAMENTAL MECHANISMS FOR ARTIFICIAL INTELLIGENCE PROGRAMMING LANGUAGES

- AN INTRODUCTION -

Philippe Jorrand

LIFIA
INPG-CNRS
46, avenue Félix Viallet
38000 GRENOBLE
FRANCE

I. INTRODUCTION

Artificial intelligence is not computer science. But computers are essential tools for research in artficial intelligence. Computers are the kind of machinery which is best fitted for mechanizing the various models for perception, reasoning, learning and control of action which are relevant to artificial intelligence.

Most artificial intelligence programs are quite complex objects and mastering the complexity of their design is a major research objective which lies at the intersection of computer science and artificial intelligence. Progress in that domain relies both on experience and on theory.

The material presented in this chapter is an introduction to the fundamental mechanisms of artificial intelligence languages and architectures. These mechanisms and the objects they involve are most of the time presented quite formally. The use of appropriate formalisms is indeed the price to pay for mastering complexity : without it, the relevant and useful properties cannot be clearly isolated nor properly used.

II. TERMS AND BASIC OPERATIONS ON TERMS

The notion of term for representing data objects, programs, computations and proofs constitutes the most primitive layer for the notions presented in this chapter. On top of it, all other mechanisms will be constructed. The material in this section is mostly drawn from [Huet 85].

II.1. Strings, trees and terms

II.1.1. Strings

Strings are well known objects. Let Σ be a countable set of objects called symbols : Σ is the alphabet with which strings will be constructed. A string u of length n on Σ is a function from $\{0,...,n-1\}$ into Σ : Σ^n is the set of all strings of length n on Σ. Let u_i denote the value of $u(i-1)$: $u_i \in \Sigma$.

Some classical notations for well understood notions :

- $\Sigma^* = \cup_{u \in N} \Sigma^n$ is the set of all strings

- Λ denotes the null string : $\Lambda \in \Sigma^0$

- $'a'$ denotes $u \in \Sigma^1$, when $u_1 = a$, for $a \in \Sigma$
- u^v denotes the concatenation of u and v
- $'abc' = 'a'\text{^}'b'\text{^}'c'$, where $a, b, c \in \Sigma$
- $u.a = u\text{^}'a'$, where $u \in \Sigma^*$, $a \in \Sigma$.
- $u \leq v$ (u "is a prefix of" v) iff $\exists\, w$ such that $v = u\text{^}w$

II.1.2. Trees

A tree has a structure and has pieces of information attached to its nodes and leaves. The structure of a tree will be represented by a set of strings on positive integers, called "positions", which enumerate in a "logical" way the nodes and leaves. Such a set of positions is called a tree domain. The information attached to nodes and leaves will be symbols from some alphabet Σ.

Thus, given N_+, the set of positive integers, $N_+{}^*$ is the set of all positions. Given a position $u = w.m$ and a position $v = w.n$, if $m<n$, u is said to be " left of" v : $u <_L v$. Then, a tree domain D is a subset of $N_+{}^*$ which is closed under both the prefix and the "left of" orderings :

- $u \in D \wedge v < u \Rightarrow v \in D$
- $u \in D \wedge v <_L u \Rightarrow v \in D$

Clearly, Λ belongs to every non empty tree domain and is the position of the root of trees. For example, the set of positions $\{\Lambda, '1', '11', '12', '121', '122', '123', '2', '21', '3'\}$ is a tree domain which represents the following structure :

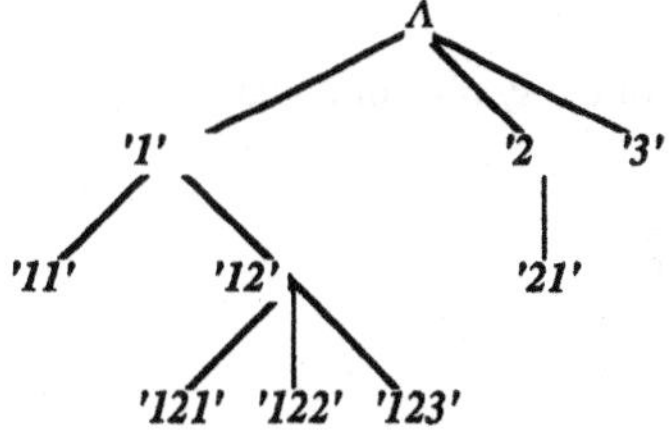

Finally, attaching information (i.e. symbols in Σ) to the nodes and leaves is done by defining a tree M as a function from its domain D into Σ. M is then called a Σ-tree : $M \in D \rightarrow \Sigma$. Given an arbitrary Σ-tree M, its domain is refered to by $D(M)$.

II.1.3. Operations on trees

Let M be a Σ-tree and u be a position in its domain $D(M)$. Two basic operations are defined on such trees : access to the subtree rooted at position u in M and grafting of a new subtree at position u in M.

The subtree rooted at position u in M is denoted by M/u. It is of course also a Σ-tree :

$$(M/u)(v) = M(u^\wedge v)$$

Given a Σ-tree N, the tree obtained by grafting N at position u in M is denoted by $M[u \leftarrow N]$. This tree is the same as M, except that the subtree which was rooted at position u in M is replaced by N in $M[u \leftarrow N]$. This tree is also a Σ-tree :

$$v \in D(M) \wedge \neg(u \leq v) \;\Rightarrow\; M[u \leftarrow N] = M(v)$$

$$w \in D(N) \wedge v = u^\wedge w \;\Rightarrow\; M[u \leftarrow N](v) = N(w)$$

II.1.4. Terms

Let M be a Σ-tree. The top-width of M is $//M// = max\{\mathbf{n} \,/\, '\mathbf{n}' \in D(M)\}$, i.e. the number of subtrees directly descending under the root of M. On alphabet Σ, a function α into the integers N, called arity function, is defined : $\alpha \in \Sigma \rightarrow N$. An alphabet with an arity function is called a graded alphabet. A Σ-term is then a Σ-tree on a graded alphabet Σ, such that the number of subtrees directly descending from every node is equal to the arity of the symbol of Σ attached to that node :

$$M \text{ is a } \Sigma\text{-term} \;\Leftrightarrow\; \forall u \in D(M) \;\; //M/u// = \alpha(M(u))$$

The set of all Σ-terms is denoted by $T(\Sigma)$. The usual parenthesized syntax for terms is defined as follows: given $F \in \Sigma$, with $\alpha(F) = n$, and $M_1, \ldots, M_n \in T(\Sigma)$, then $F(M_1, \ldots, M_n) \in T(\Sigma)$.

II.2. Variables and substitutions

II.2.1. Terms with variables

Let V be a countable set of objects called variables, disjoint from $\Sigma : V \cap \Sigma = \varnothing$, and such that the arity of all variables is 0 : $\forall x \in V,\ \alpha(x) = 0$. Variables of V can be attached to positions of terms, as is already the case for symbols of Σ. Since their arity is 0, they will always appear on leaves of terms. The set of terms with variables is denoted by $T(\Sigma,V)$ and is equal to $T(\Sigma \cup V)$.

Let M be a term on Σ and V : $M \in T(\Sigma,V)$. The set of distinct variables which occur in M is :

$$V(M) = \{x \in V \mid \exists u \in D(M),\ M(u)=x\}$$

The number of distinct variables in M is denoted by $v(M) = |V(M)|$.

II.2.2. Substitutions

As is usual in the description of computations, the purpose of variables is to be replaced by values. Here, the considered values are terms : terms can be substituted for variables in $M \in T(\Sigma,V)$. Thus, some of the leaves of M to which variables are attached will be replaced by terms. Technically, this is achieved by grafting these terms at the corresponding leaf positions in M.

The elementary form of a substitution σ is a function from the set V of variables into the set $T(\Sigma,V)$ of terms, $\sigma \in V \rightarrow T(\Sigma,V)$, and is the identity almost everywhere. The domain of a substitution σ is the set of variables where σ is not the identity :

$$D(\sigma) = \{x \in V \mid \sigma(x) \neq x\}$$

In practice, substitutions are not simply applied to variables, but are applied to terms : for performing a substitution σ on the leaves of terms of the form $F(M_1, ..., M_n)$, σ is extended to a morphism over the set of terms $T(\Sigma,V)$:

$$\sigma(F(M_1, ..., M_n)) = F(\sigma(M_1), ..., \sigma(M_n))$$

If there are several occurrences of variable x, they will all be replaced by the same term $\sigma(x)$.

II.3. The domain of terms

II.3.1. Ordering among terms in $T(\Sigma,V)$

Let M and N be two terms in $T(\Sigma,V)$. M is said to be "less instanciated" than N iff N can be obtained from M by substituting terms for some of the variables in M :

$$M \leq N \Leftrightarrow \exists \sigma, N = \sigma(M)$$

This relation is also read "N is an instance of M".

For example, with $M = F(G(x,a),y)$ and $N = F(G(H(b),a),y)$, $M \leq N$ since $N = \sigma(M)$ with $\sigma(x)=H(b)$. If $N = F(G(u,a),v)$, it would still be the case that $M \leq N$. But, in this situation, N has exactly the same structure as M and differs from M only by a consistent renaming of its variables. As a consequence, with the inverse substitution, it would also be the case that $N \leq M$. The relation defined above is thus a quasi ordering, since its is not anti reflexive : both $M \leq N$ and $N \leq M$ can hold, while M and N are different terms. Such bijective substitutions (i.e. consistent renamings of variables) are called permutations. Two terms are said to be isomorphic if one of them can be obtained from the other by a permutation :

$$\forall M, N \in T(\Sigma,V), M \equiv N \Leftrightarrow M = \sigma(N) \text{ for some permutation } \sigma$$
$$\Leftrightarrow M \leq N \wedge N \leq M$$

II.3.2. Properties of the ordering in $T(\Sigma,V)$

The strict ordering ">", defined as

$$M > N \Leftrightarrow N \leq M \wedge \neg(M \leq N)$$

is a well founded ordering. This is easy to see, using the size $|M|$ of finite terms :

$$|M| = |F(M_1, ..., M_n)| = 1 + \textstyle\sum_{i=1..n} |M_i|$$

Then, with $\mu(M) = |M| - \nu(M)$:

$$M > N \Rightarrow \mu(M) > \mu(N)$$

Thus, there is no infinite descending chain $M_1 > M_2 > \ldots$.

II.3.3. Terms form a complete lattice

Given two terms M and N in $T(\Sigma,V)$, it is always possible to find a term $M \cap N$ which is the most instanciated term such that both $M \cap N \leq M$ and $M \cap N \leq N$ hold. The term $M \cap N$ is then a greatest lower bound (g.l.b.) of M and N. This term is unique, up to the isomorphism $\equiv$.

For example, given $M = \boldsymbol{F(G(x,a),H(b))}$ and $N = \boldsymbol{F(G(y,c),d)}$, the term $M \cap N$ would be isomorphic to $\boldsymbol{F}(\boldsymbol{G}(u,v),w)$. A general definition of this operation "$\cap$" in $T(\Sigma,V)$ is as follows :

$$F(M_1, \ldots, M_n) \cap F(N_1, \ldots, N_n) \;=\; F(M_1 \cap N_1, \ldots, M_n \cap N_n)$$

$$M \cap N \;=\; \phi(M,N) \text{ in all other cases}$$

where ϕ is an arbitrary bijection which maps pairs of terms into variables :

$$\phi : T(\Sigma,V) \times T(\Sigma,V) \to V$$

For distinct ϕ, this definition of $M \cap N$ produces isomorphic results. The term $M \cap N$ is a g.l.b. of M and N under the ordering $\leq$. For identifying all isomorphic terms to a single object, the quotient of $T(\Sigma,V)$ by $\equiv$ is considered :

$$\mathbb{T}(\Sigma,V) \;=\; T(\Sigma,V) \,/\, \equiv$$

and this domain is completed by a top **T** (i.e. an element greater than all other elements). The domain $\mathbb{T}(\Sigma,V)$ is a complete lattice. It is easy to verify that the bottom of $\mathbb{T}(\Sigma,V)$ is $\perp = V$, the set of variables. Pictorially, $\mathbb{T}(\Sigma,V)$ can be represented as follows :

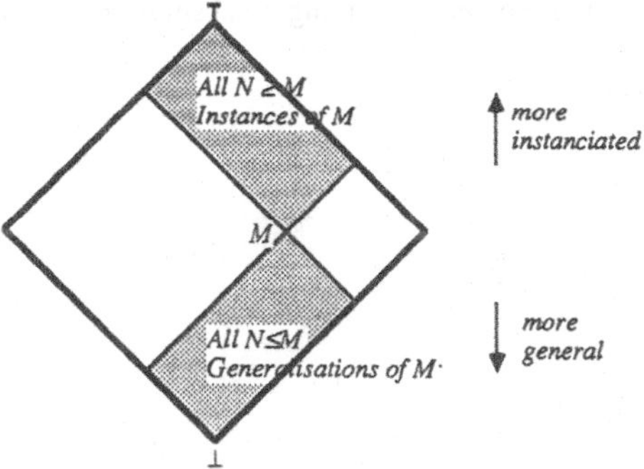

A term $\sigma(M)$ such that $V(\sigma(M)) = \varnothing$ is called a ground instance of M.

II.4. Term matching

Given two terms M and N in $T(\Sigma,V)$, N is said to match M iff N is an instance (but not necessarily a ground instance) of M, that is iff there exist a substitution σ such that $N = \sigma(M)$ (i.e. iff $M \leq N$). The problem of matching two terms is thus to find σ, if it exists, or tell that it does not exist when that is the case. In the lattice $\mathbb{T}(\Sigma,V)$, the existence of σ corresponds to the following situation :

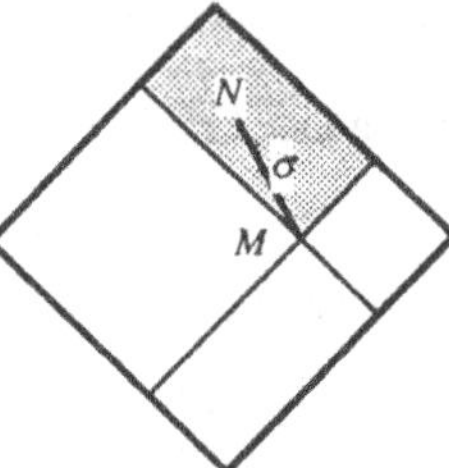

Term matching is used for term rewriting and in functional languages based on term rewriting.

II.5. Term unification

The domain $\mathbb{T}(\Sigma,V)$ is a complete lattice. As a consequence, if terms M and N have an upper bound (i.e. a common instance $\sigma(M) = \sigma'(N)$),then they have a least upper bound (l.u.b.). The l.u.b. of M and N is denoted by $M \cup N$ and it is unique up to isomorphism. $M \cup N$ is the less instanciated (or most general) common instance of M and N. Substitutions, as functions, can be composed. Given σ and σ' such that $\sigma(M) = \sigma'(N)$, there exist σ_0 , σ'_0 such that :

$$\sigma = \sigma_0 \bullet \tau \quad \text{and} \quad \sigma' = \sigma'_0 \bullet \tau$$

where τ is a substitution called a "most general unifier" of M and N : $\tau = m.g.u.\ (M,N)$. Thus, the problem of unifying M and N is the problem of finding a substitution $\tau = m.g.u.(M,N)$. Then, $\tau(M) \equiv \tau(N) \equiv M \cup N$. Pictorially :

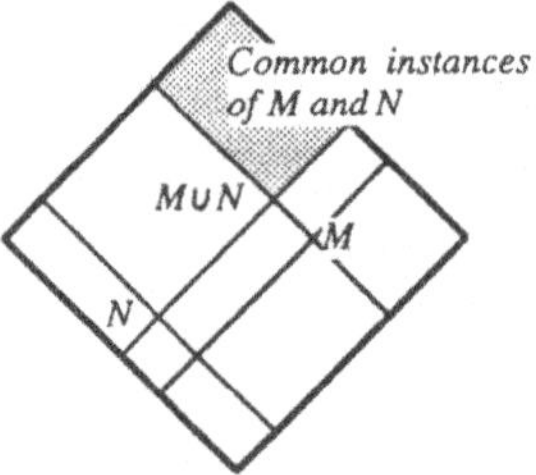

Unification is at the basis of logic programming and of "term narrowing" for solving equations.

Unification has a long history. The notion was first introduced by Herbrand, in 1930, in his thesis on "Recherches sur la théorie de la démonstration" [Herbrand 30], where he described an "algorithm" for solving equations over the "Herbrand Universe", another name for $\mathbb{T}(\Sigma,V)$. But its full significance was recognized by Robinson in 1965, where he showed a systematic treatment of terms for finding *m.g.u.*'s. Then, the theory of unification has been studied in depth and efficient algorithms have been discovered for computing *m.g.u.*'s [Huet 76, Paterson-Wegman 78, Martelli-Montanari 82, Colmerauer 84, Eder 84, Lassez 86, and many, many others].

II.6. Term anti-unification

Anti-unification is the dual problem of unification : given two terms M and N in $\mathbb{T}(\Sigma,V)$, find the most instanciated common generalization of M and N. This is finding the g.l.b. $M \cap N$, as already described in the definition of $\mathbb{T}(\Sigma,V)$. Pictorially, this can be viewed as follows :

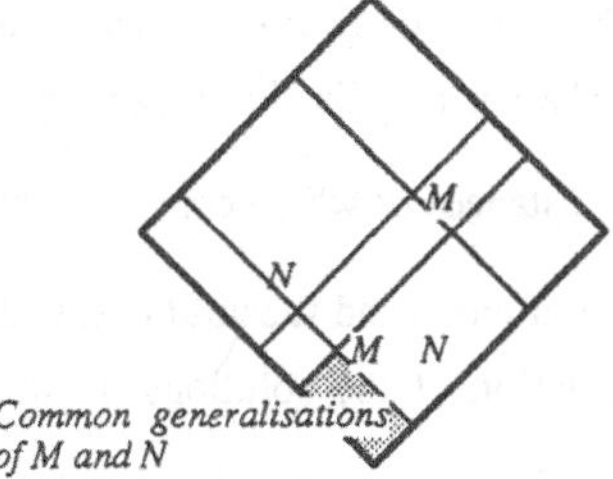

Anti-unification is used in inductive inference and in some approaches to automated learning in artificial intelligence [Plotkin 70, Reynolds 70, Plotkin 71, Vere 75]. See also [Lassez 86].

II.7. Term dis-unification

The problem of dis-unification is to find all substitutions σ and σ' such that $\sigma(M) \neq \sigma'(N)$, for M and N in $\mathbb{T}(\Sigma,V)$. Pictorially :

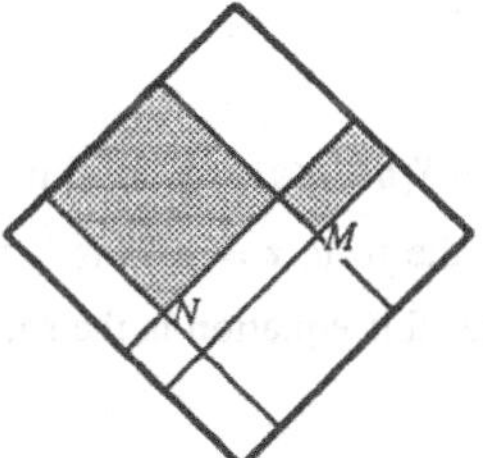

Work on that question is recent [Comon 86, Kirchner-Lescanne 87, Lassez-Marriott 87, Comon 88] and is stimulated by the use of term manipulation techniques in various domains [Colmerauer 84, Schnoebelen 87, Schnoebelen 88]. One of the difficulties is that the number of substitutions σ and σ' such that $\sigma(M) \neq \sigma'(N)$ is in general infinite. For example, with $\Sigma = \{0,S\}$ and with the terms $M = S(x)$ and $N = S(y)$, possible solutions to the dis-unification of M and N are :

$\sigma =$ identity, and

$\sigma'(y) = S(x)$, or $\sigma'(y) = S(S(y))$, or $\sigma' = S(S(S(y)))$, etc.

or :

$\sigma(x) = S(y)$, or $\sigma(x) = S(S(y))$, or $\sigma(x) = S(S(S(y)))$, etc., and

$\sigma' =$ identity.

In fact, this example amounts to find a way to characterize the subset of $T(\Sigma)\times T(\Sigma)$ which is complementary of the ground instances of the pair $(S(u), S(u))$. There is no pair of terms (nor any finite number of pairs of terms) in $\mathbb{T}(\Sigma,V) \times \mathbb{T}(\Sigma,V)$ the ground instances of which constitute the desired subset of $T(\Sigma)\times T(\Sigma)$. This requires a richer representation of terms and substitutions, with explicit constraints on variables, for having a finite representation of the solutions. In this example, the desired solution would be represented by $/(S(x),S(y))\ \&\ x \neq y/$. A theory has been developed (see [Comon 88]) for manipulating these representations.

II.8. Unification in equational theories

In general, unifying two terms M and N in $\mathbb{T}(\Sigma,V)$ is solving the equation $M = N$ in $\mathbb{T}(\Sigma,V)$, i.e. finding all substitutions σ such that $\sigma(M) = \sigma(N)$. They all are instanciations of the most general of them, which is $m.g.u.(M,N)$. For example, with $\Sigma = \{+, S, 0\}$, solve the equation :

$$+(x,S(0)) = +(S(0),y)$$

Unification, as defined thus far, would give the solution $\sigma(x) = S(0)$, $\sigma(y) = S(0)$. But everyone knows that all solutions for the equation $x+1 = 1+y$ are of the form $x = y$. This is the case, because everyone knows that addition is commutative and that this equation is the same as the equation $x+1 = y+1$, which would represented as :

$$+(x,S(0)) = +(y,S(0))$$

With the equation in this new form, the desired solution can be found : $\sigma(x) = y$ (or, identically, $\sigma(y) = x$). The commutativity of addition can be represented by an equation which defines (part of) the theory of addition :

$$\forall u, v \quad +(u,v) = +(v,u)$$

With this additional knowledge about the algebraic properties of the operations (denoted by symbols of Σ - in this example, the symbol "+") which occur in terms, it becomes possible to start by replacing $+(S(0)),y)$ by $+(y,S(0))$ in the initial equation, and then find the desired solution by unifying both members of the new equation.

Thus, in general, unifying two terms M and N is indeed solving the equation $M = N$, but modulo a theory defined by a set A of equations between terms. The simple case which has been considered thus far is the case of unification with $A = \varnothing$.

A slightly more elaborate example shows a few cases of unification in several equational theories. The alphabet is $\Sigma = \{a,F,G\}$. The equation to be solved is $F(x,G(a,z)) = F(G(y,z),x)$.

First case : the empty theory $A = \varnothing$. The solution is :

$$\sigma_1(x) = G(a,z),\ \sigma_1(y) = a$$

This solution will be part of all other solutions with non empty theories.

Second case : $A = \{F(u,v) = F(v,u)\}$, i.e. F is commutative. The solution is :

$$\sigma_2(y) = a$$

This solution is indeed less instanciated than σ_1 : $\sigma_2 \leq \sigma_1$.

Third case : $A = \{F(u,F(v,w)) = F(F(u,v),w)\}$, i.e. F is associative. There is an infinite set of unrelated solutions :

$$\sigma_3(x) = F(G(a,z),G(a,z)),\ \sigma_3(y) = a$$

$$\sigma_4(x) = F(G(a,z),F(G(a,z),G(a,z))),\ \sigma_3(y) = a$$

etc.

The case of theories with both associativity and commutativity ("AC unification") has been studied quite intensively (see for example [Stickel 81, Fages 84]) and many other cases have been explored : [Jouannaud-Kirchner 83, Kirchner 84, Fay 79, etc.]. See also [Jouannaud 85].

III. EQUATIONS AND TERM REWRITING

Term matching and unification are used as the basic operations for constructing elaborate computations on values and expressions which are represented by terms and for performing proofs on formulas which are also represented by terms.

III.1. Equational reasoning

Equational logic is a restricted form of first order logic, where :

- The only predicate symbol is "=" ;
- Axioms are equations ;
- Inference is performed by replacing equals for equals.

In what follows, terms of the form $+(u,v)$ will be written in the more usual and more readable form $u+v$. As an example, the following two axions are chosen :

(1) $x+0 = x$

(2) $x+S(y) = S(x+y)$

They define addition. Then, the following theorem has to be proved, using the principles of equational reasoning :

$$S(x)+0 = x+S(0)$$

The proof can be conducted in three steps, where "$\rightarrow$" reads "is replaced by". The proof transforms, step by step, the left side of the equational theorem, to make it identical to the right side :

$S(x)+0 \rightarrow S(x)$, using axiom (1) from left to right

$S(x) \rightarrow S(x+0)$, using axiom (1) from right to left

$S(x+0) \rightarrow x+S(0)$, using axiom (2) from right to left

Thus, at each step of an equational proof, the following questions have to be given answers :

- Choose the "good" axiom to apply ;
- Apply this axiom to the "good" sub-term ;
- Apply this axiom in the "good" direction (left to right or right to left).

III.2. Term rewriting and rewrite rules

An idea for simplifying the construction of equational proofs is to choose, for each axiom, a direction in which it will always be applied. Furthermore, this should be done in such a way that the order in which the axioms are applied one after the other, and the choice of the subterms where they are applied (i.e. the places inside the term where the replacement is done) should not be relevant : the same result should always be obtained.

This is the idea of "term rewriting", where directed equational axioms take the form of "rewrite rules".

III.2.1. Rewrite rules

In the above example, a direction can be chosen for each of the two axioms. This direction is shown by replacing the "=" sign by a "⇒"sign :

(1) $x+0 \Rightarrow x$

(2) $x+S(y) \Rightarrow S(x+y)$

Such a set of rewrite rules constitute a "rewrite system" (it should be noted that, in this example, the above proof can no longer be constructed).

Given a term M in $T(\Sigma,V)$ and a rewrite rule $L \Rightarrow R$, applying this rule to M is done as follows :

(i) Check applicability of the rule $L \Rightarrow R$ to M. It is applicable at some position u in M iff $\exists\sigma, M/u = \sigma(L)$;

(ii) Apply the rule at position u in M. This is done by grafting $\sigma(R)$ at position u in M, i.e. by "rewriting" M into a new term $M[u \leftarrow \sigma(R)]$.

Given a rewrite system S, a term can be repeatedly rewritten by using the rules of S. A term M is said to be in "normal form" (for this system) if it cannot be rewritten by any of the rule of S (i.e. no rules of S can any longer be applied to M).

III.2.2. Properties of rewrite systems

In general, it should be clear that, starting with some initial term M, the repeated applications of the rules of a rewrite system S may very well lead to different normal forms, depending in which order the rules are applied and where they are applied inside the term. Furthermore, this repeated application may also very well never stop, that is never lead to any normal form. Of course, these are not desirable situations, since the purpose of a rewrite system is to "compute" something from some initial data, i.e. lead to a unique normal form for the initial term M.

There are two desirable properties of a rewrite system S, if its purpose is indeed to compute something. They are called "confluence" and "termination".

Given a rewrite system S and terms M and $N \in T(\Sigma)$, the relation $M \rightarrow N$ holds iff N is the result of applying exactly one of the rules of S. The relation $M \rightarrow^* N$ holds if N is the result of repeatedly applying an arbitrary number (including zero) rules of S, i.e. "$\rightarrow^*$" is the reflexive closure of "$\rightarrow$". A derivation is a set of terms $\{M_1, M_2, ...\}$ such that $M_1 \rightarrow M_2 \rightarrow ...$ and M_1 is called the origin of the derivation

A rewrite system is said to be confluent iff, for all initial term M, when both relations $M \rightarrow^* N$ and $M \rightarrow^* P$ hold, with $N \neq P$, then $\exists Q$ such that both $N \rightarrow^* Q$ and $P \rightarrow^* Q$ hold. Pictorially, this situation can be visualized as follows :

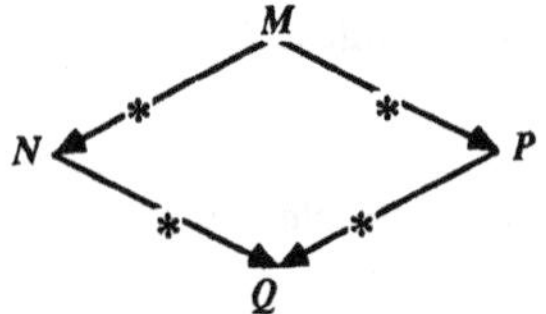

A rewrite system is said to terminate (or "is terminating") iff, for all initial term M, there is no infinite derivation with origin M. A rewrite system wich terminates is also called a Noetherian rewrite system.

A rewrite system which is both confluent and Noetherian is called a convergent rewrite system.

Convergent rewrite systems bring a great improvement to the naive form of equational reasoning presented at the beginning. Proving that $N = P$ is an equational theorem now amounts to find the normal forms of N and P and to verify that they are identical (or isomorphic if N and P belong to $T(\Sigma,V)$). Equational proofs have been replaced by computations of normal forms. But there remains a difficult pre-requisite : the convergence of rewrite systems has to be proved.

III.3. Termination

A first general remark : proving termination of rewrite systems is the same as the halting problem of Turing machines. It is an undecidable property for rewrite systems with at least two rules (decidability is still unknown for rewrite systems with exactly one rule). Fortunately, even if no algorithm will prove termination in the general case, there exist very good algorithms for proving termination in most practical cases.

III.3.1. Principle for proving termination

Given a rewrite system S, let "$\rangle$" be an ordering in $T(\Sigma)$ such that for every rule $L \Rightarrow R$ of S, every ground instance $\sigma(L)$ and the corresponding ground instance $\sigma(R)$ satisfy $\sigma(L) \rangle \sigma(R)$. Furthermore, the relation $\rangle$ should have the following two properties :

- $\rangle$ is a well founded ordering, i.e. there is no infinite strictly descending chain of the form

  $M_1 \rangle M_2 \rangle \ldots$;

- $\rangle$ is a monotonous ordering, i.e. $M \rangle N \Rightarrow F(\ldots,M,\ldots) \rangle F(\ldots,N,\ldots)$.

If, given Σ and S, such and ordering can be found, then it is the case that the derivation relation "$\rightarrow$" is contained in the ordering relation "$\rangle$" :

$$\forall M,N \in T(\Sigma), \quad M \rightarrow N \Rightarrow M \rangle N$$

Thus, there will be no infinite derivation and S is terminating. But a problem remains : find such an ordering.

III.3.2. Examples

(i) The French national flag

The French national flag is Blue, White, Red, in this order. The problem is to rearrange an arbitrary sequence of ***B***'s, ***W***'s and ***R***'s such that, at the end, the sequence is composed of a series of ***B***'s, followed by a series of ***W***'s, followed by a series of ***R***'s. For example :

$$WWBRBBWRBR \rightarrow^* BBBBWWWRRR$$

This can be done by swapping adjacent different colours when they are not in the desired order with respect to each other.

This swapping can be described by rewrite rules :

$R\,W \Rightarrow W\,R$

$W\,B \Rightarrow B\,W$

$R\,B \Rightarrow B\,R$

First, an ordering $\rangle$ can be chosen among the symbols B, W and R, where $B \rangle W \rangle R$. Then, since terms are here simply tuples of colors, this ordering can be extended to a lexicographic ordering among tuples of colors (e.g. $R\,W \rangle W\,R$). This ordering is trivially well founded and monotonous and this proves termination of the rewrite system.

(ii) Ordering with the size of terms

The size of a term M is $|M| = |F(M_1, ..., M_n)| = 1 + \sum_{i=1..n} |M_i|$. It can be chosen as a basis for defining the ordering $\rangle$: terms of larger size are greater than (according to $\rangle$) terms of smaller size. Only finite terms are considered, and this ordering is trivially well founded. Its monotonicity can be easily proved :

- if $|M| > |N|$, then $M \rangle N$

- $|F(...,M,...)| = |F(...,,...)| + |M| > |F(...,,...) + |N| = |F(...,N,...)|$

  thus, $F(...,M,...) \rangle F(...,N,...)$

However, when used with the rewrite system which defines addition :

(1) $x+0 \Rightarrow x$

(2) $x+S(y) \Rightarrow S(x+y)$

this ordering works well with the first rule (every ground instance of the left side is greater than the corresponding ground instance of the right side) but it does not work with the second rule, where the ground instances of both sides have the same size. Since this very simple rewrite system is known to terminate, this example suggests that finding a satisfactory ordering is not, in general, a trivial task.

III.3.3. Simplification orderings

Proving monotonicity of an ordering is usually easy. But proving its well foundedness may be difficult. An idea, due to Dershowitz, is then to characterize a family of orderings for which well foundedness is given : simplification orderings are such orderings.

A simplification ordering is an ordering which has two properties :

- Monotonicity : $M \rangle N \Rightarrow F(\ldots,M,\ldots) \rangle F(\ldots,N,\ldots)$
- Subterm property : $F(\ldots,M,\ldots) \rangle M$

For example, the ordering based on the size of terms and the "recursive path ordering" defined below are simplification orderings. The proof that simplification orderings are indeed well founded orderings is based on the following ideas.

An embedding "$\leq$" on $T(\Sigma)$ is a relation defined as follows :

$M = F(M_1, \ldots, M_m) \leq G(N_1, \ldots, N_n)$ is an embedding if

- either $F = G$ and $\forall i, M_i \leq N_{ji}$
- or $\exists j, M \leq N_j$

The relation $M \leq N$ contains the notion that M is "syntactically simpler" than N. For example :

$$--(0+1) < (((--(----0+1)+1)+1)+1)+1$$

Then, a rewrite system S is said to be "self embedding" if it allows a "self embedding" derivation, that is a derivation of the form :

$$M_1 \rightarrow M_2 \rightarrow \ldots \rightarrow M_j \rightarrow \ldots \rightarrow M_k \rightarrow \ldots$$

where $M_j \leq M_k$ for some $j < k$. A theorem, due to Kruskal ("Tree theorem"), shows that if S is non terminating, then it is also self embedding. In other words, if S is not self embedding, then it is terminating. Proving that a rewrite system is not self embedding is proving that all derivations are such that $M_j > M_k$ for all $j < k$. Unfortunately (and this should not come as a surprise in this evil world), self embedding is undecidable.

However, coming back to the problem of proving that S terminates, the intention is still to find a well founded ordering $\rangle$, i.e. such that there is no infinite descending chain $M_1 \rangle M_2 \rangle \ldots$, implying that there is no infinite derivation $M_1 \rightarrow M_2 \rightarrow \ldots$. This suggests that it is sufficient for the ordering $\rangle$ to hold and be well founded among terms which can be involved in the same derivations. Such a restricted ordering is called "well founded for derivation" and it has been proved that an ordering $\rangle$ is well founded for derivation if it has an extension which contains the relation $\succ$. From that, an essential result is due to Dershowitz :

Any simplification ordering is a well founded ordering for derivation.

A last problem has to be taken care of for simplification orderings to be of any practical use. The rules in the rewrite system S are written with terms in $T(\Sigma,V)$, but the ordering $\rangle$ is defined in $T(\Sigma)$. Since it is not feasable to compare all ground instances of left sides with the corresponding ground instances of right sides, the ordering $\rangle$ should also be defined on $T(\Sigma,V)$ and closed under substitution. This means that if $L \Rightarrow R$ is a rule, then $L \rangle R$ should hold and imply that, for all substitution σ, $\sigma(L) \rangle \sigma(R)$ also holds.

There are several simplification orderings which are closed under substitution. The recursive path ordering is one of them.

III.3.4. The recursive path ordering

The recursive path ordering is defined as follows :

(i) A "precedence" (i.e. a partial ordering) $\rangle$ is chosen among the symbols of the alphabet Σ.

(ii) The recursive path ordering itself is denoted by $\rangle_{rpo}$ and is defined on $T(\Sigma,V)$:

- $M = F(M_1, \ldots, M_m) \rangle_{rpo} N = G(N_1, \ldots, N_n)$ if

either $M_i \rangle'_{rpo} N$ for some i,

where $\rangle'_{rpo}$ is $\rangle_{rpo}$ modulo permutations of subterms,

or $F \rangle G$ and M $\rangle_{rpo} N_j$ for all j,

or $F = G$ and $\{M_1, \ldots, M_m\} \rangle\rangle_{rpo} \{N_1, \ldots, N_n\}$,

where $\rangle\rangle_{rpo}$ is the natural extension of $\rangle_{rpo}$ to "multisets" of terms.

As an example, the termination of a non trivial rewrite system is proved, using the recursive path ordering. This system transforms any formula of logic (i.e. using the operators $\neg$, $\wedge$ and $\vee$) into its disjunctive normal form (i.e. an equivalent formula which is a set of sub-formulas connected by $\vee$'s, where each sub-formula is a set of positive or negated atoms connected by $\wedge$'s) :

(1) $\neg\neg x \Rightarrow x$

(2) $\neg(x \vee y) \Rightarrow \neg x \wedge \neg y$

(3) $\neg(x \wedge y) \Rightarrow \neg x \vee \neg y$

(4) $x \wedge (y \vee z) \Rightarrow (x \wedge y) \vee (x \wedge z)$

(5) $(y \vee z) \wedge x \Rightarrow (y \wedge x) \vee (z \wedge x)$

(i) Chose a precedence among the symbols of the alphabet : $\neg \succ \wedge \succ \vee$.

(ii) Show that $L \succ_{rpo} R$ holds for every rule $L \Rightarrow R$ in the system :

- Rule (1) : trivial, by the subterm property, since $\succ_{rpo}$ is a simplification ordering.
- Rule (2) : by case $F \succ G$ of the definition of $\succ_{rpo}$,

  i.e. show $\neg(x \wedge y) \succ_{rpo} \neg x$ and $\neg(x \wedge y) \succ_{rpo} \neg y$

  then , because of monotonicity, show $x \wedge y \succ_{rpo} x$ and $x \wedge y \succ_{rpo} y$ which is trivial, by the subterm property.
- Rule (3) : similar to rule (2).
- Rule (4) : by case $F \succ_{rpo} G$ of the definition of $\succ_{rpo}$,

  i.e. show $x \wedge (y \vee z) \succ_{rpo} x \wedge y$ and $x \wedge (y \vee z) \succ_{rpo} x \wedge z$ which are both in the case $F = G$ of the definition,

  then show $\{x, y \vee z\} \succ\succ_{rpo} \{x,y\}$ and $\{x, y \vee z\} \succ\succ_{rpo} \{x,z\}$ which is trivially proved.
- Rule (5) : similar to rule (4).

Termination of the rewrite system is proved.

There are many results on proving termination of rewrite systems. In depth study of this question can be found in [Huet-Oppen 80, Dershowitz 85 and Jouannaud-Lescanne 86], which all contain numerous references.

III.4. Confluence

The method for proving that a rewrite system is confluent relies on an essential result, called Newman's lemma.

III.4.1. Newman's lemma

Newman' lemma uses the property of "local confluence", which is simpler than confluence : a rewrite system is locally confluent iff, for all term M in $T(\Sigma)$, when both $M \rightarrow N$ and $M \rightarrow P$ hold, with $N \neq P$, then $\exists Q$ such that both $N \rightarrow^{*} Q$ and $P \rightarrow^{*} Q$ hold. Pictorially :

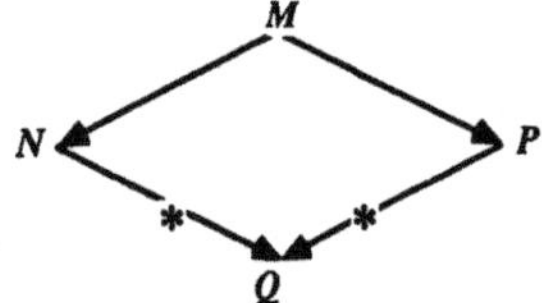

Then, Newman's lemma is the following result :

A terminating rewrite system is confluent iff it is locally confluent.

With this result, it is possible to prove confluence of a rewrite system by first proving that it terminates and then proving that it is locally confluent. The system is then not only confluent, but convergent.

III.4.2. Critical pairs

For proving local confluence of a rewrite system S, it is necessary to identify all "critical" situations, that is situations where both $M \rightarrow N$ and $M \rightarrow P$ may hold, with $N \neq P$. Critical pairs are a means of characterizing, in a general way, the immediate consequences of such possibly diverging situations. Critical pairs are found by an algorithm called the "superposition algorithm".

Let $L_1 \Rightarrow R_1$ and $L_2 \Rightarrow R_2$ be two rules in the system S and let M be a subterm of L_1 which is not simply a variable : $M = L_1/u$, for some position u in the domain of L_1. If M is unifiable with L_2, this means that the terms in $T(\Sigma)$ which match L_1 with some substitution also have a subterm which matches L_2 (in general with another substitution): both rules may be applied to such terms, and this is a critical situation.

The term obtained by unifying M and L_2 is $\sigma_1(M) = \sigma_2(L_2)$, where the substitutions σ_1 and σ_2 are chosen in such a way that this term has no variable in common with L_1.Then, terms of $T(\Sigma)$ which match L_1 can be rewritten as instances of :

either $N = \sigma_1(L_1)[u \leftarrow \sigma_2(R_2)]$

or $P = \sigma_1(R_1)$

The pair of terms $<N,P>$ is the critical pair which characterizes that situation.

III.4.3. Knuth-Bendix theorem

Proof of local confluence of a rewrite system relies on the Knuth-Bendix theorem. This theorem states that :

> A rewrite system S is locally confluent iff, for all critical pair $<N,P>$ of S, there exists a term Q such that both $N \rightarrow^* Q$ and $P \rightarrow^* Q$ hold.

As a consequence, if S is terminating, local confluence is decidable, since in that case Q will be the normal form of both N and P. Thus, with Newman's lemma, confluence is decidable for terminating rewrite systems.

III.4.4. Examples

(i) An unusual definition of addition

The following rewrite system is intended to define addition :

(1) $x+0 \Rightarrow x$

(2) $0+y \Rightarrow y$

(3) $S(x) + S(y) \Rightarrow S(S(x+y))$

One critical pair appears with rules (1) and (2), where $(x+0)/\Lambda$ is unifiable with $(0+y)$, using the substitutions $\sigma_1(x) = 0$ and $\sigma_2(y) = 0$. The corresponding critical pair is :

$$<\sigma_1(x+0)[\Lambda \leftarrow \sigma_2(y)] , \sigma_1(x)> = <\sigma_2(y) , \sigma_1(x)> = <0,0>$$

Both terms of the critical pair are in normal form and are identical : this system is confluent.

(ii) Another unusual definition of addition

(1) $0 + S(x) \Rightarrow S(x)$

(2) $y + S(z) \Rightarrow S(y+z)$

(3) $x + 0 \Rightarrow x$

One critical pair appears with rules (1) and (2), where $(0 + S(x))/\Lambda$ is unifiable with $(y + S(z))$, using the substitutions $\sigma_1(x) = z$ and $\sigma_2(y) = 0$. The corresponding critical pair is :

$$< \sigma_1 (0 + S(x))[\Lambda \leftarrow \sigma_2(S(y+z))] , \sigma_1(S(x)) > = < \sigma_2(S(y+z)) , \sigma_1(S(x)) >$$

$$= < S(0+z) , S(z) >$$

Both terms of the critical pair are in normal form, but are not identical : this system is not confluent.

III.5. Completion

Let S be a terminating non confluent rewrite system. The purpose of completion is to transform S into another rewrite system S' which is still terminating but also confluent and such that S and S' be logically equivalent, that is such that $N = P$ is an equatiional theorem in S iff $N = P$ is also an equational theorem in S'.

Completion can be performed by a procedure known as the "Knuth-Bendix completion procedure". The general idea is as follows :

- Let $<N,P>$ be a critical pair in S. By repeatedly applying the rules of S, N and P can be rewritten into their respective normal forms : $N \rightarrow^* N'$ and $P \rightarrow^* P'$. If $N' \neq P'$, the system S is non confluent. The idea is then to consider that $N' = P'$ is an equational lemma and to add that fact, in the form of a new rewrite rule, to the curent set of rules of S for obtaining a new rewrite system S'.

- For making a rewrite rule out of the equation $N' = P'$, a direction has to be chosen : either $N' \Rightarrow P'$ or $P' \Rightarrow N'$. The criteria for choosing a direction is that the adjunction of the new rule should preserve termination.

- If a direction preserving termination can be found (this is not always possible, and this is a case of failure of the procedure), the whole process is iterated, starting now with the rewrite system S' : find a new (i.e. not considered previously) critical pair in the new system, derive the corresponding lemma, etc., until no new critical pair is found.

This procedure may lead to several situations :

- Success : the procedure halts, and a convergent system has been found.
- Failure : it is impossible to preserve termination with the new rule being processed.
- Divergence : the procedure adds rules indefinitely.
- No halting : this can be due to special rules, like those which define commutativity.

As an example, consider the non confluent system which has been studied previously :

(1) $0 + S(x) \Rightarrow S(x)$

(2) $y + S(z) \Rightarrow S(y+z)$

(3) $x + 0 \Rightarrow x$

A critical pair is produced by rules (1) and (2) : $< S(0+z) , S(z) >$. Both of its terms are already in normal form. Thus, $S(0+z) = S(z)$ is an equational lemma which has to be put in the form of a rewrite rule and added to the system while preserving termination.

Termination of the initial system could be proved by a recursive path ordering obtained with the precedence $+ \rangle S$ among symbols of the alphabet. With that same ordering, a direction can be chosen which preserves termination : $S(0+z) \Rightarrow S(z)$. A new rewrite system has been obtained :

(1) $0 + S(x) \Rightarrow S(x)$

(2) $y + S(z) \Rightarrow S(y+z)$

(3) $x + 0 \Rightarrow x$

(4) $S(0+z) \Rightarrow S(z)$

All critical pairs of the initial system have been processed and no new critical pair is created by the adjunction of the new rule. The procedure halts with success and the result is a convergent rewrite system.

A comprehensive treatment of completion can be found in [Buchberger 85]. Completion serves as a basis for performing proofs by induction [Huet-Hullot 82]. See also [Jouannaud-Kirchner 84].

III.6. Narrowing

Let $L \Rightarrow R$ be a rewrite rule. As described thus far, such a rule can be applied to terms in $T(\Sigma)$, that is to terms which contain no variables. This way of applying $L \Rightarrow R$ to a term $M \in T(\Sigma)$ is called "reduction".

One step of reduction of $M \in T(\Sigma)$, at position u of the domain of M, by rule $L \Rightarrow R$ goes as follows :

(i) Applicability is checked by term matching : $\exists\, \sigma, u$ such that $M/u = \sigma(L)$.

(ii) Application : $M \rightarrow_R M[u \leftarrow \sigma(R)]$ (" $\rightarrow_R$ " stands for "is rewritten by *R*eduction").

There is another form of rewriting, called "narrowing", which applies to terms in $T(\Sigma,V)$.

One step of narrowing of $M \in T(\Sigma,V)$, at position u of the domain of M, by rule $L \Rightarrow R$ goes as follows :

(i) Applicability is checked by term unification : $\exists\, \sigma, u$ such that $\sigma(M/u) = \sigma(L)$.

(ii) Application : $M \rightarrow_N \sigma(M[u \leftarrow R])$ (" $\rightarrow_N$ " stands for "is rewritten by *N*arrowing")

With narrowing, the resulting term $\sigma(M[u \leftarrow R])$ can also be described as $\sigma(M)[u \leftarrow \sigma(R)]$. This makes explicit the principles of narrowing : M is first "narrowed", by σ, to a term which can be reduced by the rule, then it is reduced.

An essential use of narrowing is for solving equations in $T(\Sigma,V)$. For example, consider the classical rules which define addition :

(1) $x + 0 \Rightarrow x$

(2) $x + S(y) \Rightarrow S(x + y)$

Solving the equation $S(0) + z = S(S(0))$ (i.e. finding the value of z for which this is an equational theorem) can be done as follows :

(i) Attempt unification of $S(0) + z$ and $S(S(0))$: fail.

(ii) Narrow $S(0) + z$:

- by (1), the result is $S(0)$. The equation becomes $S(0) = S(S(0))$: fail
- by (2), the result is $S(S(0) + y)$, with a substitution σ_1 where $\sigma_1(z) = S(y)$. The equation becomes $S(S(0) + y) = S(S(0))$

(iii) Starting with the new equation, narrow $S(S(0) + y)$:

- by (1), the result is $S(S(0))$, which is the desired result, with a substitution σ_2 where $\sigma_2(y) = 0$.

(iv) The equation is solved and the value of z is obtained by composing the two substitutions σ_1 and σ_2 : $\sigma_2 \bullet \sigma_1 (z) = S(0)$.

References on narrowing : [Fay 79, Hullot 80].

IV. FUNCTIONAL AND LOGIC PROGRAMMING

Programming languages are tools for describing functions or relations among data objects and must be such that these functions or relations can be effectively computed and applied to some initial data for producing the corresponding results.

Two kinds of programming languages are considered here : functional programming languages and logic programming languages. Both are presented as being based on term manipulations : pieces of data are terms, functional expressions and logic formulas are terms, function application relies on term matching and reduction, logic inferencing relies on term unification and narrowing. This unifying view of two styles of programming suggests that there is a consistent way of merging them together.

IV.1. Functional programming with reduction

In functional programming, functions, in a mathematical sense, can be defined and applied to elements in their domain for producing corresponding elements in their range. Expressions can be written for describing compositions of function applications. Functional programming is also called applicative programming. The purpose here is to give a very specific (but restricted) view of functional programming, so that it will later be compared to logic programming.

IV.1.1. Values, expressions and computations

In functional programming as it is presented here, both values and expressions are terms on a graded alphabet Σ. The alphabet is partitioned into two subsets :

$$\Sigma = \Sigma_C \cup \Sigma_F$$

where Σ_C is the set of "value constructors" (or simply "constructors") and Σ_F is the set of function names. Then, two sets of terms are considered : $T(\Sigma_C)$ is the set of values and $T(\Sigma)$ is the set of expressions. As a consequence, $T(\Sigma_C)$ is a subset of $T(\Sigma)$.

Example : with $\Sigma_C = \{0, S\}$ and $\Sigma_F = \{+, \times\}$, $S(S(0))$ is a value and $(S(S(0))+S(0))\times S(S(0))$ is an expression.

The purpose of a computation is to find the value V of an expression E :

$$E \to^* V$$

For example, $S(S(0))+S(0)) \to^* S(S(S(0)))$.

Since expressions are terms in $T(\Sigma)$, computing the value of an expression E is performed by rewriting E until a normal form V is reached. This requires that the rewrite system which describes the computation steps be terminating and confluent. Furthermore, the normal form V must be a term in $T(\Sigma_C)$.

IV.1.2. Naive types

Let G be a function name : $G \in \Sigma_F$. By definition of what a computation is, every occurrence of G in an expression E is meant to disappear when the value of E is computed. This means that every subterm which is rooted at a position u in the domain of E and such that $E(u) = G$ will eventually be replaced by a value : every such subterm E/u is called an application of function G.

Every function has a domain and a range, which are subsets of $T(\Sigma_C)$. For defining the domains and ranges of functions, $T(\Sigma_C)$ is partitioned into $T(\Sigma_{S1}) \cup T(\Sigma_{S2}) \cup \ldots \cup T(\Sigma_{SN})$, where each part has its own constructors : $\Sigma_C = \Sigma_{S1} \cup \Sigma_{S2} \cup \ldots \cup \Sigma_{SN}$. The set $\{S_1, S_2, \ldots, S_N\}$ is simply a set of tags called "sorts". With the sorts, a more elaborate notion of arity can be defined for the constructors and function names in Σ:

$\alpha : \Sigma \rightarrow \langle Sort^*, Sort \rangle$ where *Sort* is the name of the set of sorts.

This defines the domains and ranges of functions : the domain is described by a string of sorts and the range by a sort. Furthermore, for constructors, α should be such that :

$\forall c \in \Sigma_{Si}, \alpha(c)$ has the form $\langle 'S_{i1} \ldots S_{ip}', S_i \rangle$

An example, defining natural integers and binary trees labelled by natural integers :

$Sort = \{Nat, Btree\}$

$\Sigma_{Nat} = \{0, S\}$, $\alpha(0) = \langle \Lambda, Nat \rangle$, $\alpha(S) = \langle 'Nat', Nat \rangle$

$\Sigma_{Btree} = \{Node, Leaf\}$, $\alpha(Node) = \langle 'Btree\ Btree\ Nat', Nat \rangle$, $\alpha(Leaf) = \langle 'Nat', Btree \rangle$

$\Sigma_F = \{+, \times, sum\}$, $\alpha(+) = \alpha(\times) = \langle 'Nat\ Nat', Nat \rangle$, $\alpha(sum) = \langle 'Btree', Nat \rangle$

It is often the case that the sort S_i is used for referring to $T(\Sigma_{Si})$. Sometimes, it is also called the "type" of the values in $T(\Sigma_{Si})$.

IV.1.3. Well formed values and expressions

The arities of constructors and function names restrict the set of terms $T(\Sigma)$ to those terms which are well formed according to the types of their subterms. Such terms are called "well typed" terms and $T(\Sigma)$ is now the set of well typed terms.

Let **F** be a symbol in **Σ** (constructor or function name). Its arity is $\alpha(F) = <'S_1...S_N', S>$:

$$dom(F) = 'S_1...S_N'$$
$$rng(F) = S$$

Then, the "well typed" condition is :

$$F(M_1, ..., M_N) \in T(\Sigma) \quad \Leftrightarrow \quad M_1, ..., M_N \in T(\Sigma) \wedge \forall i=1..N,\ rng(M_i(\Lambda)) = S_i$$

IV.1.4. Defining functions by rewrite systems

Let **G** be a function name with arity $\alpha(G) = <'S_1..S_N', S>$. A rewrite system defining **G** is a rewrite system which eventually reduces every expression containing applications of **G** to an expression which does not contain any application of **G**. A definition of **G** is written as :

$$G:\ L_1 \Rightarrow R_1$$
$$...$$
$$L_m \Rightarrow R_m$$

such that, $\forall i = 1..m$, $L_i \Rightarrow R_i$ has a form which satisfies the following conditions :

- $L_i = G(P_1, ..., P_N)$, with $P_j \in T(\Sigma_C, V)$ for $j = 1..N$
- $R_i \in T(\Sigma)$, with $rng(R_i(\Lambda)) = S$
- $V(R_i)$ is a subset of $V(L_i)$
- L_i is linear, i.e. every variable occurs at most once in L_i
- The variables in *Ri* are used consistently with the types infered for them by their occurrences in *Li*.

Examples :

$+ : \; x + 0 \Rightarrow x$ $\qquad\qquad\qquad \times : \; x \times 0 \Rightarrow 0$

$x + S(y) \Rightarrow S(x + y)$ $\qquad\qquad\qquad x \times S(y) \Rightarrow x + (x \times y)$

$sum : \; sum(Node(u,v)) \Rightarrow sum(u) + sum(v)$

$sum(Leaf(n)) \Rightarrow n$

Given the general form given above of the definition of a function G, the computation corresponding to an application of G is a derivation :

$$G(M_1, ..., M_N) \rightarrow ... \rightarrow M \in T(\Sigma_S)$$

In general, $M_1, ..., M_N$ are expressions which also contain applications of G or other functions. During the computation, these applications are of course also reduced to values. The order in which these reductions are applied should not be relevant. The rewrite systems which define functions must be terminating and confluent. Furthermore, they must be "complete" in the following sense : the left sides of the rules defining a function must cover the entire domain of the function, so that all patterns of application of the function will eventually be reduced to values.

A few references on functional programming based on equations : [Turner 82, Turner 85, Bert 82, Burstall et al. 81, Dershowitz 83].

IV.2. Logic programming

The form of logic programming which is briefly presented here is the classical one, with Horn clause logic and resolution. The purpose of this presentation is to relate logic programing to rewriting and, more precisely, to narrowing.

IV.2.1. Horn clause logic

Let $A, B_1, ..., B_n$ be atoms, i.e. elementary formulas which have the form of applications of predicate symbols to their arguments (e.g. $P(S(x),y, S(z))$). Horn clauses have one of the following two possible forms :

- Definite clauses, which, in turn can have two forms :
  - Conditional clauses : A :- $B_1 ... B_n$. A is the head the clause and $B_1 ... B_n$ is the body. A conditional clause can be read as "A is implied by $B_1 \wedge ... \wedge B_n$".
  - Assertions : A.

- Negative clauses, which can also have two forms :
    - Goals or queries : $:- B_1 \dots B_n$
    - Empty clause : $:-$

In Horn clause logic, a proof starts with one initial goal and is a sequence of goals where each goal is obtained by "resolution" from the previous goal. A proof is completed when the empty clause is reached. A resolution step operates as follows :

- One of the atoms in the current goal is unifiable with the head on a definite clause.
- This atom is replaced, in the goal, by the corresponding clause body, and the unifying substitution is applied to this new goal.

IV.2.2. Computing with Horn clause logic

In general, the initial goal of a proof contains variables. The successive resolution steps of a proof of that goal define sustitutions for these variables.

An "SLD-derivation" of goal G_0 in a set of clauses $\{C_i\}$ is a sequence of negative clauses, of the form $G_0, \dots, G_k$, such that G_j is obtained by resolution from G_{j-1}, using the definite clauses of $\{C_i\}$. Such a derivation has an associated substitution which is the composition of the *m.g.u.*'s used at each resolution step.

A derivation can be infinite or finite. When it is finite, it is a success if $G_k = :-$ otherwise it is a failure. An answer substitution is the substitution associated with a success derivation, restricted to the variables occurring in the initial goal G_0. A success derivation is also called a refutation of G_0 in $\{C_i\}$.

IV.2.3. Semantics of a set of clauses $\{C_i\}$

The notions of Herbrand universe, Herbrand base, Herbrand interpretation and Herbrand model are introduced by means of an example.

The following set of two clauses is considered :

$P(0,x,x).$
$P(S(x),y,S(z)) \;:-\; P(x,y,z)$

The symbols in the graded alphabet $\Sigma = \{0,S\}$ are used for constructing $T(\Sigma)$, the set of data, or functional terms : $T(\Sigma)$ is called the Herbrand universe.

Elementary logic formulas, called atoms, have predicate names at their outermost position and functional terms inside. The Herbrand base is the set of all ground atoms :

$$\{P(u,v,w) \mid u,v,w \in T(\Sigma)\}$$

Any subset of the Herbrand base is called a Herbrand interpretation. A Herbrand interpretation contains the atoms which are, arbitrarily, considered to be true.

A Herbrand model of a set of clauses $\{C_i\}$ is any Herbrand interpretation such that all clauses in $\{C_i\}$ can be verified by using the atoms in this interpretation. In the example :

$$\{P(0,0,0), P(0,S(0),S(0)), ...\}$$

There are several ways of defining the semantics of a set of clauses $\{C_i\}$: operational semantics, model theoretic semantics and fixed-point semantics.

The operational semantics (or success set) of $\{C_i\}$ is the set of ground atoms A_j such that the goal $:\!-A_j$ has a refutation in $\{C_i\}$. It is a Herbrand interpretation. The model theoretic semantics of $\{C_i\}$ is the intersection of all models for $\{C_i\}$. It is a "minimal" model. The fixed-point semantics associates a transformation from Herbrand interpretation to Herbrand interpretation with each clause C_i. Then, the set of clauses $\{C_i\}$ can also be viewed as a transformation : the fixed-point semantics of $\{C_i\}$ is the least fixed-point of this transformation.

These three semantics are equivalent.

IV.2.4. A term rewriting view of logic programming

A procedural metaphore is sometimes used for describing logic programming :

- Definite clauses are viewed as procedure declarations, with the predicate name of the head playing the role of the proedure name.
- A goal clause is a set of procedure calls.
- The empty clause is the halt statement.

In this metaphore, procedure calls are handled by the classical "copy rule" of procedural programming languages.

However, this view of logic programming is far from satisfactory for at least two reasons :

(i) In general, clauses define relations, not only functions.

(ii) "Parameter passing", because of unification, is "bi-directional".

These two aspects, which are essential to logic programming, cannot be represented in a procedural analogy of that sort.

Another view is proposed here, which is based on the use of term rewriting with narrowing.

A set of definite clauses and an intial goal G have the general form :

$$A_1 \ \text{:-}\ B_{11} \ \dots \ B_{1p1}$$

$$\dots$$

$$A_n \ \text{:-}\ B_{n1} \ \dots \ B_{npn}$$

$$\text{:-}\ C_1 \ \dots \ C_m$$

Each atom C_j is an element of a set of terms $T(\Sigma,V)$ where $\Sigma = \Sigma_C \cup \Sigma_P$, with Σ_C a set of constructors and Σ_P a set of predicate names (which may be used only in outermost position of terms). The goal G can be put in the form of one term, by considering that ":-" is a symbol with arity m :

$$G = \text{:-}(C_1 , \dots, C_m)$$

With this representation, $C_i = G/i$. The definite clauses are viewed as rewrite rules :

$$A_1 \Rightarrow B_{11} \ \dots \ B_{1p1}$$

$$\dots$$

$$A_n \Rightarrow B_{n1} \ \dots \ B_{npn}$$

Finally, one step of resolution is the same as one application of narrowing to the current goal :

If $\exists\, i, j, \sigma$ such that $\sigma(G/i) = \sigma(A_j)$, G can be narrowed to $\sigma(G[i \leftarrow B_{j1} \dots B_{jpj}])$

The arity of the symbol ":-" will change at each step (but this is not important : the only purpose of this symbol here is to put together all the atoms of a goal inside a single term).

The literature on logic programming is very rich. Some references : [Colmerauer et al. 73, Kowalski 79, Clocksin-Mellish 84, Lloyd 84, Robinson 83, Clark-Tarnlund 82, Colmerauer 85, Cohen 85, etc.].

IV.3. Relating functional programming and logic programming

In functional programming, a computation starts with one expression E in $T(\Sigma)$. In logic programming, a computation starts with a goal G in $T(\Sigma,V)$.

In functional programming, the computing process reduces the initial expression E to its normal form. The computed result is this normal form. In logic programming, the computing process narrows the initial goal G until the empty goal is found. The computed result is an answer substitution.

In functional programming, rules are applied by term matching and unification. In logic programming, clauses are used by unification and narrowing.

In functional programming, a function is defined and the result is unique. In logic programming, a relation is defined, and there may be several results.

This very sketchy comparison suggests that functional programming and logic programming are indeed related : matching is a special case of unification, reduction is a special case of narrowing, etc. There have been efforts for unifying these two styles of programming, with the intention of getting the best of both worlds, like :

- Get partially instanciated results in a functional style of programming.
- Simplify expressions in atoms by reducing them to normal forms.
- Get "bi-directionality" of variable bindings in a functional style of programming.

Three approaches have been taken :

- Integrate in one implementation one existing functional programming language and one existing logic programming language.
- Extend functional syntax with narrowing semantics.
- Have unification with equality in Horn clause languages.

IV.3.1. Integration of separate languages

With this approach, a functional programming language and a logic programming language are made available within a single environment, in the "most consistent way possible". Some systems of this kind are : Loglisp, based on Lisp, Qlog, also based on Lisp, and Poplog, based on Pop2. In Loglisp, for instance, Horn clause logic is implemented in Lisp and built-in Lisp functions are provided for update and query of clauses. An example of such a function is :

(ALL (X1 ... XN) C1 ... CP) where C1 ... CP is a Lisp representation of the goal and and X1 ... XN are the answer variables.

The main drawbacks of this approach is that the semantics of the resulting system are unclear and that the two languages remain separated, which makes programming sometimes uneasy in practice.

Some references on this approach : [Bowen-Kowalski 82, Robinson-Sibert 82, Komorovski 82, Mellish-Hardy 84].

IV.3.2. Extension of functional programming by narrowing

The purpose of this approach is to keep a functional style for the syntax, while achieving some typical logic programming features (i.e. essentially the "bi-directionality" of variable binding).

The means for this extension to functional programming are :

- Allow variables to be present inside expressions while they are evaluated.
- Replace reduction by narrowing.
- Change the "top level" task from one expression to be evaluated to two expressions to be unified.

This style of programming is sometimes called "equational programming" : a program is a set of directed equations (i.e. rewrite rules) and the "top level" task, which plays a role analoguous to the goal in logic programming, is indeed an equation which will be solved by using unification and narrowing by the rules of the program.

Some references on equational programming : [Reddy 85, Kahn 81, Lindstrom 85]. An essential reference on that question is [DeGroot-Lindstrom 86] where several language designs are presented.

IV.3.3. Logic programming with equality

The purpose here is to really merge in a consistent way both styles of programming, in order to allow computation of expressions, as provided by functions, while performing inferencing in a system of Horn clauses.

This is a kind of problem which had already been approached in theorem proving, under the name of "paramodulation", which is an extension of resolution theorem proving to theories with equality.

With this approach, the Horn clause part is kept unchanged and, in addition, a functional-like notation appears under the form of equations between functional terms. The main difficulty lies in the complexity of the refutation procedure (like in the case of unification in equational theories). A suitable restriction would be to stay with the kinds of equations used in functional programming languages.

Several references on this approach can be found in [DeGroot-Lindstrom 86].

V. REFERENCES

[Bert 83] D. Bert. *Refinement of generic specifications with algebraic tools*. In : IFIP Congress, North-Holland (1983).

[Bowen-Kowalski 82] Bowen and R.A. Kowalski. *Amalgamating language and meta-language in logic programming*. In : Logic programming (Clark and Tarnlund, Eds.), Academic Press (1982).

[Buchberger 85] B. Buchberger. *History and basic features of the critical-pair/completion approach*. In : Proc. 1st Conf. on Rewriting Techniques and Applications, Springer-Verlag, LNCS 202 (1985).

[Burstall et al. 81] R.M. Burstall, D.B. Macqueen, and D.T. Sannella. *HOPE : an experimental applicative language*. CSR-62-80, University of Edinburgh (1981).

[Clark-Tarnlund 82] K.L. Clark and S.A. Tarnlund (Eds.). *Logic programming*. Academic Press (1982).

[Clocksin-Mellish 84] W.F. Clocksin and C.S. Mellish. *Programming in Prolog*. 2nd Ed., North-Holland (1984).

[Cohen 85] J. Cohen. *Describing Prolog by its interpretation and compilation*. CACM 28(12) (1985).

[Colmerauer et al. 73] A. Colmerauer, H. Kanoui, R. Pasero, and Ph. Roussel. *Un système de communication homme-machine en français*. Research Report, Groupe d'Intelligence Artificielle, Faculté des Sciences de Luminy, Marseille, France (1973).

[Colmerauer 84] A. Colmerauer. *Equations and inequations on finite and infinite terms*. In : Proc. FGCS'84 (1984).

[Colmerauer 85] A. Colmerauer. *Prolog in 10 figures*. CACM 28(12) (1985).

[Comon 86] H. Comon. *Sufficient completeness, term rewriting system and anti-unification*. In : Proc. 8th CADE (J. Siekmann, Ed.), Springer-Verlag LNCS (1986).

[Comon 88] H. Comon. *Unification et disunification. Théorie et applications*. PhD Thesis, U. Grenoble (1988).

[DeGroot-Lindstrom 86] D. DeGroot and G. Lindstrom. *Logic programming - Functions, relations and equations*. Prentice-Hall (1986).

[Dershowitz 83] N. Dershowitz. *Computing with rewrite systems*. ATR-83 (8478)-1, Aerospace Corporation (1983).

[Dershowitz 85] N. Dershowitz. *Termination*. In : Proc. 1st Conference on Rewriting Techniques and Applications, Springer-Verlag, LNCS 202 (1985).

[Eder 84] E. Eder. *Properties of subtitution and unification*. JSC, 1(1) (1984).

[Fages 84] F. Fages. *Associative-commutative unification*. In : Proc. 7th CADE, Springer-Verlag, LNCS 170 (1984).

[Fay 79] M. Fay. *First order unification in an equational theory*. In : Proc. 4th Worshop on Automated Deduction, Austin, Texas (1979)

[Herbrand 30] J. Herbrand. *Recherches sur la théorie de la démonstration*. Thèse, U. de Paris (1930). In : Ecrits logiques de Jacques Herbrand, PUF Paris (1968).

[Huet 76] G. Huet. *Résolution d'équations dans les langages d'ordre 1, 2, ... ω*. Thèse d'Etat, U. de Paris VII (1976).

[Huet 85] G. Huet. *Deduction and computation*. In : Proc. Fundamentals of Artificial Intelligence (W. Bibel and Ph. Jorrand, Ed.), 1st Advanced Course in Artificial Intelligence, Vignieu, France, July 1985. Springer-Verlag LNCS 232 (1986).

[Huet-Hullot 82] G. Huet and J.M. Hullot. *Proofs by induction in equational theories with constructors*. JCSS 25 (1982).

[Huet-Oppen 80] G. Huet and D. Oppen. *Equations and rewrite rules. A survey*. In : Formal languages : Perspectives and open problems (R. Book, Ed.), Academic Press (1980).

[Hullot 80] J.M. Hullot. *Canonical forms and unification*. In : Proc. 5th CADE, Springer-Verlag, LNCS 87 (1980).

[Jouannaud 85] J.P. Jouannaud (Ed.). *Proceedings of 1st Conference on Rewriting Techniques and Applications*. Springer-Verlag, LNCS 202 (1985).

[Jouannaud-Kirchner 83] J.P. Jouannaud, C. Kirchner, and H. Kirchner. *Incremental construction of unification algorithms in equational theories*. In : Proc ICALP'83, Springer-Verlag, LNCS 154 (1983).

[Jouannaud-Kirchner 84] J.P. Jouannaud and H. Kirchner. *Completion of a set of rules modulo a set of equations*. In : Proc. 11th ACM POPL (1984).

[Jouannaud-Lescanne 86] J.P. Jounnaud and P. Lescanne. *La réécriture*. AFCET TSI 5(6) (1986).

[Kahn 81] K.M. Kahn. *Uniform - a language based upon unification which unifies (much of) Lisp, Prolog and Act1*. In : Proc. Workshop on Logic Programming for Intelligent Systems (1981). Also appears in [DeGroot-Lindstrom 86].

[Kirchner 84] C. Kirchner. *A new equational unification method : a generalisation of Martelli-Montanari's algorithm*. In : Proc. 7th CADE, Springer-Verlag, LNCS 170 (1984).

[Kirchner-Lescanne 87] C. Kirchner and P. Lescanne. *Solving disequations*. In : Proc. 2nd IEEE Symp. on Logic in Computer Science (1987).

[Komorovski 82] Komorovski. *QLOG - The programming environment for Prolog in Lisp*. In : Logic programming (Clark and Tarnlund, Eds.), Academic Press (1982).

[Kowalski 79] R.A. Kowalski. *Logic for problem solving*. Artificial Intelligence Series, North-Holand (1979).

[Lassez 86] J.L. Lassez, M.J. Maher, and K. Marriott. *Unification revisited*. Research Report RC 12394, IBM T.J. Watson Research Center (1986).

[Lassez-Marriott 87] J.L. Lassez and K. Marriott. *Explicit representation of terms defined by counter examples*. J. of Automated Reasoning (1987).

[Lindstrom 85] G. Lindstrom. *Functional programming and the logical variable*. 12th ACM POPL (1985).

[Lloyd 84] J.W. Lloyd. *Foudations of logic programming*. Springer-Verlag (1984).

[Martelli-Montanari 82] A. Martelli and U. Montanari. *An efficient unification algorithm*. ACM TOPLAS, 4(2) (1982).

[Mellish-Hardy 84] C.S. Mellish and Hardy. *Integrating Prolog in the Poplog environment*. In : Implementations of Prolog (J.A. Campbell, Ed.), Ellis Horwood (1984).

[Paterson-Wegman 78] M.S. Paterson and M.N. Wegman. *Linear unification*. JCSS, 16(2) (1978).

[Plotkin 70] G. Plotkin. *A note on inductive generalization*. In : Machine intelligence 5, (1970).

[Plotkin 71] G. Plotkin. *A further note on inductive generalization*. In : Machine intelligence 6, (1971).

[Reddy 85] Uday S. Reddy. *Narrowing as the operational semantics of functinal languages*. In : Proc. IEEE Symposium on Logic Programming (1985).

[Reynolds 70] J. Reynolds. *Transformational systems and the algebraic structure of atomic formulas*. In : Machine intelligence 5, (1970).

[Robinson 65] J.A. Robinson. *A machine oriented logic based on the resolution principle*. JACM 12(1) (1965).

[Robinson 83] J.A. Robinson. *Logic programming, past, present and future*. New Generation Computing 1 (1983).

[Robinson-Sibert 82] J.A. Robinson and Sibert. *LOGLISP : an alternative to Prolog*. In : Machine Inteligence 10 (1982).

[Schnoebelen 87] Ph. Schnoebelen. *Rewriting techniques for the temporal analysis of communicating processes*. In : Proc. PARLE Conference, Springer-Verlag, LNCS 259 (1987).

[Schnoebelen 88] Ph. Schnoebelen. *Compilation of pattern matching*. Research Report LIFIA, Grenoble (1988).

[Stickel 81] M. Stickel. *A unification algorithm for associative-commutative functions.* JACM 28, (1981).

[Turner 82] D.A. Turner. *Recursion equations as a programming language.* In : Functional programming and its applications (D.A. Turner, Ed.), Cambridge University Press (1982).

[Turner 85] D.A. Turner. *Miranda : a non-strict functional language with polymorphic types.* In : Proc. 2nd Conf. on Functional Programming Languages and Computer Architecture, Springer-Verlag, LNCS 201 (1985).

[Vere 75] Vere. *Induction concept in the predicate calculus.* In : Proc. IJCAI'75, (1975).

Advanced Topics in Automated Deduction

W. Bibel

University of British Columbia and
Canadian Institute for Advanced Research

1 Introduction

This chapter deals with a number of issues in Automated Deduction that have recently attracted some attention in this area. The presentation is *not* meant to provide an introduction to this area. Rather its purpose is to supplement the introductory articles [5,24] contained in a preceding volume. In other words, the reader is expected to be familiar with the basic techniques used in Automated Deduction either from these or from other sources. This requires, for instance, a familiarity with resolution and the connection method. Also, the importance of deduction for Artificial Intelligence is not discussed here again. The reader who lacks motivation (or is confused by some ongoing discussions) in this respect might wish to read the introduction to [5].

In recent years there has been a remarkable progress in the field of automating deduction which is mainly due to the success of PROLOG. The number of logical inferences per seconds (LIPS) now ranges between 300K and 500K for the most advanced systems. Ironically, this dramatic speed–up in deductive performance has not yet produced any significant result such as the proof of a longstanding conjecture in Mathematics, or the like. Rather it occasionally happened that seemingly simple deductive problems cause these systems difficulty. This, for instance, happened with Schubert's steamroller problem [12] that we will briefly discuss in Section 3.

We see the following three different main problems in the current technology of Automated Deduction.

- Control regimes such as those used in PROLOG are too simple–minded.
- The expressive power of PROLOG is too poor.
- Certain phenomena arising in human reasoning are badly understood for an adequate representation within some logical formalism.

In this chapter we will not address the last item, only briefly discuss issues related with the second item, and focus mainly on the first of these points. Indeed, a more elaborate control regime for deductive systems may enhance their performance without affecting the virtues of the architecture of PROLOG–like systems as has been demonstrated in [12]. In order to establish a basis for the discussions of this issue, we begin our presentation with studying various possible control regimes. First, we review the standard arguments in Section 2 that favor top–down in comparison with bottom–up control. Then we show in Section 3 that a reasonably restricted bottom–up regime is actually superior in its performance. The gist of this regime consists of the application of several reduction operations, notably what we call DB– and ISOL–reductions. Only after their application is the control handed over to a top–down regime. One may think of this approach as a way of eliminating some of the redundancy involved in the representation of a logic program in order to then work on the harder core of it.

Section 4 extends these discussions to programs that contain recursive rules. Such rules give rise to deductive cycles. So Section 4.1 first characterizes such recursive cycles and distinguishes them from tautological ones. Section 4.2 then describes an algorithm that compiles a certain class of programs into iterative mechanisms. The application of this algorithm is then demonstrated with more complicated problems, namely the Fibonacci program and the rule expressing the associative law that both illustrate specific features. Factoring plays a significant role for the first and a resulting organization of the database does so for the second of these problems. Since there is a great similarity with the work done in datalogic, but also some terminological confusion in the database literature, we include a clarification of some notions in Section 4.5. Finally, the limitations of our approach are discussed.

Note that the approach we take is quite different in its spirit from that aiming at LIPS performance records. An elaborate analysis like the one required for the algorithm just mentioned needs quite a bit of execution time, which might slow down the performance for simple problems. We gain a more intelligent behavior this way, however, so that in more elaborate problems the advantages will outweigh the overhead.

Although quantifiers are present in most of human reasoning, current deductive systems of the PROLOG-type do not even mention them. In Section 5 we recall a way dealing with them that has long been neglected. It does not take recourse to skolemization, but rather takes advantage of the logical operators in their relative positions within the formula. While this is already attractive in the case of first-order logic, it has recently led to an extremely elegant solution to treating deduction in various modal logics [26] that we briefly summarize. A brief section reminding of the importance of building-in theories and mathematical induction concludes the whole chapter.

In our treatment we use standard notation as much as possible. In cases of doubt the reader might wish to check with [3].

2 Bottom-up vs top-down execution

The control regime of a PROLOG system is strictly top-down. It takes the goal clause (considered to be at the top of a search tree), selects its first literal, searches for a matching head, performs resolution on the pair of literals (i.e. on the connection) thus located, yielding a modified goal clause for which this process is carried out in exactly the same way again, and so forth. This regime, which is actually based on *ordered input resolution*, works fine for many problems. At the same time for many other problems it is just not appropriate and often fails badly. Consider first why it works pretty well in many cases, which will be illustrated by the following two programs.

$$
\begin{array}{lll}
Pa_1 . & & \\
\vdots & & \\
Pa_m . & & \\
Q_1 x & \leftarrow & Px . \\
 & \vdots & \\
Q_n x & \leftarrow & Px . \\
 & \leftarrow & Q_n a_m ?
\end{array}
$$

Top-down this program would succeed with two inference steps in the obvious way. An unintelligent bottom-up execution would need $m \cdot n$ inference steps, not counting in both cases the identification of pairing predicates. As we can see, top-down execution in PROLOG outperforms bottom-up execution in this kind of program.

$$
\begin{array}{lll}
P0. & & \\
Q0. & & \\
P(x+1) & \leftarrow & Px. \\
Q(x+1) & \leftarrow & Qx. \\
 & \leftarrow & Qn\,?
\end{array}
$$

Top–down this program would succeed with $n+1$ steps (see below for the built–in arithmetic) while, again, an unintelligent bottom–up execution might actually run forever. These two programs seem to be typical for programs involving a number of facts and "chaining" rules on the one hand and recursive rules on the other. Since facts, chaining and recursive rules are the main components of any logic program, it seems that in general top–down execution provides a much better performance. This is not always true as we will see upon closer inspection in the following sections.

Let us start considering this other side of the coin with a look at the factorial program below which is actually a variant of the recursive program above.

$$
\begin{array}{lll}
FAC(0,1). & & \\
FAC(x+1,(x+1)\cdot y) & \leftarrow & FAC(x,y). \\
 & \leftarrow & FAC(n,z)\,?
\end{array}
$$

In the discussion of this and similar examples we allow theory connections and theory unifications [3], i.e. terms like $0+1$ and $1\cdot 1$ are considered unifiable on the basis of the theory of arithmetic. In this sense this theory is *built into* the deductive mechanism. Now, if this program is executed top–down, any of the instances of the variable y cannot be assigned a value until the whole process reaches the bottom which requires the intermediate storage of n expressions associated with these n instances that cannot be evaluated. In contrast, the bottom–up execution allows the immediate computation of the value of any instance of each occurring variable. Since this value is all that is needed in order to compute the value of the next instance, this next instance may make use of the same storage location as the previous one, which altogether amounts to three storage locations for the three occurring variables. Even without a more detailed quantitative analysis it should be obvious from this discussion that here bottom–up execution results in a much faster computation of the final value for z than top–down execution.

In [9] (see also [7]) it was first shown that bottom–up execution corresponds to the execution of iterative programs in conventional programming languages, and top–down to recursive ones. The implementation of recursion in general requires maintaining a data structure (called a stack–frame) for every recursive call that has not terminated yet. A recursive computation involving n recursive procedure calls requires, therefore, space linear in n. On the other hand, an iterative program typically uses only a constant amount of memory, independent of the number of iterations. These observations apply for any programming language, and have been illustrated for PROLOG above with the factorial program.

This demonstrates that there seem to be virtues in bottom–up execution as well. This is true not only for recursive programs but also for programs with a focus on facts and chains. An example is Schubert's steamroller problem that will be described in the following section. So the natural question arises whether one might combine the virtues of both kinds of regimes. We devote the following sections to a discussion of exactly this question. This discussion will result in a much more attractive control regime than the one provided by either top–down or bottom–up execution.

3 Bottom–up reductions

As we know from [24] (or from [3] for that matter) the problem of finding a proof consists of identifying an appropriate subset among the connections of the given formula. Obviously, the smaller the set of connections the easier this task can be achieved. There are many possibilities to reduce this set in a given formula. A number of them are treated, for instance, in [3] such as pure literal reduction, subsumption, tautology reduction, and elimination of simple circuits, that all remove connections and possibly clauses. Here we concentrate on further reductions of a less familiar sort. Let us consider an example for illustration.

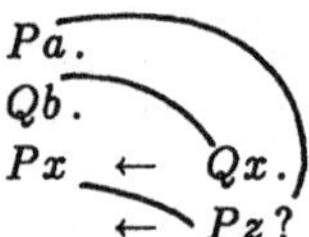

Concentrating on the Q–connection we observe that both literals engaged occur in no other connection of the whole formula. We call connections with this property ***isolated***. Note that the remaining connections are not isolated in this sense, since Pz occurs in both of them. The isolated connection in question may be eliminated by substituting the affected clauses by their resolvent, which amounts to a (bottom–up) resolution step with elimination of the parent clauses and has the following result.

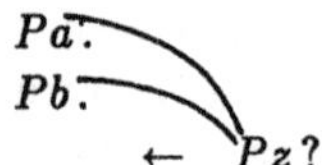

Clearly, this reduction step, called ***ISOL–reduction***, decreases the complexity of the initial formula and retains provability in general.

It can easily be seen that the definition of isolated connections may be liberalized by allowing literals to occur in more than one connection if they are ground literals in unit clauses (i.e. facts). For details on this and for several ways to produce isolated connections see [12]. Here we only discuss one further reduction that is based on the following valid equivalence.

$$Pr \leftarrow r \in \{c_1, \ldots, c_k\} \;\leftrightarrow\; Pc_1 \wedge \ldots \wedge Pc_k$$

The substitution in a logical formula of the right side of this equivalence by the left side will be called a ***DB–reduction***. Note that the literal $r \in \{c_1, \ldots, c_k\}$ may be tested for its truth–value by database operations. For that reason we will take the convention to drop such a literal from this kind of logic program and treat the range that it defines separately (or even implicitly). In fact we take the view that this range is actually represented in a database table not presented explicitly in the following examples.

DB–reduction properly reduces the size of a formula. But more importantly, it often results in new isolated connections which may then in turn be eliminated. For instance,

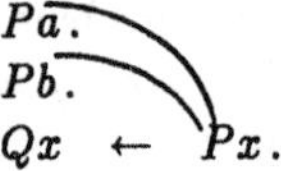

has no isolated connection, while after DB–reduction, yielding

with $r \in \{a, b\}$, indeed an isolated connection appears.

In conjunction with ISOL–reduction DB–reduction in general requires the use of all the usual database operators such as union $\cup$, intersection $\cap$, projection π, and the (natural equi–) join $\bowtie$. Since they are standard [25], we only demonstrate them by use of a few simple examples. For instance, consider the following program in which $r_1 \in R_1$ and $r_2 \in R_2$.

$$\begin{array}{lll} Pr_1. & & \\ Qr_2. & & \\ Px & \leftarrow & Qx. \\ Sy & \leftarrow & Py. \end{array}$$

Here only the Q–connection is isolated which upon removal yields

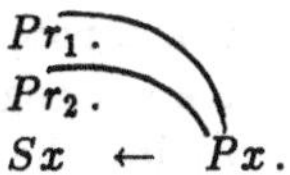

The obvious next step is a further DB–reduction that takes the union $R_1 \cup R_2 = R$ for the range of r.

$$\begin{array}{lll} Pr. & & \\ Sx & \leftarrow & Px. \end{array}$$

obviously producing a new isolated connection. It is well–known in logic programming that two subgoals in a clause sharing common variables correspond to the join in databases which in the simplest case of unary predicates is identical with the intersection $R_1 \cap R_2 = R$. For instance, if r ranges over R thus defined then ISOL–reduction upon the two connections in the program

$$\begin{array}{lll} Pr_1. & & \\ Qr_2. & & \\ Sx & \leftarrow & Qx, Px. \end{array}$$

simply results in Sr. Had the subgoals been Qyx, Pxz, we would have had $R_1 \bowtie R_2 = R$ instead with everything else remaining the same. The projection, finally, comes into play if Pr is connected with a clause of the form $Qx \leftarrow Pxy$. ISOL–reduction here leads to Qr_1, where $r_1 \in \pi_1 R$.

With these reductions at hand, an enhanced control regime would now operate on a given logic program in the following way. All the possible connections will first be determined. Then possible reductions will be performed until none is applicable any more. To some extent these operations may already be performed even at compile time. Note that they never require more than linear time (otherwise they should not be subsumed under the notion of a reduction, cf. [6]). Thereafter, the usual top–down execution will be carried out on the remaining program. Note that in this last phase a form of unification is needed that incorporates database operations.

As a technical remark we mention that in performing ISOL–reduction with a literal Pr in a unit clause this literal would not actually be removed from the program. As a reference to a database table it might be needed for further queries to the system that might involve the predicate P.

A proof system for Horn clause logic, PROTHEO, that follows this whole scheme of operation has been developed in the author's former research group [12]. In [12] the power of this approach has been demonstrated with Schubert's steamroller problem. This problem describes the eating habits of a number of animals, and asks for the existence of an animal among these characterized by certain properties. As a logical formula it consists of 26 clauses (in one of the possible formalizations). For most proof systems operating in a purely top–down oriented way the search space of this formula turned out to be infeasible. DB– and ISOL–reduction reduces these 26 clauses to merely 4 remaining clauses with altogether 7 literals. There is nearly no search left so that the solution can be computed in a straightforward way mainly as a deterministic sequence of fast database operations.

A number of other proposals have been made to cope with the problem that was demonstrated by the steamroller formula. Most if not all of them involve the declaration of sorts, requiring a sorted logic theorem prover. In effect this eventually results in a behavior very similar to the one in our solution. This is because a DB–reduction actually collects several items into the same "sort". By ISOL–reduction these sorts are then propagated through the remaining formula. In sorted logic we have a more elaborate unification procedure that additionally has to care for the sorts of the terms. In our solution the analogue complication is the incorporation of database operations into the unification mechanism mentioned above.

While no one has studied these similarities and potential differences in further detail, it seems to be obvious that technically the differences are negligible. However there is a major drawback for the sorted logic approach insofar as it requires the programmer to provide the system with the information as to which among the unary predicates are to be treated as sorts, an unpleasant extra burden on the user. Also it does not seem to provide a solution for "sort"–predicates with more than one argument, while obviously our reduction mechanism is completely general in that respect. Since first–order logic is already complicated enough, particularly in view of more general applications like in non–monotonic reasoning, the extra technical complications involved in sorted logic cannot be regarded as a particular virtue either. Hence for all these and other reasons the reduction mechanism described in this section is our favorite solution to this issue.

By now the reader may have noticed that the first program in the previous section, which was meant to witness the supposed superiority of top–down vs. bottom–up execution, with DB– and ISOL–reduction (i.e. bottom–up) behaves as efficiently as the usual top–down execution. In other words the arguments given there — for the case of facts and chaining rules — have lost their credibility. On the contrary, a bottom–up regime like the one we just described is at least as good as a purely top–down one, and sometimes (like in the steamroller problem) even dramatically better. It replaces deep search trees by shallow ones, thus reducing the need for costly backtracking substantially.

In [4] it is shown that the same technique leads to the reduction of any kind of a constraint satisfaction problem to the problem of executing a nested term consisting of database operations. Since constraint satisfaction problems play a particularly important role in Intellectics[1], we see that the seemingly simple ideas presented in this section apparently have important applications beyond those represented by the steamroller problem.

In spirit the Q^* algorithm [19] addresses exactly the same problem as the one dealt with in the present section. The authors actually emphasize their view of Q^* as a problem reduction mechanism which is exactly what our reduction rules provide as well. While here we presented a very few and simple reduction rules, Q^* seems to be a collection of a number of ideas built into this algorithm. As far as it can be taken from the way Q^* is presented in [19] all these ideas are actually covered in a technical sense by our reductions, so that our approach appears to be much more satisfactory because of its simplicity, generality, and uniformity. But it might still be worthwhile to look into the (unpublished) algorithm Q^* itself in order to possibly detect features that might further enhance our technique perhaps by way of a further reduction rule.

[1] the field of Artificial Intelligence and Cognitive Science

4 Recursion

So far we have discussed a number of reduction operations that simplify a given logical problem and sometimes already provide even the whole proof. We now study the logical structure of the formulas that result from such a sequence of reductions, aiming at the identification of further possibilities for their efficient treatment. Such formulas will typically contain cycles of connections possibly indicating some sort of a recursive structure. The present section will hence be devoted to the topic of recursion.

4.1 Cycles

We begin our discussion of recursion with the definition of the more general concept of a cycle.

Definition. In a set of clauses a *cycle* is a set $\{c_1, \ldots, c_n\}$ of connections $c_i = \{L_i, R_i\}$, $i = 1, \ldots, n$, such that R_i and L_j with $j - i = 1 \bmod n$ are different literals in one clause. A cycle is called *linear* if there is no literal that occurs in more than one of its connections.

Recall that unifiability of the terms in the literals is not inherent in the notion of a connection, that is, only the predicate symbols determine connections. Our notation $\{L_i, R_i\}$ is meant to indicate an implicit existential quantification that orders the otherwise unordered pairs of literals in the connections. The following example illustrates a cyclic set of connections that would not qualify as a cycle in the sense of our definition, since Px is contained in two connections next to each other.

$$\begin{array}{l} Px. \\ Qfy \leftarrow Py. \\ \quad\leftarrow Qz, Pz? \end{array}$$

The cycle formed by the two connections in $Axz \leftarrow Axy, Ayz$ is not linear since Axz occurs in both of them. There are two different types of such cycles, the tautological and the recursive ones. Let us first consider tautological cycles.

Definition. A cycle is called *tautological* if there exists a clause C involved in the cycle and a substitution which on C is the identity substitution, such that all connections in the cycle become complementary pairs of literals.

For instance, the cycle in each of the following clause sets is tautological,

$$\{\{Px \leftarrow Qy, Px\}\}, \quad \{\{Px \leftarrow Qy\}, \{Qz \leftarrow Pz\}\}, \quad \{\{Pxy \leftarrow Qyx\}, \{Qza \leftarrow Pza\}\}$$

while this does not hold for the following clause sets.

$$\{\{Px \leftarrow Py\}\}, \quad \{\{Axz \leftarrow Axy, Ayz\}\},$$

$$\{\{Px \leftarrow Qx\}, \{Qa \leftarrow Pb\}\}, \quad \{\{Pxy \leftarrow Qxy\}, \{Qza \leftarrow Pua\}\}$$

In no case can tautological cycles ever give rise to a recursion since the identity substitution on C in the definition prevents any progress while traversing the cycle in a deductive process. Under certain conditions even some or all of the connections in a tautological cycle may be deleted without affecting provability. On the ground level such conditions have been stated in Lemma 3.6 of [6] for a class of tautological cycles called simple circuits (mentioned before in section 3). The generalization to the first-order level follows standard techniques [3], which always require some care, however. The deletion of such connections may leave some of the previously connected literals pure in the sense of [6] so that whole clauses may become obsolete. Altogether this is a powerful generalization of the well-known reduction of deleting tautologies mentioned already in the previous section. It may be used to further reduce a given program beyond what was already achieved with the techniques described in the previous section, and in this sense it is indispensable for the restriction of the search space.

Definition. A cycle is called *potentially recursive*, if it is not tautological and if there exists a weak unifier for all its connections.

Weak unification was defined in [15] and captures whether in a proof a pair of literals is potentially unifiable by possibly renaming variables so that a variable occurring at both ends of a connection adopts a name at one end that is different from the one at the other. For instance, the connection in

$$Pfx \leftarrow Px.$$

is weakly unifiable in this sense since x will be renamed to, say, x' in one of the two literals. The obvious idea behind this concept is to take into account the possibility of considering more than a single copy of the clauses involved.

Definition. A cycle is called *recursive* if there is a proof of the formula with a spanning set of connections that contains a fixed number of instances of the whole cycle, i.e. of all its connections.

For instance, there are two such instances (depicted here with one connection only) from the potentially recursive cycle of the previous example in the following proof.

$$\begin{array}{lll} Pa. & & \\ Pfx & \leftarrow & Px. \\ & \leftarrow & Pfffa? \end{array}$$

If the instances of the clauses involved in a recursive cycle are represented explicitly, then there is actually no cycle anymore. This may be seen in the following picture where, along with the substitutions involved, the three instances of the rule in the previous proof here are represented explicitly.

$$\begin{array}{lllll} Pa. & & & & \\ Pfx & \leftarrow & Px. & & x\backslash a \\ Pfy & \leftarrow & Py. & & y\backslash fa \\ Pfz & \leftarrow & Pz. & & z\backslash ffa \\ & \leftarrow & Pfffa? & & \end{array}$$

Nevertheless there is this cyclic property of coming back again and again to a copy of the same clause. In the following we will often briefly speak of a recursive cycle even if we actually mean a potentially recursive one. This notion of a recursive cycle, usually introduced with resolution in mind, is generally accepted although there are differences in the details of the definition given by various authors such as our exclusion of tautological cycles; this will be further discussed in Section 4.5 below.

The restriction in our definition of cycles, whereby the literals in the same clause have to be different ones, excludes other types of cycles (like the example shown above) that might as well be considered in our context. Although I lack a striking argument I nevertheless feel that the notion captured here is the more productive one for our purposes. Indications of this are the following two observations. First, a tour through a cycle, that ends in the same literal where it started from, indeed returns to this point of departure in quite a different state than it started from since, for instance, it could not run through the same cycle again in a deductively meaningful way. Second, these types of cycles seem better attacked with the reduction provided by factoring, which reduces them to the cycles we have defined above, or the cycle can at least be broken into two parts associated with the deductive solution of two independent subgoals. Both actually applies to the example of a "non-cycle" given above.

Recursive cycles as defined above may still include cycles that are tautological in nature (but of course not tautological in the sense of our definition). We may only conjecture that our definition of tautological cycles covers all the cycles that are indeed tautological in nature. It is actually somewhat of a surprise that no one seems to have bothered before to clarify such a basic distinction.

4.2 Compilation of recursive cycles

In a given formula (or logic program) all cycles can be detected fast by well–known algorithms. Once the cyclic structure is known, this insight may be used for a much faster proof detection than the one that could be achieved by a straightforward depth–first search as in PROLOG. This observation was known for a long time and has been made, for instance, in [9]. Special attention was given recently to this possibility by the researchers working in datalogic, i.e. in the field on the boundary between logic and databases that will be reviewed in more detail in Section 4.5 below.

The most attractive approach among those taken in this kind of work is the one that aims at a compilation of the whole proof process [17]. For instance, the compilation of a program such as the one in our last example in the previous section should result in a code that checks the term in the goal for an arbitrary number of consecutive f's followed by an a, rather than performing any deductive steps at all [9]. We will now outline such an approach for a limited class of programs. First, let us illustrate the idea with the familiar factorial problem.

$$\begin{array}{lcl} FAC(0,1)\,. & & \\ FAC(x+1,(x+1)\cdot y) & \leftarrow & FAC(x,y)\,. \\ & \leftarrow & FAC(n,z)\,? \end{array}$$

We have discussed this program already in Section 2. Recall from there that we allow theory connections and theory unifications [3], i.e. terms like $0+1$ and $1\cdot 1$ are considered unifiable on the basis of the theory of arithmetic. There are four unifiable connections in this program and one of them forms a potentially recursive cycle. How could one, with such a knowledge at hand, head for a compilation such that any reasonable goal may be executed fast without explicit (more time-consuming) deduction steps?

Recall that running a logic program means finding and executing a proof. Also recall that in terms of the connection method a proof consists of a spanning set of connections. The cycle does not itself form a spanning set of connections. The single connection formed by the fact $FAC(0,1)$ and the top goal would satisfy this requirement, but in this simple case the cycle connection would not even be involved in the proof. Another spanning set of connections is set up by the connection formed by the fact $FAC(0,1)$ and the rule subgoal, the cycle connection, and the connection formed by the rule head and the top goal. Let us examine more closely this second alternative.

Since the cycle connection is not tautological, it must connect two different instances of the rule which we may assume to be the i–th and the $i+1$–th instances. The unifications that are implied by this connection may be expressed as the following equations.

$$x_{i+1} = x_i + 1\,,\;\; y_{i+1} = (x_i+1)\cdot y_i$$

The $FAC(0,1)$–connection may be used to determine a value for the base case.

$$x_1 = 0\,,\;\; y_1 = 1$$

The top goal connection determines the value for the output.

$$z = (x_k+1)\cdot y_k$$

where k is such that $x_k + 1 = n$. It is a simple step from these equations to the following destructive assignment program.

$$x \leftarrow 0;\ y \leftarrow 1;\ \ell : x \leftarrow x+1;\ y \leftarrow x \cdot y;\ \text{if } x \neq n \text{ goto } \ell;\ \text{output } y$$

This program clearly outperforms any deductive mechanism, or, to put it differently, it provides the fastest way to carry out the proof for the above formula (except for parallel executions). So is there a mechanical way to extract it from the formula? We claim that the following *compilation algorithm* may be refined so as to achieve this for a limited class of formulas.

1. Identify cycles in the problem (the single connection in the rule above).

2. Select one of the cycles (only one choice above).

3. Add unifiable connections necessary to form a spanning set (the two additional connections above).

4. Select appropriate "base" connections (the $FAC(0,1)$–connection above) providing the initialization for the variables involved.

5. Extract the cycle equations (as done above).

6. Possibly normalize these equations (not needed above; for an example see next section).

7. Extract the termination equations from the remaining connections (as done above).

8. Transform the resulting set of equations into a bottom–up destructive assignment algorithm (the result was shown above).

Selections in this algorithm have to be interpreted as non–deterministic features that have yet to be transformed into some sort of a while–loop (or, in other words, some sort of backtracking). The present example is so simple that no alternatives are possible.

There is an alternate way of looking at the equations resulting from the unification of the connected terms which will be helpful as a guide to the more refined version of the algorithm. Namely, the cycle's effect may be seen as that of a function f that takes a pair (x,y) as input and returns the resulting pair $f(x,y)$ as output. Let us call f the *cycle function* associated with the cycle in question (a way to determine and represent such a function will be shown shortly). This observation holds for any cycle although one would have to consider arbitrary tuples rather than just pairs in the general case.

If the cycle is traversed k times then the output will be $f^k(x,y)$. If the initial values for (x,y) have been obtained in step 4, viz. $(0,1)$ in the present case, then step 7 provides a single equation that is $(n,z) = f^k(0,1)$ in our case. Actually this is a vector equation and therefore consists of two equations, one for each component. Since this makes two equations with two unknowns, k and z, they can be solved, that is, z may be provided in a functional form dependent on the input only. So z may as well be computed in a functional way which is what we are aiming for.

The extraction of f is particularly simple in our case where the pair (x,y) is explicitly contained in the subgoal (i.e. without any further function symbols) and where the cycle contains only a single connection. In this simplest case f can just be read off from the other literal in the connection. That is, here the function consists of a pair where the left component is the $+1$–function and the right one the $\cdot$ –function with appropriate argument–functions. Using the primitive functions and operations from recursion theory and following the notation in [13], then for the factorial program the full equation is the following.

$$(n,z) = [(\varsigma \circ \pi_2) \times (\cdot \circ < \varsigma, \pi_2 \circ {}_1\xi_2 >)]^{\#}((0,1),k)$$

Since $n = \varsigma^{\#}(n)$, it is straightforward to determine k and z in this case. The reader not familiar with this functional language should not worry too much. The only lesson to be learned from this exercise is that the compilation of recursive cycles indeed boils down to solving equations. If we take the present alternative way of determining the cycle function then step 8 in the algorithm becomes even superfluous since the primitive functions and operations used on the right side of the equation above provide a perfect and highly efficient programming language.

Note that the resulting functional program in the present example is iterative in the sense of a DO–loop rather than a WHILE–loop. So the performance of the resultant program is even better than the algorithmic program shown further above (by using a register rather than a termination test to be executed in each cycle). This may be achieved in general following this approach as long as we are computing primitive recursive functions which is done anyway most of the time.

Coming back to the algorithm itself, let us emphasize once more that we are not claiming to handle *all* recursive problems this way, of course. The point is that we aim at an identification of a class that consists of a rather simple, but popular kind of problems to be treated this way. Simple problems in this sense are those that have *linear* cycles only. In fact the present version obviously has only a single *cycle* in mind. Another feature that makes problems simple is given when the output tuple (the pair (n, z) in the present example) may be represented in closed form as in the equation above which of course is not always possible (the Ackermann function is the classic example). We will refer to this as to the *solvability* feature.

Note that the approach taken here with compiling logic programs is different from what is usually considered in the compilation of logic programs. There, no transformation into an iterative form takes place as here. Of course, the program might be presented in an iterative way by the user himself (see programs 8.3 and 8.4 in [23] for computing the factorial in an iterative way in PROLOG). Although possible, we would *not* like to have the programmer bother about this issue.

The transformation we suggest is also not provided by the technique of tail recursion optimization used in PROLOG. This optimization re–uses the memory area allocated for the parent goal for the new goal if this is the last call in the body of a rule. Although this technique can be used in our program above it does not provide a cure to the problem under discussion. The memory requirements still grow linearly with n, since the result variable z has to store the intermediate symbolic results $n \cdot y$, $n \cdot (n-1) \cdot y$, etc., whereby y cannot be evaluated. In addition there are the extra efforts needed for building each of the frames associated with the procedure calls. The fact that here this growth could actually be prevented by computing the result of the subexpressions like $n \cdot (n-1)$ is accidental with this particular example, and would not apply in all cases where our approach would still work. In summary, we claim that the compilation techniques used in PROLOG could be enhanced by the bottom–up compilation we are proposing here.

4.3 The incorporation of factoring

The factorial problem is too simple to illustrate all the features that have to be taken into account in our approach. Therefore we analyze a more complicated example in the present section, viz. the Fibonacci problem, and test the previous algorithmic steps with it. Thereby we prefer the more illustrative first alternative of representing the equations resulting from the unifications.

$$\begin{array}{lll} FIB(0,1). & & \\ FIB(1,1). & & \\ FIB(k+2, x+y) & \leftarrow & FIB(k+1, x),\ FIB(k,y). \\ & \leftarrow & FIB(n,z)\,? \end{array}$$

There are two connections in the rule that may both, separately or together, be used to form a recursive cycle. If we consider using them both for a single cycle then this one would no more be linear (hence much more complicated) since the head literal would occur in both connections of the cycle. So we try to succeed by using only one of them and select the one containing the rule's first subgoal (the other alternative being briefly mentioned later). This completes the first two steps of the compilation algorithm.

Step 3 requires determining a spanning set of connections. Ignoring the trivial alternatives that do not involve the cycle connection, we proceed in a mechanical way as follows. There is only a single connection possible that involves the rule head and does not interfere with the cycle, namely the one with the program's goal; so this must be taken. Similarly, there is no choice with the first subgoal which only unifies with $FIB(1,1)$. This literal is also contained in the connection with the other subgoal to be taken into consideration. $FIB(0,1)$ is sort of an "isolated literal" since for the spanning set of connections to be assembled there is no other connection that contains this literal. It must be selected as the connection required for $FIB(k,y)$ since otherwise unifiability fails for one of the two connections that contain $FIB(1,1)$.

This selected set of connections is now spanning except when the cycle connection is involved since then the second subgoal literal is pure in instances other than the first two ones (not unifiable anymore with $FIB(0,1)$ and $FIB(1,1)$). This is where this problem differs significantly from the previous ones. At this point we recall the factoring technique in Automated Theorem Proving [3], that is, we consider factoring the first and second subgoals in the rule (illustrated as a factoring connection) as the only possibility left to settle the spanning property requirement. So altogether we arrive at the following situation.

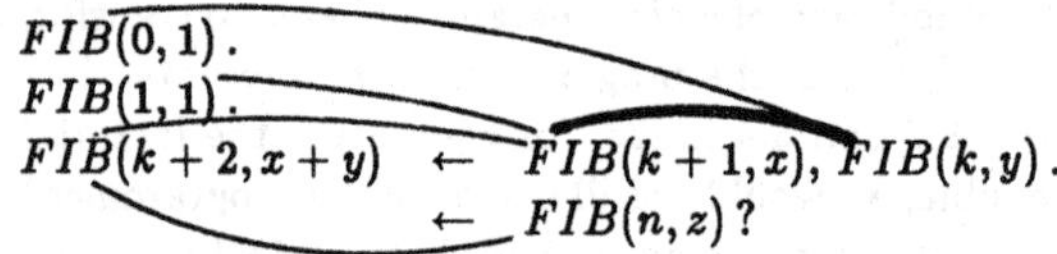

Step 4 in the algorithm now yields the equations $k_1 = 0$, $x_1 = y_1 = 1$. The equations $k_2 = 1$, $y_2 = 1$ in a refined version of the algorithm might result not before step 5 has been performed since only then this assignment becomes obvious to a mechanical procedure. Step 5 yields $k_{i+1} + 1 = k_i + 2$ and $x_{i+1} = x_i + y_i$, where the first one in step 6 will be reduced to $k_{i+1} = k_i + 1$. This equation now determines the instances that are linked together by the factoring connection. Hence in addition we obtain $y_{i+1} = x_i$. From now on the situation is the same as in the factorial problem so that we may proceed exactly as demonstrated there with performing the remaining steps 7 and 8. In other words, our compilation algorithm succeeds also in solving this more complicated problem if factoring is included in the proof technique as it certainly should.

Above we mentioned the other alternative of selecting a linear cycle. Had we selected this one then the resulting equation $k_{i+1} = k_i + 2$ would turn out to be inconsistent with the constraints resulting from the factoring connection, which discards this alternative.

4.4 A datalogic example

As we mentioned before, a lot of work has already been done to compile recursion for the access of a database. By treating the transitivity problem frequently studied in that area we first want to demonstrate the relevance of our algorithmic approach to this sort of application. A more detailed evaluation of the relationship with that area and its terminology will then follow.

$$
\begin{array}{lll}
Aab\,. & & \\
Abc\,. & & \\
Acd\,. & & \\
Ade\,. & & \\
Axz & \leftarrow & Axy,\ Ayz\,. \\
 & \leftarrow & Avw\,?
\end{array}
$$

Before we apply our algorithm from Section 4.2 to this example we clarify the circumstances under which it is meant to be applied. One alternative would be to run this algorithm at compile time with the query already available. Another one would consider the compilation prior to the queries being available. It actually makes quite a difference which of these two alternatives is assumed since in the first case we would have the information about the specific input, its argument position and its value, while in the second one neither are known. For real applications we have to provide solutions for both of these situations. Prior to any query available the database has to be organized for a fast access via the recursive rule. But once the query is available its particular features should be used once more to speed up the access even further. In the following we thus first consider the case where it is not known which of v and w actually carries the input and what this input is.

As a second remark note that it is not this particular problem for which we strive to provide a particularly smart database solution. Rather our algorithm (in its refined version) is meant to handle any such problem similarly well, obviously a much more ambitious goal. In the present case the result should be that for a given input, say on v, the compiled algorithm would just start at the appropriate point in the list (c, d, e) to just read off all the possible outputs from the remainder of that list. With these preliminaries in mind let us now see how our algorithm would proceed with this particular program whereby a number of issues will be mentioned that will have to be incorporated in the envisaged refined version of the algorithm.

The program has a structure very similar to that of the Fibonacci program. So if we again restrict our considerations to linear cycles then the first step produces the two obvious alternatives from which we select (in step 2) the first one. In order to put together a spanning set of connections in step 3, the technique of factoring from the previous section would be naturally attempted in this case again. It would fail, however, in the present case, since the resulting unifications would transform our cycle into a tautological one (so a test for tautological cycles as a consequence of unifications being, for instance, among the necessary refinements of the algorithm mentioned above). The only way to assemble a spanning set is by solving the second subgoal in the rule in each instance with a fact from the database. All other connections are then obvious. So we obtain the following equations (step 5).

$$x_{i+1} = x_i = v\,,\; y_{i+1} = z_i\,,\; z_{i+1} \in \lambda u A z_i u\,,\; w = z_k$$

There are two cases to be considered. Assume the first where v carries the input which in step 7 yields

$$y_1 \in \lambda u A v u\,,\; z_1 \in \lambda u A y_1 u\,,\; w = z_i\,,\; i \in \{1, 2, \ldots\}$$

So indeed the algorithm provides a precomputation for this case so that for a concrete v the resulting w–values may just be read off the z–list assuming that a further refinement of the algorithm has provided the maximal list which is (c, d, e) as noted before.

The other case where w carries the input goes similarly. Both cases may be prepared by the compiler without having the actual input. Once the input is available the appropriate choice will be made. The second alternative in the choice of the two cycles by symmetry leads to the same solutions, an insight that at this point we would not expect from the compiler in mind (rather it would – redundantly – handle it as an alternative).

In summary, it turns out that our proposed algorithm provides the adequate framework for this kind of problem as well.

4.5 A logical view of datalogic

A *database* is a collection of explicitly given data organized in some way (see [22] for a more detailed definition). There has been an agreement on this notion for decades; only recently various authors are producing notational confusion that we will try to clarify in the following.

There is no need for a definition of *logic*, since it is well–known, not only for decades but even centuries. *Horn clause logic* is a more recent concept (denoting a certain part of logic) but still predates the emergence of the concept of databases. *PROLOG* is a programming language based on Horn clause logic. From a logical point of view databases are concerned with that part within (Horn clause) logic, that concerns the facts (i.e. the clauses consisting of a ground literal) only.

Given this common ground it is natural that there has always been an interaction between logic and the database field; let us just mention three logical papers [16,10,22], from three rather different periods, with an emphasis on databases. This interaction has recently intensified considerably so that it is justifiable to speak of a whole area in its own right. In [20] the term *datalog* is used that we slightly modify to the more elegant *datalogic*; either of these two terms is adequate since there is no doubt that we are dealing with (Horn clause) *logic* once rules are added, but at the same time the emphasis within logic is on the *data*.

Other names such as deductive databases (or even simply databases [1]) are ill–conceived. Since there is only the most trivial form of deduction possible in a database, which is the matching of a query (typically a literal) with a fact (another literal) in the database, what could be "deductive" about it? This remains true even though some deductions may be compiled into database or relational algebra operations as we have shown further above. It is not the database operations themselves that gain more power by this compilation, rather it is the compilation that in certain cases encodes the deductive steps with a combination of such simple operations.

The features behind the important notions of datalogic are quite familiar in the literature of Automated Theorem Proving for many years. For instance, [6,3] survey the origins of the notion of a cycle in the early seventies and even before. As we have shown above, the cyclic feature is the essence of a recursive rule. It should therefore be simple to restate the definitions of some datalogic notions (cf. [1,20]) in terms of cycles, a fact that will be demonstrated now. Of course, all the following definitions are restricted within datalogic to the Horn clause case while the cycle notions actually apply to the general case.

Definitions A predicate P is said to be *recursive* if there is a potentially recursive cycle containing P (i.e. P appears in a literal in some of its connections). Two predicates P and Q are called *mutually recursive* if there is a potentially recursive cycle containing both P and Q. A rule in a set of rules is called *recursive* if there is a potentially recursive cycle containing the rule's head. A recursive rule is *linear* if all potentially recursive cycles containing its head are linear. A set of rules is *linear* if all its recursive rules are linear. Two rules are *mutually recursive* if there is a potentially recursive cycle containing both their heads.

All these so–defined notions coincide with those in datalogic at least in spirit, but not always in the fine details. For instance, the two rules

$$\begin{array}{lcl} Px & \leftarrow & Qx. \\ Qy & \leftarrow & Py. \end{array}$$

contain a tautological cycle which therefore is not potentially recursive; hence the two rules are not mutually recursive in our terminology while they usually fall into that category in datalogic. Since the cycle here truly is a tautological, not a recursive one, we prefer our refined notion. Also note that a non–linear rule may still be treated in a linear way with linear cycles, as we have demonstrated with the Fibonacci and transitivity examples above, which once again shows an advantage of our refined terminology.

On the other hand we do not at all claim that this short subsection covers all the relevant techniques for treating recursion in the context of a database with maximal efficiency. For instance, concepts such as *adornments*, *magic sets*, *counting*, and others [1,20] would have to be discussed in a more comprehensive survey. Nevertheless we are convinced that these might preferably be incorporated on the basis outlined in the previous sections whenever they add truly new concepts to those introduced above.

4.6 Limitations

The technique for treating recursion efficiently, that has been described in the last few subsections, will, of course, not succeed in all cases. On purpose we have restricted ourselves to the treatment of a limited class of problems. This class is determined by the following two characteristics.

A Only linear and single cycles are considered, that feature

B the solvability property (see Section 4.2).

This limited class clearly contains all the tail recursion problems that have been mentioned in Section 4.2. On the other hand, there are many recursive problems that cannot be treated with our technique. An example is the following quite complex non–Horn problem [21].

$$\begin{array}{lcl} Pxz & \leftarrow & Pxy,\, Pyz\,. \\ Qxz & \leftarrow & Qxy,\, Qyz\,. \\ Qyx & \leftarrow & Qxy\,. \\ Pxy \vee Qxy\,. & & \\ & \leftarrow & Pab \vee Qcd\,? \end{array}$$

This formula allows nearly no reductions of the sort we mentioned so far. It has many different cycles and gives no indication which of them should be preferred in order to find the proof. In fact the proof is made up by a recursive cycle that involves all possible connections; so in any case the cycle is highly non–linear. Moreover, this cycle is traversed by the proof in a way that does not suggest any obvious regularity and further requires three instances of each rule except the first one where two suffice. So we would say, its apparent non–obviousness (just try to proof it by hand) is manifested by these characteristics: non–reducibility, non–linearity (or –regularity in a more general sense), and need for a relatively high number of instances. In the early work of the present author the last property was taken as the only characteristic parameter (see the *degree* in [2]). With the deeper insight gained over the years we now propose a more refined "degree" of non–obviousness that takes into account the other two parameters as well. To formalize such a more complicated degree in a logically convincing way might not be that easy a task, though.

This example illustrates that there are formulas that need non–linear cycles to be proved. So the restriction to linear cycles properly limits applicability. On the other hand it is a very natural restriction worth exploring, since "most" practical problems may be treated this way (whatever this means).

From a theoretical point of view one would like to have a syntactic characterization of the class of problems that may be treated with our technique, such that for a given formula it can be determined whether it is a member or not (like the characterization of Horn formulas). So far we can only offer the characterization that is provided and may be applied by carrying out the proposed algorithm. Since the algorithm is reasonably efficient, we think that this characterization is actually good enough for practical purposes, although it certainly would be useful if someone in Theoretical Computer Science would find a more explicit one.

In [8] we have presented an alternate way of functionalizing a logic program that takes into account an appropriate induction scheme. It seems that the proposal made here is more direct, at least for relatively simple programs. The other proposal might then be useful in cases where a linear cycle does not provide the solution, i.e. in more complicated cases. But a more elaborate comparison has yet to be carried out.

5 Quantifiers and modal operators

Logic will not forgive inaccuracy while people are fond of their little mistakes. This is one reason why logic has not really attained popularity to an extent it certainly should. Being the single available formalism capturing essential features of human thought it should be taught at elementary schools already in some way or another. But even Mathematics professors question any relevance of logic to their work.

Logic has now gained a little popularity through PROLOG particularly for applications in the knowledge-based systems area. As we have seen PROLOG is limited to the simple logical structure of rules. It is interesting to watch the field, how it currently stretches its limbs in order to try to fit into the jacket that obviously is too tight. Negation is one cause for discomfort, quantifiers are another.

Indeed quantifiers are never mentioned in PROLOG. Nevertheless they are present by the nature of human logic. We just do not mention them explicitly (for the psychological reason mentioned above), assuming a default structure in this respect instead. Unfortunately, there are even very practical examples where the original default jacket simply does not fit. [20] mentions some of these and proposes an improved default instead. While this is fine, the principal problem does not disappear which is that quantifiers are essential and cannot be defined away. They abound in natural language in particular. So we have to deal with them in a conscious way, even in the default case. Let us have a brief look at this default case.

It is achieved by skolemization (see [3]). Instead of saying "Everyone has a father" which all-quantifies by way of the "everyone" and existentially quantifies by way of the "a", a "father"-function is introduced which substitutes the existential quantifier. This way only all-quantifiers are left which then are ignored by default. There are a number of reservations with this solution.

First of all, the meaning actually has changed slightly by this transition. While the natural statement did not rule out the possibility of having more than one father, the functional version actually does by the nature of functions. Second, in a nested quantificational structure the skolemization gives up quite a bit of information about this structure retaining only the relative position of the existential quantifiers with respect to the all-quantifiers. Thirdly, the length of the formula may increase by the transition, quadratically in the worst case which in turn causes an increased overhead in the performance. Finally, in view of advanced unification techniques skolemization actually turns out to be a redundant step. More on these points can be found in [3].

Raising these issues means begging for alternatives. As just indicated, the main function of skolemization is to record the relative occurrences of the different types of quantifiers within a formula. The proof technique most sensitive for the position of any logical operation within a formula is that based on the Gentzen-type natural deduction systems. And indeed an analysis of these systems has provided such an alternative. Rather than introducing Skolem functions, this alternative achieves the right way of unification by taking into account the structure of the relation that is provided by the operational symbols within the formula the way they occur in relation to each other. While there have been other approaches to the automation of deduction on the basis of calculi of natural deduction, this one is unique insofar as it does not dispense with the concern for efficiency comparable to that of resolution. An outline of this whole approach is given in [5]. For a comprehensive treatment the reader has to consult [3].

The technique used in this approach is not dependent on the logical operators involved. So in a sense it does provide an efficient treatment of deduction in (to some extent) *any* logistic calculus. [3] further presents the treatment of higher-order logic this way. Very recently now Wallen [26] has picked up these ideas and applied them to various modal logics, specifically to the modal systems K, K4, D, D4, T, S4, and S5. He succeeded in providing efficient proof mechanisms for all these systems. Actually, since the technique is as general as it is, one may expect its successful application to other systems as well along exactly the same lines. Since we did not want to spoil the beauty of Wallen's work by giving a sketchy overview of it, the remainder of this section will just state a few observations in this context. The interested reader might find it extremely rewarding to read the original source itself, perhaps start with [27] as an appetizer.

The work is done on the basis of a sequent calculus [5]. All the modifications needed to extend the classical calculus to cope with these modal systems still preserve the property of being cut–free, which is of vital importance for the automation of deduction. Also they retain the subformula property and, of course, the basic structure of the sequents.

One central part in establishing provability is an analysis of the propositional structure of the given modal formula. In fact, it turns out that this part is in essence identical with the analogue part in first–order logic. That is, a spanning set of connections has to be identified. What is different are the conditions under which a pair of literals can be deemed complementary.

The key observation is that an appropriate notion of complementarity can be defined by noting the context of atoms relative to the modal operators in the endsequence, and considering mappings of representations of these contexts, called prefixes, which render the prefixes of the components of connections identical. The first part of this is similar to incorporating the relation among occurrences of logical operators into the unification process, while the second part, which makes it actually work, is an original contribution of extreme elegance. These mappings can in fact be seen as substitutions in the usual sense. Their exact definition depends on which modal system we are dealing with.

Testing a formula for validity in any of these modal logics thus is in a sense the same as in classical logic, so that any kind of search strategy developed so far is applicable without alteration. For instance, all the material presented in the previous sections have full relevance to modal logic this way. What changes is the unificational part, which, for instance, does not always produce a single most general unifier, although the set of such unifiers is always finite.

It should be noted that this seems to be the first proof mechanism for such modal systems that is both fully general and (comparatively) efficient. Its compatibility with first–order proof techniques makes it even more attractive. One has to get serious with quantifiers and modal operators, though, in order to appreciate this beauty.

6 Building–in theories

All the material in the previous sections focused on the purely logical part of deduction. For practical purposes it is essential though that in a certain context advantage is taken of deductive structures that occur in a stereotype way again and again (resulting from the theory defined by the context). Equality has to be treated this way to mention just one example. The previous volume contains much material on this topic [18,24]. This is the only reason why no additional attention is given to this area here, so the reader should not draw false conclusions about the importance of this area.

In addition there has been some progress in the meantime with the treatment of mathematical induction in the context of a theorem prover based on the connection method reported in [14]. There a special sort of connection is introduced that links literals if they reoccur in a proof with an inductive nature. A system based on this approach is actually operative.

The restriction to literals in this inductive setting seems not be that harmful since more complicated formula parts may be abbreviated with literals by inclusion of appropriate definitions as also Wallen (private communication) suggests.

7 Conclusions

This chapter is meant to provide an update on the material contained in a previous volume [11] on the topic of Automated Deduction. As has to be expected for such a wide and active area, only a few major issues could be discussed at some length and to some degree of detail here. We have chosen these to be the following ones.

A bottom–up reduction technique has been suggested that enhances the performance of top-down theorem provers such as PROLOG systems. It is well-known that bottom–up executions may quickly result in an exponential combinatorial explosion. This is avoided here by carefully restricting the bottom–up execution to those deductive parts of the program that are guaranteed to be settled in linear time. These parts are identified in a syntactic way with the notion of isolated connections along with other preparatory features like DB–reductions. It is felt that this kind of technique has a great importance, in particular for practical applications.

The program resulting from these operations typically is recursive in nature. Such recursive programs have been analyzed in some detail, in particular by way of the basic concept of a (deductive) cycle. On the basis of this analysis the framework of an algorithm is given that achieves the compilation of a recursive logic program into code of a purely iterative nature (basically a DO–loop), at least for a class of practically important cases. This algorithm is illustrated with selected examples demonstrating key issues such as the need for factorizing and the incorporation of databases.

The remaining two sections are more of the nature of providing pointers to material of particular interest in the literature, such as an extremely elegant approach to the automation of deduction in modal logic.

References

[1] F. Bancilhon and R. Ramakrishnan. An amateur's introduction to recursive query processing strategies. In *Proc. SIGMOD Conf. on Management of Data*, pages 16–52, ACM, 1986.

[2] W. Bibel. An approach to a systematic theorem proving procedure in first-order logic. *Computing*, 12:43–55, 1974.

[3] W. Bibel. *Automated Theorem Proving.* Vieweg Verlag, second, 289 pages edition, 1987.

[4] W. Bibel. *Constraint Satisfaction from a Deductive Viewpoint.* Technical Report, Forschungsgruppe Künstliche Intelligenz, Technische Universität München, 1987 (submitted).

[5] W. Bibel. Methods of automated reasoning. In W. Bibel and Ph. Jorrand, editors, *Fundamentals of Artificial Intelligence — An Advanced Course*, pages 173 - 222, Springer, LNCS *232*, Berlin, 1986.

[6] W. Bibel. On matrices with connections. *Journal of ACM*, 28:633–645, 1981.

[7] W. Bibel. Prädikatives Programmieren. In *GI — 2. Fachtagung über Automatentheorie und Formale Sprachen*, pages 274–283, Springer, Berlin, 1975.

[8] W. Bibel. Predicative programming revisited. In W. Bibel and K. Jantke, editors, *MMSSSS'85 — Mathematical Methods for the Specification and Synthesis of Software Systems*, pages 24–40, Springer, Berlin, 1986.

[9] W. Bibel. *Programmieren in der Sprache der Prädikatenlogik.* (Rejected) thesis for "Habilitation" presented to the Faculty of Mathematics, Technische Universität München, January 1975.

[10] W. Bibel. *A Uniform Approach to Programming.* Bericht 7633, Technische Universität München, Mathematische Fakultät, 1976.

[11] W. Bibel and Ph. Jorrand, editors. *Fundamentals of Artificial Intelligence. Study Edition,* Springer, Berlin, 1987.

[12] W. Bibel, R. Letz, and J. Schumann. Bottom–up enhancements of deductive systems. In I. Plander, editor, *Proceedings of 4th International Conference on Artificial Intelligence and Information–Control Systems of Robots,* North–Holland, Smolenice, CSSR, October 1987.

[13] W. S. Brainerd and L. H. Landweber. *Theory of Computation.* Wiley, New York, 1974.

[14] M. Breu. *Einbeziehung einfacher Induktionsbeweise in den Konnektionenkalkül.* Diplom–thesis, Technische Universität München, 1986.

[15] E. Eder. Properties of substitutions and unifications. *Journal for Symbolic Computation,* 1:31–46, 1985.

[16] C. Green. Theorem proving by resolution as a basis for question–answering systems. In B. Meltzer and D. Michie, editors, *Machine Intelligence 4,* Edinburgh University Press, 1969.

[17] L. J. Henschen and S. A. Naqvi. On compiling queries in recursive first-order databases. *Journal of ACM,* 31:47–85, 1984.

[18] G. Huet. Deduction and computation. In W. Bibel and Ph. Jorrand, editors, *Fundamentals of Artificial Intelligence — An Advanced Course,* pages 39–74, Springer, LNCS *232*, Berlin, 1987.

[19] J. Minker, D. H. Fishman, and J. R. McSkimin. The Q^* algorithm — a search strategy for a deductive question–answering system. *Artificial Intelligence,* 4:225–243, 1973.

[20] K. Morris, J. D. Ullman, and A. van Gelder. Design overview of the NAIL! system. In E. Shapiro, editor, *Proc. 3rd Intern. Conf. on Logic Programming,* pages 554–568, Springer (LNCS *225*), Berlin, 1986.

[21] F. J. Pelletier and P. Rudnicki. Non–obviousness. *AAR Newsletter,* 6:4–5, 1987.

[22] R. Reiter. Towards a logical reconstruction of relational database theory. In M. L. Brodie et al., editor, *On Conceptual Modeling,* pages 191–238, Springer, Berlin, 1983.

[23] L. Sterling and E. Shapiro. *The Art of Prolog.* MIT Press, Cambridge MA, 1986.

[24] M. E. Stickel. An introduction to automated deduction. In W. Bibel and Ph. Jorrand, editors, *Fundamentals of Artificial Intelligence,* pages 75–132, Springer, Berlin, 1987.

[25] J. D. Ullman. *Principles of Database Systems.* Computer Science Press, Rockville MD, 1982.

[26] L. Wallen. *Automated Deduction in Modal Logics.* PhD thesis, University of Edinburgh, 1987. PhD Thesis.

[27] L. Wallen. Matrix proof methods for modal logics. In *IJCAI'87,* pages 917–923, Morgan Kaufmann, Los Altos CA, 1987.

Qualitative Reasoning

Anthony G Cohn

Department of Computer Science
University of Warwick
COVENTRY
CV4 7AL
UK

1. Introduction

The purpose of this chapter is to introduce the field of Qualitative Reasoning and survey the state of the art as it appears in the summer of 1987. The field is presently exploding and inevitably I shall not be able to cover all relevant work or even everything to the same level of detail.

First we must make clear what is meant by the term 'Qualitative Reasoning'. In view of the oft repeated claim that AI is not (principally) concerned with quantitative reasoning but with symbolic reasoning it might seem that all, or at least most of AI, might be viewed as qualitative reasoning. However the term has come, in some quarters at least, to have a more precise meaning. In particular, for domains which have a standard quantitative treatment (such as physics), the aim of the enterprise we are discussing here is to provide a purely qualitative approach to problem solving in the domain.

Some examples may be of help in explaining what we intend by the term qualitative reasoning; much of the work to date has been concerned with building models of naturally occurring physical situations or (more usually) constructed physical systems and performing various kinds of reasoning tasks on such models and the four simple examples below are all taken from this literature.

Forbus (1984b) cites the example of a super heated steam boiler (see figure 1): If the input water temperature is increased what happens to output temperature? Although the answer (which is left as an exercise for the reader) may appear counter intuitive at first, it does not require any quantitative knowledge or reasoning.

An example which appears frequently in the literature – for example Forbus (1984b) or Kuipers (1986) – is that of a mass on a spring sliding on a frictionless surface in one dimension (see figure 2): we want to be able to answer the question 'what happens if the mass is extended and then released'? We would expect a qualitative reasoner to be able to predict an oscillation even though the precise period could not be determined.

Figure 3 shows a rather different kind of situation: what happens when a mixture of water, sand and pebbles is poured through a sieve? Common sense tells us that the water will fall through, the pebbles will stick and the sand may fall through or not depending on their size relative to the sieve grain and that in order to get the sand to fall through it may be necessary to agitate the sieve.

The final example we will present here is again one that is cited frequently – for example de Kleer and Brown (1984). Figure 4 depicts a pressure regulator: we want our qualitative reasoning program to be able produce an explanation of how it works such as:

> "An increase in source pressure increases the pressure drop across the valve. Since the flow through the valve is proportional to the pressure across it, the flow through the valve also increases. This increased flow will increase the pressure at the load. However, this increased pressure is sensed, causing the diaphragm to move downward against the spring pressure. The diaphragm is mechanically connected to the valve, so the downward movement of the diaphragm will tend to close the valve thereby pinching off the flow. Because the flow is now restricted the output pressure will rise much less than it otherwise would have" (de Kleer and Brown 1984, page 10).

Other examples in the literature include reasoning about electronic circuits (for example Williams 1984) and physiological systems (for example Kuipers and Kassirer 1983).

In each of the above examples, both the problem and the output are expressed in qualitative terms, even though the problem might traditionally be described using continuous real valued parameters and differential equations which might then be solved analytically or numerically. However it is clear that one does not need to have a knowledge of differential equations in order to be able to provide answers at the level of abstraction

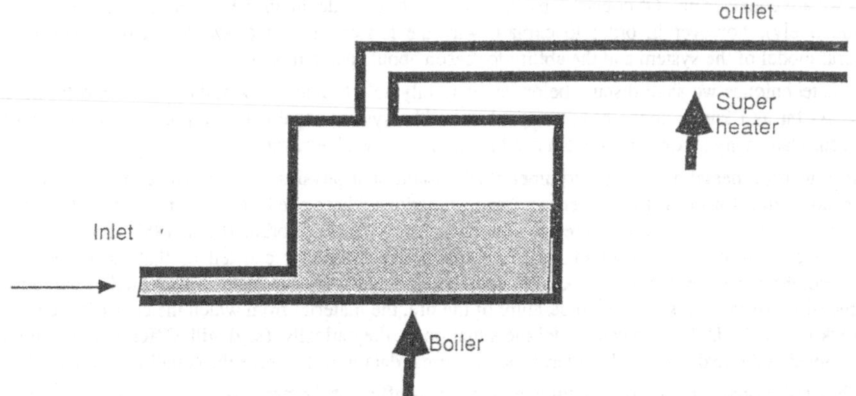

Super heated steam boiler: what will happen if the inlet water temperature increases?

Figure 1.

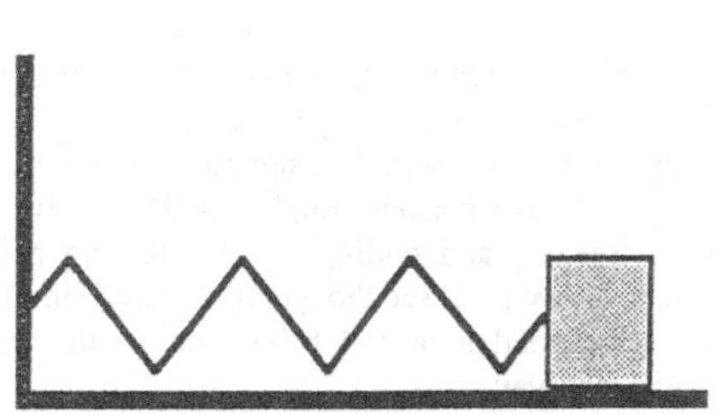

Mass on a spring sliding on a frictionless surface: what happens if it is extended and then released?

Figure 2.

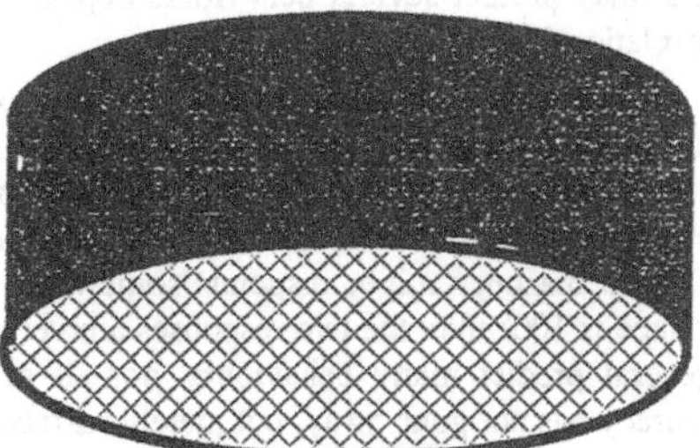

What happens when a mixture of water, sand and pebbles is poured through the sieve?

Figure 3.

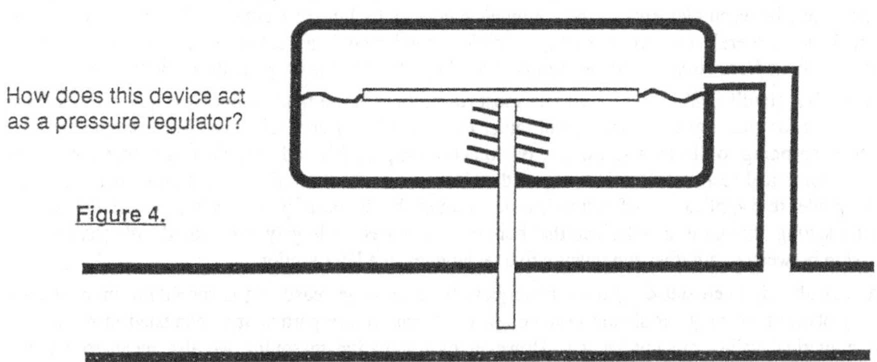

How does this device act as a pressure regulator?

Figure 4.

which we are considering. Of course one might be able to provide an answer purely on the basis of experience (ie inductively); however in order to explain why the answer is correct would seem to require a deeper, structural model of the system and the ability to reason about such a model.

The techniques we shall discuss below are certainly able to reason about the second and fourth examples above. As far as I know, noone has attempted to build a system capable of reasoning about the sieve and we will discuss later why no existing system can handle the first problem yet.

It is worth rehearsing here the arguments why traditional physics may be inadequate in order to provide further motivation for the sequel. There are many situations where one can reason from 'first principles' about likely futures but without knowing precise data about the scenario. Forbus (Badii 1987) gives the example of seeing someone throw an aerosol into a fire – qualitative reasoning can tell us that since the container is pressurised, it is possible that it may explode upon being heated. We can make this prediction without knowing the dimensions of the canister, the temperature of the fire, the material from which the canister is constructed or how thick it is, or ... Unless we can model the situation mathematically, (say) with differential equations which can be solved analytically we will not have the numerical data in order solve the equations numerically.

Thus traditional quantitative techniques may be insufficient for problem solving because we may not be able to build a precise model (for example the exact relationship between two variables may not be known). Further difficulties may be caused because the initial values of some or all of the parameters are unknown or too expensive or difficult to obtain. If the initial conditions for all variables are not precisely given then one will have to guess a precise initial value and the resulting behaviour prediction may be very dependent on this; moreover usually only a single behaviour is predicted at a time; by contrast the qualitative techniques we shall look at may predict several behaviours depending on different assumptions about the value of variables and their relationships.

A quantitative solution by successive approximation or simulation will give an exact answer or behaviour prediction but there may be an error coefficient due to rounding or too large interval steps. By contrast qualitative reasoning should give a less precise, but totally accurate answer; for example, to the question 'what is the temperature of the substance in the container?' a quantitative reasoner might say 91.47°±10% whilst a qualitative reasoner might respond 'somewhere between freezing and boiling'. If the boiling point of the substance is 100° then the two responses are very different. As we shall see though, qualitative simulation will in general predict many behaviours, not all of which correspond to a real behaviour, so the problem of inaccuracy has not gone away, but merely surfaces in a different way.

In summary therefore we may say that quantitative techniques may be unsatisfactory because of the requirement for a very detailed model, the need for precise initial conditions to be known and the computational expense typically engendered by numeric problem solving techniques.

Further motivation for studying qualitative reasoning comes from the observation that people seem to be able to reason qualitatively, thus it is a valid AI or Cognitive Science task to investigate this. There is a growing literature (for example Gentner and Stevens 1983, Falkenheiner et al 1986, Roshelle 1987) on applying representation schemes such as we shall describe below to the task of mental modelling. As with other formal approaches to mental modelling one may take the strong view that there is a fairly direct correspondence between elements of the computer model and a human mental model or the weaker view that the formal model merely circumscribes the possible mental models a human might have. However we shall not particularly address ourselves to the mental modelling applications of qualitative reasoning here.

As Forbus (Badii 1987) has pointed out, most researchers in the field do not view qualitative reasoning as a *replacement* for quantitative reasoning but rather as a *complementary* technique. For example one might use qualitative reasoning to discover if a dangerous outcome is *possible* and only then use more computationally expensive numerical techniques to investigate the situation in more detail. Or qualitative reasoning might be used to guide the application of numerical techniques by helping with quantitative model selection or parameter setting, though it must be said that both of these ideas are largely unexplored. We shall return to the relationship between qualitative and quantitative techniques in a later section.

As has already been stated what we mean here by qualitative reasoning is something more specific than merely symbolic reasoning. It should now be apparent that we are particularly interested in reasoning when precise numerical values are not known. However by qualitative reasoning we also mean something more specific than just any approximate reasoning scheme; in particular it is not anything to do with 'fuzzy' reasoning (Zadeh 1983), at least at present. The value of any particular qualitative variable will not be at all 'fuzzy' but will be a precise (possibly interval) value, though there may be several parallel 'worlds' in which the same variable may have different values. The fact that different possible values for a qualitative variable do not overlap is used crucially when building and reasoning about an *envisionment.*

Also worth commenting on at this juncture is the variety of terminology used to describe the field. The following terms all seem to be very closely linked: qualitative reasoning, qualitative simulation, qualitative physics, qualitative analysis, qualitative modelling, deep knowledge, naive physics, commonsense reasoning; and there are no doubt other similar terms in the literature. The present author's view is that qualitative reasoning usually operates on a qualitative model; that qualitative simulation is a particular kind of qualitative reasoning (the most common in the literature); that qualitative analysis is another kind of qualitative reasoning; that qualitative physics is qualitative reasoning in the physics domain; that qualitative modelling is *a* technique for encoding deep knowledge; the emphasis in naive physics is to build model of a layman's understanding of everyday physics – this might be done using qualitative modelling and reasoning techniques.

What is certainly true is that all these fields are quite young though rapidly expanding; this is not a mature subject with a well agreed theory, approaches and methodology. In the sequel I shall try to make comparisons, draw out common threads and unify the field as much as I can, but this seems an impossible task at present.

An early collection of Qualitative Reasoning papers appears in a special issue of the AI journal (volume 24) which has also been published as a book (Bobrow 1984). Another collection of papers is Hobbs and Moore (1985) and the recent IJCAI and AAAI conferences, amongst others, also have many relevant papers.

1.1. Qualitative Modelling and Deep Models

Most current expert systems are very specific in the kind of problems they can solve. Typically if they do diagnosis they cannot predict or tutor as well. Moreover they can not solve simpler or more abstractly stated versions of the problems they were designed to solve. This is often because the knowledge is all 'compiled' – much knowledge is implicitly represented and no irrelevant knowledge for the particular task is present. Usually there is no justification or supporting knowledge – each fact or rule stands on its own as an underivable 'axiom' and it is not possible to question the validity or the basis of it. Such systems are unable to reason from 'first principles'; for example a typical medical expert system for diagnosis will have rules which enable it to conclude about (say) the presence of a particular organism from particular lab data and other observations without any underlying knowledge or reasoning about the physiological pathways, processes or causal connections involved. Now, although diagnostic problem solving can be and normally is conducted in such a manner by using so called 'surface' or 'compiled' knowledge, other problem solving activities in the same domain are not usually possible with the same knowledge base as has been found (for example Clancey and Letsinger 1981). Moreover the inadequacy and lack of satisfaction frequently expressed with the explanations proffered by such systems is endemic to a system which has no deeper level of understanding or knowledge than the pure 'how to do it' knowhow of surface rules. Much of the interest in qualitative reasoning systems and qualitative modelling comes from the possible application of these techniques to expressing deeper models to act as underlying models supporting conventional expert system rulebases.

1.2. Desiderata for a Qualitative Reasoning System

From the above discussion we can start to enumerate the features we should like a qualitative reasoner to have. No existing theory entirely meets these specifications.

The modelling language should be capable of describing complex physical systems to varying levels of detail and granularity. Consequently the grain of the output of the reasoner may vary as the input grain changes. Processes and interactions must be describable and moreover the reasoning system must be capable of instantiating such descriptions and, what is much more difficult, generating new descriptions to describe the (dynamic) behaviour of an entire system from the descriptions of the parts.

The system should provide a unified structure for supporting a variety of different tasks such as design, diagnosis, planning and prediction.

In view of the requirement to build descriptions of, and reason about, complex systems it must be possible to model individual parts of a system separately and have the system reason about the behaviour of the complete system. Thus the modelling language should support descriptions which are *composable.* Support should also be provided to help the user of the system to model their problem using the primitives. Such help might be provided partly by making the language sufficiently expressive, partly by providing a library of primitive descriptions (for processes, components, and their cause. Of course the problem of helping a user express their problem in a particular knowledge representation formalism is not unique to qualitative modelling.

Finally, one would like to be able to integrate quantitative knowledge and inference into a qualitative reasoner when available and link a quantitative reasoner to a traditional 'surface' system. In fact one comes to realise that the deep/surface dichotomy is false and in reality there is a continuum of 'deepness' along several scales.

1.3. (Some) History

Most of the work in the field and everything that we shall discuss here has been published in the 1980s. There is however some earlier important work from which much of the work presented here descends and which is worth describing briefly.

Perhaps the earliest published work in the area is de Kleers' NEWTON system (de Kleer 1977). NEWTON is a system which attempts to solve simple mechanics problems qualitatively and only uses quantitative methods if qualitative reasoning fails to provide a solution; however even in this case, the results of the qualitative reasoner may guide the selection of equations and the way they are solved quantitatively. NEWTON introduced the important idea of *envisioning* which is a qualitative state transition graph and captures the possible qualitative behaviour sequences. However NEWTON was very limited in its representation and inference techniques and seemed very tied to the simple mechanics domain in which it operated. Moreover, it had virtually no notion of time.

The other, now almost classical, research referenced by almost all papers in the literature is Hayes' work (1979, 1985a, 1985b) on *Naive Physics*. Hayes is particularly interested in axiomatising our commonsense knowledge of the physical world (within a logical framework). He is more concerned with the modelling problem, ie the conceptualisation and the ontological problems rather than with the reasoning aspects; he is concerned with *what* knowledge is represented, not *how* it is to be manipulated. The idea which we shall meet shortly of a *qualitative quantity space* is due to Hayes. His first paper, the *Naive Physics Manifesto* (Hayes 1979), and the revised version (Hayes 1985a) give the motivation for trying to build Naive Physics axiomatisations, the advantages of doing it in first order logic, and discuss the methodology and some particular problem areas. His first foray was into the world of liquids (Hayes 1985), a subject he had argued as being particularly hard to formalise in (Hayes, 1974). Briefly, the problem is hard because in a formal, propositional, representation, liquids are denoted by mass terms and the semantics of mass terms has been the subject of much philosophical debate (Bunt 1985). Moreover liquids can divide, combine and deform with incredible ease compared to solid objects which are much more sharply individuated. He introduced what he called the *contained space ontology* which has been extensively used since.

Another concept introduced in these papers is the idea of a *history,* which is a piece of 4D space time describing the 'life' of a particular object. He argues that histories can be of great help in solving the frame problem (McCarthy and Hayes 1969) because if histories do not intersect then (assuming 'no action at a distance') the histories can be evolved separately; in a state based system such as the situational calculus, there is only a global state so all actions have to be reasoned about globally which can create great inefficiencies and problems in specifying what is affected by any action. Of course in the history based approach the problem becomes one of computing history intersection. We will return to histories when discussing the work of Forbus (1984a) and Williams (1986).

Hayes argued that although ultimately all Naive Physics concepts are related, they tend to form closely linked clusters which are only sparsely interlinked. We have already mentioned liquids as being one cluster; others which he identified include measuring scales, shape, assemblies, support and substances.

Although these papers have been very influential in the field of qualitative reasoning as a whole, Naive Physics itself remains relatively unexplored. Other forays include Hobbs et al (1985) and Cunningham (1985a). Hayes' investigation of the liquids cluster is only an initial investigation and there are many difficulties and inadequacies with his axiomatisation and many unanswered problems (see, for example, Hayes and Welham 1984, Cunningham 1985a, Hayes 1987). McDermott (1987) has come to believe that the whole enterprise is impossible, at least within the confines of formal logic. It should be noted however that the journal issue containing the (McDermott 1987) also contains extensive peer commentary and criticism including a rejoinder by Hayes (1987b) himself.

1.4. Approaches to Qualitative Reasoning

Broadly speaking there are three main approaches to qualitative modelling and reasoning. Perhaps the simplest from an ontological view is the so called *constraint centred* approach in which an entire system is described by a homogeneous set of constraints; typical of such an approach is the work of Kuipers (1984,

1986). A more structured approach is the *component centred* one where a system is modelled by instantiating components from a library which are then connected together explicitly. The work of de Kleer and Brown (1984) and Williams (1984) is typical of this approach. Finally, the *process centred* approach builds on the component centred approach by modelling not only individual components explicitly but also the processes which act on them. Forbus' (1984a) work exemplifies this approach.

The next three sections will describe a constraint based system, a component centred system and a process centred system respectively. Then I will try to compare and contrast the three approaches and draw some general conclusions. The next two sections will investigate some uses of qualitative reasoning and the problem of building efficient qualitative reasoners. The final sections will discuss time in more detail, qualitative spatial reasoning, order of magnitude reasoning, approaches to extracting higher level behaviour descriptions, various modelling problems and some current and future research directions.

2. Constraint Based Qualitative Reasoning

The first approach to qualitative reasoning we shall examine is that presented by Kuipers (1986) which built on his earlier work (Kuipers 1984). For Kuipers, a physical situation is modelled by a single set of constraint equations which are, essentially, qualitative differential equations. Thus a model consists of a number of parameters, or variables, and some specified relationships between them.

The main issues addressed by Kuipers (1986) are the provision of a qualitative representation for quantities, an efficient qualitative simulation algorithm, a method for selecting state transitions, the fidelity of quantities to standard mathematical analysis, and the question of the fidelity of computed qualitative behaviours to real world (ie whether all possible behaviours are generated and whether any extraneous behaviours are generated). We shall cover all these issues below.

First we will describe the representational apparatus Kuipers uses. At the heart of this is the notion of a *qualitative variable* – ie a variable which can take one of a finite number of qualitative values and which is a function of time. The first section below describes the representation of values for qualitative variables. The way the behaviour of a system is described is through a set of constraints which relate the various qualitative values. The second section below describes the various primitive constraint types. Perhaps the most interesting of these are the so called *monotonic function* constraints ($M^{\pm}$) since these can be viewed as a 'qualitisation' of more quantitative constraints; however quantitative constraints would be of little use given the purely qualitative variable values. We then proceed to define Kuipers notion of a qualitative simulation which will generate sequences of states, where each state is corresponds to a constraint-satisfying assignment of values to the qualitative variables and where the transition between one state and a neighbouring one obeys certain general continuity constraints.

2.1. The representation of qualitative variables

Landmarks are distinguished points on the real line. A *quantity space* is a finite set of totally ordered landmarks. Landmarks may be either numeric (eg 0) or symbolic (eg capacity42) – it is their ordinal relationship which is important. A quantity space thus defines an alternating sequence of points and open intervals on **R**. A quantity space always includes the landmarks {minf, 0, inf} where inf and minf are plus and minus infinity respectively. New landmarks may be discovered dynamically (eg when a decreasing oscillation is predicted).

At any time t a function f is described by a pair *<qval,qdir>*. The value *qval* may be a landmark l or two adjacent landmarks *(l1,l2)* if f is between landmarks at t. The value *qdir* is one of {dec, std, inc}, standing for decreasing, steady or increasing, and is the qualitative derivative of f. Thus a qualitative derivative is of low fixed resolution while the qualitative value may be of higher, though still finite resolution.

2.2. Constraint Equations

Kuipers allows a variety of constraint primitives (two or three place):

arithmetic: ADD(x,y,z), MULT(x,y,z), MINUS(x,y)
functional: $M^+(x,y)$, $M^-(x,y)$
derivative: DERIV(x,y)

ADD(x,y,z) constrains z to be the sum of x and y and similarly for MULT(x,y,z). MINUS(x,y) constrains x to be $-y$. $M^+(x,y)$ states that x is some function of y which is strictly monotonically increasing. Similarly $M^-(x,y)$ states that x is some function of y which is strictly monotonically decreasing. DERIV(x,y) predicates that y is the derivative (with respect to time) of x. (The older formulation (Kuipers' (1984) ENV system) also had inequality and conditional constraints).

M^+ and M^-can also have *correspondences* specified. A correspondence is a pair of landmarks $l1$ and $l2$ such that x is $l1$ when y is $l2$. If <0,0> is a correspondence we usually write M_0^+ or M_0^-.

Earlier we said that Kuipers' constraints can be viewed as qualitative differential equations. The following example shows how a particular ordinary differential equation (ODE) can be transformed to a set of qualitative constraints in Kuipers' formalism. Suppose we have the ODE

$$\frac{d^2u}{dt^2} + \frac{du}{dt} = cot(cu)$$

We can rewrite this as the set of simultaneous equations displayed below on the left, whilst the corresponding qualitative constraints are on the right.

$f_1 = du/dt$	DERIV(u,f_1)
$f_2 = df_1/dt$	DERIV(f_1,f_2)
$f_3 = cu$	MULT(c,u,f_3)
$f_4 = cot\ f_3$	M^-(f_3,f_4)
$f_2+f_1 = f_4$	ADD(f_2,f_1,f_4)

The set of qualitative constraints so derived will always be equivalent to, or (more usually) less restrictive than, the original ODE, so any solution to the ODE will also satisfy the qualitative constraints.

2.3. Describing a Situation

A physical situation is described by

- a set of parameters (which represent continuous and continuously differentiable real-valued functions) each of which has an associated quantity space, and possibly range limits which define the operating range of constraints.
- a set of constraint equations.
- a set of qualitative values for each of the parameters at the specified time point.

2.4. Qualitative Simulation

A qualitative simulation differs from a standard numerical simulation in several ways. For example, in a quantitative simulation each simulation step is usually a fixed, metric, time after the previous one. By contrast in all the qualitative simulation algorithms we shall examine, including Kuipers' which we shall describe now, the successive simulation steps are determined by establishing when 'something interesting happens' rather than by any fixed time steps.

For any individual function f, the *distinguished time points,* ie the places of interest, are those points in the domain of f where f reaches an extremum or passes a landmark. The set of distinguished time points of a complete system is the union of the distinguished time points of all the functions comprising the system description. At every distinguished time point of the system at least one individual function will have reached or passed a landmark or achieved an extremum.

The QSIM algorithm which we describe below will incrementally compute all the distinguished time points given an initial value for every function at some time point.

2.4.1. Qualitative State Transitions

For Kuipers, (qualitative) time consists of a series of alternating points and open intervals between the points. Each state of the system predicted by QSIM will thus either be an instant or will endure for some open ended interval. Successive state to state transitions are thus alternately from an time interval to a time point *(I-transitions)* or from a time point to an time interval *(P-transitions).*

The driving force behind QSIM is a set of transition rules which match against individual function values and posit possible transition values for the 'next' state. Depending on the value and qualitative derivative there may be more than one possible transition for an individual variable (though global considerations may later rule some or all of these out). These transition rules are subdivided depending on whether we are considering I-transitions or P-transitions. At any time (interval or point) a quantity may be at a landmark or in the open interval between them; thus there rules for both I- and P-transitions for dealing with quantities at a landmark

(I1, P1, P2, P3, P4, P6) and rules for dealing with quantities between landmarks (I2 - I9, P5, P6). The initial state is always given at a time point at it can be seen that there are P-transitions for every possible *<qval,qdir>*. (To describe a quantity initially between two landmarks and steady requires a new landmark to be added to the appropriate quantity space). After a P-transition a quantity is either at a landmark and steady, in which case I1 will be applicable next, or the quantity will be between landmarks and non steady, in which case rules I2, I3, I4, I8 or I5, I6, I7, I9 will be applicable.

P-Transitions (transitions from a time point to an interval):

P1 $<l_j, \text{std}> \quad \rightarrow \quad <l_j, \text{std}>$

P2 $<l_j, \text{std}> \quad \rightarrow \quad <(l_j, l_{j+1}), \text{inc}>$

P3 $<l_j, \text{std}> \quad \rightarrow \quad <(l_{j-1}, l_j), \text{dec}>$

P4 $<l_j, \text{inc}> \quad \rightarrow \quad <(l_j, l_{j+1}), \text{inc}>$

P5 $<(l_j, l_{j+1}), \text{inc}> \quad \rightarrow \quad <(l_j, l_{j+1}), \text{inc}>$

P6 $<l_j, \text{dec}> \quad \rightarrow \quad <(l_{j-1}, l_j), \text{dec}>$

P7 $<(l_j, l_{j+1}), \text{dec}> \quad \rightarrow \quad <(l_j, l_{j+1}), \text{dec}>$

I-Transitions (transitions from a time interval to a point):

I1 $<l_j, \text{std}> \quad \rightarrow \quad <l_j, \text{std}>$

I2 $<(l_j, l_{j+1}), \text{inc}> \quad \rightarrow \quad <l_{j+1}, \text{std}>$

I3 $<(l_j, l_{j+1}), \text{inc}> \quad \rightarrow \quad <l_{j+1}, \text{inc}>$

I4 $<(l_j, l_{j+1}), \text{inc}> \quad \rightarrow \quad <(l_j, l_{j+1}), \text{inc}>$

I5 $<(l_j, l_{j+1}), \text{dec}> \quad \rightarrow \quad <l_j, \text{std}>$

I6 $<(l_j, l_{j+1}), \text{dec}> \quad \rightarrow \quad <l_j, \text{dec}>$

I7 $<(l_j, l_{j+1}), \text{dec}> \quad \rightarrow \quad <(l_j, l_{j+1}), \text{dec}>$

I8 $<(l_j, l_{j+1}), \text{inc}> \quad \rightarrow \quad <l^*, \text{std}>$

I9 $<(l_j, l_{j+1}), \text{dec}> \quad \rightarrow \quad <l^*, \text{std}>$

The rationale underlying these state transitions (which are taken from table 1 of Kuipers (1986)) is that functions are assumed to be continuous and differentiable and thus qualitative versions of the mean value theorem and intermediate value theorem restrict the possible state transitions. Transitions P4, P5, P6 and P7 uniquely determine the next value of a variable which matches their left hand side; if a function is increasing or decreasing at a landmark then in an instant it will move to the adjoining open interval in the direction of change and a function cannot reach the endpoint of an interval instantaneously. I1 also uniquely determines a next value since a function moves away from a landmark instantaneously rather than over an interval. The situation where a function is steady at a landmark at an instant is three ways ambiguous and the situation where a function is non steady in an interval and is transitioning to a time point is four ways ambiguous. In the latter case the possible cases are that it stays non steady in the interval, that it reaches the landmark at the end of the interval either steady or not, or it may become steady within the open interval thus splitting the open interval in two by dynamically creating a new landmark (l^*) (rules I8 and I9).

2.4.2. The QSIM Algorithm

The top level of the QSIM algorithm consists of selecting an active state, generating possible successor states, filtering these and repeating. If more than one successor state results then a branching tree of states is generated. Initially the set of active states consists of a single specified state.

The possible successor states are generated thus: first, possible individual function transition rules from the set P1 to P7 or I1 to I9 are selected; functions may have invariant assertions (eg always positive, always constant) and any potential rule applications violating these invariants are discarded. Then, for each constraint, two or three tuples of value pairs are built, using the previously selected transition rules, according to the strictures of the constraint. Consistency between each pair of constraints is checked using a Waltz (1975) filtering algorithm (the constraints are the nodes, variables in common between two constraints are the arcs and tuples of variable assignments consistent with each constraint are the node labels). Complete state descriptions are now generated from the filtered tuples and these new states are made children states of current state. Finally, global filters are applied to these states and any which pass are added to the set of active states. Global filters are *no change* (is the new state identical to parent state?), *divergence* (some function reaches infinity – this might correspond to some component breaking in the modelled world), *cycle* (is the new state identical to some earlier state?). In addition heuristic filters such as *quiescence* (the state is a time instant and all qdirs are std) may be activated.

The individual constraint checks mentioned above are of two kinds: the directions of change must be consistent and corresponding values must be adhered to. For example M^+ requires both functions to have the same direction of change, ADD requires that if the first two arguments are increasing then so is the third, DERIV(f,g) requires the sign of g (determined with respect to landmark 0) to agree with the qdir of f and $M^{\pm}$ requires both functions to reach specified corresponding values at the same time instant.

2.5. Complexity of QSIM

Kuipers considers the complexity of QSIM and concludes that the complexity of each step (except generating global interpretations) is a linear function of the number of parameters.

However, although generating a single global interpretation only takes O(n) there may (in the worst case) be exponentially many of them. In practice the runtime seems to be about O(mt) where m is number of constraints and t the length of the longest generated behaviour.

Owing to landmark generation, QSIM may never terminate.

2.6. "Soundness" and "Completeness"

Kuipers proves that all actual possible behaviours (ie all solutions to all ODEs which translate to a particular set of qualitative constraints) are found by QSIM. This is a kind of completeness result.

QSIM may produce extra behaviours, ie behaviours which do not correspond to any actual behaviour of a physical system modelled by the constraints. Thus, in a sense, QSIM is "unsound". The problem seems to be that simulation is local and a qualitative state description may not have enough information to determine the next state appropriately.

For example, the system of the mass on a spring sliding on a frictionless surface quoted at the beginning of this paper might be represented to QSIM as a three variable system (a, v, x) representing the acceleration, velocity and x-coordinate of the mass with three constraints, two specifying the derivative relationships between a, v and x and a third which expresses the relationship between a and x: $M_0^+(a,x)$. If the initial state is x=0, a=0, v=v*, where v* is some positive landmark, then the simulated behaviours include stable oscillation, increasing oscillation, decreasing oscillation, increasing then decreasing oscillation,... Only the first is an actual behaviour. In order to force QSIM to predict a unique behaviour further constraints specifying the conservation of energy must be added. We will return in a later section to Kuipers' more recent work on reducing the ambiguity in QSIM's behaviour predictions.

Thus QSIM will not generate false negatives but may give false positives. It is easy to see that if a unique behaviour is predicted then it must be the real behaviour. Kuipers claims this "unsoundness" theorem must apply to any purely local qualitative simulation algorithm.

3. A Component Centred Approach

The second approach to qualitative modelling that we shall examine is the so called component centred approach as exemplified by de Kleer and Brown (1984). Others who have taken a similar approach include de Kleer and Bobrow (1984), Williams (1984) and, in the digital domain, Davis (1984).

De Kleer and Brown are particularly interested in building a qualitative physics which will provide explanatory and predictive power. They view a physical situation as a device, composed of individual components connected together. This is essentially the approach taken by the field of System Dynamics (Cochin 1980) which de Kleer and Brown take as the theory for which they wish to develop a qualitative version.

The main idea is to develop a library of device/component models, each with an associated behaviour description. However it is very important that these behaviour descriptions do not make assumptions about how the components will be 'used' in a particular device so that the library is truly generic and moreover so that the behaviour of the overall circuit is not predetermined by purely local considerations. This prime assumption which de Kleer and Brown discuss at some length is the *no function in structure* principle. For example the description of a valve must not say that liquid will flow if it is opened because this will depend upon, amongst other things, whether there is liquid in the pipes leading to the valve. However any behaviour description must make some assumptions which can be reasonably assumed to hold across a sufficiently wide class of systems of interest. Such assumptions are known as *classwide assumptions;* for example one might assume that liquids are incompressable, that flows are laminar, that currents are low enough not to induce currents in other wires. Many classwide assumptions are about granularity, particularly with respect to time, ie a decision is made to ignore certain effects which only last a short time, such as settling behaviours.

3.1. Device Structure

The total behaviour of a complex system is computed from the behaviours of the primitive constituents. There are three kinds of basic entity: *materials* (such as water, air, electrons), *components* (which operate on materials to alter their form and/or properties) and *conduits* (which merely transport material). A system may be viewed as a graph where the nodes are components and the edges are conduits. The behaviour of a component is described using two basic attributes of materials: 'pressure' and 'flow'. These two attributes may be termed differently depending on the domain; for example in electrical circuits, pressure is voltage and flow, current. Obviously not all physical systems are representable easily or at all in this view (consider a game of pool or billiards for example).

3.2. Qualitative Variables

De Kleer and Brown also define a qualitative quantity space for variables which is a finite total ordering of intervals. These intervals must cover the real line. However, by far the most commonly occurring quantity space in the paper under discussion and elsewhere, is the quantity space {–, 0, +}, ie the only qualitative distinctions made are between negative numbers, strictly positive numbers and zero. Every attribute (such as pressure or flow) is represented by a set of variables, $x, \partial x, \partial^2 x, \ldots$ where ∂ denotes a derivative with respect to time. ∂ variables *always* have the quantity space {–, 0, +}.

Like Kuipers, de Kleer and Brown can also induce a qualitative description of time; however their model of time is non *dense:* two consecutive states may both be time points (recall that Kuipers time line consisted of alternating points and open intervals). The consequences of this change do not seem to be great in de Kleer and Brown's system – however see the discussion below concerning the possibility of *stutter cycles* in Forbus' system. All variables are assumed to be continuous and thus can not 'jump' a qualitative value. For example, if $x = 0$ at two successive times, then $\partial x = 0$ at the first time.

De Kleer and Brown define and use a qualitative calculus which is essentially the same as the qualative constraints of Kuipers. The tables for addition and multiplication are given below.

plus	–	0	+
–	–	–	?
0	–	0	+
+	?	+	+

times	–	0	+
–	+	0	–
0	0	0	0
+	–	0	+

Notice that although multiplication is everywhere well defined, addition is sometimes ambiguous and this will lead to branching in the behaviour predictions.

3.3. Specifying Component Behaviours

The behaviour of each part of a system is specified by a set of *confluences,* which can be viewed as qualitative differential equations. Each confluence is an equation of form:

$$t1 \pm t2 \pm \ldots \pm tm = c$$

where c is a constant (ie a member of a quantity space) and the ti are terms which are of the form: variable or constant * variable. Confluences are *satisfied* by particular assignments to variables providing the confluence evaluates correctly in the qualitative calculus or cannot be evaluated because of ambiguity.

3.4. Qualitative States

A set of confluences alone may be insufficient to describe the behaviour of a device because a device may have different operating regions each of which may require a different set of confluences to describe the behaviour with that operating region. *Qualitative states* are introduced in order to increase the power of the modelling system. Each qualitative state for a component consists of a set of confluences and a precondition which determines when the operating region is active. The precondition may only test non derivative variables (in order to satisfy the 'no function in structure principle', because operating regions are a structural device and derivative variables give information about behaviour over time) and has the form of a conjunction of inequality relationships between such variables and quantity space constants.

For example the pressure regulator system depicted at the start of the article has a valve component which can be modelled as a three state component.

state OPEN:

precondition: $a = amax$; confluences: $p = 0, \ \partial p = 0$

state WORKING:

precondition: $0 < a < amax$; confluences: $p = q, \partial p + p^* \partial a - \partial q = 0$

state CLOSED:

precondition: $a = 0$; confluences: $q = 0, \partial q = 0$

However the definition of a term given earlier did not allow for two variables being multiplied together; a model with multiplication signs occurring in the confluences is known as a *mixed model*. A *pure model* with no multiplication can be obtained by expanding the WORKING state to three states depending on the qualitative value of p (assuming a $\{-, 0, +\}$ quantity space for p). One might call these states CLOSING, OPENING and STEADY. This has the benefit of being able to subsequently provide a finer grain description of the system and of simplifying the calculus.

3.5. Conduits

Conduits are assumed to be always full of incompressable material. Their internal structure is just a set of n terminals ($n \geq 2$), each of which has an associated flow parameter qi. There is just a single pressure parameter p for an entire conduit. Every conduit has a *continuity* confluence which captures the notion that material is conserved: $q1 + \cdots + qn = 0$ which also holds for the derivative variables: $\partial q1 + \cdots + \partial qn = 0$. There is also a *compatibility* confluence for every three conduits which have a path between them. If $p1$ and $p2$ are the pressures between conduits C1 and C2, and C2 and C3 respectively, then the pressure, $p3$ between C1 and C2 must be the sum of $p1$ and $p2$; i.e. the compatibility condition is: $p1 + p2 - p3 = 0$. Again the compatibility condition may also be formulated for the derivative variables.

Care is needed in identifying the parts of the system which are to be modelled as conduits. For example consider a simple two tank system connected by a pipe as depicted in figure 5.

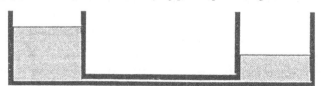

Two tanks connected by a pipe: what are the components?

Figure 5.

If we model the pipe as a conduit then the pressure at each end must, by definition, be equal, so the levels in each tank must be equal! In order to reason about a situation where the two levels may be different we must model the pipe as a valve not as a simple conduit.

3.6. Producing an Envisionment

De Kleer (1977) coined the term *envisioning* to describe the process of inferring a behaviour description from a structural description. The resulting behaviour description, the *envisionment*, is also known as the *qualitative state diagram*, for it describes the possible transitions between component states. If a system comprises k devices and each device d has s(d) states then the state diagram for the entire system has $\prod_{i=1}^{i=k} s(d_i)$ states; ie the system states are formed from the cross product of all the constituent component states. The envisionment thus completely describes all the possible *inter* state behaviours and certain system wide properties may be determined by inspection of the envisionment such as existence of a cycle (eg oscillation) and that certain states cannot be reached from certain other states.

What is not made explicit in an envisionment is the *intra* state behaviour, ie the changes within a state. A state is specified by conditions on certain variables (those which appear in the qualitative state preconditions in the individual component specifications) and it can be that more than one assignment of values to the complete vector of variables is consistent within a global state. The qualitative state diagram does not make transitions between these *interpretations* explicit, nor does it show how some variables constrain the values of others.

Each internal description of each state of the envisionment is determined partly by simple constraint propagation; however this is not sufficient because the confluences may be simultaneous. Algebraic manipulation is not appropriate because qualitative arithmetic does not satisfy the field axioms (and hence multiple solutions may exist). So ENVISION uses a combination of constraint propagation and 'generate and test' (which they subsequently call *plunking*) in order to determine completely the possible interpretations of a state. (In an appendix, de Kleer and Brown briefly explain how an expanded envisionment where every state has a unique interpretation can be constructed).

QSIM had explicit generating rules which when applied to a particular variable would posit 'next' values which satisfied the underlying continuity constraints. In ENVISION these constraints are specified explicitly. Thus any value generated for a variable must satisfy (inter alia) the following constraints. The *limit rule* states that if time t immediately precedes t' then $x(t') = x(t) + \partial x(t)$. (The notation $x(t)$ means the value of x at time t). This effectively prohibits 'standing starts' (eg a quantity becoming non zero when its derivative is zero). The *continuity rule* states that if t immediately precedes t' then $x(t)$ must be adjacent to $x(t')$ – ie variables are continuous. The *equality change rule* ensures that if x=0 (or any other point), and $\partial x \neq 0$, then a new state is created immediately, with x having a different value. Finally, the *ordering rule* is used in situations such as the following: suppose $\partial x = +$ and $y - z = +$ (ie $y > z$). If one component has a state specification s.t. $x < y$ and another component has a state specification $x < z$, then the global state will alter with only the second component changing state.

In their paper de Kleer and Brown show the complete envisionment for a model of the pressure regulator where the mass of the valve is explicitly modelled and thus the velocity and force of the valve are represented. The valve component has nine states because the preconditions depend on the force and velocity, each of which may have one of three qualitative values. The other components in the system (ie the sensor, spring and sump) only have a single state so there are only nine states in the total envisionment. The state diagram can be used to answer 'what if' type questions and make predictions. Various different models are analysed with different assumptions (whether there is a continuing input signal or not and whether there is friction). If there is no friction then their program ENVISION correctly predicts that there is no final state and the behaviour is cyclic. If there is friction then a possible predicted behaviour is that the oscillation may terminate (ie the envisionment contains a path that has a node which has no successor node). However there is also a behaviour which is oscillatory, although the real device will always settle to a final state. Note that analysis of the envisionment is 'outside' the theory – ie ENVISION leaves it up to a human to interpret the envisionment.

3.7. Explanation

De Kleer and Brown spend some time discussing what constitutes an explanation of behaviour and whether such an explanation is a causal explanation. They develop the notion of an *explanationproof,* which is a natural deduction style proof of why a particular variable has a particular value; the axioms are the confluences and any input signals. An explanationproof explains intra state behaviour, ie it can be used to complete interpretations from the input signals. Obviously in a different state a different set of axioms (confluences) would apply.

However de Kleer and Brown are not entirely happy with explanationproofs as a causal explanation for a number of reasons. Firstly, introduction of premises may be required, even if there is no ambiguity (ie the state has a unique interpretation) and these may appear unmotivated. Secondly, indirect proofs *(reductio ad absurdum)* are sometimes required and they consider these to be non causal, though others may disagree and be happy with explanations of the form "this variable has this value because if it's this value we get a contradiction and similarly for these values". The question is whether the proof has to 'simulate reality' or merely explain why a device operates in the way it does. However since we are now treading on very deep philosophical waters we shall not discuss this point further. See, for example, Sosa (1975) or Lucas (1984) for essays on the subject. Another problem that de Kleer and Brown identify with explanationproofs is that they may be non-unique, which they again find unsatisfactory for a causal explanation; the non-uniqueness is of course not surprising, much of the effort of the computational logic community during recent decades has been devoted to reducing the redundancy found in the search spaces induced by a logic. Finally, explanationproofs may be 'causally misordered'; eg the steps in the proof may not be in the same order as the intuitive causal ordering. Thus, we can say that explanationproofs explain *why* a system operates in a particular way, not *how*.

When one considers qualitative physics as a modelling process it is perhaps not surprising that a (qualitative) model does not provide a perfect explanation, for any model makes assumptions about the modelled system and abstracts it; anything beneath the grain size of the model will not be explainable and the abstraction process will inevitably lead to ambiguity.

3.8. Mythical Causality

In order to try and introduce a more compelling form of causal explanation, de Kleer and Brown introduce the notion of *mythical causality*. The idea is to regard change of state as: equilibrium state followed by a sequence of non equilibrium states followed by an equilibrium state. Mythical causality 'explains' the sequence of non equilibrium states which cause the equilibrium state change. Assuming the device is initially at equilibrium (ie satisfying all the confluences of the state), a *single* disturbance is introduced (ie a parameter change) and constraints are propagated until a new equilibrium is reached. The infinitesimal time this takes in the actual device is called 'mythical time'. As already discussed, propagation may halt before all variables are determined; in order for propagation to continue, three heuristics (all of the form "places where disturbances haven't yet reached aren't changing") are introduced. These are the *component heuristic*, the *confluence heuristic* and the *conduit heuristic*. For details of these refer to de Kleer and Brown (1984).

However it is still possible for the mythical causal account not to be unique (perhaps because it may be possible to use heuristics in several ways – ie introduce alternate assumptions). ENVISION produces *all* mythical causal explanations in the envisionment and thus (unless there is no ambiguity) does not 'causally simulate' the device but rather constructs 'reasonable explanations of how it might work'. Of course, the above heuristics may not be the only ones that could be used when making assumptions, however de Kleer and Brown claim that they are natural in the sense that they were formulated as a result of analysing descriptions of device behaviour given by humans.

3.9. The Iwaski and Simon Debate

An extended debate took place in the AI Journal in 1986 (de Kleer and Brown 1986, Iwasaki and Simon 1986a, 1986b) concerning the work we have been describing here. The main thrust of Iwaski and Simon's (1986a) commentary was to question the applicability, validity and suitability of de Kleer and Brown's Qualitative Physics and in particular the work on mythical causality.

They suggested an alternative methodology for reasoning about equations, such as those to be found in a de Kleer and Brown model, which comes from the mathematical economics literature. A system of equations can be analysed to determine the *causal ordering*. If no feedback is present then this will give a directed acyclical graph where each variable of the model is a node and the directed arcs are 'causal links'. Variables that depend on no others (ie with in-degree 0) are the 'uncaused causes' – ie they can be regarded as *exogonous* variables. Actually the causal ordering technique requires n (independent) equations for n variables; if this requirement is not met then additional equations, of the form x=constant will be required. No advice on how to choose such equations however is given.

Causal ordering is purely a structural analysis of the equations to determine a direction for each equality, and does not manipulate the functors – ie no equation solving is performed; also no input signals are needed (unlike the mythical causality technique). Causal ordering is a one off static process, while determining mythical causality is a dynamic (runtime) computation requiring an input signal. The mythical causality will also determine the direction of change but Iwasaki and Simon claim that this could be added to the causal ordering method as an orthogonal technique.

If there is no feedback then all concerned seem to agree that mythical causality and causal ordering are approximately equivalent. However when a feedback loop is present then mythical causality will determine all the interpretations and a (mythical) causal direction round the loop.

In order to analyse systems with feedback loops Iwasaki and Simon advocate the method of *Comparative Statics* where 2nd order equations are (manually) added (ie as part of the process of building the model) and these will usually give a unique solution (provided the feedback loop is stable). However it doesn't determine an ordering for variables in loop: a feedback loop just *is;* according to Iwasaki and Simon there is no sense in which one event can be said to precede another in a feedback loop.

Iwasaki and Simon conclude that Causal Ordering and Comparative Statics are more general than the Mythical Causality technique and also give a formal justification to it (eg the assumptions that are introduced by the plunking heuristics are that certain variables are exogonous as determined by the Causal Ordering technique).

De Kleer and Brown (1986) constitutes a reply to these comments. They remark that the concerns of those modelling Economics and those modelling physical systems seem to be different. They argue that whereas the form of equations in Economics may be somewhat arbitrary, in physical systems there are *real* components which naturally give rise to particular kinds equations and that it is natural to think of physical feedback systems having an ordering round the loop. (Of course some physical systems might be modelled by having virtual sub components (eg physiological models are often like this) and the argument may lose some of its force in such systems). They also comment that, as we have already seen, qualitative reasoning generally makes multiple predictions owing to ambiguity; in such cases ENVISION will determine all globally consistent interpretations whereas Iwasaki and Simon's method will only determine a single labelling leaving ambiguous variables unlabelled.

They point out that Iwasaki and Simon don't address the problem of how to produce a model (whereas they appeal to their component library). ENVISION is also implemented as a computer program while Iwaski and Simon's method is not (though for some progress in this direction see Iwasaki (1987)).

De Kleer and Brown also make the somewhat controversial claim that ENVISION is a general procedure for solving (possibly non linear) sets of qualitative differential equations. However in their reply, Iwasaki and Simon (1986b) dispute this and state that ENVISION will only deal correctly with non linear differential equations when the model is close enough to equilibrium for linear assumptions to apply.

They also ask for a more precise definition of Qualitative Physics: they find it too *ad hoc,* but perhaps it is too early on to hope for this. They take de Kleer and Brown to task for unstated assumptions behind ENVISION. Finally they ask for clarification of the 'no function in structure' principle. What does it really mean and how can one tell if one has followed it?

4. A Process Centred Approach

We now turn to the final commonly found approach to qualitative modelling in the literature, based on an explicit representation of processes. This approach is due to Forbus (1984a); he is still working on it (Forbus 1986a, 1986b), and others are now taking a similar approach including Weld (1985), Ambrosio (1987), Manzo and Truco (1987) and Bredeweg (1987). Here, we shall concentrate on the original theory, called *Qualitative Process Theory (QPT)* as described in Forbus (1984a) and (1984b).

Unlike Kuipers and de Kleer and Brown who seem to be primarily interested in building a qualitative version of conventional physics, Forbus is more interested in following on from the ideas of Naive Physics (Hayes 1979, 1985a, 1985b); however unlike Hayes he is interested not only in representational issues but also in the computational aspects. He is influenced by the histories idea from Hayes' work and views QPT as being a Hayes style *cluster*. From de Kleer's work he uses the idea of envisioning and the qualitative quantity spaces. Of the three approaches we have examined, QPT has the most sophisticated conceptual mechanisms for modelling. Not only do we find representational apparatus for qualitative quantity spaces, differential equations and function descriptions, but also a way of viewing collections of individuals satisfying certain conditions as aggregates with particular behavioural properties. There is also an explicit representation for processes of course.

4.1. Modelling Primitives

Forbus assumes Allen's (1983) interval calculus as an underlying temporal basis. Thus 'instants' are just intervals with no subintervals and there are certain primitive relationships between intervals such as *starts, ends* and *meets*. Time is not dense because two intervals may have no intervening interval. Forbus defines two functions *start* and *end* which map intervals to instants denoting their 'endpoints'. The function *during* maps an interval to the set of intervals in it, and *duration* maps an interval to a number (which is 0 for intervals which are instants). T(x,y) means x is true at/during time y.

A *quantity* q represents a continuous function of time which has an *amount* (A[q]) and *derivative* (D[q]) (both numbers); numbers are represented by a *sign* and *magnitude* (notated by s[ ] and m[ ] respectively); a sign is one of −1, 0 or 1 but there is no way of directly representing a magnitude: only a partial ordering on symbolic magnitudes can be given by defining a *quantity space*. Two points in a quantity space are *neighbours* when they are no intervening points in the partial order; (determining neighbours is important for detecting when processes start/stop). All quantity spaces include zero so that a connection can be made to the sign of a number. This sign and magnitude representation of quantities helps Forbus disambiguate addition of signs which was ambiguous in the positive + negative case in de Kleer and Brown's algebra because if the magnitudes of the two numbers being added are totally ordered in the quantity space then the addition is not ambiguous.

Individual views are the modelling device for describing an object (or more usually a collection of objects) satisfying certain conditions which have a particular behaviour. For example individual views might be created to describe an extended spring, a compressed spring and a relaxed spring. There are four parts to an individual view: *individuals* – the objects that must exist for the individual view to exist; *quantity conditions* – inequalities between individuals and predications on other individual views (or processes); *preconditions* – other conditions; *relations* – things that are true when the individual view is active.

The difference between preconditions and quantity conditions is that the former conditions may be affected by the system, the latter are 'external' conditions which cannot be affected by any process. (For example amount of current drawn v. a switch being on or off – the former quantity may be affected by other quantities but the latter can only be changed by an external agent). An individual view instance will exist whenever a set of individuals satisfies the *individuals* conditions; it will be active whenever the *preconditions* and *quantity* conditions are satisfied. Certain kinds of creation and destruction of objects can be modelled by the activity level of an individual view. In particular Forbus (1985) discusses the modelling of *quantity conditioned existence*. Thus an individual view may be of use even if the relations field is null (no behaviour is specified) because we can use it to model the conditions when an object will cease to exist (for example Forbus (1984a) models states of matter this way).

Normally Forbus represents individual views using a kind of frame notation. He does give an example translation of an individual view so represented into first order logic syntax; however in the absence of a formally specified translation procedure and much greater discussion of the ontological status of entities such as liquid objects or pieces of stuff which he quantifies over, and without an axiomatisation of the envisionment procedure, it is not clear how much this is worth.

Some mechanism is required in the relations field of an individual view in order to express the behaviour of the objects in the view and in particular the functional relationships that may hold between quantities when the conditions specified in the view are satisfied. Forbus introduces *qualitative proportionalities* in order to fulfill this need. $q1 \propto_{Q+} q2$ means that $q1$ is qualitatively proportional to $q2$ and is monotonically increasing in its dependence. $q1 \propto_{Q-} q2$ means that $q1$ is qualitatively proportional to $q2$ and is monotonically decreasing in its dependence. For example one might write level(p) $\propto_{Q+}$ amount-of(p) to express that the level of water in a container increases as the amount increases. Qualitative proportionalities are similar to Kuipers' monotonic function constraints but differ in that $q1 \propto_{Q+} q2$ means that $q1$ will increase if $q2$ increases *and everything else relevant stays the same* (relevant quantities are all those which *influence ql* – see below). Thus $q1$ may be a function of more than just $q2$ – this is not expressible by Kuipers' $M^{\pm}$ constraints. Furthermore, the implied function behind a qualitative proportionality can be named so that it can be used more than once if desired; thus one can express the fact that two (or more) qualitatively expressed functions are the *same* function. This could be used, for example, to enable the system to infer that if there are two containers whose bottoms are at the same height and which have fluid at the same level then the pressure at the bottom of each container is identical (provided of course the liquids have the same specific gravity). It is also possible to specify that the functions behind qualitative proportionalities are dependent on things other than quantities (eg shapes), so that one could restrict the qualitative proportionality concerning the level of fluid above to depend on the shape and size of the container remaining the same (to stop an incorrect prediction being made, when filling a balloon, for example). Correspondences can also be used to further specify the implied function in the same way as we saw with Kuipers' system.

Forbus builds on Hayes' (1979) idea of using 4D pieces of space time called *histories* to describe the behaviour of an object over time. In fact, it would seem that Forbus' histories are *configuration space* (Lozano-Perez 1983) histories rather conventional 4D histories, for an object's possible histories include all of the histories of its parameters which measure some linear attribute of the object. The other histories of an object are the histories for the processes it participates in.

Hayes' original motivation for introducing histories was to try and provide a more tractable approach to dealing with time and change in order get round the frame problem which is traditionally associated with situational calculus type approaches. The advantage claimed for the histories approach is that by spatially delimiting change one would not have to evolve a complete global sequence of changes and compute the effects of a change on the whole universe; rather one could evolve a set of parallel local histories which could be reasoned about separately until they intersect. Forbus briefly discusses how one might try to separate out what histories can be reasoned about separately and suggests that the frame problem has now been changed to the problem of computing history intersections. However in all the examples he gives, the state is still a global state. Hayes (1987) briefly discusses some further problems with the histories approach.

We can now turn our attention to describing how a process is to be represented in more detail. In fact a process is represented in the same way as an individual view except that there is an additional part which specifies the *influences* which are the source of any change to a quantity in a model. One may write I+(q,n) to specify that the number n positively influences the quantity n; similarly one may write I–(q,n) with the obvious meaning; I±(q,n) defines an influence with an unspecified sign. For example in the definition of a heat flow process one might write I+(heat(destination),A[flow_rate]) and I–(heat(source),A[flow_rate]). Specifying these influences does not mean that the destination will heat up or the source will cool when the process is active, because there may be other competing influences (from other processes). The influences specified in the influences section of a process are *direct* influences. Indirect influences on quantities arise because of propagation through qualitative proportionalities. The system manipulates the influences on a quantity in order to determine its derivative which will in turn affect the amount of the quantity over time through an integration procedure called *limit analysis*. If a quantity is directly influenced then its derivative is the sum of all the direct influences (it is illegal to write process and view specifications which result in a quantity being simultaneously directly and indirectly influenced). If a quantity is directly influenced both positively and negatively then unless the quantity space can be used to determine whether the positive influence has a greater magnitude than the negative influence (or vice verse) then the situation is ambiguous and the envisioner will have to fork.

Resolving positive and negative indirect influences is more difficult because the lack of information about the exact functions behind the qualitative proportionalities means that the quantity space cannot be used to resolve ambiguities in the same way as when combining direct influences. (However see Ambrosio (1987) for some ideas on how to extend QPT to help in this situation by providing a mechanism for specifying which indirect influences dominate).

A process instance will exist whenever a set of individuals satisfies the individual's conditions component of the process specification; it will be active whenever preconditions and quantity conditions are satisfied just as is the case with individual views. New individuals may also be introduced in the relations field so that, for example, the steam produced by a boiling process can be explicitly represented.

QPT rests on the assumption that "all changes in physical systems are caused directly or indirectly by processes", what Forbus calls the *sole mechanism assumption*. A consequence of this is that provided we make a *closed world assumption* that the model contains all definitions of all relevant processes then we can reason by mutual exclusion about what can change and how.

The final modelling primitive provided by QPT is the *encapsulated history*. Some phenomena (such as collisions between moving objects) are not easily represented by processes; rather Forbus uses encapsulated histories which have the same syntax as individual views (ie individuals, preconditions, quantity conditions and relations) but where the relations specify pieces of histories (ie slices) for the individuals involved.

For example a simple encapsulated history for a collision event *e* (in one dimension) between a moving object *b* with direction *dir* and an immobile object *c* might have a relations field which specified

M[A[velocity(*b*)],start(*e*)] = –M[A[velocity(*b*)],end(*e*)]
M[velocity(*b*),during(*e*)] = ZERO
duration(*e*) = ZERO
T(direction-towards(*c*,*b*,*dir*),end(*e*))
T(contact(*b*,*c*,*dir*),end(*e*))

where M[*x*,*t*] denotes the magnitude of *x* at time *t*.

Encapsulated histories are somewhat 'adhoc' since they violate the principle of composibility; we are not describing a situation by describing its parts but by describing a behaviour which refers to times explicitly. Forbus does not describe how encapsulated histories are integrated into or used by the deductive mechanism described below.

4.2. Deductive Apparatus

We will now examine the machinery which manipulates the modelling primitives we have been describing in order to produce a behavioural description. The main activities are as follows.

Instantiation of processes and individual views creates individual view and process instances given a particular domain description of individuals which exist and a library of process and individual view definitions (the process and individual view *vocabulary*).

Given a collection of process and individual view instantiations then the *process structure* can be created, ie the quantity and pre-conditions of these instances are examined to determine which instances are currently active.

Given a process structure, the influences (both direct and indirect) must be *resolved* to determine the derivatives of all the quantities. Note that feedback loops will always contain a process which will start an influence chain, so there is no possibility of a circular loop of indirect influences causing problems in the implementation.

Limit analysis is a procedure which determines how quantities being influenced will change their amount, which may in turn lead to changes in the process structure because activation conditions may be altered.

Finally, a complete *envisionment* can be built where each node of the envisionment has a unique process structure. Forbus also describes a *summarisation procedure* on an envisionment.

The limit analysis procedure mentioned above deserves a little further explanation. Most elements of a quantity space will come from (be used in) the quantity conditions of processes and individual views. Such conditions act as boundary conditions and these elements are called *limit points*. For each changing quantity q (ie $s(D[q]) \neq 0$) all neighbouring points in quantity space to $A[q]$ are found (these are other quantities). The signs of the derivatives of the quantities involved are examined to determine if inequality can change. (Rates (derivatives) are assumed not be infinitesimals so a quantity 'moving' towards a point in the quantity space will eventually reach it). The set of single such changes plus consistent combinations are the *quantity hypotheses*. Quantity hypotheses which change the process structure are called *limit hypotheses*.

Ambiguity (ie several quantity hypotheses) can occur for several reasons: for example the quantity space may not be a total ordering; a process may influence more than quantity; more than one process may be active. QP theory cannot disambiguate in general except in the special case when the *equality change law* helps: "With two exceptions a process structure lasts over an interval; it lasts for an instant only when either (1) a change from equality occurs in a quantity condition or (2) a change to equality occurs between two quantities in a quantity condition and they were only influenced from equality for an instant". Thus change from equality only takes an instant, but to equality usually takes some interval of non zero duration. For example, if $b=c$ and $d \neq e$ and all the derivatives are non zero then b and c will change from equality before $d=e$.

The equality change law means that it is possible for two consecutive states to be instants and more generally for there to be a cycle in the envisionment consisting entirely of such instantaneous states. Forbus calls such cycles *stutter cycles* since they do not reflect true oscillations but rather dynamic equilibrium behaviours such as a rising heat equilibrium between a series of objects with heat flows between them. His program summarises such cycles into single states.

4.3. Causal Reasoning in QPT

Forbus observes that traditionally equations and constraints are not used in all directions when reasoning 'causally'. Thus in QPT there are no bidirectional equations, only influences and qualitative proportionalities which are unidirectional. Therefore when building a model one has to decide in which direction(s) causality can operate across an equation which will in turn decide which quantities are directly influenced by processes and those only indirectly via qualitative proportionalities.

The fact that all changes originate from some process gives a very strong direction of propagation of change in the system (compared to the other systems we examined earlier). Forbus discusses this and sees it as a strong point of QPT and embodies this way of dealing with change and causality in his *Causal Directedness Hypothesis:* "Changes in physical situations which are perceived as causal are due to our interpretation of them as corresponding either to direct changes caused by processes or propagation of those direct effects through functional dependencies". Thus, unlike the situation in de Kleer and Brown's theory where mythical causality and plunking heuristics were introduced, in QPT we never have to guess or make assumptions about whether a variable is changing or not, only whether a process is active and the best way to resolve influences.

4.4. Building Domain Theories

Although we have so far been concerned with the development of QPT, Forbus was originally motivated to develop this representational and inferential apparatus in order to develop a naive physical theory of the world. He envisages a library of general process and individual view descriptions which can be used to model and then reason about physical situations. His doctoral thesis (Forbus 1984b) contains the beginnings of such a library.

5. Comparison of Approaches

It is appropriate to step back and try to review the three approaches we have described and compare and contrast them. Apart from the obvious differences of whether the approach is component, constraint or process centred, we could identify a number of other dimensions along which the systems could be compared including the representation of quantities, the language for describing behaviour, the nature of the qualitative simulation, the extent to which the theory makes predictions which are faithful to reality and the treatment of causality. We shall examine each of these.

5.1. Qualitative Quantity Spaces

Common to all the approaches we have examined is the idea of a qualitative quantity space. It turns out that even only making the distinction between +, – and 0 can be very effective: de Kleer and Brown always use this quantity space for derivatives (and for non derivative variables as well usually) and Kuipers uses this quantity space for his 'qualitative directions'. It has the advantage of making computation easy and faster because there are fewer possible states and thus fewer branches when ambiguity occurs. However it is less expressive. In order to make more distinctions using this three valued quantity space, extra variables have to be introduced; for example if we wanted to have a quantity space for some variable x which represented possible temperatures and we wanted to distinguish the regions separated by absolute zero, freezing/melting, boiling/condensing, then we would have to introduce a further three variables (called, say, az, fm and bc) and defining equations, eg: bc – fm = +, fm – az = +, az = 0. Three regions and three landmark values (not counting infinity) are now possible compared to the normal two regions and one landmark value. A precondition on a qualitative state, could now depend on the condition x>fm (in this example all states would obviously have the precondition x≥az). However introducing extra variables seems to be less natural and perhaps less efficient compared to building additional divisions into the quantity space itself. Moreover the results of Struss (1987) concerning the special status of the quantity space {-,0,+} would seem to imply that we have lost absolute expressive power.

Forbus alone allows partially ordered quantity spaces, which is more expressive, though of course the above auxiliary variable mechanism could be used to code up partial orderings.

A distinguishing feature of Kuipers' quantity spaces is the dynamic landmark creation. This enables him to distinguish between increasing, steady and decreasing oscillation but means that his simulation may never terminate and thus he can only simulate from a starting state and cannot consider producing an envisionment as can Forbus and de Kleer and Brown. Kuipers does point out that it is very easy to change his transition tables to stop dynamic landmark creation if desired.

The crucial point about a qualitative quantity space it is that is a finite, discrete space which is much more amenable to reasoning about than the underlying continuous quantitative space. In particular sets of equations can be solved by a finite number of guesses if required and the number of possible states and behaviours is also finite (unless dynamic landmark creation is allowed).

5.2. Behaviour Specification Language

All three languages include plus and minus but only Kuipers includes multiplication (de Kleer and Brown prefer to eliminate multiplication by creating more states). All three languages have explicit three valued derivatives. Both Kuipers and Forbus have abstract function descriptions which may have corresponding values; Forbus' representation is the more general and powerful. Forbus also has a mechanism for the partial specification of functional relationships through his mechanism of influences. De Kleer and Brown do not have a monotonic function constraint, but it would be less useful with only {+,–,0} quantity spaces. A weak form of monotonic function constraint between two variables can be encoded in their system by saying $\partial x = \partial y$. In all three systems there is a mechanism provided so that different operating regions can be specified. This can be used to break up a non monotonic function into series of monotonic operating regions. In Kuipers' case this is only at the global level – an entire model is swapped in or out; in the other approaches individual components can have different qualitative states and behaviour specifications (de Kleer and Brown) and different individual views can be specified with different relation fields (Forbus).

5.3. Constraint vs Component vs Process Centred Approaches

A comparison of different approaches to qualitative modelling including the component, constraint and process centred approaches can be found in Bonissone and Valavanis (1985) who survey the field briefly and build a model of a coffee maker in each of the theories.

The constraint centred approach is certainly the simplest in many ways but unfortunately provides no explicit help with the hard task of modelling, nor is there any attempt to build a qualitative physics; the main emphasis is on the simulation algorithm. Of course one could imagine building an interface which helped with modelling and in fact this has been done for the case of physiological compartmental systems (Leaning and Nicolosi 1986).

The device centred approach aids modelling, not only by encouraging a user to modularise the system description but also by having a component library available. Causal connections between components are made explicit in the model by specifying the linking conduits. Provided the component descriptions obey the 'no function in structure principle', descriptions should be composable. Of course it may still be a problem for the modeller to choose component descriptions from the library to fit the system (cf the discussion earlier about a pipe needing to be modelled as a valve). Some systems (for example electronic circuits or pneumatic systems) can be very naturally viewed as networks of standard components; however it is not clear that all physical systems fall into this category, even such a simple system as a ball bouncing on a table top.

Forbus' Qualitative Process Theory certainly has the most sophisticated set of modelling features and the most complex ontology. Arguably, this allows better explanations of device behaviour because, for example, processes can be explicitly discussed. Causal connections are not explicitly built in, but are discovered dynamically by influence resolution. Moreover the explicit representation of processes and the sole mechanism assumption seems to allow for a more natural representation for causal reasoning compared (say) to de Kleer and Brown's mythical causality. Moreover, because all influences and qualitative proportionalities have a built in direction, there is no need for any input assumptions or causal ordering as required in bi-directional equational systems.

QPT can also explicitly represent and reason about state changes such as turning water to steam which can be at best implicitly represented in the other systems. Of course the underlying machinery is much more complicated, difficult to implement and would seem to be more computationally expensive. Moreover, while both QSIM and ENVISION are based on traditional mathematical theories, QPT has a much less well defined formal semantics. ENVSION can display a logical derivation of the envisionment, while the inferential procedure of QPT is defined purely procedurally. (Forbus displays informal logical translations of some process and individual view descriptions but does not attempt to axiomatise the envisionment procedure). However Forbus is particularly interested in modelling *naive* physics and thus is perhaps less concerned as to how or even whether his theory corresponds to traditional theories or to reality. Of course, in the absence of a semantics, one can not even *ask* such questions. (See Hayes (1974, 1977), Israel 1985 and McDermott (1978) for further discussion of this last point). The question of correctness of qualitative simulation algorithms is further discussed below.

Other approaches to structuring qualitative models include Addanki and Davis (1985) and Bylander and Chandrasekaran (1985).

5.4. Qualitative Simulation

Although this article is entitled "Qualitative Reasoning", the actual reasoning techniques we have discussed have been mainly limited to some form of Qualitative Simulation. In each case this has lead to an induced qualitative description of time (though QPT also allows some explicit description of time via encapsulated histories). In de Kleer and Brown's system, mythical causality also induces a finer level of qualitative time, consisting entirely of instants, within a qualitative state, which they call mythical time.

Owing to the low grain of resolution in qualitative quantity spaces, qualitative simulation may give rise to ambiguous predictions, unlike a standard quantitative simulation.

A distinction can be drawn (see Forbus (1986a)) between a *total* envisionment and an *attainable* envisionment. In the latter only all states attainable from some initial start state are generated (as in the programs NEWTON (de Kleer 1977), QUAL (de Kleer 1979) and GIZMO (Forbus 1984b)). In a total envisionment all possible start states are considered (eg ENVISION (de Kleer & Brown 1984) and QPE (Forbus 1986b)). A history is just a path through an envisionment. Kuipers' QSIM does not produce an envisionment since there are potentially infinitely many states owing to landmark generation. If there were no dynamic landmark creation then the simulation structure would resemble an attainable envisionment.

Each state in a QSIM simulation is distinguished by being a unique assignment of values to variables, in de Kleer and Brown's representation by being a unique selection of individual component qualitative states and in Forbus' system by being a unique process structure (ie collection of active processes and individual views).

Cycles in a simulation represent oscillation (possibly a rising equilibrium if a QPT cycle contains only instantaneous states).

A distinction that could be made between qualitative and quantitative simulation, is that the latter produces an exact (within the precision of the machine) answer which is possibly inaccurate owing to rounding error, whilst the former produces an exact prediction, but at lower precision.

5.5. What are Valid State Transitions?

All systems we have discussed so far enforce continuity constraints on the qualitative quantity space. Corresponding value constraints may be present in Forbus' and Kuipers' systems. Obviously any new state must be internally consistent (all equations and conditions must be satisfied).

De Kleer and Brown enumerate a number of transition rules between qualitative states. These have analogs in the other two representations. The limit rule is encoded in Kuipers' transition tables and in QPT by the fact that variables don't change unless influenced. The adjacency rule is encoded in QSIM's transition tables and because of the total ordering of his quantity spaces and in QPT's use of neighbours during limit analysis. The ordering rule has no real analog in QSIM because there are no components but has an analog in QPT in the partial orderings of the quantities specified in quantity conditions and the neighbourhood relation. The equality change rule is encoded into Kuipers transition tables and Forbus' equality change law; however in QPT there is a second part to the equality change law which has no analog in the other systems.

5.6. Correctness

Kuipers asks the question: do the behaviours predicted by qualitative simulation correspond to reality? Although he can show QSIM to be complete (ie all real behaviours are predicted), QSIM may also predict extraneous behaviours. This analysis depends on the assumption that the qualitative model is an abstraction of an underlying quantitative ODE and the notion of correctness is relative to this semantics. Since a set of qualitative constraints may represent more than one quantitative ODE, behaviour predictions may relate to any of these. However it is also possible, because of the local nature of the simulation, for genuinely spurious behaviours to be predicted. Neither Forbus nor de Kleer and Brown explicitly discuss the mathematical correctness of their theories.

Struss (1987) has investigated the correctness of the qualitative arithmetic in a variety of systems including QSIM and ENVISION. Assuming that the correctness is defined with respect to standard arithmetic on the real numbers and qualitative constraints or equations are to be viewed as abstractions of standard equations on the reals then he produces a number of important negative results about qualitative reasoners in general. In particular, he shows that no qualitative reasoning method which has finite quantity spaces preserves the associativity of the arithmetic operators unless the quantity spaces are all just –/0/+. Lack of associativity means that different orders of computation may yield different solutions. He defines notions of soundness and completeness for qualitative reasoners with respect to an underlying gold standard of the reals and shows that no qualitative reasoning method can be sound (even what he calls 'weakly sound') for sets of even very simple kinds of equations. He demonstrates that this unsoundness arises due to the same variable occurring more than once. Of course transforming a set of equations to satisfy this requirement amounts to virtually solving them and we would expect variables to occur many times in general so this is a very strong limitation on the soundness of qualitative arithmetic. The number of spurious solutions can be reduced by ensuring that each equation or constraint does not contain more than one occurrence of a variable but this does not ensure global soundness.

Apart from algebraic manipulations to transform equations locally, he suggests combining quantitative knowledge and qualitative knowledge where available using a formalism such as that in Simmons (1986).

Struss also wonders whether the condition enforcing the exclusivity of qualitative values (ie existing qualitative reasoners always assume that the intervals denoted by values in a qualitative quantity space are pairwise non intersecting sets) could be relaxed. He points to the work on qualitative quantity spaces based on non standard analysis (Raiman 1986, Lutz and Goze 1981) as a possible step in this direction. He also suggests using *Partial Sets* (Klaua 1969) as a representation technique which might help.

6. Uses of Qualitative Reasoning

We have already come across some uses to which qualitative reasoners might be put, in particular explanation (how does this system work) and prediction (what might happen if). Other tasks that one might want to use qualitative models for include diagnosis (why does the system behave in this way and how could we make it behave in that way), measurement interpretation (what is the system doing if we observe these parameter values – clearly this might form part of the diagnosis task), verification and mental modelling. One can obviously imagine combinations of these tasks such as what Forbus calls a 'Doubting Thomas' system (= measurement interpretation + explanation), which could be used in critical applications to help avoid the human operator of a physical system being blinkered.

We have already discussed explanation of behaviour using qualitative models when discussing de Kleer and Brown's work. Other work on explanation using qualitative models which has not been mentioned includes Forbus and Stevens (1981) and Laughton (1985).

6.1. Diagnosis

One approach to diagnosis is to build in faulty behaviours into component descriptions – as is done in, for example, Kardio (Bratko et al 1986) which we will describe below. This is not the same as a global list of faults for the entire system, for it is much easier and more viable to imagine specifying a fault list for every component type rather than globally for an entire system. The process of envisioning would then build a description of all ways in which faults or combinations of faults affect the global system behaviour. One obvious disadvantage of such an approach is that it will not deal with assembly or design errors or with faults not explicitly foreseen in any component description. Nor will it deal with changes in structure (owing perhaps to a short circuit). However a greater problem in practice is likely to be the combinatorial explosion. This results from considering all the possible interactions of faulty and correct behaviours of individual components. Of course one can imagine certain strategies to help here, such as multi level models, or making a single fault assumption at first but there is still something rather inelegant about having to pre-ordain all the ways in which all the components can fail. Also note that this technique is only applicable in a component centred approach (where one would have a different qualitative state within each component state for each faulty behaviour) or the QPT approach (where one would have a different individual view for each faulty mode of behaviour of a component), but not in the global constraint model of Kuipers.

The alternative approach is to dispense with explicit fault models and dynamically infer which components are faulty. This is the technique Davis (1984) used. More recently this approach has been investigated by de Kleer and Williams (1987) and, independently, Reiter (1987), with particular attention to the problem of diagnosis in the presence of multiple faults. Reiter's approach is more formal, whilst de Kleer and Williams have implemented a system, based on the ATMS (de Kleer 1986a, 1986b, 1986c; Reiter and de Kleer 1987). Their program, called GDE (General Diagnostic Engine), tries to manipulate sets of candidate assumptions about which components are faulty, as efficiently as possible. Moreover GDE will propose further measurements to help distinguish between candidate sets. Given information about the likely failure of candidates, it will do this optimally (from the standpoint of the likely number of such tests). The input to GDE consists of the structure of the system, the component behaviour definitions, the *a priori* probabilities of every component failing and an input vector of observations. So far, the technique has only been applied to digital domains (though see Dague et al (1987)).

Other work on diagnosis in a qualitative reasoning setting includes Bareiss and Farquhar (1986) who built a diagnostic engine on top of QSIM (the report includes the Prolog code) and Chandrasekaran et al (1987) who discuss diagnosis using a deep model of the domain.

6.2. Measurement Interpretation

An interesting use of a qualitative envisionment to help interpret numerical data is described by Forbus (1986a). The technique itself is domain independent but assumes that a total envisionment can be generated and the availability of some (probably domain specific) technique for translating numerical values to qualitative values. The input to the measurement interpretation procedure is a set of sequences of measurements of certain parameters which occur in the envisionment (the relative times of all the measurements must be known). Initially, an assumption is also made that all measurement sequences are *close*, ie are taken often enough not to miss anything 'of interest'.

The input measurements for each variable are grouped into a sequence of maximal intervals (which meet, since closeness is assumed), during which the parameter does not change qualitative value; these intervals are called *segments*. Each such interval may or may not be associated with a single qualitative state in the envisionment.

Global segments (ie which contain all the observed parameters) are constructed from these individual parameter segment sequences. During each such global segment, no individual measurement changes, and every global segment starts some individual segment and finishes some individual segment. Each global segment is likely to correspond to a single qualitative state in the envisionment.

A global segment can be viewed as a partial description of one or more qualitative states in the envisionment. The *p-interps* of a global segment are the qualitative states which are consistent with it (these can be computed dynamically or simply looked up if the total envisionment is already built). If the system is large and only a few variables are being measured then each global segment is likely to have many p-interps so some kind of pruning is required. Domain specific knowledge can be used if available; however a Waltz filtering algorithm can prove remarkably effective. Since the data is assumed to be close, for every pair of global segments g1 and g2, such that g1 meets g2, any p-interps of g1 which do not have a successor in the p-interps of g2 can be discarded from the set of possible p-interps for g1. Similarly any p-interps of g2 which are not a successor of some p-interp of g1 can also be filtered out. This procedure is repeated as usual until it can be applied no longer or some global segment has no p-interps left; in this latter case either the initial data was inconsistent, the assumption that the data was close is false or there is a hidden transition problem. A hidden transition problem occurs when two adjacent states in envisionment are identical with respect to the measured variables – this can be dealt with by including extra states in p-interps. If the Waltz filtering algorithm terminates normally, then the remaining p-interps can be used to construct possible behaviour sequences.

Forbus describes a simple example which demonstrates this technique very effectively. The system consists of a beaker whose temperature can be measured and which contains liquid. The only liquids in the world are alcohol and water. The model states that the boiling temperature of alcohol is lower than that of water (but the absolute temperatures are not known). The only processes modelled are heatflow and boiling. The model ignores heat flow to the atmosphere, any gasses produced, and possibility of the beaker exploding or melting.

A sequence of temperatures of the beaker are available but only the derivative of this parameter is any use since the absolute boiling points are not known. Thus the global segments are trivial to compute and consist of (as it happens) six intervals during which the derivative of the temperature is alternatively positive and zero. There are alternately seven and four p-interps for each of the global segments. However after Waltz filtering a unique prediction of the behaviour which produced the observation set is made. First there is water and alcohol in the beaker and heat flow to the beaker. Next the alcohol starts boiling. Then there is just water left in the beaker. Then the water starts boiling. After that the beaker is empty and finally the heat flow stops when the beaker reaches an equilibrium temperature.

It is worth making a small aside here: Michael Mavrovouniotis (personal communication) has pointed out that the input data Forbus gives could not be actually obtained in the real world: the temperature of a beaker containing water and alcohol being heated will not have an alternating sequence of zero and positive gradients; such behaviour will only occur when the two liquids are not miscible (e.g. mercury and water).

If sparse data is given or detected Forbus suggests using the above procedure to try and detect close sub-sequences and then finding a path in the envisionment to close the gap. He admits that cycles in the envisionment may cause problems but does not make any particular suggestions to cope with this.

6.3. Other Applications of Qualitative Reasoning.

Other applications of qualitative reasoning which we do not have the space to describe further here include control, planning and design. Clocksin and Morgan (1986) describe a qualitative controller. Hogge (1987) is an account of his investigations into building planning operators from QPT theories. Dyer et al (1986, 1987) is a fascinating account of their theory of 'naive invention'.

7. Efficiency Issues

So far we have talked little of the practicality of the techniques we have been describing for large problems – almost all the examples in the literature are limited to small systems (this perhaps applies less to those working in digital domains such as Davis (1984) or Barrow (1984)). However even for small systems the qualitative simulation can be quite expensive; for example GIZMO, Forbus' first implementation of QPT took one and three quarter hours to produce a 14 state attainable envisionment of a problem involving just three containers (Forbus 1986b). Of course it is reasonable to expect that large systems will have complex behavioural descriptions and will thus give rise to large envisionments; however the problem of qualitative ambiguities may result in a combinatorial explosion of possible state transitions.

Work on improving the efficiency of qualitative reasoners has proceeded on a number of fronts. For example the basic implementations have been improved. Methods are being developed to reduce the problem of qualitative ambiguities. Hierarchically organised qualitative models have been shown to be of help. If the model is fixed then one can produce the envisionment once and for all and subsequently use it for tasks such as explanation, diagnosis or measurement interpretation – this effectively amounts to a compilation of the model. We will discuss all these approaches below.

Progress on the basic implementation of qualitative reasoners includes Forbus' new implementation of QPT (called QPE) using de Kleer's ATMS (de Kleer 1986a, 1986b, 1986c; Reiter and de Kleer 1987) which appears to run approximately 95 times faster (Forbus 1986b). Thus QPE takes less than four minutes to produce an envisionment for the three container problem mentioned above. (Moreover QPE produces a total envisionment, rather than an attainable envisionment, which has more states (66 in this example)).

The QSIM implementation of Kuipers' theory described in Kuipers (1986) runs some 30 to 60 times faster compared to his earlier program (Kuipers 1984) – in part attributable to the use of Waltz filtering.

An important part of qualitative reasoning involves manipulating constraints and reasoning about inequalities – it is clearly important that this kind of reasoning is efficiently implemented. Forbus (1987a) describes the inequality reasoning in QPE using an ATMS. Simmons (1986) describes a constraint reasoning system in which both qualitative and quantitative information can be combined and integrated efficiently. The systems described in Simmons and Davis (1983) and Mohammed and Simmons (1986) both use the *quantity lattice* representation developed in Simmons (1986).

Sacks (1987a) describes his program BOUNDER which reasons about inequalities efficiently. In fact Bounder contains four different inequality reasoning algorithms, arranged hierarchically from the point of view of both efficiency and the range of problems they can solve. Davis (1987) reviews a number of constraint propagation algorithms and analyses them from a theoretical viewpoint.

One approach to reducing qualitative ambiguities is to use higher order derivatives. The use of higher order derivatives in qualitative reasoning was first investigated by de Kleer and Bobrow (1984). More recently, Chiu and Kuipers (1987) have extended Kuipers' representation in order to reduce the qualitative ambiguities which can be particularly harmful in his system because unnecessary landmark creation may result.

They consider coupled systems such as two cascaded tanks. QSIM exhibits *chatter* with this system; ie a variable (representing the net flow into the second tank) remains positive but its derivative wanders between the three qualitative values and new landmarks also get created. Very many behaviours are thus predicted. The problem is that not enough is known about the function behind a monotonic function constraint to know what to do at *critical points* (ie when the derivative is std).

Two solutions are proposed. The first collapses behaviours, by telling QSIM to ignore derivatives of the chattering parameter. The second involves making additional assumptions about all the variables and automatically analysing the set of constraints to derive additional rules for what to do at critical points.

In order to collapse behaviours, an extended version of QSIM can be told that the qdir of certain parameters can only have a new value *ign*. Thus, for these parameters, values of the form <α,inc> <α,std> <α,dec> are collapsed to <α,ign> eliminating the possibility of chatter occurring. Certain checks are still required to ensure that continuity conditions are not violated. For the two cascaded tanks, only two behaviours are now predicted: (i) both tanks reach equilibrium simultaneously and (ii) tank A reaches equilibrium before tank B. It turns out that (ii) is spurious and that (i) represents several real behaviours.

The second technique involves trying to use higher order derivatives. In a quantitative linear ODE, the behaviour at a critical point is determined by first non zero higher order derivative (the curvature of the parameter). However unless care is taken, introducing higher order derivatives may just increase opportunity for ambiguity and increase the complexity of simulation because more variables are present. Higher order derivatives are only needed when the first order derivative is zero (ie std).

The essential idea of Chiu and Kuipers' method is to find automatically the highest order derivatives (HODs) of a system and then automatically derive constraints on the second derivatives of these when their first derivative is zero, in terms of the other existing parameters. (Of course if the second derivative is also zero the ambiguity is still present).

Finding HOD(s) is easy: the constraints are represented as a network, and paths from DERIV constraints are traced through M± and MINUS constraints and further DERIV constraints until blocked by an ADD or MULT constraint; maximal derivatives in these paths are the HODs. (If a path is circular and thus there is no HOD then the curvature constraint is already encoded in the system). A simple algorithm is given to define the second derivative of HODs in terms of other parameters. The algorithm assumes that the functions behind monotonic function constraints are approximately linear locally. For example in a two tank coupled system, the HODs are the netflows through the two tanks and the method derives expressions for the second derivative of each of these in terms of the first derivative of the other. QSIM then predicts a unique behaviour.

The first method must be hand applied (at present); the second method is automated, but makes stronger assumptions. Chiu and Kuipers claim that both these techniques are more generally applicable than just to QSIM.

In further work jointly with Lee (Lee, Chiu & Kuipers 1987) they continue the development of the technique of using higher order derivative constraints for reducing ambiguity. They also give consideration to the use of extremum constraints and system properties. For example when QSIM simulates a damped spring the behaviour tree is very explosive (at depth eight, approximately half an oscillation, there are already 35 leaves in the simulation tree!). Applying second order derivative constraints gives a unique behaviour at depth eight, but 21 behaviours at depth 16. Analysis of the underlying ODEs implies that oscillation should decrease. They derive *extremum constraints* which then restrict the number of behaviours to six at depth 16 (including one cycle of length 11).

Analysis of system properties can also have a dramatic effect on QSIM's branching behaviour. For example when the first branch occurs in the simulation of the damped spring the state is x=<(0,inf),dec>, v=<(minf,0),inc>, a=<(0,inf),inc>. QSIM predicts three successor states:

x=<(0,inf),dec>	v=<(minf,0),inc>	a=<(0,inf),std>
x=<0,dec>	v=<(minf,0),inc>	a=<(0,inf),std>
x=<0,dec>	v=<(minf,0),inc>	a=<(0,inf),inc>

However any given spring will behave in the same way so the same decision should be made subsequently. This yields a simulation with one cycle and three infinite branches. Analysis of the initial state can constrain simulation to predict unique behaviour.

At present none of the above analysis and application of extremum and system property constraints is implemented.

7.1. The Kardio Project

An interesting piece of work which deserves study especially given our current concerns with efficiency is the Kardio project (Bratko et al 1986, Mozetic 1987a, 1987b).

Kardio is a qualitative model of the electrical control system of the heart. An ECG measures electrical activity and can be used to help diagnose electrical disorders of the heart. The question is, if an ECG is not normal, what disorders could have caused it. There are 30 basic disorders (cardiac arrhythmias). However what complicates the issue is that multiple arrhythmias (up to seven) are not uncommon. Bratko et al (1986) report that it has proved difficult to construct a conventional 'surface' rule base from clinical interviews. So they constructed a qualitative model of heart where electrical signals are not represented as voltages but symbolically, specifying qualitative features of signals.

The model is a component model consisting of a network of components such as impulse generators, conduction pathways, impulse sumators and ECG generators. Normal and abnormal behaviours were associated with components (eg blocked, block every 3rd impulse,...). A dictionary of simple arrhythmias also formed part of the model.

A qualitative simulation algorithm was implemented which would predict an ECG from a given combination of arrhythmias. Running the simulation backwards would enable diagnosis but proved to be much too inefficient because of the higher branching in this direction. Their solution was to compile the qualitative model to create a surface style rule base. The simulation algorithm was run on all possible legal combinations of arrhythmias (2419 out of 2804011 mathematically possible combinations). This was rather expensive computationally, but was a 'one off' computation. This produced a set of 8314 <arrhythmia, ECG description> pairs which could be used for diagnosis or prediction equally efficiently.

Also described in the paper is an interesting application of an inductive learning algorithm which was used to compact this rule set by a factor of about 200.

More recently Mozetic (1987b) has reformulated the qualitative model as a three level hierarchical qualitative model. The abstraction levels are created by varying the component granularity (ie a component at one level may be a set of components at another level), by introducing more variables and by making the qualitative quantity spaces finer grained (for example at level one there is only the distinction as to whether an electrical pulse is present or not; at the second level the pulse type is distinguished and at the most detailed level the precise shape of the pulse is represented).

It turned out that with this hierarchical model it was computationally feasible to do diagnosis directly from the qualitative model rather than having to compile a set of surface rules because the solutions at more abstract levels could be used to constrain the solution process at the lower levels.

7.2. Temporal Abstraction

Kuipers (1987a) describes an interesting way of improving the efficiency of reasoning about an equilibrium system. It depends on being able to view a device as a set of interacting sub-devices which operate at very different speeds. An intermediate speed device can then regard a faster one as operating instantaneously and a slower one as constant. He outlines a technique for exploiting such a temporal device hierarchy and gives an example drawn from medical physiology: the water sodium balance system.

8. Time

As just indicated temporal reasoning can be very important when reasoning about physical systems but has somewhat second class status in most of the systems we have described. Only in QPT are there explicit primitives for referring to temporal intervals. Temporal knowledge and constraints are generally built into the systems at a very low level such as continuity assumptions.

Unsatisfied with this state of affairs, Williams (1986) has tried to separate out the temporal reasoning component of a qualitative reasoner. He built a temporal constraint propagator (TCP) which can be used as the temporal reasoning component of a qualitative reasoner such as his earlier system (Williams 1984).

His major motivation for this is to be able to reason more efficiently about time and to be able to change and experiment with different ontologies for time without having to change the rest of the qualitative reasoning system. Thus there should be a clean and well defined interface to the temporal reasoner.

He notes that all the qualitative reasoners we have been describing here (and others) are essentially based on a single global state and thus suffer from all the problems of the situational calculus; in particular unnecessary temporal distinctions have to be made as to the temporal ordering of essentially unrelated events. This in turn leads to extra states and therefore larger envisionments and more inference. The problem is essentially the well known frame problem.

Moreover in existing systems (perhaps with the exception of Forbus' measurement intepretation procedure) prediction, diagnosis and other tasks always assume an input with no temporal extension; ideally one would like to be able to describe time varying inputs. Another problem Williams identifies is the difficulty of describing actions (or processes) with a delayed effect.

In TCP every variable is represented by a sequence of <interval,value> pairs such that the intervals are contiguous and no two adjacent intervals have the same value (ie the intervals are maximal). He calls such a sequence a *concise value history* for the variable. The basic inference mechanism in TCP is constraint propagation, where the values being propagated are <interval,value> pairs. Values can be propagated through constraint equations provided the intervals involved intersect in which case the propagated value will refer to the interval which is the intersection of the values involved in the deduction. It is also possible to associate a (possibly infinitesimal) delay with a rule so that the new interval starts later. TCP checks consistency by ensuring that overlapping episodes for the same variable have the same value. TCP also ensures that all histories are maintained in a concise state.

The inputs to TCP are any input histories and of course the equations defining the model and the qualitative description of the domain. The outputs are the value histories for all the variables and their *justification histories* ie the reasons why they have the values they do (in terms of the deductions made). TCP will make calls to a special interval reasoner which will answer questions about relationships between intervals (for the same variable). Special care is required for disjunction (eg intersection is expressed using disjunction and start and end points): because reasoning with disjunctive intervals is potentially explosive; the algorithms exploit the fact that the disjunctions have a common time point. His interval reasoner is polynomial (but unfortunately incomplete!).

In order to build a Qualitative Physics system on top of TCP one has to specify the details of the representation for time (eg whether intervals are open or closed) and write constraints which define the qualitative arithmetic to be used, the continuity constraints in variables across adjacent intervals and of course the particular system to be modelled.

In his paper he gives an example from the digital domain of an SR-latch built with crosscoupled NOR gates and also the mass on a spring example we have seen before.

We mentioned above that an explicit theory of time is required by TCP. Work on building temporal logics and axiomatising theories of time suitable for qualitative reasoners and naive physics includes McDermott (1982), Allen (1983), Allen and Hayes (1985), Ladkin (1987) and Hayes and Allen (1987). Shoham has published extensively on time and causality. Shoham (1985c) discusses criteria for a good theory of time and change. Shoham (1985d) discusses temporal representations for reasoning about causation.

9. Qualitative Spatial Reasoning

It will be noticed that none of the examples which we have discussed so far require any sophisticated spatial reasoning or representation. In particular all spatial reasoning and representation has been one dimensional (for example the level of a liquid, the 'x' position of a spring on a surface). Moreover all derivatives have been with respect to time. To develop a general qualitative physics would obviously require more powerful qualitative spatial reasoning.

There has been very little work in this area. Much of the work in AI generally on spatial representations, for example for Robotics or Vision, has been explicitly quantitative. Moreover Saund (1987) argues for a much richer representation language than one based on generalised cylinders because qualitatively useful information is not made explicit in such representations: a greater number of shape primitives and attributes should be available. What work there has been has lead some researchers to believe that it is impossible to develop purely qualitative spatial reasoners. Davis (1986) discusses some of the difficulties and poses a set of deceptively simple challenge problems for a qualitative spatial reasoner. In (Davis 1987) he describes the kind of representation and reasoning which would solve these problems. He reports on an axiomatisation of geometry, motion and simple physics which allows him to infer that, given certain conditions, an object thrown into a steep sided funnel will come out of the bottom. The reasoning required is surprisingly complex given this apparently simply stated problem. There are about 140 axioms and ninety nonlogical symbols. No actual implementation of the theory exists yet, so the proof is done by hand. What should be noted is that the reasoning is not a simulation of any kind but rather a proof that the object must come out of the bottom because no other behaviour is possible.

Following the earlier work of Shoham (1985a, 1985b), Forbus, Nielsen and Faltings (1987) have been investigating the possibility of producing a qualitative *kinematics*. A qualitative kinematics would be a qualitative theory for spatial reasoning about the geometry of motion. However Forbus, Nielsen and Faltings conjecture (their *Poverty Conjecture)* that there is no purely qualitative general purpose kinematics. They base this surmise on the following premises: nobody has done it yet; people tend to use diagrams when doing such tasks; and quantity spaces rely on transitivity and most higher dimension relations aren't transitive. They suggest that any qualitative kinematics must be backed up by a complementary quantitative representation – essentially a diagram. They call this paradigm the *Metric Diagram/Place Vocabulary* model. The former is an oracle for answering simple spatial questions and contains both quantitative and symbolic knowledge; the latter is a purely qualitative representation of shape and space and is created by abstracting from the metric diagram. This view of qualitative spatial reasoning is based on Forbus' earlier FROB system (Forbus 1980) which reasoned about a bouncing ball in 2D space using a qualitative vector representation.

In kinematics, the basic criterion for differentiating states would seem to be connectivity, since changes in connectivity usually imply changes in force. The potential connecting points of the various objects must be found from the metric diagram (Forbus, Nielsen and Faltings liken this to computing process and view instances). The problem of finding kinematic states, ie computing all possible consistent combinations of connections may also require the metric diagram (they liken this to computing the process and view structure). The analogue of influence resolution is the process of completing the qualitative kinematic state descriptions by computing all the active forces and freedoms of movements. Computing possible state transitions to produce an envisionment can be done purely qualitatively without consulting the metric diagram.

Faltings (1987) has been working on the metric diagram computations whilst Nielsen (1987) has concentrated the latter stages of reasoning within this paradigm which do not require any use of the metric diagram.

They choose to view the world using *configuration space* (Lozano-Perez 1983) which enables the motion of an arbitrary shaped object to be viewed as the motion of a point. Configuration space has as many dimensions as there are parameters of motion in the situation of interest; (eg a cog and ratchet has two dimensions). In order to specify a place vocabulary the configuration space has to be divided up into a finite number of regions (the places) and their connectivity has to be specified (the place vocabulary can be thought of as a kind of qualitative quantity space).

Constraints on the motion of objects divide configuration space into free and filled space. Faltings gives requirements for places (eg separate contact points must be different places; multiple equivalent paths through free space must be collapsed) and specifies how to compute places from configuration space to meet these requirements. Faltings (1987) gives an example of the place vocabulary obtained by his methods for a simple two dimensional, two component cog and ratchet system and shows the envisionment which can be obtained. Places can be distinguished according to how many degrees of freedom there are (eg in the cog and ratchet system there are two degrees of freedom if the parts are not touching, one degree of freedom if the parts are touching and able to slide without changing connectivity and zero degrees of freedom if neither part can move without a change of connectivity – for example if the ratchet is touching a point of the cog).

It is possible to inspect the envisionment and check that, provided the initial state is appropriate the system will indeed function as a ratchet; it is also possible to infer that the system may lock from certain other initial places.

Other qualitative spatial reasoning research includes Shoam's (1985) foray into naive kinematics where he analyses fit and freedom and starts to formulate a first order logical theory of this.

Simmons and Davis (1983) built a system for reasoning about geological formations and inferring how particular structures might have occurred. Their work uses an explicit representation of process, a quantitative data representation analagous to the metric diagram discussed above, and both quantitative and qualitative simulations.

Stanfill (1985) built a program (MACK) to reason about devices such as pistons based on a library of standard shapes. Joskowicz (1987) presents an investigation into rotational devices and unusually considers a three dimensional world rather than the simplified 2D world that others are currently working in.

Hayes (1985) started to formulate a first order theory of naive geometry which has been continued in Hayes and Welham (1984) and Cunningham (1985a).

10. Order of Magnitude Reasoning

Suppose we are trying to model a system with a partly full tank which is being filled but also has two open outlets at the bottom, and we want to know what might happen. Any of the theories we have described so far will predict (at least) three basic behaviours (ie the tank will fill, empty or stabilise at some partly full level). Suppose further that the rate of filling is very much greater than the rate at which each of the outlets is emptying – we would want our system to be able to predict that the tank will definitely fill to the top. However we cannot represent this order of magnitude difference in the quantities to any of the theories we have described so far. If there had been only one outlet then we could have solved the problem using techniques we have already presented because the fact that the input rate was greater than *the* output rate would have been sufficient to disambiguate the situation; however unless we explicitly tell the system that the inflow is greater than the *sum* of the outflows the qualitative reasoner will not be able to predict a unique behaviour. Of course we would prefer only to give local information to the system (eg the inflow is very large, the outflows are all very small). So it would be valuable to be able to represent and reason about order of magnitude information, which is of course still essentially of a qualitative nature.

Sometimes the problem to be solved cannot be expressed using simple partially ordered qualitative scales; for example a system may be faulty, but the symptom is that two quantities are greatly differentiated; in normal operation they are never exactly equal but are never very far apart.

Raiman (1986) built a system called FOG (Formal System for Order of Magnitude reasoning). He defines three binary relations whose intuitive interpretations are thus:

A ne B: A is negligible compared to B
A vo B: A is close to B (ie A–B ne B)
A co B: A is the same sign and order of magnitude as B

There is one axiom (A vo A) and 30 inference rules (eg transitivity of ne, vo, co). It turns out that vo and co are both equivalence relations, and that vo implies co, but not vice versa. Raiman uses Non Standard Analysis (Lutz and Goze 1981) to provide a theoretical foundation for FOG. Basically, the idea is to add very small 'numbers' called *infinitesimals* to the reals. An infinitesimal is a number with the property that a real multiplied by an infinitesimal is still an infinitesimal.

The way the above defined relations relate to the qualitative reasoning techniques we have been discussing is that they could be used to structure qualitative quantity spaces. The co and vo relations group quantities with the same order of magnitude while the ne relation sets up the partial ordering hierarchy. One needs to define how the standard arithmetic operators operate in the context of these relations, for example A ne B → (A+B) vo B 'defines' addition across equivalence classes and A ne B ∨ C co D → A*C ne B*D 'defines' multiplication across equivalence classes.

Raiman's intended applications include trouble shooting analog circuits (he is constructing a program called DEDALE (Dagne et al 1987) to perform this task) and building a qualitative model of macroeconomics (from a text book).

More recently Mavrovouniotis and Stephanopoulos (1987) have come up with an alternative formulation. They enumerate certain problems they see with Raiman's FOG, in particular the lack of well defined semantics, an apparently arbitrary set of rules, no methodology given for how to extend the rules to cope with other functions apart from addition and multiplication and no defined way to integrate quantitative information. They also point out that the co relation combines sign and magnitude information and would prefer to keep sign information separate from order of magnitude information (we have already seen the benefits Forbus derived from this separation). Finally disjunction and negation are required even to express quite simple problems and they point to the computational complexity these connectives tend to engender.

Actually, notwithstanding Raiman's intuitive definition of co and the consequent criticisms of Mavrovouniotis and Stephanopoulos, the semantics that Raiman (1986) gives, means that co does not carry any sign information. The problem with non standard analysis as a semantics for FOG is not that it does not provide a sound basis for FOG, but rather that there is a danger that this semantics might not correspond to the intuitions a human user might have about the relations.

Mavrovouniotis and Stephanopoulos go on to present their O[M] formalism for order of magnitude reasoning. Quantities have a sign, magnitude and dimension. Links relate pairs of quantities giving all the known relative order of magnitude information between them. Reasoning involving the sign of a quantity is done as in conventional qualitative reasoning systems. They define seven primitive order of magnitude relations to relate magnitudes. These are: A<<B (intuitively: A is much smaller than B), A–<B (intuitively: A is moderately smaller than B), A-<B (intuitively: A is slightly smaller than B) and A==B (intuitively: A is exactly equal to B). The first three relations also have their obvious duals making seven in all. A further 21 compound relations (ie their semantics are defined as disjunctions of primitive relationships, though implemented in the system as primitives) are also defined and given an intuitive semantics.

They claim that their system subsumes FOG (ne is <<; vo is -<..>- and co is –<..>–, where <op1>..<op2> means the disjunction of all relations between op1 and op2, where the relations are ordered as given above; note that not all disjunctions of operators can be thus expressed; this restriction is for efficiency reasons). Some, but not all negations can be expressed (eg there is no representation for 'not roughly equal to'; again this restriction is for efficiency reasons; Mavrovouniotis are Stephanopolous are particularly concerned to create an efficient reasoning system).

They also give a precise semantics for the primitive relations in terms of an arbitrary accuracy parameter e. The truth of A op B (where op is one of the primitive relations) is defined in terms of A/B which is compared against e, 1/(1+e), 1, 1+e, 1/e. These expressions effectively divide the real line into six intervals and the single point (unity) which correspond to the seven relations.

They discuss whether this semantics is too strict to conform to 'naive' order of magnitude reasoning. For example a human would probably want to conclude A>-C from A>-B and B>-C, but the formal semantics just given only allows the weaker inference A>-..>–C. They go on to define a more "aggressive" semantics which effectively loses accuracy but might be construed as a more natural system. (They point out that FOG's reasoning is even more "aggressive").

Finally they overview their ATMS based implementation, some strategies for dealing with contradictions due to aggressive inferences and their application of the system to reasoning about biochemical pathways. They also claim that the formalism allows an easy integration of quantitative and qualitative knowledge. The formalism and its application is discussed in greater detail in Mavrovouniotis et al (toappear) Mavrovouniotis and Stephanopolous (toappear).

We have already briefly mentioned the work of Kuipers (1987a); this can also be seen as an application of order of magnitude reasoning (at the meta level) – by declaring one system to operate an order of magnitude faster or slower than another, the qualitative simulation of a complex device can be made faster and simpler.

11. Recognising Higher Level Processes

In the case of a reasonably complex system, an envisionment can be very large and complicated and it may be difficult for a human to interpret an overall behavioural description from it. The only summarisation process we have mentioned is the stutter cycle recognition procedure of Forbus which replaces cycles of instantaneous nodes by a node describing a dynamic equilibrium.

In general one might hope to make progress on this problem in a number of ways. Multiple models at different levels of abstraction is clearly likely to be of help. One could also imagine having a library of 'cliches' (cf the Programmer's Apprentice project – Rich et al (1979)) which envisionment fragments could be matched against.

Weld (1986) has also done some interesting work on cycle extraction in the case where the cycle is not maintaining an equilibrium (ie he will recognise a cycle even if the state at the end of the cycle is not exactly the same as an earlier state). He terms this cycle extraction procedure *aggregation*.

Weld concentrates on recognising and extracting serial cycles in a process centred representation. In order to see if a currently active process is the same as a previously active process, each variable in the quantity conditions of the processes involved must be identical if the quantity space is unordered and the two values must not be distinguished by the conditions otherwise. For example, from the simulation of a cascaded clocked decade counter, Weld shows how aggregation will recognise and summarise the events which cause the least significant digit to count to zero, and subsequently for other more significant digits. Thus there is some ability to deal with nested cycles. The entire lengthy simulation is eventually summarised to a few instances of automatically created countdown processes and the definition of the countdown process itself.

The work reported is at an early stage and there are still problems for example with deadlock in multiple cycles and determining an appropriate theoretical foundation.

12. Multiple Models

We have already mentioned the work of Mozetic (1987b) in employing a hierarchy of models for qualitative modelling and reasoning. It seems to be very important to investigate and use multiple and hierarchical models further in order to improve the efficiency of qualitative inference, the size of problems that can be tackled, and also, by employing models with different views or ontologies, enable problems to be solved that could not be solved with reference to a single model.

For example Forbus (1984b) suggests that reasoning about the superheated steam boiler referred to at the beginning of this chapter requires not only a contained liquid ontology but also the ability to reason about a particular bit of water (the *molecular collection* ontology) in order to solve the problem.

Collins and Forbus (1987) investigate the molecular ontology and describe an extension to QPE which reasons about fluid granules. They argue that it is not possible to reason about fluids using the molecular collection ontology in isolation but that it must be parasitic on a contained fluid model. Thus they first compute a standard envisionment using a contained liquid model and then reason about the history of particular 'bits of liquid'. Although they have not yet built a system which can actually solve the superheated steam boiler problem, they argue that they are now much closer; all that remains is to perform automatically a *differential qualitative analysis* (Forbus 1984b) on the computed histories.

In unpublished work Weld has been developing hierarchical models of a refrigerator so that it can be represented and reasoned about at a variety of levels of deepness and detail. The topmost model might thus be of a box with a cold interior. Successively more detailed models might be: an insulated box with heat being pumped out; a model where refrigerant is circulated by a pump which carries heat to an outside radiator; a model where the evaporation of the refrigerant in low pressure tubing inside the refrigerator, its absorbtion of heat and its subsequent compression to hot liquid in an outside radiator by a pressurising pump is detailed. The most detailed model might enable a behaviour description such as the following to be produced: in the evaporator, high pressure liquid is released into near-vacuum; since the boiling point is much lower, the liquid evaporates and cools; the temperature inside the refrigerator is above the new boiling point, so the liquid continues to evaporate absorbing heat from the refrigerator interior; eventually all the liquid will have evaporated and the box temperature will be cooler.

Klein and Finin (1987) discuss how different models can be according to the 'depth' of the knowledge represented and illustrate the distinctions with several examples.

Of course one can imagine a variety of ways in which models of the same system may differ. A hierarchical model may have a varying level of component granularity (a primitive component at one level may be expanded to a whole subsystem at another level). This is the kind of model to be found in for example Davis (1984), Genesereth (1984) or Barrow (1984).

A hierarchical model can also be built by simplifying at different levels and leaving out certain attributes of concepts (for example as in the classical ABSTRIPS (Sacerdoti 1973) planning system).

One might also obtain a hierarchy by having different grained quantity spaces at the different levels. At one end of this hierarchy all the quantity spaces might just have +/0/– values, at the other end we have a normal quantitative model. An important study into the theory of creating abstraction hierarchies by varying the granularity of the model is Hobbs (1985).

We have already mentioned the possibility of changing the ontology entirely, for example from a continuous to a discrete representation when discussing the super heater example above. Other work on models differentiated thus includes the work of Bunt (1985) and the work of Gentner and Gentner (1983) where they investigate peoples mental models of electricity using a continuous 'pneumatic' model and a discrete 'moving crowd' model. Raulefs (1987) describes a system for reasoning about continuous objects and processes built using Bunt's *ensemble theory*.

Some models will provide support for others in the sense that they provide justifications (eg proofs) of assumptions in other models. Having such models may be important for providing good explanations of physical systems.

Of course difficulties will arise where models are inconsistent with each other (ie make different predictions) and developing models of the utility of models is an important subject for future research in this area. If different predictions are made then it may be appropriate to intersect the solution set if this is non null, otherwise a more detailed model might be of use in resolving the contradiction.

The most appropriate model(s) must be selected to help solve a particular problem. If the problem involves reasoning about the effects of a particular parameter perturbation then a good first choice might be to choose the simplest model(s) which mention that parameter.

If several models are required to solve a particular problem then the question of how the models communicate has to be addressed (perhaps via a shared vocabulary or via support/justification links).

13. How are Qualitative Models Generated?

We have not paid any particular attention so far on the problem of how to actually construct a qualitative model for a given situation or system. Of course if a library of generic components, processes or individual views is available this will help at the detailed level though there will still be the problem of choosing items from the library, instantiating them and connecting them together appropriately. However there is still the problem of how to construct or add to the library. This problem is not peculiar to qualitative modelling but is faced by anybody trying to build a model. To state the problem succinctly I can do no better than to quote Letovsky (1983): "A major unsolved question for reasoning systems of this type is, where are the causal models supposed to come from? All these models are descriptions of situations that carefully include certain features and ignore others in order to produce descriptions that are precisely tailored for the performance of a specific task. How is such a model extracted from a richer description? How does the extractor know which features are worth including in the causal model, and which can be neglected for the current purposes? This question definitely deserves further consideration".

Of interest in this context is Mozetic's work (Mozetic 1987a) on learning a qualitative model from a set of behaviour observations. Given the structure of the model only (ie the network structure but with no component behaviours specified), Mozetic used a learning algorithm to induce the component behaviours. Twenty five observations were input originally and after eight learning cycles during which a further nineteen behaviour observations were supplied by a human the complete model was acquired. The computation required approximately one week on a SUN2. Interestingly, if no structure was given (ie the task was to learn a black box behaviour) then the same observation set resulted in a model which would correctly predict ECGs for 80% of all possible arrhythmia combinations.

Selfridge et al (1985) describe an interactive program which acquires qualitative causal models by comprehending explanations of behaviour stated in natural language.

It is also worth mentioning briefly the experiences learned by those attending "Commonsense Summer" (Hobbs et al 1985). The participants were particularly interested in model building within a Naive Physics framework and their methodology is obviously affected by this. They worked on a number of domains including Naive Kinematics (Shoham 1985) and properties of stuff (Hager 1985). When first investigating an area (a Naive Physics cluster) it is obviously important to clarify the conceptual structure of the domain. A thesaurus can be a useful tool here, but they point out that a classification of concepts is not an end in itself: it is important to extract the principles behind the classifications – ie why these distinctions are relevant.

In order to limit the area of investigation it is important to isolate the cluster of interest and to circumscribe it. They advise looking for typical examples rather than pathological examples which tend to cloud the issue (and which, they suggest, may be 'cross cluster' examples). Of course this begs the question of what a pathological example is.

In order to make progress, the participants felt it important to devise target problems at the outset otherwise the problem of trying to model a moving target might occur. They did not try to aim for 'psychologically real' models, the problem seemed to be hard enough in any case! Nor did they stick to standard mathematical theories of, for example, space.

Like Hayes' original foray into Naive Physics they tried to avoid thinking of implementation which they felt was a distraction to the modelling process.

They also tried to avoid some well known 'black holes' such as the 'I need to invent a new knowledge representation language in order to describe this situation' syndrome. (In fact most, but not all, of the work over the summer was done in first order logic).

The participants tried to be 'ontologically promiscuous' and not worry about whether possible worlds, points, or any other virtual object really existed, but just to use whatever ontology seemed to be helpful. They realised that always giving exact definitions with necessary and sufficient conditions can be difficult and were content to write down partial definitions of concepts, at least in the first instance.

The problem of the real world always seeming to provide counterexamples to a theory was discussed. They felt perhaps the best approach here was to hope that some higher level process may be able to help by choosing the appropriate model and knowing the limitations of a theory. However they did not research what such a higher level process might really look like at all.

One problem which affects any modeller is to know precisely what has been captured by ones axiomatisation – ie what interpretations satisfy it, and indeed to know whether the theory is in fact consistent. This is a very hard and difficult problem particularly as the theory becomes larger and less trivial. Cunningham (1985a) points out that Hayes failed to realise in his liquids paper (Hayes 1985b) that his 'toso' function ('the other side of') wasn't a function at all (eg toso(room1,wall2) may be cupboard22 *and* room3).

Cunningham also writes of the difficulty he found in writing large consistent sets of axioms for a Naive Physics cluster, and built a program to find (finite) satisfying interpretations of his axioms (Cunningham 1985a, 1985b). Note that the notion of a model being inconsistent presupposes a clean representation language with a well defined semantics – for further discussion on this see (Israel 1985, Hayes 1985a and McDermott 1978).

Of course any language with the expressive power of full first order logic is only semi decidable so determining consistency in general is not actually possible. However there are still research opportunities for building (possibly interactive) consistency checkers which may be constrained by partitioning of the theory and by results of verification of higher or lower level models. Jackson's game theoretic approach (Jackson 1988) to consistency checking is another avenue of attack. Features of the representation language such as a powerful sortal apparatus may also be of help (see Cohn (1985) for further discussion of this point).

14. Current and Future Trends

Rather than trying to summarise the preceding text, we will finish by drawing attention to some current work not mentioned elsewhere and possible future trends.

It will have been observed that all the examples discussed have been rather simple and much simpler than any system to be found in an industrial setting. In fact there has been some work applying techniques such as we have described here to industrial and real life systems. We have already mentioned the DEDALE system (Dagne et al 1987) which is reported to troubleshoot failures on complex analog circuits occurring in actual systems. Rajagopalan (1984) describes his work on qualitative modelling of turbojet engines and Gallanti et al (1986) report on their system which reasons both qualitatively and quantitatively about a condenser in a power plant in a diagnostic setting. Lepetit and Vernet (1987) describe their experience with qualitative modelling using a constraint model in a process control domain. Hamilton (1987) describes a diagnostic system based on de Kleer and Brown's work for reasoning about mechanical subsystems of a helicopter. A hierarchy of models (of depth four at present) is created by representing a subsystem of components by a single component; the behaviour confluences for the higher level component are formed by equation solving on the confluences of the constituent lower level components. Diagnosis is performed by constraint suspension in a similar fashion to Davis (1984). Mohammed and Simmons (1986) describe their approach to qualitative reasoning about semiconductor fabrication which is built using the same system as Simmons and Davis (1983) earlier used to reason about geological structures. Preliminary investigations of qualitative reasoning techniques in financial applications include Apte and Hong (1986) and Hart et al (1986).

No doubt with increasing awareness of qualitative reasoning techniques and as further technical progress is made exploitation of the ideas in applications may increase.

There is certainly much work still to do at a theoretical level, for example providing secure foundations for existing theories such as QPT and in developing and extending qualitative reasoning methods to cope with a wider range of problem types. The results of Struss (1987) mentioned earlier provide an important impetus for doing this. Kokar (1987) discusses the problem of determining a landmark set (ie the set of points in the quantity spaces) for a problem and remarks that it is often not possible to find a finite set of such points; he suggests that quantity conditions should be specified not by particular values of certain parameters but by "some hypersurfaces in the cross-product of the parameters". He presents a way of determining such 'critical hyperspaces'. Forbus (1987b) discusses the formal relationship between specific histories and envisionments such as he used informally in Forbus (1986a). All the systems discussed thus far have assumed that variables are continuous (except for Forbus' encapsulated histories technique). Nishida and Doshita (1987) consider methods for reasoning about discontinuous changes.

We remarked in the introduction that qualitative reasoning is seen as a complement rather than a replacement for quantitative reasoning. However the interface between the two reasoning paradigms still needs to be researched. Some work has been done in this area, for example Simmons and Davis (1983), Gallanti et al (1986) and Forbus (1986a). However a proper theory still needs to worked out.

Another area which is important to research further is the relationship between deep (qualitative models) and surface style knowledge bases. The Kardio work on producing the latter from the former has already been mentioned but a more thorough investigation of how a qualitative model can and should be used as an underlying deep, supporting representation for (perhaps several different) surface knowledge bases is certainly needed.

Reasoning about space and shape seems to be a very difficult and still largely unexplored area but is very important, for solving problems about many physical systems requires sophisticated spatial reasoning. All the derivatives in the systems we have described have been with respect to time – could one build a qualitative reasoner which represented partial derivatives with respect to a spatial dimension?

Finally we might remark that most of the work in qualitative reasoning seems to have involved simulation. However there are clearly other possible reasoning modes and in particular one might like to do problem solving by reasoning about the model rather than simulating it. To take a very simple and classical example, consider McCarthy's mutilated chessboard and the computational efficiency achieved by reasoning about what a solution would look like rather than actually trying to achieve it by a process akin to simulation.

Similarly, Davis (1986) has suggested that the problems alluded to earlier concerning the difficulty of building a qualitative spatial reasoner might be overcome, not by attempting to simulate the physical system, but by looking for a *proof* of the correct behaviour. He does however admit that finding and reasoning with such proofs would be non trivial.

Sacks (1987b) also eschews qualitative simulation and describes a methodology for reasoning about dynamic systems by constructing piecewise linear approximations of systems of non linear differential equations and thus building a phase diagram.

Bylander and Chandrasekaran (1985) describe a technique they call *consolidation* which computes a behavioural description for a composite system, not by qualitative simulation but by composing behaviour descriptions. They see their technique as a complementary technique to qualitative simulation.

Also relevant is the work of Weld (1987) who has built a system which will take the results of a qualitative simulation (QSIM's) and reason about the effects of a perturbation. For example it can answer the question about what would happen to the period of the mass on the spring system previously discussed if the mass were heavier.

15. Acknowledgements

There are many people with whom I have discussed the issues presented in this chapter and I should like to thank them all. In particular I am grateful to all the members of the Alvey DKBS SIG. Moreover Ivan Bratko, Ben Kuipers, Ken Forbus and Brian Williams all gave invited papers to various Alvey DKBS workshops and I have benefited tremendously from these and discussions in the working groups afterwards. I should also like to thank the participants at ACAI87 in Oslo where the lectures on which this chapter is based were first given for their comments and feedback. Bert Bredeweg falls into both these last two categories and I thank him for the detailed comments he made on an earlier version of this paper. Members of the AI group at Warwick University have given helpful comments and criticism on the material presented here – in particular, Kathy Courtney, Felix Hovsepian and Guy Saward. Especial thanks are due to David Randell for his careful reading and criticism of the manuscript and the discussions I have had with him. I have also benefitted from the comments provided by an anonymous referee. Some of the material presented here was presented at the tutorial on qualitative reasoning at ECAI 1986 which was presented jointly with Pat Hayes. I would like to thank my wife, Gillian, for help with proof reading. Of course I take full responsibility for any remaining errors or misrepresentations in the work.

This work was partly financed by the SERC under grant G/E/00273. I should also like to thank the Alvey Directorate for the funding of the DKBS workshops.

References

Addanki, S and Davis, E, "A Representation for Complex Physical Domains," *Proc. IJCAI*, Morgan Kaufmann, 1985.

Allen, J F, "Maintaining knowledge about temporal intervals," *CACM*, vol. 26(11), 1983.

Allen, J F and Hayes, P J, "A Common-Sense Theory of Time," *Proc IJCAI*, Morgan Kaufmann, 1985.

Apte, C and Hong, S, "Using Qualitative Simulation to Understand Financial Arithmetic," in *Proc AAAI*, Morgan Kaufmann, Los Altos, 1986.

Badii, A, *Proc DKBS3*, IEE, Farnborough, 1987.

Bareiss, R and Farquhar, A, "Fault Diagnosis Using Qualitative Simulation," AI TR86-25, University of Texas at Austin, 1986.

Barrow, H G, "VERIFY: A Program for Proving Correctness of Digital Hardware Designs," *Artificial Intelligence*, vol. 24, 1984.

(Ed), D Bobrow, *Qualitative Reasoning about Physical Systems*, North Holland, 1984.

Bonissone, P P and Valavanis, K P, "A Comparative Study of Different Approaches to Qualitative Physics Theories," *2nd AI Applications Conf*, IEEE, 1985.

Bratko, I, Mozetic, I, and Lavrac, N, "Automatic Synthesis and Compression of Cardiological Knowledge," in *Machine Intelligence 11*, ed. J Hayes, D Michie, J Richards, Oxford University Press, 1986.

Bredeweg, B, *Modelling Physical Systems with QP Theory*, University of Amsterdam, 1987.

Bunt, H, "The Formal Representation of (Quasi-) Continuous Concepts," in *Formal Theories of the Common Sense World*, ed. J R Hobbs & R Moore, Ablex Publishing Corporation, 1985.

Bylander, T and Chandrasekaran, B, "Understanding Behavior Using Consolidation," *Proc. IJCAI*, Morgan Kaufmann, Los Altos, 1985.

Chandrasekaran, B, Smith, J W, and Sticklen, J, *Deep Models and Their Relation to Diagnosis*, Ohio State University, 1987.

Clancey, W J and Letsinger, R, "Neomycin: Reconfiguring a Rule Based Expert System for Application to Teaching," *IJCAI 7*, 2, 1981.

Clocksin, W and Morgan, A, "Qualitative Control," in *Proc ECAI*, 1986.

Cochin, I, *Analysis and Design of Dynamic Systems*, Harper and Row, New York, 1980.

Cohn, A G, "Deep Knowledge Representation Techniques," in *Expert Systems 85*, ed. M Merry, Cambridge University Press, 1985.

Cunningham, J, "Comprehension by Model Building as a Basis for an Expert System," in *Proc Expert Systems 85*, ed. M Merry, pp. 259-272, Cambridge University Press, 1985b.

Cunningham, J, "A Methodology and a Tool for the Formalization of "Common Sense" (Naive Physical) Knowledge," PhD Thesis, University of Essex, 1985a.

D'Ambrosio, B, "Extending the Mathematics in Qualitative Process Theory," *Proc. AAAI*, Morgan Kaufmann, 1987.

Dague, P, Raiman, O, and Deves, P, "Troubleshooting: when modelling is the trouble," in *Proc AAAI*, Morgan Kaufmann, Los Altos, 1987.

Davis, E, *Conflicting Requirements in Reasoning about Solid Objects,* Courant Institute, New York University, 1986.

Davis, E, "Constraint Propagation with Interval Labels," *Artificial Intelligence*, vol. 32, pp. 281-331, 1987.

Davis, R, "Diagnostic Reasoning Based on Structure and Behavior," *Artificial Intelligence*, vol. 24, 1984.

Dyer, M, Flowers, M, and Hodges, J, "Naive Mechanics and Comprehension in EDISON," in *Proc IJCAI*, Morgan Kaufmann, Los Altos, 1987.

Dyer, M , Flowers, M, and Hodges, J, "Edison: An Engineering Design Invention System Operating Naively," in *Proc 1st Conf on AI in Engineering*, ed. Sriram D & Adey R, Springer Verlag, 1986.

Falkenhainer, B, Forbus, K D, and Gentner, D, "The Structure-Mapping Engine," UIUCDCS-R-86-1275, University of Illinois, 1986.

Faltings, B, "Qualitative Kinematics in mechanisms," in *Proc IJCAI*, Morgan Kaufmann, Lost Altos, 1987.

Forbus, K D, "Spatial and Qualitative Aspects of Reasoning about Motion," in *Proc. AAAI*, 1980.

Forbus, K D, "Qualitative Process Theory," *Artificial Intelligence*, vol. 24, 1984a.

Forbus, K D, "Qualitative Process Theory," Tech. Report 789, MIT, 1984b.

Forbus, K D, "The Problem of Existence," UIUCDCS-R-85-1239, University of Illinois, 1985.

Forbus, K D, "Interpreting Measurements of Physical Systems," *Proc. AAAI*, Morgan Kaufmann, 1986a.

Forbus, K D, "The Qualitative Process Engine," UIUCDCS-R-1288, University of Illinois, 1986b.

Forbus, K D, "The Logic of occurrence," in *Proc IJCAI*, Morgan Kaufmann, Los Altos, 1987b.

Forbus, K D, *Inequality reasoning with an ATMS,* University of Illinois, 1987a.

Forbus, K D, Nielsen, P, and Faltings, B, "Qualitative Kinematics: a Framework," in *Proc IJCAI*, Morgan Kaufmann, Los Altos, 1987.

Forbus, K D and Stevens, A, "Using Qualitative Simulation to Generate Explanations," Report No. 4490, Navy Personnel Research & Development Center, 1981.

Gallanti, M, Gilardoni, L, Guida, G, and Stefanini, A, "Exploiting Physical and Design Knowledge in the Diagnosis of Complex Industrial Systems," in *Proc ECAI*, 1986.

Genesereth, M R, "The Use of Design Descriptions in Automated Diagnosis," *Artificial Intelligence*, vol. 24, 1984.

Gentner, D and Gentner, D R, "Flowing Waters of Teeming Crowds: Mental Models of Electricity," in *Mental Models*, ed. Gentner D & Stevens A, Lawrence Earlbaum, 1983.

Hart, P E, Barzilay, A, and Duda, R O, "Qualitative Reasoning for Financial Assessments: a Prospectus," *Artificial Intelligence Magazine*, vol. 7(1), 1986.

Hayes, P J, "Some problems and non-problems in representation theory," in *Proc AISB*, 1974.

Hayes, P J, "In Defence of Logic," in *Proc. IJCAI 5*, Morgan Kaufmann, Los Altos, 1977.

Hayes, P J, "The naive physics manifesto," in *Expert Systems in the Micro Electronic Age*, ed. D Michie, Edinburgh University Press, 1979.

Hayes, P J, "The Second Naive Physics Manifesto," in *Formal Theories of the Common Sense World*, ed. J R Hobbs & R Moore, Ablex Publishing Corporation, 1985a.

Hayes, P J, "Ontology of liquids," in *Formal Theories of the Commonsense World*, ed. J Hobbs and R Moore, Ablex, 1985b.

Hayes, P J, "The Frame Problem in Histories," in *The Frame Problem in Artificial Intelligence*, ed. F M Brown, Morgan Kaufmann, Los Altos, 1987.

Hayes, P J, "A Critique of Pure Treason," *Computational Intelligence*, 1987b.

Hayes, P J and Allen, J, "Short Time Periods," in *Proc IJCAI*, Morgan Kaufmann, Los Altos, 1987.

Hobbs, J R, "Granularity," *Proc. IJCAI*, Morgan Kaufmann, 1985.

Hobbs, J R, Blenko, T, Croft, B, Hager, G, Kautz, H A, Kube, P, and Shoham, Y, "Commonsense Summer: Final Report," CSLI-85-35, Stanford University, 1985.

Hobbs, J R and Moore, R C, *Formal Theories of the Commonsense World,* Ablex Publishing Corporation, New Jersey, 1985.

Hogge, J, "Compiling Plan Operators from Domains Expressed in Qualitative Process Theory," *Proc. AAAI*, Morgan Kaufmann, 1987.

Israel, D, "A Short Companion to the Naive Physics Manifesto," in *Formal Theories of the Common Sense World*, ed. J R Hobbs & R Moore, Ablex Publishing Corporation, 1985.

Iwasaki, Y, "Generating Behaviour Equations from Explicit Representation of Mechanisms," in *Proc AAAI Worshop on Qualitative Physics*, University of Illinois, 1987.

Iwasaki, Y and Simon, H A, "Causality in Device Behavior," *Artificial Intelligence*, vol. 29, 1986a.

Iwasaki, Y and Simon, H A, *Theories of Causal Ordering: Reply to de Kleer and Brown*, 29, 1986b.

Jackson, P, "On Game-Theoretic Interactions with First-Order Knowledge Bases," in *Non Standard Logics*,

ed. P Smets et al, Academic Press, London, 1988.
Joskowicz, L, "Shape and Function in mechanical Devices," *Proc. AAAI*, Morgan Kaufmann, 1987.
Klaua, D, "Partielle Mengen und Zahlen," *Monatsberichte der Deutschen Akademie der Wissenschaften*, vol. 11, 1969.
Kleer , J de and Williams, B, "Diagnosing Multiple Faults," *Artificial Intelligence*, vol. 32 (1), pp. 97-130, 1987.
Kleer, J de, "Multiple Representations of Knowledge in a Mechanics Problem-Solver," in *Proc IJCAI*, Morgan Kaufmann, Los Altos, 1977.
Kleer, J de, "Causal and teleological reasoning in circuit recognition," Report AI-TR-529, MIT, 1979.
Kleer, J de, "An Assumption-based TMS," *Artificial Intelligence*, vol. 28, 1986a.
Kleer, J de, "Extending the ATMS," *Artificial Intelligence*, vol. 28, 1986b.
Kleer, J de, "Problem Solving with the ATMS," *Artificial Intelligence*, vol. 28, 1986a.
Kleer, J de and Bobrow, D G, "Qualitative Reasoning with Higher-Order Derivatives," *Proc AAAI*, Morgan Kaufmann, 1984.
Kleer, J de and Brown, J S, "A Qualitative Physics Based on Confluences," *Artificial Intelligence*, vol. 24, pp. 7-83, 1984.
Kleer, J de and Brown, J S, "Theories of Causal Ordering," *Artificial Intelligence*, vol. 29, 1986.
Klein, D and Finin, T, "What's in a Deep Model?," in *Proc IJCAI*, Morgan Kaufmann, Los Altos, 1987.
Kuipers, B, "Commonsense Reasoning about Causality: Deriving Behavior from Structure," *Artificial Intelligence*, vol. 24, 1984.
Kuipers, B, "Qualitative Simulation," *Artificial Intelligence*, vol. 29, 1986.
Kuipers, B, "Abstraction by Time-Scale in Qualitative Simulation," *Proc. AAAI*, Morgan Kaufmann, 1987a.
Kuipers, B and Chiu, C, "Taming Intractible Branching in Qualitative Simulation," in *Proc IJCAI*, Morgan Kaufmann, Los Altos, 1987.
Kuipers, B and Kassirer, J P, "How to Discover a Knowledge Representation for Causal Reasoning by Studying and Expert Physician," in *Proc IJCAI*, Morgan Kaufmann, Los Altos, 1983.
Ladkin, P, "Models of Axioms for Time Intervals," in *Proc AAAI*, Morgan Kaufmann, Los Altos, 1987.
Laughton, S, "Explanation of Mechanical Systems Through Qualitative Simulation," AITR85-19, University of Texas at Austin, 1985.
Leaning, M S and Nicolosi, E, "MODEL – Software for knowledge based modelling of compartmental systems," *Biomed. Meas. Infor. Contr*, vol. 1, pp. 171-181, 1986.
Lee, W, Kuipers, B, and Chiu, C, "Steps toward constraining qualititative simulation," TR-87-44, University of Texas, 1987.
Lepetit, M and Vernet, D, "Qualitative Physics Applied to a Depropanizer in Process Control," in *Proc AAAI Worshop on Qualitative Physics*, University of Illinois, 1987.
Letovsky, S, "Qualitative and Quantitative Temporal Reasoning," YALEU/DCS/RR*296, Yale University, 1983.
Lozano-Perez, T, "Spatial planning: A Configuration space approach," *IEEE Transactions on Computers*, vol. C-32, 1983.
Lucas, J R, *Space, Time and Causality*, Oxford University Press, 1984.
Lutz, R and Goze, M, *Non Standard Analysis, Lecture Notes in Mathematics vol. 881*, Springer Verlag, 1981.
Manzo, M di and Trucco, E, "Commonsense Reasoning about Flexible Objects: A Case Study," in *Advances in Artificial Intelligence*, ed. C Mellish & J Hallam, 1987.
Mavrovouniotis, M, Stephanopolous, G, and Stephanopolous, G, "Formal Modelling of Approximate Relations in Biochemical Systems," *Biotechnology and Bioengineering*, toappear.
Mavrovouniotis, M and Stephanopolous, G, "Formal Order of Magnitude Reasoning in Process Engineering," *Biotechnology and Bioengineering*, toappear.
Mavrovouniotis, M and Stephanopoulos, G , "Reasoning with Orders of Magnitude and Approximate Relations," *Proc. AAAI*, Morgan Kaufmann, 1987.
McCarthy, J and Hayes, P J, "Some philosophical problems from the standpoint of AI," in *MI4*, ed. B Meltzer & D Michie, Edinburgh University Press, 1969.
McDermott, D, "Tarskian semantics, or no notation without denotation," *Cognitive science*, vol. 2, 1978.
McDermott, D, "A Temporal Logic for Reasoning about Processes and Plans," *Cognitive Science*, vol. 6, 1982.
McDermott, D, "A Critique of Pure Reason," *Computational Intelligence*, vol. 3, 1987.
Mohammed, J and Simmons, R, "Qualitative Simulation of Semiconductor Fabrication," in *Proc AAAI*, Morgan Kaufmann, Los Altos, 1986.

Mozetic, I, ''Learning of Qualitative Models,'' *Proc 2nd EWSL*, Sigma Press, 1987a.

Mozetic, I, ''The Role of Abstractions in Learning Qualitative Models,'' *Proc 4th Int Workshop on Machine Learning*, 1987b.

Nielsen, P, *A Qualitative Approach to Mechanical Constraint*, University of Illinois, 1987.

Raiman, O, ''Order of Magnitude Reasoning,'' *Proc. AAAI*, Morgan Kaufmann, 1986.

Rajagopalan, R, ''Qualitative Modelling in the Turbojet Engine Domain,'' *Proc AAAI*, Morgan Kaufmann, 1984.

Raulefs, P, ''A Representation Framework for Continuous Dynamic Systems,'' in *Proc IJCAI*, Morgan Kaufmann, Los Altos, 1987.

Reiter, R, ''A Theory of Diagnosis from First Principles,'' *Artificial Intelligence*, vol. 32 (1), pp. 57-95, 1987.

Reiter, R and Kleer, J de, ''Foundations of Assumption Based Truth Maintenance Systems: Preliminary Report,'' in *Proc AAAI*, Morgan Kaufmann, Los Altos, 1987.

Rich, C, Shrobe, H, and Waters, R, ''Overview of the programmers apprentice,'' *Proc. IJCAI 6*, MIT, 1979.

Roshelle, J, ''Qualitative Processes and Scientific Reasoning,'' in *Proc AAAI Worshop on Qualitative Physics*, University of Illinois, 1987.

Sacerdoti, E D, ''Planning in a Hierarchy of Abstraction Spaces,'' *Proc IJCAI*, Morgan Kaufmann, 1973.

Sacks, E, ''Piecewise Linear Reasoning,'' in *Proc AAAI*, Morgan Kaufmann, Los Altos, 1987b.

Sacks, E, ''Hierarchical Inequality Reasoning,'' *Proc. AAAI*, Morgan Kaufmann, 1987a.

Saund, E, ''Qualitative Physics and the Shapes of Objects,'' in *Proc AAAI Worshop on Qualitative Physics*, University of Illinois, 1987.

Selfridge, M, Daniell, J, and Simmons, D, ''Learning Causal Models by Understanding Real-World Natural Language Explanations,'' *Proc Conf. on Applications of AI*, IEEE, 1985.

Shoham, Y, ''Naive Kinematics: One Aspect of Shape,'' *Proc. IJCAI*, Morgan Kaufmann, 1985a.

Shoham, Y, ''Naive Kinematics: Two Aspects of Shape,'' in *Commonsense Summer: Final Report*, ed. J Hobbs et al, University of Stanford, 1985b.

Shoham, Y, *Ten Requirements for a Theory of Change*, Yale University, 1985c.

Shoham, Y, ''Reasoning about Causation in Knowledge-Based Systems,'' *Proc Conf. on Applications of AI*, IEEE, 1985d.

Simmons, R, '''Commonsense' Arithmetic Reasoning,'' *Proc. AAAI*, Morgan Kaufmann, 1986.

Simmons, R G and Davis, R, ''Representation for Reasoning about Change,'' AI Memo No. 702, MIT, 1983.

Sosa, E, *Causation and conditionals*, Oxford University Press, London , 1975.

Stanfill, C, ''MACK, a Program which Deduces the Behavior of Machines from their Forms,'' *SIGART Newsletter*, vol. 93, 1985.

Stevens, A L and Gentner, D, *Mental Models*, Lawrence Earlbaum, New Jersey, 1983.

Struss, P, ''Problems of Interval-Based Qualitative Reasoning - a preliminary report,'' in *Wissenrepraesentation und Schlussfolgerungsverfahren fuer technische Expertensysteme*, ed. Fruectenicht et al, Munich, 1987.

Waltz, D, ''Understanding line-drawings of scenes with shadows,'' in *The Psychology of Computer Vision*, ed. P Winston, McGraw Hill, 1975.

Weld, D S, ''Combining Discrete and Continuous Process Models,'' *Proc. IJCAI*, Morgan Kaufmann, 1985.

Weld, D S, ''The Use of Aggregation in Causal Simulation,'' *Artificial Intelligence*, 1986.

Weld, D S , ''Comparative Analysis,'' in *Proc IJCAI*, Morgan Kaufmann, Los Altos, 1987.

Welham, B and Hayes, P, *Notes on Naive Geometry*, HP Labs Bristol & Schlumberger Palo Alto Research Labs, 1984.

Williams, B C, ''Qualitative Analysis of MOS Circuits,'' *Artificial Intelligence*, vol. 24, 1984.

Williams, B C, ''Doing Time: Putting Qualitative Reasoning on Firmer Ground,'' *Proc. AAAI*, Morgan Kaufmann, 1986.

Zadeh, L A, ''Commonsense Knowledge Representation Based on Fuzzy Logic,'' *IEEE Computer*, 1983.

Knowledge Acquisition for Expert Systems

B.J. Wielinga, B. Bredeweg & J.A. Breuker

University of Amsterdam
Department of Social Science Informatics (S.W.I.)
Herengracht 196
1016 BS Amsterdam (The Netherlands)
Phone: +31-20-245365

1. Introduction

The development of knowledge based ("expert") systems is a difficult and often time consuming task. The acquisition of the knowledge necessary to perform a certain task -usually through a series of elicitation sessions with a domain expert- is considered one of the main bottlenecks in building knowledge based systems. In this chapter we will provide an overview of approaches and techniques that are currently in use for the knowledge acquisition process in knowledge based system development.

Sections 2 and 3 set the scene by defining the scope of knowledge based systems, expertise and models of knowledge and knowledge use. Sections 4 through 6 discuss various approaches to knowledge acquisition. In sections 7 and 8 we describe a specific method -the KADS method- for KBS development in more detail. Sections 9 and 10 present an overview of the most commonly used techniques for eliciting data from human experts and for interpreting them in such a way that a formal specification of a knowledge base results. Because of lack of space, several relevant topics related to knowledge acquisition had to be omitted from this paper: tools for knowledge acquisition (see Anjewierden, 1987), knowledge base refinement, validation and maintenance and issues related to taxonomies for problem solving tasks.

2. Knowledge and Expertise in Expert Systems

Before addressing the problem of knowledge acquisition itself, we need to define and explain a number of terms. This section discusses the objectives and scope of knowledge based systems and provides some of the working definitions that will be used throughout this paper.

2.1. Expert Systems

An important trend in current Artificial Intelligence (AI) research concerns the development of *expert systems*. Buchanan and Shortliffe (1984) define expert systems as computer programs that are able to solve complex problems at a high level of expertise. One of the very first expert systems, and without doubt also the most well known one, is the MYCIN system (Shortliffe, 1976). This program performs medical diagnosis. In particular it selects an antimicrobial therapy for treating a patient suffering from a bacterial infection.

Although many would agree that MYCIN is an expert system, a precise definition of expert systems is not available. There is, however, a growing consensus in the AI community about what characteristics a computer program should have in order to be called an expert system. As mentioned before, the first and most important characteristic is the ability to provide expert-level solutions to complex problems.

Besides this primary performance capability, a second characteristic is understandability, i.e. its problem solving behaviour should be understandable for the person who is using the system. A third characteristic is flexibility. The system must be flexible enough to allow accommodation of the knowledge easily to to be applicable to varieties of problems. Finally, most expert systems seem capable of explaining *why* and *how* they came to a particular solution. The why-question refers to what knowledge supports the conclusion, whereas the how-question refers to reasoning steps in solving the problem.

Obviously, this list of characteristics can be further specified and enhanced. For instance, Hayes-Roth et al. (1983) use in their definition of expert systems seven semi-independent dimensions. One of those is *reasoning by symbol manipulation*, which is commonly recognised as a general feature of AI research. Hayes-Roth et al. also mention some characteristics which currently are not addressed by expert systems, but which should be incorporated in future expert systems. One of those characteristics is learning from past experience. If expert systems are to resemble human experts more closely, then they should also be able to learn from their own problem solving behaviour.

2.2. Knowledge Based Systems

The term expert system has gained some negative connotations over the past few years, because it suggested misleading notions and features about what these systems could do and what kind of applications were appropriate (Rauch-Hindin, 1986). Moreover, from a historical point of view expert systems dealt with intuitive and academic expertise, instead of ordinary knowledge. The term *Knowledge based system* has therefore been introduced as an alternative. This is probably a more appropriate term, because it refers to a broader range of systems and has less pretentious connotations as to what these systems are capable of. We define both terms as follows (and bear this definition in mind when we use either of those terms). Knowledge based systems are systems that solve problems using knowledge about the domain. Expert systems are knowledge based systems, that solve real-life problems which require a considerable amount of expertise, when solved by humans.

2.3. Types of Expertise

Knowledge based systems use expertise as the basis for their problem solving behaviour. It is possible to identify a number of different types of expertise and it appears that not all of these are currently used in knowledge based systems. A tentative classification of types of expertise is shown below.

- Automated skills. An example of this form of expertise is a piano player, who has an enormous amount of automated skills which together constitute the piano playing behaviour.

- Lots of facts. Some professions require the knowledge of a lot of facts, like for instance in the case of a store manager.

- Empirical associations. For instance, operators who control (partly) automated plants. These experts know exactly what behaviour is associated with a particular manipulation on the control board, but are usually not familiar with the underlying process.

- Knowledge based problem solving, in semanticly rich domains. An example of this can be found by a physician who is able to discriminate between different diseases on the basis of knowledge about those diseases. Both, knowing *why* a particular disease matches a particular set of symptoms and knowing *how* to arrive at that conclusion, are part of the knowledge that is needed to perform problem solving behaviour.

- Knowledge Broking. Hawkins (1983) describes a form of expertise that consists of the ability to abstract from partial solutions to a problem, data and constraints that are relevant to solve other parts of the problem by using knowledge from other domains (e.g. geological and geophysical properties in exploratory drilling).

- Aesthetic Expertise. Aesthetic qualities may play an important role in the design and in the evaluation of artifacts.

In knowledge based systems one finds often some combination of empirical association and 'semantically rich' problem solving. The empirical associations represent the heuristic character of many expert systems. Aesthetic and knowledge broking expertise are in general beyond the state of the art in system design, while large amounts of factual knowledge are the domain of data base systems. Automated skills are typical for perceptual (e.g. vision) systems and robotics.

2.4. Modalities of Knowledge Based Systems

The modality of a knowledge based system refers to the role that the system plays in the overall activity of the user. User and system can be viewed as cooperating to accomplish some task which is more global to the specific tasks that the system performs. There is a distribution of tasks between system and user(s). This distribution may be another distribution than may have existed before the introduction of a knowledge based system, because it will hardly be ever the case that a human expert is simply replaced by a system.

There are several reasons for not simply mimicing the human expert. The most important one is that a in good task distribution the specific abilities of the participating agents are optimally exploited: the capabilities of (knowledge based) computer programs are different from those of human beings, as is illustrated by the list of expertise that is typical for human beings. Computers are good in routine tasks, i.e. for knowledge based systems: typical problems. Difficult problems are often left for human experts because they are far more flexible. This flexibility also includes the ability to perform a large variety of tasks. A human physician may not only be consulted for a medical problem. x may also provide emotional support and consider the overall well being of the patient.

The role of a system, e.g. an expert problem solver, teacher, coach, or advisor, defines to a large extent about what and how the system should communicate with the user, and which parts of its processing should be transparent to the user. This leads to the distinction between the problem solving tasks and the communication tasks of an expert system. In the simplest case, the communication consists only of obtaining data from the user and a presentation of the solution. A typical example of such an 'autistic' problem solver is XCON, which takes a computer order and produces a configuration specification of the system (McDermott, 1980). Users may want the solutions to be justified, or have explained the way the solution is achieved. Sometimes these explanations are also needed as an input for a task that is outside the scope of the system/user interaction. Often they have only a secondary function to make the user have confidence in a solution, or to satisfy his curiosity. The user may want to present his solution to the system to ask for an opinion. This is both the case in so called 'critiquing' (Miller, 1984) and in coaching systems (e.g. Breuker et al., 1987): the difference being the time perspective to learn.

The autistic problem solver and intelligent coach are two extremes on the modality dimension of expert systems, which is independent of type of problem solving that is performed by the system. The coach may monitor and advise about diagnostic, design, planning etc. tasks. This distinction between the problem solving functions and the communication functions is hardly made explicit in the literature (e.g. Hayes Roth et al, 1983; cf Breuker & Wielinga, 1987). It is obvious that the complexity of the communication tasks increases towards the coaching end of this dimension. This is a reason why intelligent coaching (teaching) systems are often viewed as incorporating everything the state of the art has to offer in constructing knowledge based systems (Sleeman & Brown, 1983; Self, 1988).

3. Generations of Knowledge Based Systems

The characteristics as discussed in section 2 do not apply to all types of knowledge based systems. Flat, rule based systems like MYCIN may be able to perform at the level of human experts for typical problems, but they lack many of the remaining characteristics. These types of systems are sometimes called "first generation" systems. Their knowledge is not transparently structured (understandable), and, hence, their reasoning trace may not provide a "how" explanation at all. In this *shallow* nature of representing knowledge, (heuristic) rules only associate data with solution classes, but do not allow for "why" explanations. Moreover, these rules often contain mixtures of different types of knowledge, e.g. domain knowledge and control knowledge (see also Clancey, 1985; Keravnou & Johnson, 1986). For instance, many 'screening conditions' in MYCIN are used to control communication with the user in preventing weird or redundant questions to be asked, and appear among conditions which describe states (hypotheses) of the diagnosis, and to be obtained evidence, as the following example shows: (table: 3-1):

Table 1: Shallow Rule
IF the infection is meningitis and the subtype of meningitis is bacterial and only circumstantial evidence is available and the patient is at least 17 years old and the patient is an alcoholic **THEN** there is suggestive evidence for diplococcus-pneumonia

Even if explanation capabilities are not an important function -as in XCon- and the system can be employed as an autistic problem solver, the performance of first generation systems is often unacceptably brittle. This means that the system is not capable to adapt its reasoning to the type of problem at hand. As a consequence, the system may simply get stuck in an atypical problem, or worse, come up with a wrong solution, which may have very costly consequences. In other words, first generation systems lack the flexibility for *graceful degradation*, i.e. the capability to recognise which type of problems require which strategy, or are beyond the scope of its capabilities. As pointed out by Steels (1987) flexibility requires self-, or meta-knowledge.

In second generation expert systems different types of knowledge are distinguished, and separately represented; often by using hybrid formalisms which enhance the tractability of the inference capacities (cf. Levesque & Brachman, 1985). A major distinction is between domain knowledge and strategic knowledge. The strategic knowledge -and its reasoning- controls the use at the domain level. Another distinction is between heuristic knowledge and 'domain theory'. The former can be viewed as an efficient, compiled out version of the latter. The compiled out knowledge is used for efficient performance: it condenses the crucial steps in the reasoning process on the basis of structured domain concepts (domain theory). The domain theory can be used to justify or evaluate solutions, and, for deriving new solutions when the compiled out knowledge is inadequate. Examples of second generation systems are NEOMYCIN (Clancey & Letsinger, 1981), XPLAIN (Swartout, 1983), CONCLAVE (van der Velde, 1988), and StatCons (De Greef et al., 1988). Second generation systems allow for the use of far more advanced AI techniques like qualitative reasoning (see e.g. Bobrow, 1984) and learning from experience (e.g. DISCIPLE, Kodratoff & Tecuci, 1987), than currently employed in the construction of expert systems. In fact, one may state that there is an unwarranted time lag in applying state of the art AI techniques in most expert system building environments (Clancey, 1985). However, this is also due to the fact that many approaches in knowledge acquisition simply do not allow for distinguishing between various types and levels of knowledge.

4. Knowledge Acquisition in General

Knowledge acquisition is the process of obtaining, structuring and formalising the knowledge of one or more human experts, in order to construct a program that can perform a difficult task adequately. Knowledge acquisition is generally seen as difficult and considered to be the major bottleneck in expert systems development. The difficulties arising during the knowledge acquisition process are primarily the result of the gap that must be bridged between the linguistic level (language) on one hand and the implementation level (programming languages) on the other hand (Brachman, 1979). Often it is not self evident how a complex reasoning processes, as performed by human experts, can be implemented into programming languages.

4.1. Modalities of Knowledge Acquisitions

As described by Hayes-Roth et al. (1983), the process of the knowledge acquisition can be carried out in a number of different ways. Currently most practiced is knowledge acquisition by means of a *knowledge engineer* (see figure 1). In this approach the person who does the the knowledge acquisition interrogates the expert in the field, structures and formalises the expertise of the expert and in most cases also builds the expert system. However, if the knowledge is formalised in a proper way then the actual implementation can also be done by somebody else.

In an other version of the acquisition process, called *knowledge editing*, the expert himself puts the

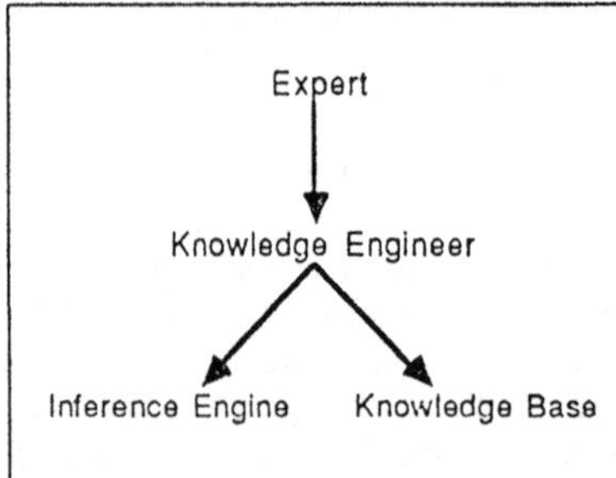

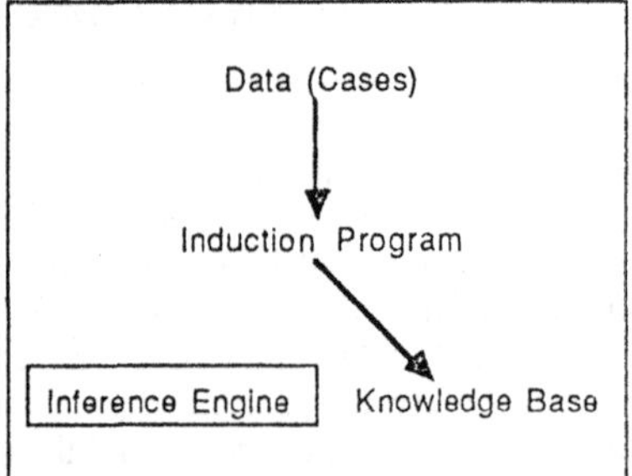

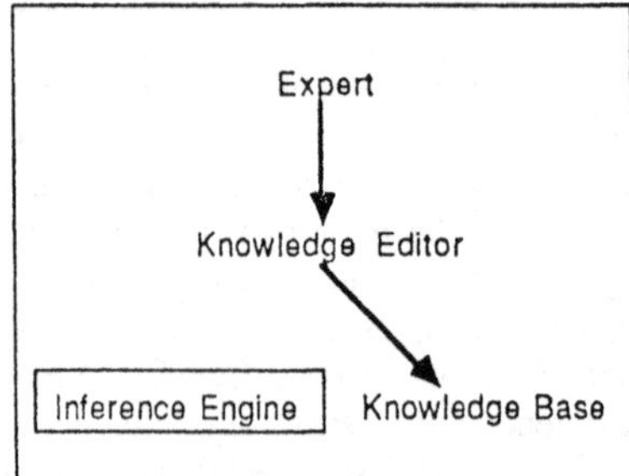

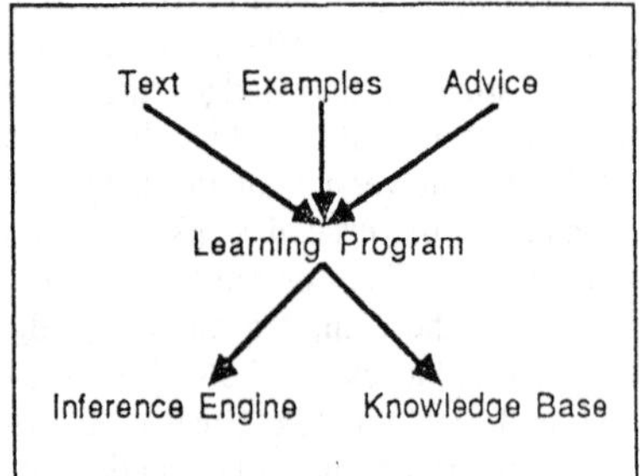

Figure 1: *Modalities of Knowledge Acquisition*

knowledge in the expert system by using an editing program that facilitates manipulation of the contents of the knowledge base. The scope of this approach is limited compared to knowledge acquisition done by an knowledge engineer, but may in some situations be very suitable. In particular, when the structure of the knowledge base is largely predefined and easily understood by the expert, and the inference engine is fixed.

A more tentative, and currently not so often used, approach to the knowledge acquisition process is the use of an *induction program.* A computer program is used to generate the knowledge. It examines the input for generalities that can be used in the knowledge based of the expert system. This way of doing knowledge acquisition may be applyable when large amounts of data (or cases) must be examined in order to generate the contents of a knowledge base. For example, in the domain of medical diagnosis it might be worthwhile to examine a large number of cases in order to identify the characteristics that go along with particular diseases. The knowledge generated in this way can then subsequently be used to diagnose particular diseases on basis of their characteristics.

Finally, a *learning program* may be used. In this approach a computer program consults the expert, or is fed with textual material or examples. It generates (or refines) the expert system on the basis of this interaction. Although this way of doing knowledge acquisition is being examined at a large scale in the research laboratory, its potential for use in real life settings is currently far from sufficient.

4.2. The Role of the Knowledge Engineer

In the following we will mostly be concerned with knowledge acquisition carried out by a (human) knowledge engineer. A knowledge engineer has to *elicit* verbal data from the expert. Standard techniques, such as asking the expert to formulate rules or provide think-aloud protocols, are available for this purpose. However, obtaining data may be difficult, because the expert is not used to verbally express his knowledge, or to give an on line report of his reasoning (thinking aloud).

Once data have been obtained from the expert the knowledge engineer has to abstract the knowledge that is implied in the data. This is in fact the major difficulty. The verbal data do not speak for themselves, because they are hardly ever expressed as explicit structures of knowledge. The knowledge engineer has to interpret the data by abstraction into types and structures of knowledge. This process is to be viewed as a modelling enterprise, rather than as a 'mining' enterprise (Hayward, 1987). This modelling may be complicated by the fact that the data may be incomplete. Moreover, when more experts have been consulted, multiple sources of data must be integrated. Just explicating the knowledge will therefore in general not be sufficient. The knowledge needs to be analysed critically in order to point out omissions and/or contradictions.

During the knowledge acquisition special attention should be paid to the structure of the reasoning. Even in think-aloud protocols this structure is implicit, because they only show a particular path the expert traverses during the problem solving process. It is likely that large parts of the total search space, as well as in what way the traversal of this space was constrained, do not necessarily evolve from the protocol.

Finally, two additional points are relevant for the knowledge acquisition process. First, a knowledge engineer should, while doing the acquisition, take care not to become an expert himself. Beside the fact that this would be too time consuming, it is not what the acquisition is about. The knowledge engineer should identify the different *types* of knowledge that are used by the expert and put them into an appropriate structure, which is different form actually *knowing* all the contents of that knowledge. Second, the knowledge engineer should be aware of the fact the building expert systems depends highly on the techniques and tools developed in the field of AI. As this field is still subject of research, it may well be the case that particular techniques or tools are simply not available, because current research has not yet reached that level. Some applications might therefore appear to be impossible.

5. Methodologies for Knowledge Based System Development

Currently the development of knowledge based systems proceeds much like traditional AI programming. The knowledge engineer has hardly any idea of the problems that are going to be encountered during the knowledge acquisition process, nor of the way these problems can be solved. The whole enterprise is therefore rather experimental and non-structured, characterised by an incremental and ad-hoc analysis of the domain, often in combination with what has become known as *rapid prototyping*. In this section we will investigate this traditional approach, describe its problems and outline a framework for more appropriate methodologies for building knowledge based systems.

5.1. Rapid Prototyping

Using rapid prototyping means that the knowledge engineer tries to build a part of the perceived system as early as possible. Given some small piece of knowledge, obtained during the analysis, the knowledge engineer starts building a system which may have the function of an initial model of the knowledge based system. This prototype is meant to give an illustration of what the final system will look like and how it is supposed to behave. In order to build the prototype the knowledge engineer is forced to elicit a particular piece of the knowledge from the expert, say a detailed description of solving one or two cases.

Rapid prototyping has some important benefits. Building a prototype will focus the elicitation and interpretation process carried out by the knowledge engineer. Moreover, the expert, who may initially be somewhat sceptical about the idea of building a knowledge based system, may get more motivated, because the prototype illustrates the feasibility. Also the management is often more likely to be convinced of the effectiveness of the enterprise.

However, there are a number of drawbacks on the rapid prototyping approach as well. The most important one is the fact that a solution is constructed without an encompassing analysis of the problem: the surest sign of inadequate problem solving, which is accompanied by frequent and drastic backtracking. Throwing away prototypes is recommended as a standard practice. To cut losses, an apparently inadequate design should be discarded as soon as possible. This has as a consequence that the domain is not explored in depth: it remains terra incognita. Rabid rapid prototyping is an underestimation of the knowledge acquisition problem. This problem is the fact that there is a very large gap between the verbal data on expertise and the implementation constructs used to build the artifact: the knowledge based system. There is certainly no simple mapping between these data and the constructs. The verbal data have to be interpreted and abstracted to enable the construction of a system. This interpretation and abstraction process can be viewed as a number of drastic transformations of the verbal data. In this sense the knowledge based system is a model that interprets or explains the (relevant) verbal data on expertise. Clearly this is not something that can be done easily. An implementation language has simple and unambiguous semantics, whereas natural language is semantically very rich and flexible. Often it is possible to make a prototype that copes with some detailed part of the knowledge of the expert, because the alternatives are limited. When larger parts of the knowledge of the expert have to be taken into account this may become quite troublesome, because the number of variations within the problem solving process grows, for which generic solutions have to be found within the existing framework, which may not fit at all. This contrasts one of the assumptions underneath prototyping, i.e. that it facilitates at a very early stage the uncovering of the basic structure of the expertise.

5.2. Software engineering

The experimental approach in developing knowledge based systems is useful in research environments, but is less acceptable in commercial environments. It is expensive, hardly manageable, and does not fit with the careful life-cycling of traditional software engineering practice. However, traditional software engineering techniques and task decompostions (life cycle models) do not straightforwardly apply to the domain of knowledge engineering. One of the reasons is that building a knowledge based systems has to do with *knowledge*. It is not simply a set of algorithms that needs to be taken into account, but the development of knowledge based systems deals with knowledge, different types of knowledge, and how to use this knowledge. Software engineering methodologies do not specify activities, nor have the techniques and tools to uncover knowledge and reasoning. More or less as a result of this, these methodologies underestimate the complexity of the knowledge acquisition process and do not support this, if the problem is even identified.

5.3. Stage based Approaches

More structured approaches (Hayes-Roth et al, 1983; Frieling et al., 1985) overcome some of the omissions in the experimental approaches. In order to make the knowledge acquisition more easy and controlable, they decompose the knowledge acquisition into a number of stages and specify the order in which these stages should be carried out. Stages are a rudimentary *life cycle model*. A typical example of such an approach is shortly described below (from: Hayes-Roth et al, 1983).

The knowledge acquisition starts with *problem identification*. During this stage the participants that are somehow related to the problem solving process are identified, together with an informal description of that problem. The second stage is *problem conceptualisation*. During this stage a description of the overall problem structure is described. The relevant concepts within this structure are pointed out and the general feasibility of building the knowledge based system is determined. The third stage is *knowledge formalisation*. During this stage the prototypical problem solving process is identified and a selection is made of the overall representation framework. During the fourth stage, called *representation*, the requirements of the representation are further specified, tools supporting the chosen representation are selected and a first design of the system is made. During the fifth stage, *prototype construction*, a subdomain is selected, a prototype with respect to this domain is implemented and a test on a case library is carried out. During the sixth stage, called *review*, the prototype is judged on performance, acceptability, and validity. During the seventh stage, *knowledge refinement and extension* the prototype is augmented with more knowledge of the domain, eventually resulting in the final knowledge based system.

Two more phases may follow. First, it is possible that the structure of the prototype is insufficient to cope with the augmentation and extension of the knowledge and that therefore the structure of the prototype has to be *reformulated*, or redesigned. This would then more or less enforce backtracking to the representation phase (stage four). If on the other hand the architecture appears to be sufficient for the augmentation and extension of the knowledge then reformulation is not needed, and the knowledge based system will eventually emerge from the augmentation and extension stages. Given the complete system one final activity must be carried out, namely the *field test*. The system is introduced in its real operating environment and again reviewed for its performance, its acceptability, and its validity. Obviously, the results from this test can enforce backtracking to one of the previous stages.

Although the stage approaches, like the one described above, are a considerable improvement over the experimental approaches, they still have some mayor problems. For a start, there are hardly any tools available to support the different activities. Furthermore, the specifications of the intermediate results are vague. It is not clear, at least not explicitly specified, what the output of a particular activity should be. Related to this is the lack of documentation, because the outputs have not been pointed out precisely there is also no emphasis on documenting the intermediate results. This makes the backtracking as troublesome as in the prototyping approach. Moreover, there is still an important reliance on prototyping. Finally, and this is in contrast to traditional software engineering, the requirements of the user, the organisation, and the characteristics of the operational environment are largely ignored during the development process.

6. The KADS Methodology

KADS (see e.g. Hayward, 1987) aims at the development of a methodology for the construction of knowledge based systems. KADS is a stage based approach which also incorporates aspects of software engineering in the sense that it specifies a life cycle model of activities. It differs from software engineering, because it also contains tools and techniques which are typical for knowledge engineering, such as elicitation techniques (see section 9) and modelling languages for the specification of knowledge and reasoning (see section 7). Building an expert system is in fact building a model of some real life expertise, or "model of a system in the real world" (Clancey, 1985). Therefore, in the methodology a modelling language has to be specified. The modelling language may consists of implementation formalisms, as is the case in rapid prototyping, but these formalisms are at too low a level to conceptualise the structure of reasoning and knowledge. The languages should allow for a high level of abstraction: at the knowledge, or epistemological level (Newell, 1982; Brachman, 1979). In the next two sections, the modelling languages used in KADS are described. These modelling languages preserve the coherence of the analysis of the expertise, and are a simple but powerful alternative to rapid prototyping.

In KADS the analysis of the expertise is separated as a distinctive stage from the design, implementation, and other successive stages. Within these stages detailed activities and the use of techniques, documentation and tools are specified (Edin et al., 1987). Here we will focus on a global description of the analysis and design stages.

An important principle on which the KADS life cycle model and the use of techniques is based, is best illustrated by the knowledge based system development curve (see figure 2). The Y-axis indicates different levels of abstraction, whereas on the X-axis the order of the different modeling activities is specified. The points on this curve indicate the positions of the products which are the result of the analysis, resp. design stages in KADS as intermediary steps in going from the data on expertise to the artifact. As discussed before, the bridging of this gap constitutes the mayor problem in knowledge acquisition.

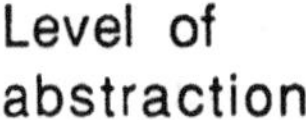

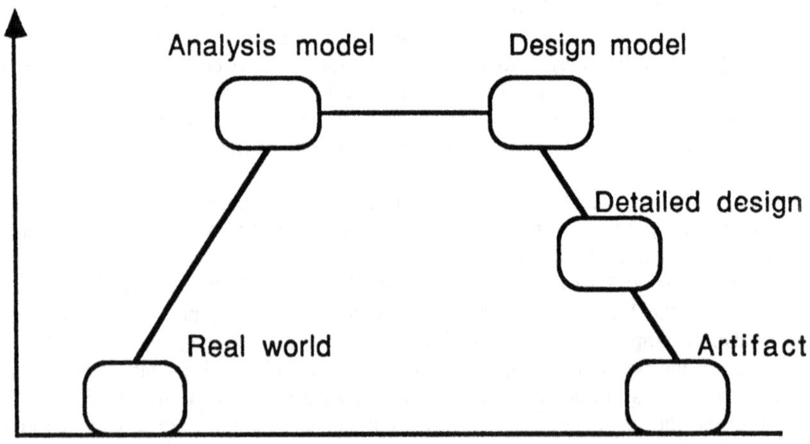

Figure 2: *The knowledge based system development curve*

The *conceptual* model is a model of the expertise, as observed (or synthesised) in the real world. It is one of the results of the Analysis stage. The *design* model is at the same level of abstraction as the conceptual model, but it is a model of the artifact, rather than a model of the real world. This model is constructed on the basis of the conceptual model and 'external requirements' as specified in the analysis stage. The design model is similar to what is called logical or abstract design in more traditional software development methodologies. Between the design model and the artifact one additional model has been specified, the *detailed* or *technical design* model, which can be transformed by simple mappings into the final artifact. This is in fact a further specification of the design model.

Using these two intermediate languages is useful because of a number of reasons. As mentioned before, it reduces the overall complexity of the knowledge acquisition process (Wielinga & Breuker, 1986). Second, because (informal) languages have been specified for each intermediate model, the output of each activity can be monitored and reviewed explicitly. Third, the conceptual model serves as a record of knowledge that is independent of the current technology and is therefore not biased or distorted by some particular implementation (Young, 1987). Fourth, the intermediate descriptions of the system can be used for debugging, maintenance, and/or refinement of the final knowledge based system, i.e. in its most optimal case a path through the intermediate models can be identified that relates the problem solving behaviour and knowledge of the expert on one hand, to the problem solving behaviour and knowledge of the artifact on the other hand. So, if the artifact, during a particular problem solving process, fails to show the correct problem solving behaviour, then it should not be too hard to trace this failure back to a particular part of the knowledge of the expert, which in turn makes the debugging, maintenance and refinement more easy and more focussed. Finally, the conceptual model, the design model and their relations can be used to give explanations at a higher level than just paraphrasing code by relating a particular piece of code back to the higher level concept that originated it.

6.1. The Analysis Stage of KADS

The analysis stage in KADS consists of two streams of activities: an internal stream which is concerned with the development of the conceptual model, and an external stream. The external stream is strongly similar to the analysis stages in traditional software engineering methodologies, and produces a description of the external requirements of the system. External requirements are performance specifications, implementation constraints, and interface desiderata.

The internal analysis constitutes the major and critical part of the knowledge acquisition. It should be noted that knowledge acquisition may occur at other stages as well: in particular during detailed design, implementation and maintenance, but in these cases, the knowledge acquisition process consists of a refinement, rather than a constructing activity. In the next section we will describe the modelling language for the conceptual model.

7. What's in a Conceptual Model

Developing a KBS involves modelling of expertise, i.e. the structuring of the required knowledge, inference competence and (flexible) use of knowledge. This model is the conceptual model. Conceptual model is a term borrowed from Norman (1983) denoting the model the designer of a computer system (KBS, conventional software) has in mind and/or specified when implementing a system. The role of a conceptual model is a high level functional specification that is used in designing and implementing a KBS.

Flexibility refers to the control of complexity. Current views consider the distinction between domain knowledge and 'meta knowledge' to control the reasoning at the domain as a viable, but problematic solution (Davis, 1980; Clancey, 1983). This solution is problematic for various reasons: it is computationally inefficient, and moreover, there is no theoretical boundary to prevent proliferation of metalevels. In the framework we propose, we distinguish 4 layers of describing expertise: each level has a different functionality, and, moreover, it seems that the fourth level is a top-level: not in a formal sense, but in a psychologically valid sense. A summary of these four layers is presented in table 2.

Table 2: Layers of a Conceptual Model (after Breuker & Wielinga, 1986)		
Layer	*Elements*	*Relation with lower layer*
Strategy	Plans, meta rules	
		controls
Task	Goals, task structures	
		applies
Inference	Meta classes, knowledge sources	
		describes
Domain	Concepts, relations	

The first layer contains the static knowledge of the domain: domain concepts, relations and complex structures, such as models of processes or devices. First generation expert systems contain only descriptions of expertise at this level: often incomplete, because the domain knowledge may not only consist of knowledge to perform specific tasks, but also knowledge that contains underlying principles and justifications (i.e. 'support' knowledge: Clancey, 1983, or: 'domain theory'). Formalisms for describing domain knowledge are the classical knowledge representation paradigms, which distinguish e.g. concepts and relations.

The second layer is the inference layer. It describes the inference making competence that is required for solving a problem based upon the domain knowledge. It states *what inferences* can be made: not how or when they are made. The how is dependent on the structures in the domain layer that allow for methods to be applied. For instance, if at the inference layer some classification competence is specified, this may be based on is-a structures in the domain knowledge, or may be ad-hoc, based upon a number of heuristic classification rules. The 'when' is specified at the next, task layer (sse below). The inference structure provides a flow of data view; the task structure a flow of control view superimposed on this inference structure.

The 'vocabulary' for the inference layer consists of three elements: knowledge sources, metaclasses and dependencies between these. A structure of these elements is called an inference structure (cf. Clancey, 1985). Because this layer is different from other metalevel reasoning descriptions in which the domain knowledge does not have a competence description, but is immediately controlled by a flexible task description or strategic reasoning components, we will discuss this level in some more detail.

7.1. Inference layer: knowledge sources and metaclasses

A knowledge source can be defined as a primitive inference making function, in which the metaclasses are the roles or input/output parameters of this function. Metaclasses stand for domain concepts that may play various roles. Well known instances of those roles are: hypothesis, evidence, factor, diagnosis, plan, etc. Distinguishing the role of a concept in some problem solving or reasoning process from what the concept "means" is very important. It provides an almost orthogonal view on domain structures in the sense that some domain concept may play various roles. For instance: the concept that is a hypothesis (e.g. a disease) at a certain moment in the problem solving process may turn out to be the diagnosis, because it is supported by evidence. These dependencies between terms like hypothesis, evidence and diagnosis are not accidental: they form a pattern in reasoning. Metaclasses are "handles" which mediate between domain knowledge and control, or strategic reasoning.

A knowledge sources (KS) identifies a type of inference. An inference is an operation on some input state producing a new, output state. The relation between the input state and the output state denotes the type of inference and is expressed by an action term like 'assemble' or 'specify'. For instance, in 'abstraction' the input state consists of some concept and the output state is another concept, which contains less attributes than the input concept. In other words in 'abstraction' irrelevant features are deleted and the remaining structure is mapped upon an existing concept, or a new concept is created. This simplified description shows that in the type of a KS the details of how this abstraction is made, what irrelevance means, what the abstract concepts are, etc. is not included. In this respect a KS is an abstraction of the inference process, that simply describes that an inference can be made. How it is made can be specified as a method that is applied to the domain knowledge, but it appears to be more practical to specify the precise method in the Design model (M2) (see next section).

The typology of KSs -or inferences- is based upon the epistemology of concepts. Inferences are operations on concepts, so knowledge sources can be viewed as abstracted operations (functions) on abstracted concepts, i.e. their naked structures, not filled with their particular types. This is what is meant by the fact that the inference layer is a metalevel of the domain level. KSs can be classified according to which elements of the structure of a concept, or structures of concepts it manipulates. In other words, inferences can be typed in terms of "what can happen to a concept". A concept can be either part of a description (say: generic knowledge) or of a set of instances.

In figure 3 an overview is presented of KS as identified up till now (for further details: see Breuker et al., 1987, chapter 5.1.2.). Between brackets the transition between the types of knowledge is summarised. This typology is probably not exhaustive, but in practice it has been sufficient to model a large variety of domains.

Knowledge sources can be viewed as functions in the problem solving process; the metaclasses are the arguments or *roles* in this process. A metaclass has therefore no structure; it is a slot that can be filled with a domain concept (i.e. its actual reference to the domain layer). Because roles are dependent on the stage in the problem solving process a typology of metaclasses is difficult to construct, because the structure of the problem solving process (e.g. inference structure and task structure) varies. Therefore, we have only used a very crude leading principle in viewing the problem solving process in a pseudo temporal/causal way. An important reason the typing of metaclasses has caused us much problems is

Change concept

- assign_value
- compute

Generate concept

- instantiate (description -> instance)
- classify | identify (instance -> description)
- generalise (set -> description)
- abstract (description -> description)
- specify (description -> description)

Differentiate between concepts

- compare (values)
- match (structures)

Structure manipulation

- assemble (set -> structure)
- sort (set -> set)
- decompose (structure -> set)
- transform (structure -> structure)

Figure 3: *A Typology of Knowledge Sources*

that the vocabulary in our natural languages contain only few terms to denote roles in reasoning. Therefore, many metaclasses have a newspeak flavour as a consequence of a lack of a well structured naive cognitive psychology in our society. In figure 4 this provisional typology of metaclasses is presented.

Knowledge sources and metaclasses and their dependencies form inferences structures. A simple example of an inference structure is presented in section 2.3. -Example of a Conceptual Model.

7.2. Control: the task and strategy layers

The third layer is the task layer. At this level the basic objects are goals and tasks. Tasks are ways in which knowledge sources can be combined to achieve a particular goal. A task structure is a fixed strategy that controls the use of KSs and the interactions with the environment/user. The ingredients for task structures are *goal statements* and *control statements*. Goal statements are specified as an action term and one or more objects, e.g. 'obtain (data)'. At the lowest level a goal statement may refer to the invocation of a knowledge source. Goal statements may consist of structures of (sub)goal statements.

Although models of fixed strategies are very powerful in problem solving, they do hardly account for the flexibility of expert behaviour. Flexibility in strategic reasoning would require a planning component that dynamically generates a goal tree. Such a planner would use knowledge about general problem solving methods, such as means-end analysis, heuristic classification, etc., and adapt its planning on the

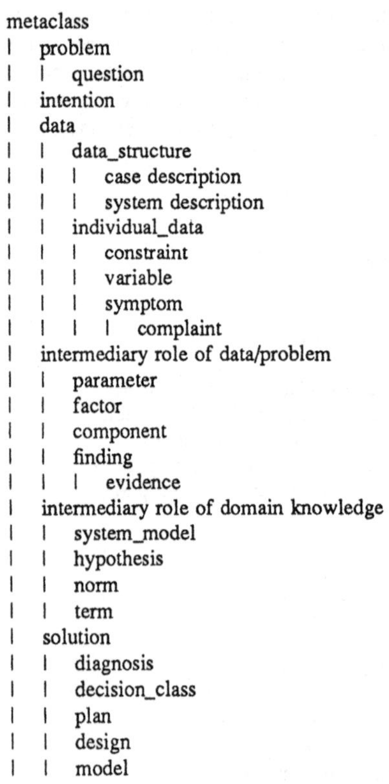

metaclass
| problem
| | question
| intention
| data
| | data_structure
| | | case description
| | | system description
| | individual_data
| | | constraint
| | | variable
| | | symptom
| | | | complaint
| intermediary role of data/problem
| | parameter
| | factor
| | component
| | finding
| | | evidence
| intermediary role of domain knowledge
| | system_model
| | hypothesis
| | norm
| | term
| solution
| | diagnosis
| | decision_class
| | plan
| | design
| | model

Figure 4: *Typology of metaclasses (tentative)*

basis of interactions with the user and/or monitoring its own progression in the course of the problem solving process.

A full description of competences at the strategic level is impossible. The strategic level represents "problem solving and knowledge acquisition *abilities*", or "intelligence" in the psychometric sense. Strategic reasoning is of utmost importance in attacking new types of problems, but for expert -i.e. highly overlearned- problem solving skills, strategic reasoning compiles out in a semi-fixed task structure, which varies over known types of problems. Thus in practice a full description of strategic reasoning is not required for building an expert system. The strategic level in the conceptual model is therefore only specified by some rules which often have the form that if some type of problem occurs, the task structure should be modified in a particular way. Only if we want to have a highly flexible and intelligent system which will acquire knowledge knowledge and skills for new types of problems (e.g. in new, adjacent domains), the specification of the strategic level becomes essential. This is obviously far beyond the state of the art. In the simple example of a conceptual model in the next section no specifications of the strategic level occur, because such a degree of flexibility is not required.

8. The Design Model of KADS

In describing the design of knowledge based systems a distinction can be made between the *elements* of the design description and the *process* of how to arrive at a design description in terms of these elements. They are respectively referred to as as the *elements of the design notation* and the *design process*.

Figure 5 below, illustrates the overall design activity. The top of this figure depicts the *analysis model*, which consists of the *conceptual model* and the *external requirements* and is the input for the overall design process. (Notice, that the modality requirements are basicly part of the conceptual model.) The different steps in the design process are, in this picture, represented as ovals, whereas the elements of

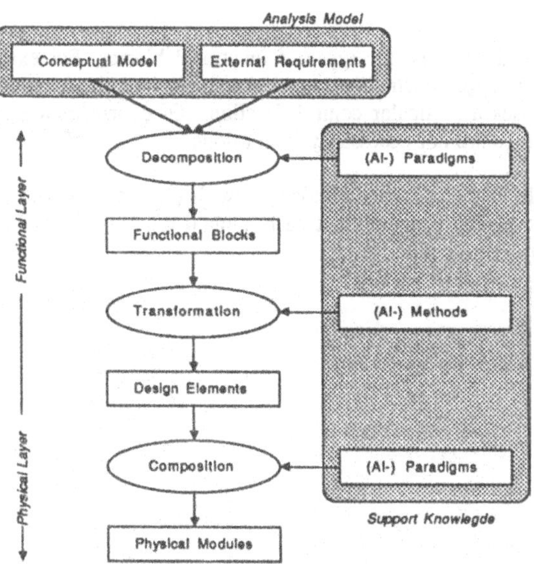

Figure 5: *The design process*

the design notation are displayed as boxes. The elements of the design notation can be divided into three main layers, namely, the *functional* layer, the *behaviour* layer and the *structural* layer. In the next sections each layer will be described briefly. A more detailed description can be found in Schreiber et al. (1987) and Bredeweg et al. (1988).

8.1. Functional Layer

This layer is concerned with the *functional description* of the system. The functional description should encompass a specification of the internal and external behaviour of the perceived system. Or to put it differently, it should specify *what* behaviour is required of the final artifact.

The functional description consists of a conversion of the conceptual model into a set of functional blocks. During this process the external requirements are integrated. Each functional block represents a distinct functional unit of the final artifact and can be classified according to a number of features. The most relevant features are the *function type* and the *relations with other functional blocks*. The function type is a characterisation of the role that the function plays in the perceived system (e.g. problem solving, data storage). The relations of a functional block with other functional blocks are *consist-of* relations, *input-output* relations, and, *control* relations. These relations can be used to specify that: a functional block can be decomposed into other functional blocks; a functional block can use output from, or provide input for, other functional blocks; a functional block may control other functional blocks.

8.2. Selection of Methods or Behaviour Layer

Selecting methods is one of the significant difference between knowledge based system development and conventional system design. Methods specify the way in which the functions are realised by the artifact and usually refer to AI methods like: search algorithms, classification using isa-relations, and others. Methods should be seen as abstract entities, associated with a set of design elements, which are the physical parts that make up the method. The *hierarchical classification* method, for instance, is made up of the design elements: *classify procedure*, *subsumption relations*, *class definitions* and *attribute value pairs*.

Methods can be associated with specific types of functional blocks. For example: a truth maintenance method realises a data storage function; a natural language interpreter realises a data I/O function; a blackboard method realises a particular control function. Of course, relations between a particular AI method and a function type are not necessarily 'one-to-one'

In table 3 some example methods are listed, together with the function type(s) that each method can be associated with, and the design elements that each method requires. A *library* of AI methods (Bundy, 1985) would be a useful tool for KBS design.

Table 3: Methods and their Design Elements

Method	*Function Type*	*Design Element*
Hierarchical Refinement	Problem Solving	Classifier Subsumption relations Class definitions Attribute value pairs
STRIPS	Planning/Problem solving	operators - add-list - delete-list - precondition propositions operator selector subgoal administrator
ATN parsing	Data I/O	Parser ATN grammar Lexicon Text string Parse tree
ATMS	Data storage	scheduler nodes - datum - labels - justifications consumers

The methods thus link the functional layer with the behavioural layer by describing the behaviour selected for a functional block. The link between the behavioural layer and the structural layer is established by the design elements.

8.3. Structural Layer

At the structural layer, the design elements of the chosen methods are composed into modules. The objective of this layer is to provide the basis for detailed design and implementation. Or to put it differently, the structural layer specifies *how* the functional requirements at the functional layer can be addressed in the final artifact. The structure of modules represents the *architecture* of the artifact.

At the structural layer the notion of *environment* is introduced. An environment is an off-the-shelf software system 'containing' a set of methods and the corresponding design elements. Examples are: EMYCIN, KES, and Prolog. Environments can be divided into *open* and *closed* environments. In a closed environment the set of methods and design elements is not expandable, whereas an open environment has possibilities for expanding the set of methods and design elements. Open environments can be further specified as being *weak* or *strong* environments, depending on the size of the set of predefined methods and design elements. Prolog can in this sense be viewed as an example of a weak environment, whereas KEE can be seen as an example of a strong environment.

In the case of a closed environment the module structure of the artifact is largely fixed. Closed environments can thus be seen as *skeleton architectures* of the artifact. A special category of (closed) environments are the *shells*. A shell is an environment, containing a set of methods and corresponding design elements necessary to carry out a specific task. The shell is a complete system except for the domain dependent part of the design elements.

8.4. Role of Paradigms

To guide the overall process of transforming the analysis model into the design model, a paradigm can be selected. A paradigm refers to a principle, or a set of principles, which is based on a theory or a methodology. An example of such a paradigm, comming from the field of structured system design, is that of *minimising coupling* and *maximising coherence* (Yourdon & Constantine, 1978). However, only using conventional software engineer paradigms will not be sufficient for the development of knowledge based systems. For that purpose *AI-paradigms* are needed which take different aspects of the *knowledge*, that is going to make up the final artifact, into account.

There are three ways in which a paradigm can support the conversion of the analysis model into the design model. First, by advocating a particular functional block structure for representing the functions that need to be addressed by the final artifact. Second, by pointing out appropriate methods that can be used to achieve the behaviour needed to address particular functions. Third, by suggesting a particular physical block structure for aggregating the design elements that go along with the used methods. However, not all paradigms necessarily apply to the total design process. A distinction can be made between *weaker* paradigms, which only apply to a particular part of the design process, and *stronger* paradigms, which apply to the design process as a whole. Obviously, strong paradigms will constrain the design process to a much greater extent the weak paradigms, i.e. the stronger the paradigm the more constraints it will put on the design decisions.

From the AI literature it appears that the notion of paradigms is often used implicitly. To illustrate this, consider the following two briefly described paradigms. A more extensive description of these paradigms can be found in (Schreiber et al, 1987). The first example of a paradigm, that is used intensively, is the *production system* paradigm. This paradigm refers to the whole class of rule-based systems that are build in analogy with the traditional MYCIN system (Shortliffe, 1979). Basicly, this paradigm supports at the top level two typical functions: consultation and explanation (which can be further decomposed into subfunctions) The method most often used in the context of this paradigm is a backward search of an implicit AND/OR tree. It provides the overall behaviour that is needed to address the consultation and explanation function. The physical modules that are suggested by the production system paradigm are a knowledge base, an inference engine, a database, and an explainer, each containing a number of the design elements. The knowledge base, for instance, contains, among others, rules that are applied by the backward search method, whereas the inference engine contains the procedures, which are the physical parts of the backward search method that applies the rules.

An other example of a paradigm is the *state-space* paradigm. This paradigm is of particular interest because the SOAR system (Laird et al., 1987), that is currently gaining in popularity, is based on this paradigm. As mentioned before, we will not describe paradigms in detail, but only focus on some typical features of the paradigm. Here we will focus on the set of design elements and corresponding methods that are supported by the state-space paradigm.

Systems build with the state-space paradigm in mind, are characterised by explicitly representing the states in the problem solving process, consequently there is an initial state, a goal state, and a whole area of intermediate states. The initial state is transformed into intermediate states, in order to arrive at the goal state. Each state can, with help of heuristics, be analysed and classified as being more or less appropriate for achieving the final goal state. Typical for this paradigm is that the operators, which change states into other states, can as such not be classified as being good or bad. Finally, search procedures are needed to guide the search trough the state-space, i.e. to apply the available operators in a particular way. These search procedures are most typical for identifying the different methods. Some of those methods are: depth-first search, breadth-first search, hill-climbing, and others. More complex methods, within the context of this paradigm, are: GPS (General Problem Solver), A* (A-start),

MiniMax, and others.

We are aware of fact that the descriptions of the paradigms presented here, have a tentative character. However, they clearly illustrate that a general framework can be identified which, on one hand, describes the general characteristics of many systems that have been build in the past, and on the other hand, provides support knowledge for systems to be build in the future. We therefore think it is essential that, like in the case of SOAR, more effort is put in formulating AI-paradigms. They could benefit the development of knowledge based systems to a large extent.

9. Elicitation Techniques

Knowledge analysis requires data which have to be acquired in some way. Some data are publicly available in a written or machine-readable form. Most data relevant for KBS development are not available in written form, but have to be obtained through a process of *elicitation.* In particular data concerning the reasoning process of an expert will in general not be publicly available, but will have to collected using special techniques.

Different types of data relevant for KBS development can be distinguished. *Verbal data* are the most commonly used type of data for the simple reason that natural language is the most evolved and flexible medium for expressing knowledge. The relationship between knowledge and language is very intimate. This does not mean that for specific purposes other media may not be more adequate, but natural language is at least the most universal one.

Graphical data are graphs, diagrams, sketches, technical drawings, etc. Many graphical data are employed to focus on structural or organisational aspects of knowledge. The specific advantage of graphical data over verbal data in this respect is not the fact that organisation or structure is made explicit: words can do this too. It is the fact that it is easier to abstract the intended structure from a 2 dimensional presentation, than from a 1 dimensional one (Breuker, 1984). Like language, the use of graphical data is based upon conventions. These conventions may be part of our culture (e.g. the use of bar charts), others of some subculture (e.g. "semantic" networks), but the conventions may also be domain specific (electronic circuit diagrams).

Observational data are records of or codes for events and actions (behaviour). In analysing expertise, observational techniques are not often used. They are however useful when verbal accounts may easily get out of tune with mental and situational events, e.g. in operators performing process control.

Quantitative data give information about relevant variables in the domain, relationships between concepts in a domain or about certainty of knowledge elements. Quantificational data can be obtained in interviews, but a more common way of eliciting quantitative information is to have the expert perform some task, which produces quantifiable data, such as sorting, indicating differences or conceptual distances or by asking the expert to assess the certainty of a certain piece of knowledge.

Different techniques produce different type of data. In the following sections we will discuss a number of well known techniques and the type of data they elicit. Table 9-4 gives an overview of these elicitation techniques.

Table 4: Elicitation techniques

METHOD	*DESCRIPTION*	*SPECIFIC DATA ON*
Focussed interview	sequence of topics	factual knowledge
Structured interview	deep probing	structure of concepts models
Introspection	hypothetical task performance	global strategies
Self-Report	thinking aloud as second task	reasoning strategies inferences
User-dialogues	mock-up/real dialogues	modality/interaction
Review	interview on processed data	additional data justifications
Laddering	use of graphical tools	concept structures
Scaling & sorting	multidimensional scaling	structure of concepts structure of problems structure of solutions

9.1. Interviewing Techniques

Most information that is used in the analysis phase is obtained by interviewing. Interviewing is a skill that requires more than asking the right questions in the right way. It also implies adequate preparation, recording and documentation. Although extensive training in interviewing techniques may not really be needed in knowledge engineering, a minimal requirement is at least some days experience in interviewing, which may be obtained by role playing, e.g. by having interviews with colleagues about expertise in domains like cooking, holiday planning, audio equipment troubleshooting, etc.

A major question for any data collection technique is whether the data obtained are reliable and valid. Reliability refers to the question whether the same elicitation actions will produce the same data. Validity refers to the degree to which the collected data cover the intended phenomena. In "normal" interviewing reliability is in general very high: e.g. in responding to a factual question the content of the answer will be essentially the same. Validity is another, more complex issue. If the aim of the knowledge acquisition is to capture expertise in action, i.e. its operational knowledge and reasoning procedures, data collection should be directed towards eliciting or observing data from the tasks as used in practice. This is the reason why one can assume that thinking aloud (or "self report") as elicitation method yields far more valid data than for instance sorting and rating. This does not mean that data on domain knowledge obtained by less valid methods is useless. Often this knowledge plays a very specific role in a system, for instance for explanation, and other supportive functions.

If data are reliable and valid, they may still be incomplete. In knowledge engineering, verbal data are almost by definition incomplete. First, many data are "invisible" to the minds eye. Automated processes do not require conscious control; only their results become available in working memory. In practice this means that only some intermediate states of inferences can be reported; not the full chain of inference steps, because the hailmark of expertise is a high degree of automated inferencing. These small "black boxes" in the data may particularly occur in thinking aloud data. These local gaps in the data may often easily be filled by a "rational reconstruction", because there are often sufficient contextual constraints. The problem is somewhat similar to reading a text in which -not completely randomly- sentences are deleted.

Inaccessibility of inference procedures is one reason for incomplete data, unreportability is another one. The expert may know about the data, but is not able to express his knowledge. This may be due to time constraints. For instance, in thinking aloud he may think "much faster" than he can talk. A complicating factor is the fact that some "conscious" knowledge states may require more transformations before they can be expressed in natural language than others. For instance, the verbal description of a mental picture requires far more transformation than some "abstract" thought. Incompleteness may turn into invalidity if task demands require an answer, when there is no direct information available. In some cultures it may be very impolite to sell ignorance as an answer: rather a wrong answer than no answer. In a more subtle way this may also occur -probably less consciously- in interviewing experts (cf. Ericsson & Simon, 1984).

A factor that plays a role in obtaining as valid and complete data as possible is the motivation of the expert to supply data. If there is lack of motivation on the part of the interviewee, this can become manifest in subtle ways, among which refusal or direct expressions of irritation are rare. Major indicators of lack of motivation are: under-reporting, taking over initiative from the interviewer, diverting from the topic at hand to side issues.

Motivating factors can be distinguished as intrinsically and extrinsically motivating ones. Motivation is intrinsic when the activity itself -responding in an interview- is rewarding. In extrinsic motivation the reward is outside the activity itself, but in general the activity serves as a means to achieve the reward. Making the expert *feeling understood* or *recognising* the expert's competence can increase the motivation. Defining a *common goal* between the expert and the knowledge engineer is a good way of motivating the expert by extrinsic means. Such a common goal may be to build a system that takes over some of the more boring tasks of the expert's duties.

9.2. Focussed Interview

Focussed interview is a "normal" interview. It is the most widely employed elicitation technique at present, although its effectiveness is highly limited, because it does not probe for data on "expertise in action". This may be one of the reasons that there is a widespread belief that "real expertise remains implicit, because it is automatised". This is certainly true for a focussed interview, but in self-report (thinking aloud) important parts, or manifestations of automised knowledge can be uncovered. Focussed interview is an insensitive data elicitation method. On the other hand it is very simple and provides the following type of data, which are particularly relevant in the initial activities in the analysis phase, i.e. up to the analysis of expertise and the user analysis.

(1) Factual domain knowledge. (This is particularly relevant for domains where the static knowledge is not documented.)

(2) Types of problems. (see also Sorting & rating)

(3) Functions of the expertise within the environment: this may partly coincide with a description of the expert's job and how it is performed

(4) Objects and agents in the environment.

(5) Some characteristics of users.

The focussed interview is the interviewing technique most akin to normal conversation. In general the interviewer asks questions on topics of conversation he has prepared in advance (hence the term "focussed"), and the interviewee provides the answers. Although the interviewee is free to follow his own train of thought, the interview is clearly steered by the interviewer. The global structure of an interview consists of three parts: an introduction explaining the purpose and structure of the interview, a series of questions focusing on a sequence of topics, and a closing summary possibly reviewing some of the topics discussed earlier in the interview.

Addressing a topic can be performed in a "breadth first" way, so that the most general topics are discussed first. This approach is very advantageous for a first orientation in a domain, but it runs counter to the usual form of conversation which is more, "depth first" oriented: i.e. topics which are addressed, lead naturally to various sub-topics, which are themselves discussed in some depth, before the conversation returns to the higher level of discussion. In normal conversation the focusing of topics may occur in a rather associative manner. In a focussed interview, it is the task of the interviewer to prepare meaningful associations between topics, and to evaluate whether the topic structure of the conversation is flowing more or less according to the plan. The most valid answers are obtained by specific questions, rather than general ones. preferably following a chronological sequence.

9.3. Structured interview

The purpose of a structured interview is to get a detailed insight into the static aspects of the domain. This technique may uncover the structure of a concept in more detail than any other technique, and is preferred to the focussed interview for the elicitation of factual knowledge.

While a focussed interview is comparable to normal conversation, a structured interview is much like an interrogation. In a structured interview the knowledge engineer tries to elicit all knowledge relating to some concept or model by continuously asking for clarification, explanation, consequences, justifications, instances and equally, counter-instances. The transition between the focussed interview and the structured interview can be quite smooth. The principal difference is, that in the structured interview, the dialogue consists mainly of a large variety of questions put by the knowledge engineer to probe a few topics in depth, rather than a number of topics in breadth.

The success of the interview depends heavily upon the question list, which must therefore be constructed carefully. The preconditions for using the structured interview are quite demanding. Firstly, the knowledge engineer must be well acquainted with the domain terminology, and have a fair but "passive" insight into the domain, (i.e. he must be able to understand explanations, although he is not required to perform the task). Secondly, the knowledge engineer must have good interviewing skills, and particularly, be able to improvise. Thirdly, the expert must be really motivated to answer all kinds of potentially "annoying" questions.

There is the danger that the knowledge elicited is an artifact of the technique: i.e. one cannot be sure whether the information is constructed ad hoc, under the pressure of the questioning, or is evoked by the presentation of a large variety of retrieval cues and probes. More generally speaking: too much probing may lead to invalid data where the knowledge is inaccessable or simply lacking. The ordering of questions and of topics discussed can influence results significantly.

9.4. Introspection

The conversational analogue for introspection is telling stories, anecdotes, or giving testimony. It is essential to introspection that the expert is asked how he solved some problem/case, or to imagine how he would solve a class of problems. As pointed out in Breuker & Wielinga (1983a, ch 4. see also Ericsson & Simon, 1980), the validity of data obtained by introspection is not as high as that of data obtained from self report. Introspection often occurs "spontaneously" as part of a focussed interview. The main difference with a focussed interview is, that in an interview an expert is not explicitly asked to think aloud, but may answer a question by "running a mental model" of some task.

Introspection is a form of thinking aloud, of solving an imagined problem. Notice that, it is not thinking aloud while solving the problem, because there is no actual problem solving, as in self report. A typical instruction for introspection would be: "How would you solve this (kind of) problem". By this, the knowledge engineer may not expect the expert to engage in problem solving activities, but in explaining what he would do or had already done, in similar cases. Introspection protocols are shorter than self report protocols and contain a large amount of "meta-descriptions" and process comments (Newell & Simon, 1972).

The pre-conditions which apply for introspection are similar to those required for a focussed interview, except for the fact that the expert should feel free to present the information in an uninhibited way.

The type of data that can be obtained are:

- A global description of the strategies that the expert (believes he) employs in solving some set of problems.

- Some justifications for the solutions, or decisions in the problem solving process.

- Some global, but also, potentially unreliable information on the types of knowledge (knowledge sources) the expert uses in solving problems.

  There are several specific strategies for introspection. In a *retrospective case description* the expert is asked to give a detailed account of how he has handled one or more typical cases, preferably recent ones. One potential problem here however, is that the expert may pick interesting, rather than typical cases. These are usually better remembered than typical, run of the mill, cases but in general are atypical, or at least may contain atypical elements. Therefore, the knowledge engineer should have sufficient information to assess typicality of cases.

  A second strategy is *forward scenario simulation (hypothetical cases)*. Here the expert gives a detailed account of how he would solve a given problem, or class of problems: i.e. the cases are hypothetical (Grover, 1983). This may however, introduce another source of invalidity, because the correspondence between the hypothetical cases and real life cases may be poor.

  The *critical incident* method has been applied since the fifties in industrial psychology (Flanagan, 1954). It is almost identical to the retrospective case description, except that the cases are selected for being remarkable or difficult, and although this strategy may reveal little about the hard core of expertise in action, it may be very relevant to ask for difficult cases, and how these were solved. This may provide information on the limits of performance characteristics of a prospective knowledge based system, and on typical bottlenecks in expert functioning. The latter may lead to the identification of a prospective knowledge based system which will support the functioning of the expert by preventing the occurrence of bottlenecks.

9.5. Self Report

In self report, the expert thinks aloud, while solving a problem. Contrary to what occurs in other interviewing situations, giving verbal report is a task secondary to problem solving. In other interview situations, there is no additional task for the expert. By actually solving problems, task performance is much more truthful to real life than other interview situations. Self report sessions are different from other interview situations, because the interviewer is supposed to adopt an unobtrusive role. Except when presenting an instruction the role of the interviewer is restricted to motivating the expert so that he performs both tasks. Most interviewer actions are therefore aimed at keeping the expert talking.

The selection of problems in self report sessions is crucial. The selected problems should be representative of the domain and not too easy or too difficult for the expert. Asking experts beforehand to sort problems into some order (Chi, Feltovitch & Glaser, 1981) may give an insight in the relative difficulty of problems.

The expert should not feel embarrassed of describing his expertise in detail, and should have, preferably, some experience in thinking aloud. One or two short training sessions in which simple tasks like puzzles are performed in a self report condition, may be sufficient. It is often beneficial to inform the expert about the function of self report data, since he himself may consider normal interviews sufficient or even more effective.

Self report techniques are particularly suited to elicit information about the control aspects (task structure and strategy) of the reasoning process. Detailed chains of inferences can often be found in protocols, even though they are only valid for the problem at hand.

9.6. User-Expert Dialogues

In many cases, the expert's problem solving (or that of the prospective knowledge based system) proceeds in close interaction with the client (or prospective user). For instance, most consultations can only be performed if expert and client can exchange information, especially when specifying and negotiating a problem, when explaining solutions, and when presenting the justification for a solution. Coaching is, almost by definition, an interactive affair. In such cases, straightforward self report sessions are impossible, because the problem statement and data have to be obtained interactively. This does not preclude taking self report protocols simultaneously (see below: "Mock-up dialogues").

Data from user-expert dialogues are used particularly for analysing the roles (modalities) of the prospective system; for modelling the interactive capabilities of the system (discourse and user models); and for requirements for the man-machine interface (cf. Moran, 1979; Pollack, 1986).

The way to apply this technique should be self-evident, in that the interaction between expert and client is recorded. Types of problems may be varied with the type of client, i.e. the "user-characteristics". Sometimes, the knowledge engineer may play the role of client, dependent on the nature of the domain. Otherwise, the role of the knowledge engineer is even more passive than in a self report session. Sometimes he may not even be present at all, i.e. he only analyses the transcripts.

A particular method in arranging user-expert dialogues is the Mock-up dialogue. This method is also known as the "Wizard of Oz" technique. The expert mimics as much as possible the (functions) of the prospective system. The typical set up for this method of data collection is to have the user and the expert in different rooms, and to have them communicate via terminals. In general, the communication protocol provides machine readable data. There are more, important advantages of this technique. In a normal dialogue it is not possible to have to combine the dialogue with self report of the participants, but the room separation and the writing instead of talking in the mock-up dialogue make such combination quite natural. Therefore, the mock-up technique produces three parallel streams of data: self reports by expert and by user, and the communication protocol (cf Winkels, Sandberg & Breuker, 1987). Another advantage of this technique is that prototypes of (elements) of the user interface can be tried out as well before the actual system has been build.

From the point of view of validity of the data this technique provides the most valid data, because the actual tasks (both problem solving and communication) can be almost identical with those to be performed by the system. The only -small- problem is the fact that this way of communicating may initially appear somewhat strange to participants who normally would engage in a face to face dialogue, and that some typing skill is required. Mock-up dialogues are certainly the most adequate and powerful elicitation technique for constructing expert systems.

9.7. Review

In itself, review is not an interview technique, but a way of assessing the data collected by some other interview technique. Reviews are particularly relevant for repairing gaps in self report protocols (De Groot, 1965). Moreover, transcripts may contain many uninterpretable episodes, which may only be explained adequately, by the expert, afterwards. Reviewing may introduce ad-hoc, after-the-fact justifications, which can be a source of error for psychological modelling. However, for constructing a knowledge based system, such "distorsions" can hardly a source of invalidity, because these explanations and justifications may be required in the prospective system anyway.

It should be noted, that reviewing may occur at all stages in the process of knowledge acquisition. It may be used both for checking on (gaps) in the data, and for assessing interpretations of data. The latter may take the form of discussing for instance the conceptual model (expert analysis) with the expert. Experiences with KADS have shown this to be very effective. In an extreme form, the evaluation of a prototype by the expert can be viewed as a review technique as well.

9.8. Sorting and Rating

Sorting and rating elicitation tasks are often discussed under the header of multi dimensional scaling techniques. Multi dimensional scaling techniques are statistical analysis techniques: sorting and scaling are the elicitation tasks. In fact, for simple sorting tasks no statistical, multi dimensional analysis techniques are required. Sorting tasks consist of grouping a set of objects -e.g. names of concepts written on cards- into subsets. The constraints of grouping may be "syntactic" (e.g. the number of subsets; distribution over sets, etc.), or "semantic" (e.g. cities vs villages, types of vehicles, etc.), or "pragmatic" (e.g. important vs unimportant; typical vs atypical). In rating tasks, the relations between objects are attributed some quantitative value on some attribute. Typically, in rating tasks pairs or triads of objects are presented successively, instead of the full set, because all combinations (or a strategic subset) of objects have to be given a value. Rating tasks require multi dimensional scaling techniques for analysis.

Sorting and scaling can be employed in many ways and for various purposes, but their use for knowledge acquisition is more limited than is suggested by current literature (e.g. Shaw & Gaines, 1987; Boose, 1985, Gammack, 1987). A major limitation of the techniques is that the nature of the elicited relations remains implicit. In addition, multiple views on the structure of domain concepts may contaminate the data obtained by sorting or rating methods. In relatively simple domains -such as simple classification problems- these techniques are effective, in particular because they can be automated to a large extent. In more complex domains sorting and rating are often used in combination with other elicitation techniques, and may play the role of "initial organiser" of (large) sets of objects (e.g. Gammack, 1987).

The sorting of problems along dimensions such as difficulty or typicality, are useful means for determining the scope of human expertise and for defining the scope of the prospective system. Data obtained from such sorting tasks, can be used in determining optimal cases to be used in self report sessions.

A popular technique which combines some of the advantages of sorting and eliminates the disadvantage of too implicit attribution is the repertory grid method, developed by Kelly (1955) to map out personal beliefs (constructs) about "elements". In the practice of knowledge acquisition for expert systems these elements are in general domain concepts. The most effective use of this technique requires that elements are presented in triads. The expert is asked to state a distinction that separates one element from the other two, and to name this distinction. Or he may be asked to name the attribute that makes the other two similar. Often, this is a two valued attribute or dimension (big, small). Then the expert rates the other elements of the set of elements with respect to that dimension on a 5 or 7 point scale. All combinations of triads are presented, so that $(n-1)^3$ combinations have to be evaluated. The matrix (or grid) can be analysed by statistical techniques, such as cluster analysis. The advantage of this procedure is that there is a kind of consistency checking provided in applying "uncovered" attributes to all elements. The focusing on differences between concepts may indeed reveal unattended (rather than "implicit") attributes, but it is highly dependent on the sample of elements which attributes can be uncovered. Because the number of combinations grows combinatorically only a limited number of concepts can be processed in this way.

10. Interpretation of Verbal Data

The data that are elicited using any of the techniques described in the previous section do not provide knowledge in a form which allows direct use in a knowledge base. Data have to be interpreted in order to make them suitable for current knowledge representation techniques. Two stages can be distinguished in this process: *knowledge identification*, where elements in the data are identified as relevant pieces of knowledge, and *knowledge interpretation*, where knowledge elements are structured and are assigned a role in the problem solving process.

Data interpretation can proceed in a data-driven way or in a model-driven way. The data-driven way proceeds through a bottom-up analysis of the data, slowly -and often painfully- finding a structure for the data that can support a problem solving process. The model driven interpretation starts with a generic model of the problem solving process and attempts to find the relevant knowledge elements in the data. In this section we will first describe the data-driven techniques and subsequently discuss top-down data-analysis methods.

10.1. Data-driven Analysis

Data-driven analysis of verbal data usually begins with the construction of a *lexicon* and a *glossary*. Techniques for lexicon and glossary construction are based on simple textual analysis techniques for identification of domain terms. Invariably in a domain of expertise some terminology is used to refer to domain specific concepts. Often, the complexity of a domain can be estimated by the number of domain specific terms. A relatively simple domain contains between 100 and 300 domain specific terms. Complex domains may have more than 2000 domain terms.

Often, domain specific terms may be new interpretations, or combinations of established, general world terms: they have a real 'newspeak' flavour. Among these general world terms there may be terms which occur in a large variety (or a class of) domains, because they are powerful general *abstractions*: examples are: "procedure", "process", "variable", "signal", etc. Many of these abstractions may have a more specific meaning in a particular domain. For instance, the term "variable" has another meaning in statistics than in computer science, although there is a large amount of overlap in meaning. These abstractions play a often pivotal role in constructing hierarchies of domain concepts (see section on Structure of domain concepts). They can be used as high level "organisers" of domain concepts.

Other terms that require special attention are terms which denote *roles* in the problem solving process. They correspond to domain specific meta-classes. In fact, finding meta class terms is rare: our vocabulary to specify roles in thinking and problem solving is rather limited. These role terms should be documented in the analysis, but they will be used in the inference structure as referring to a set of domain terms, rather than as high level concepts in the structures of domain concepts. The difference between roles and abstractions can be very subtle. For instance the term "factor" will in general stand for a role, but there are many examples of domains where it stands for an abstract concept (e.g. in statistics).

Distinguishing domain specific terms from other terms is often quite easy: they are in general unfamiliar to the KE. Assuming that the interviews are transcribed in an electronically readable form, various filtering tools may be used. For instance, domain specific terms may be filtered out by applying matching procedures with vocabularies which contain (frequently occurring) general world terms (e.g. the 'spell' vocabularies as provided in many word processing systems). This kind of filtering is in general rather coarse, but may be viewed as a preprocessing method which should be supplemented by handcrafted selections.

The **glossary** consists of domain terms as entries, but may contain in their 'bodies' all kind of descriptions. These descriptions may range from 'definitions' to references to statements in the data. To a large extent, the 'structures of concepts may imply semi formal, high level definitions of domain terms ("an X is an A, and consists of Y and Z" is a very powerful standard format for describing terms, as can be verified in encyclopedia). Definitions of terms can often be found in written documentation rather than in elicited data. The glossary has a documentation (communication) function but may also be used to identify 'local' bits and pieces of the structures of concepts (and vice versa; structures of concepts may shape or reshape definitions).

An important data-driven analysis activity is concerned with structuring the domain specific concepts. Structures are build using general relations such as ISA or CONSISTS-OF. Such structures of domain concepts reflect the static structure of the domain knowledge. Structuring the domain concepts is often guided by general world concepts which are used as top nodes in the concept tree. Examples are physical object, action, process, state etc. It is unlikely that in a domain of any complexity a single major structure will cover all of the domain concepts. Multiple, and partial hierarchies will be the rule. Hierarchies in which a number of the same concepts reappear are quite normal. Multiple occurrence reflects the fact that there are multiple views in the domain (as formalised in multiple inheritance). As a heuristic for building concept hierarchies we advise to build -initially- small hierarchies of concepts, which may be extendable by combining these with other hierarchies.

Verbal data often contain simple facts, rules or formulae. Although identification of such knowledge elements is usually not difficult, their administration is tedious and bound to cause confusion if no interpretative framework is available. Special purpose editors (Anjewierden, 1987) can provide some help in indexing these knowledge elements, but using a model of the reasoning process as a guide for indexing the domain knowledge is a better solution.

A similar advise can be given with respect to bottom-up analysis of self-report protocols. It is possible to encode statements in a protocol as a manifestation of a certain type of inference, e.g. abstraction. It is very difficult, however, to assign such inference steps their appropriate place in the reasoning process. A consequence of this approach may be a long and painful debugging process of the knowledge base.

10.2. Model-driven Analysis

Verbal data do not speak for themselves. Hence, the bottom-up interpretation of verbal data is often very difficult. In cognitive psychology it is good practice to construct a tentative model of a reasoning process -e.g. on the basis of rational task analysis- before analysis of self report protocols is attempted. Such an initial model acts as a template to compare the protocol with. Differences between model and data indicate how the model should be changed. In knowledge acquisition models can be used as a framework for the elicitation and interpretation of data. A model of the domain, for instance, can guide the elicitation of concepts and structures, by providing super or meta concepts of the relevant domain concepts. Knowledge acquisition tools like OPAL (Shortliffe, 1987) are based on such strong domain models. The model provides domain categories such as therapy to be applied to a patient and related attributes. The expert fills in the domain specific therapies and attributes.

In KADS generic models of reasoning processes are used as a guide for elicitation and interpretation of verbal data. Such *interpretation models* consist of the inference, task and strategic layer applicable to a class of tasks such as diagnosis or design. A library of such models has been developed (Breuker et al., 1987), which allows the knowledge engineer a choice of models to select from. Practice shows that these models -even though they are rarely used without modification- greatly help the knowledge acquisition process. The categories of concepts and inferences that an interpretation model provides make the space of possible interpretations of verbal data manageable.

Generic tasks such as "pure" diagnosis occur seldom in real life situations. More often than not the knowledge engineer has to combine several generic reasoning models into a model of the task at hand. For instance an accountant judging the viability of a company may construct a model of the company (a synthesis task), perform assessments of certain aspects of the company and may diagnose reasons for certain problems.

11. Final Remarks and Conclusions

The methods and techniques for knowledge acquisition described in this paper have been used in a number of KBS development projects, including a statistical advisor project, a network monitoring project and equipment design projects. In general these projects have shown that the KADS approach is a viable framework for KBS development, even though different ways of operationalising the methodology may exist. In KBS projects and AI research in general, ideas are emerging that are similar to KADS. For instance the use of strong models of the reasoning process as a basis for knowledge acquisition is the basic idea behind knowledge acquisition tools like OPAL (Shortliffe, 1987) and MOLE. The use of models and languages at the knowledge level is gaining ground in the KBS community. For example recent work of Chandrasekaran and others (1987) proposes to use generic models for problem solving tasks as a framework for knowledge acquisition and as building blocks for actual systems. The difference with the KADS interpretation models is that the latter only model the problem solving behaviour, but are not concerned with the actual AI methods used to realise that behaviour.

The techniques for knowledge elicitation that we have described in section 9 are well established in the social sciences. Recent work by Burton and Shadbolt (1987) provides new insights in the efficiency and applicability of these techniques. More experimental work, however, is needed to give knowledge engineers clear guidelines how to proceed in the data collection process.

An important development -we think- is the development of libraries of generic models of problem solving behaviour and of computational methods to realise such behaviours. Even though these libraries are subject to criticism of all sorts, they appear to provide -even inexperienced- knowledge engineers with sufficient support to perform the knowledge acquisition process efficiently.

Finally, we conclude that the current insights in the knowledge acquisition process allow us to start developing powerful tools for knowledge acquisition that will enable both the domain expert, the knowledge engineer and possibly the end-user of the KBS to create, access, modify and enhance the knowledge base.

Acknowledgement

Guus Schreiber, Massoud Davoodi, Paul de Greef, Simon Hayward, Robert de Hoog, Maarten van Someren, Anjo Anjewierden and Jan Wielemaker contributed to the research reported here. Many other co-workers of Esprit Project 1098 participated in discussions, applications and validations of the ideas presented here.

This research was supported in part by the ESPRIT programme of the Commission of the European Communities, as Project 1098. The partners in this project are STC plc, Scicon Limited, SCS GmbH, Cap Sogeti Innovation S.A., University of Amsterdam and the Knowledge Based Systems Centre of the Polytechnic of the South Bank.

12. References

Anjewierden, A., (1987), *Knowledge acquisition tools*, AI-Communications, 0, p.29-39.

Barthelemy S., Edin G., Toutain T., Becker S., (1987), *Requirements Analysis in KBS Development*, Cap Sogeti Innovation, Esprit Project P1098, Deliverable D3.

Bobrow D.G. (ed.), (1984), *Qualitative Reasoning about Physical Systems*, Elseviers Science Publishers B.V., Amsterdam.

Brachman R.J., (1979), On the Epistemological status of semantic networks, In: *Associative Networks*, N.V. Findler ed., p. 5. Academic Press, New York.

Brachman R.J., Schmolze J.G., (1984), An overview of the KL-ONE knowledge representation system, *Cognitive Science*, 9, p. 171-216.

Bredeweg B, & Schreiber G., & Wielinga B.J., (1988), *Towards a framework for KBS Design*, University of Amsterdam, Amsterdam.

Breuker, J.A. and Wielinga, B.J. (1983) *Analysis techniques for knowledge based systems*, Report 1.2, University of Amsterdam.

Breuker, J.A. and Wielinga, B.J. (1984) *Techniques for knowledge elicitation and analysis*, Report 1.5, University of Amsterdam.

Breuker J. (ed.), Wielinga B., van Someren M., de Hoog R., Schreiber G., Bredeweg B., Wielemaker J., Billeault J-P., Davoodi M., Hayward S., (1987), *Model Driven Knowledge Acquisition - Interpretation Models*, University of Amsterdam, Esprit Project P1098, Deliverable D1.

Breuker, J.A. & Wielinga, B.J. (1987), *Use of models in the interpretation of verbal data*, In: Knowledge elicitation for expert systems: a practical handbook, A. Kidd, (ed.), Plenum Press, New York.

Buchanan B.G., Shortliffe E. H., (1984), *Rule-based expert systems*, Addison-Wesley Publishing Company, Reading Massachusetts.

Bundy A. (ed.), (1985), *A Catalogue of AI techniques*, Springer-Verlag, New York.

Burton, A.M., & Shadbolt, N.R., & Hedgecock, A.P., & Rugg, G., (1987), *A formal evaluation of knowledge elicitation techniques for expert systems: Domain 1*, Proceedings of the workshop: knowledge acquisition for knowledge-based systems, Reading University, UK.

Chandrasekaran B., (1987), *Towards a functional architecture for intelligence based on generic information processing tasks*, Proceedings of IJCAI-87, Milano Italy, p1183-1192.

Clancey, W. J. (1985), *Heuristic classification*, Artificial Intelligence, 27, p215-251.

Ericsson, K. A., and Simon, H. A., (1980), *Verbal reports as data*, Psychological Review, 87, p215-251.

Greef, P. de, & Breuker, J., & Schrieber, G., & Wielemaker., (1988), *StatCons: knowledge acquisition in a complex domain*, Proceedings of the ECAI-88, Munich, Germany, (forthcoming).

Hayes-Roth, F. & Waterman, D.A. & Lenat, B.D. (eds), (1983), *Building expert systems*, Reading, MA: Addison-Wesley.

Hayward S.A., (1987), *The KADS Methodology: Analysis and Design for Knowledge Based Systems*, STC, Esprit Project P1098, Synthesis Report Y1.

Hayward S.A., (1987), *How to build knowledge systems; techniques, tools, and case studies*, Proceedings of 4th annual Esprit conference, p665-687, North-Holland, Amsterdam.

Hayward, S.A., & Wielinga, B.J., & Breuker, J.A., (1987), *Structured analysis of knowledge*, Int. J. Man Machine studies, 26, p487-498.

Hawkins, D., (1983), *An analysis of expert thinking*, Man-Machine Studies, 18, p1-47.

Keravnou, E.T., & Johnson, L., (1986), *Component expert systems: A case study in fault diagnosis*, Kogan Page Ltd, London.

Laird, J.E. & Newell, A. & Rosenbloom, P.S., (1987), *SOAR: An architecture for general intelligence*, Artificial Intelligence, 33, p1.

McDermott, D., (1980), *R1: An expert in the computer systems*, Proceedings of the AAAI-80, p269-271.

Miller, P.L. (1984), A critiquing approach to expert computer advice: ATTENDING, *Boston: Pitman.*

Moran, T.P., (1981), The command language grammer: a representation for the user interface of interactive computer systems, Int. J. Man Machine Studies, 15, p3-50.

Musen, M.A., & Fagan, L.M., & Combs, D.M., & Shortliffe, E.H., (1986), *Using a domain model to drive an interactive knowledge editing tool*, Proceedings of the knowledge acquisition for knowledge-based systems workshop, p33-0, Banff, Canada.

Newell, A., (1982), *The knowledge level*, Artificial Intelligence, 18, p87.

Newell, A., & Simon, H.A., (1972), *Human problem solving*, Prentice-Hall, Englewood Cliffs.

Pollack, M., & Hirschberg, J., Weber, B., (1982), *User participation in the reasoning processes of expert systems*, Proceedings of the AAAI-82, Pittsburgh, p358-361.

Rauch-Hindin, W.B., (1986), *Artificial intelligence for business, science, and industry, vol 1-fundamentals*, Prentice-Hall.

Rich E., (1983), *Artificial Intelligence*, McGraw-Hill, Singapore, London.

Schreiber G., & Bredeweg B., & Davoodi M., & Wielinga B., (1988), *Towards a design methodology for KBS*, Deliverable task B2, Esprit Project P1098, University of Amsterdam, Amsterdam.

Shortliffe E.H., (1979), *Computer-based medical consultations: Mycin*, American-Elsevier, New York.

Sleeman, D., & Brown, J.S., (1982), *Intelligent tutoring systems*, New York, Academic press.

Steels L., (1987), *The Deepening of Expert Systems*, AI-Communications, 0, p9-16.

Wielinga B., Breuker J., (1986), *Models of Expertise*, In: Proc. ECAI, Brighton, UK, p306-318.

Young R.M., (1987), *Role of intermediate representations in knowledge elicitation*, Proceedings of the Expert Systems '87 (BCS), Brighton, UK.

Yourdon E., Constantine L., (1978), *Structured Design: A discipline of Computer Program and System Design*, Yourdon Press.

Fundamental Mechanisms in Machine Learning and Inductive Inference: Part 2

Alan W. Biermann
Department of Computer Science
Duke University
Durham, NC 27706

1. Introduction

A system is said to *learn* if

(1) it has one level of performance quality at a particular time,

(2) it undergoes a subsequent interaction with its environment or its own cognitive mechanisms, and

(3) it self modifies as a result of the interaction to achieve improved quality of performance.

Learning mechanisms can be divided into two categories, those which operate by *rote* memorization and those which use *inductive inference*. A rote memory system simply stores facts about its target behavior and operates by referencing those facts directly. An inductive system summarizes the observed facts in some way and operates by utilizing a more compact representation of its experience. This paper will be concerned primarily with the later type of system.

An inductive system observes examples that represent a given class of objects or behaviors and possibly examples known to be outside the class, and it constructs a general rule to characterize that class. Inductive inference produces a best guess of the defining rule for the unknown class; however, it is quite typical that its best guess is not logically justifiable even though it may be pragmatically necessary. Thus, for example, animals in nature learn, on the basis of relatively few examples, to seek the necessities of life and avoid the pitfalls, even though there may be no formal proof of the correctness of their actions. Induction has been studied in the literature under many names including "generalization", "concept formation", "categorization", "theory formation", and others.

The literature on learning is both extensive and diverse so that attempts to comprehend the field completely may be frustrated. The approach of the current paper is to propose a single model which can be used to comprehend most learning systems and to study them with respect to this model. While it may be necessary to bend or modify its parts occasionally in order to match some example learning machines, the model still provides a good foundational point from which to begin the study.

The general model for learning is shown in Figure 1 where the two major portions represent nature (in the upper half) and the learning machine (in the lower half). The learning machine has the ability to receive inputs and to yield outputs and its learning task is to discover which outputs are appropriate under every possible input condition. That is, the learning machine is supposed to discover a function that represents "correct" behavior. The learning

---

Supported in part by the U.S. Army Research Office under grant DAAG-29-84-K-0072.

problem is thus posed in terms of the current machine's function, the target function to be learned, the class of learnable functions, and the class of possible target functions.

Specifically, beginning at the top of Figure 1, it is assumed that there is a known class of functions C_t from which the target function will be chosen. This class represents the fact that, while the target function is not necessarily known, much may be known about its properties. For example, it may be known in a given situation, that the laws of Newtonian mechanics will hold and that C_t need only contain those target behaviors that are compatible with this solution. All known information about the target class is embedded in C_t.

What is unknown about the target behavior is represented by the assumption that nature selects a member of C_t called the target function f_t. This function f_t is unknown to the learning machine and the fragmentary information that the environment provides will be the only information available about it. The learning environment will, however, provide samples of f_t's input-output behaviors (positive information) and it may also include samples known to be outside of f_t's behavior (negative information). The presentation of these examples is represented in Figure 1 by the downward forked arrows below f_t.

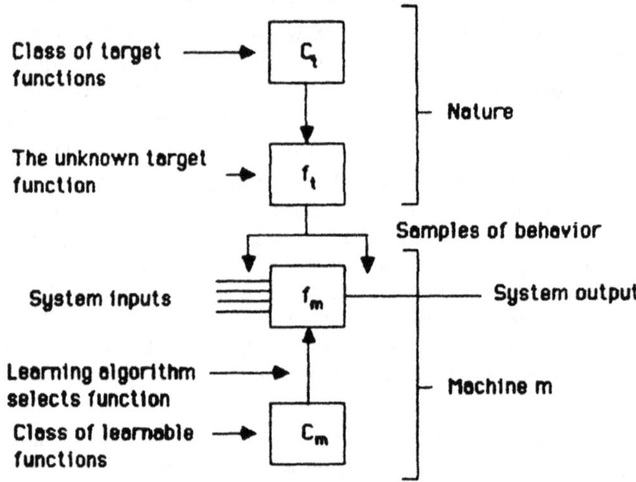

Figure 1: A model of learning systems.

The learning machine, on the other hand, is capable of learning only a limited class of behaviors. Thus C_m represents the set of all possible functions that the machine may be capable of learning. The learning machine will have a learning algorithm that effectively selects one of the members of C_m and uses that as its operating hypothesis for correct action. This algorithm will use the available information about f_t to select f_m and its goal is to make these two match on as many inputs as possible. The learning procedure may be able to construct its hypothesis f_m from the known behaviors in an efficient way or it may have to enumeratively search through C_m to find a hypothesis.

While many learning machines may take the form described here, their details serve to differentiate them in some dramatic ways. We will examine five dimensions for measuring such systems and build a topological decomposition of the field based on them. The dimensions measure

(1) whether the learning is parametric or structural,

(2) the nature of the information presentation for the algorithm,

(3) the dependence on a teacher or lack thereof,

(4) the execution time of the algorithm, and

(5) whether the algorithm solves a known and well specified class of problems.

Concerning the first dimension, the learning algorithm might select f_m by setting parameters or it could include a structure building mechanism for constructing f_m. In the former case, there will be a set of constants, c_i, that affect the machine behavior, and learning is done by finding the best values for these c_i's. The perceptron is an example of such a machine as described in the next section. In the later case, the algorithm creates f_m by building a structural entity such as a program, a network, or a grammar.

Learning systems may also differ on the presentation of the information they receive about the target. The types of presentation will be classified as *data, input-output,* and *trace*. A *data* presentation is the weakest form of information in that only the inputs to f_t are known without any samples of its output. This is the so called "clustering problem" in which a function is sought that identifies natural partitions in sets of data. For example, one could ask a machine to discover a "reasonable" classification for the data

AABAAAAB
ABAAAA
BBBBBBBA
AAAAA
ABBBBBBBAB
BB
AAAAAABA

and expect the machine to create f_m which yields one value, say 1, on the first, second, fourth, and last examples, and another value, say 2, on the others. Thus the machine would be said to have "learned the concepts" of mostly A's and mostly B's so that it differentiates between them. The second form of presentation, *input-output,* includes examples of the input-output behavior with the proper markings as to whether they are positive or negative.
Thus the samples

input	output	classification
AABAAAAB	2	+
ABAAAA	1	+
BBBBBBBA	3	-

might be given to represent an f_t that counts the number of B's. An even stronger form of presentation is designated as *trace* information. It provides the learning algorithm with information telling how the output is found from the input. In the case of counting B's, a computation trace could be given as follows.

C = 0
read A
C = 0
read B
C = 1
read A
C = 1
read A
C = 1
read B
C = 2

Such strong information makes it possible to build much more efficient learning algorithms than would be otherwise possible.

The third dimension for measuring systems concerns the care with which the examples must be selected for presentation to the learning algorithm. There may be a teacher who chooses exactly the needed cases to illustrate the target f_t or the examples may be selected randomly. Clearly, the former case leads to faster learning and models some practical situations. The later case is more general but also more demanding for the machine.

The fourth dimension concerns the execution time required to learn, low or high order polynomial or exponential. Some methodologies, by attacking rather narrow classes, achieve extremely fast learning while others may solve a harder problem and require proportionally more resources.

The last dimension simply specifies whether or not the learnable class C_m is well specified or not. If heuristic programming is used to create the machine, the class of learnable behaviors may be only vaguely describable. But if the principles of operation for the machine are well understood, it may be possible to precisely characterize the set C_m.

Figure 2 shows a decomposition of the field of learning and inference using these five dimensions. A number of learning machines from the literature are shown in the approximate positions where they belong. In some cases, their exact location may not be clear because specific properties may not be known. For example, it may not be clear whether a particular methodology will run in polynomial or exponential time. It may be arguable whether a particular type of presentation should be classified as input-output or trace since information which is syntactically input-output may contain considerable trace information. It may also be arguable whether the presentation contains an implicit teacher. Thus while the precise placements on the chart should not be taken too seriously, its general form does provide an organization for the field.

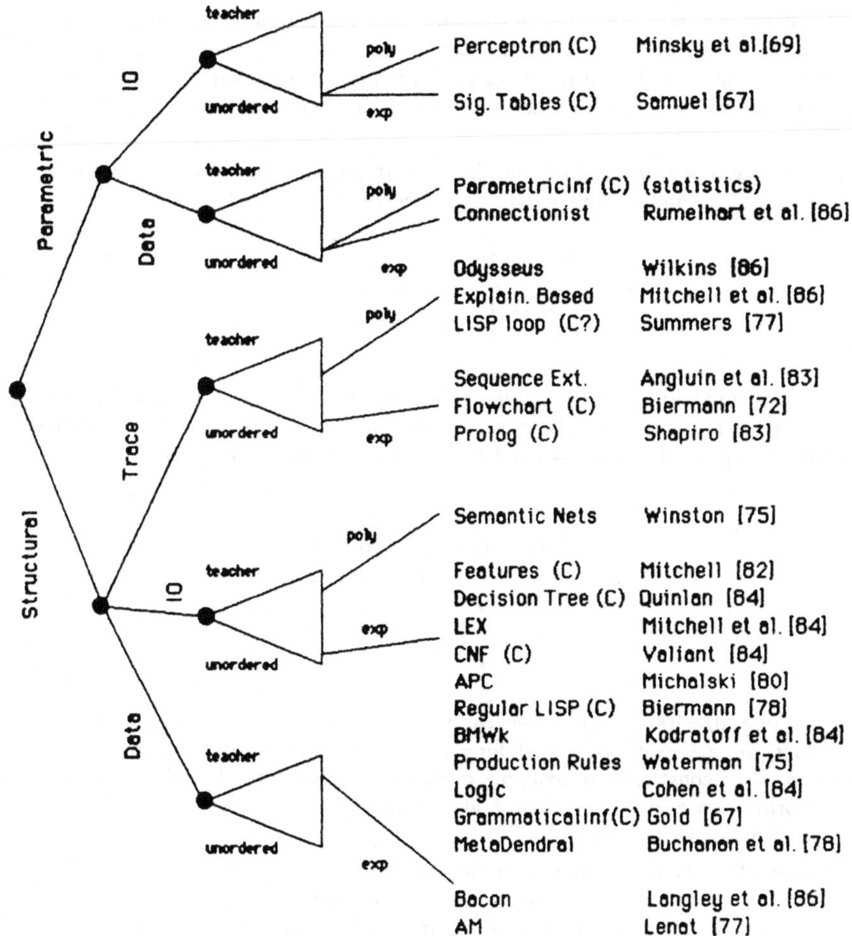

Figure 2. Organizing the learning literature. A system is marked C if its learnable class can be characterized mathematically.

A proper overview needs to include a discussion of a representative subset of the systems given in Figure 2 or other systems, their design, their capabilities, and their relationships to each other. This coverage was given in Part I of this paper (Biermann [85]) or the reader might wish to examine other surveys such as Carbonell et al. [84], Michalski [86], or the articles in the *Encyclopedia of Artificial Intelligence* (Shapiro [87]) on concept learning, inductive inference, and learning. This paper will consider general properties of some learning machines from the point of view of our model and will briefly examine some connectionist machines.

2. The Learning Machine as a Set of Learnable Behaviors

The set C_m of learnable behaviors specifies the capabilities of a learning machine so an understanding of its properties leads to an understanding of the complete machine. One should ask what is the nature of C_m, how large is it, how are its members spread across the space of all possible behaviors, and how does it compare with the learnable classes for other machines. This section will consider these properties for the case of the perceptron (Minsky and Papert [69]) in order to illustrate the nature of the such a study. Then it will make some general observations about the size of learnable classes, the errors machines will make, and the time required to learn.

The perceptron will be defined, for the current purpose, to be a machine with p binary inputs $x_1, x_2, \ldots, x_p$ and a single binary output y where

$$y = \begin{cases} 1 & \text{if } \sum_{i=1}^{p} c_i x_i > c_0 \\ 0 & otherwise \end{cases}$$

and the c_i's are constants set by the learning algorithm. Learning is done by examining target input-output pairs and adjusting the c_i's until the machine behaviors match as well as possible the observed examples. Thus if $p=4$ and the following examples are given,

x_1	x_2	x_3	x_4	y
1	0	1	0	1
0	1	0	0	0
0	0	0	1	1
1	1	0	0	1
0	1	1	0	0

then the learning algorithm might select the values $c_0=0$ and $(c_1,c_2,c_3,c_4)=(2,-1,0,1)$. These values, in fact, are satisfactory for matching the target behavior, and if they are discovered by an algorithm, they constitute an example of successful learning. The details of some specific learning algorithms are given by Minsky and Papert [69], and Part I (Biermann [85]) of this paper. They will not be repeated here.

The issue of concern here is the characterization of the complete function that has been learned. That is, given the c_i's specified, what is the complete function computed by the perception? Let us compute y for every possible input and examine the function.

x_1	x_2	x_3	x_4	y
0	0	0	0	0
0	0	0	1	1
0	0	1	0	0
0	0	1	1	1
0	1	0	0	0
0	1	0	1	0
0	1	1	0	0
0	1	1	1	0
1	0	0	0	1
1	0	0	1	1
1	0	1	0	1

1	0	1	1	1
1	1	0	0	1
1	1	0	1	1
1	1	1	0	1
1	1	1	1	1

The column below y is a complete specification of the learned behavior; it gives the learned function and here it will be called a *learnable vector*.

So, for perceptrons, the set C_m is the set of learnable vectors, and a study of C_m is a study of a set of such vectors. Specifically, what is the nature of these vectors, how many of them are there, how are they scattered in the set of all possible vectors of length 16, and how are they related to other sets of learnable vectors.

Graphically, one can think of the learnable vectors as a set of points scattered across the space of all possible vectors as shown in Figure 3. Suppose the target function f_t is some vector as shown. The task of the learning algorithm is to select the learnable vector f_m that is closest to f_t. Ideally f_t would be in C_m and f_m could be chosen to be identical to f_t. Otherwise f_m can be chosen to minimize the Hamming distance between the associated vectors. Then f_m would be identical to f_t on all but, say, e entries.

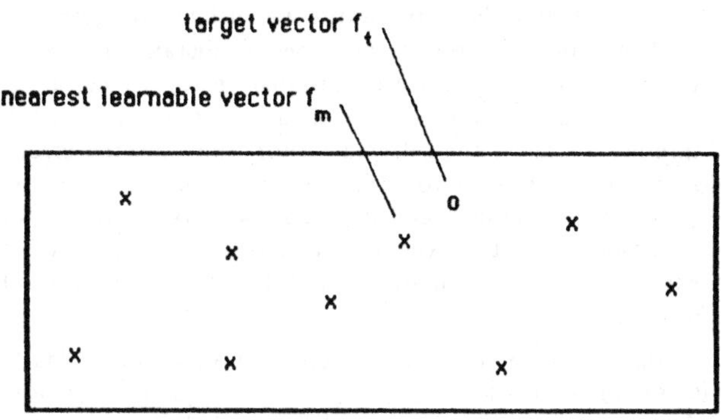

Figure 3. The set of learnable vectors (indicated with x's) spread across the space of all possible vectors. The learning algorithm attempts to select the learnable vector that is nearest the target o.

One can then ask, what is the nature of the set of learnable vectors for the perceptron. This has been partially answered by scholars of these systems such as Muroga [71]. For example, one can define the set of *completely monotone* functions and then prove that every perceptron learnable function is completely monotone. It has also been shown that every completely monotone function with $p \leq 8$ is learnable. This means that if C_t is made up of completely monotone functions, the learning machine will have a good chance of learning f_t. It will certainly acquire f_t if $p \leq 8$ and if its learning algorithm converges properly.

But how many learnable functions are there for the perceptron? This question has also been answered in Muroga [71] for $p \leq 8$. The answers are given here along with a computation of the total number of functions.

Number of inputs p	Number of learnable vectors L	Total number of such vectors
1	4	4
2	14	16
3	104	256
4	1882	65536
5	94572	4,294,967,296
6	15,028,134	1.844×10^{19}
7	8,378,070,864	3.403×10^{38}
8	17,561,539,552,946	1.1158×10^{77}

From this information, we can infer that the total number of learnable functions is rather small compared to the total number of functions. If one chooses randomly from the set of all possible vectors, the probability that the machine can learn it will be small. This is especially true if p is large.

One also wonders whether the learnable vectors are evenly spaced throughout the class of all possible vectors; or are they clustered? Biermann et al. [86] have shown that for the perceptron they are moderately clustered. This can be discovered by examining the *expected error* for the learning machine. The expected error is the expected distance (in the probabilistic sense) from a randomly selected vector to its nearest learnable vector. That is, if many vectors are selected from the space of all possible vectors, and if in each case, the machine chooses the vector nearest (using Hamming distance) the selected vector, the expected error is the average distance from the randomly selected vectors to their individual nearest learnable vectors. The perceptron, for the case $p = 4$, was examined and it was shown that if the vectors were evenly distributed to achieve minimum error, the expected error would be about 1.8 bits. However, for the perceptron, the expected error is actually about 2.1 bits indicating a substantial variation from a perfectly uniform distribution.

Thus for any learning machine that receives binary inputs and yields binary outputs, the characterization of its set of learnable vectors C_m leads to an understanding of its behavior. The most important feature of C_m is its size L and Figure 4 shows the relationships between L and the expected error and the number of examples required to learn. Suppose L is very large; then the space of all possible vectors will be nearly filled and a randomly selected vector will always be near a learnable vector. But the amount of information required to learn will be large since there are so many vectors to choose from. This corresponds to a point at the right side of Figure 4. The extreme case would be the machine that can learn every function but would then need to observe every possible input to acquire its associated output.

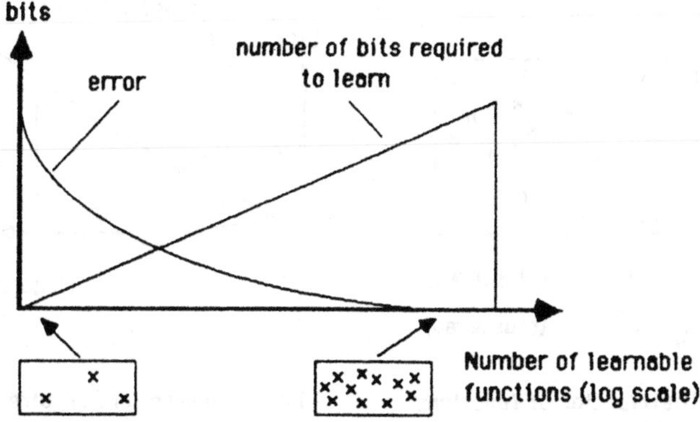

Figure 4. The tradeoff between error and information required to learn.

On the other end of the spectrum, the learning machine may have a small L and thus a larger expected error. In this case, learning will require few examples. The table above indicates that the perceptron is nearer the left end of this spectrum as are many other well known learning machines (see Biermann et al. [86]).

Once the ideas are clear, the effect of clustering can be understood as shown in Figure 5. Suppose the learnable vectors are clustered as indicated by the x's but the set of target vectors are not as indicated by the 0's. Then the number of examples required to learn will be the same as before, but the expected error will be higher. Randomly selected 0's from the set C_t will, on the average, be farther from their nearest x-labelled neighbors.

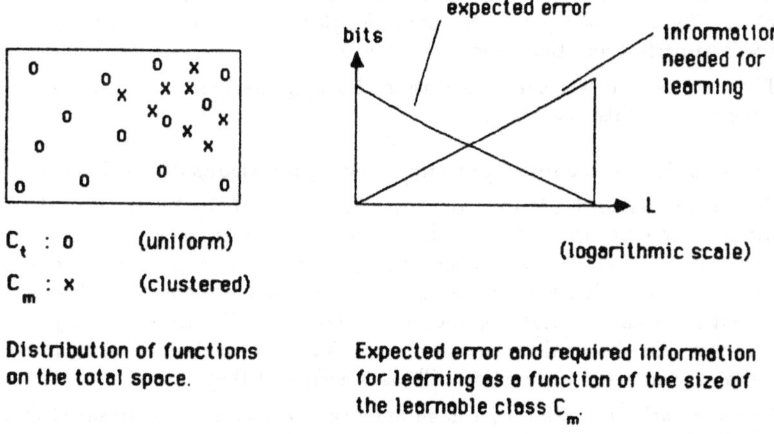

Figure 5. Learning performance where the target class is uniformly distributed and the learnable class is clustered.

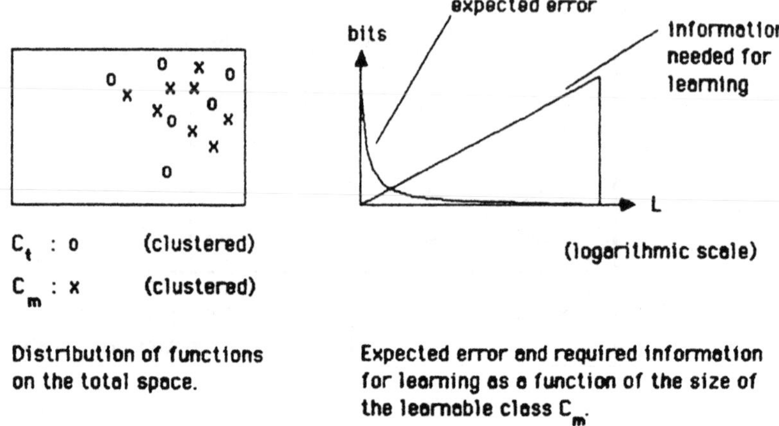

Figure 6. Learning performance where the target class and the learnable class are similarly clustered.

However, it may be that the target class C_t is itself clustered as shown in Figure 6. Then the best learning machine is the one with its class C_m clustered similarly with C_t. Then a machine with relatively small L will have both a fast learning time and a low expected error. This corresponds to what is called *impedance matching* in electrical engineering. The maximum power is transmitted to a loud speaker if its internal impedance matches the internal impedance of the driving amplifier. In learning theory we have the general law: *The expected error is minimized for any L, if the target and learnable classes are maximally matched.* This provides a standard for learning machine design that leads to the best possible achievable performance.

Returning to the example of the perceptron, suppose an application is found in which the completely monotone restriction is known to hold. Then the perceptron will provide an excellent solution because its capabilities closely match the target class. In fact, if $p \leq 8$, then the match will be perfect and the expected error will be zero.

The next section will survey a class of learning machines not discussed in Part I of this paper, the connectionist machines.

3. Connectionism and some Contemporary Applications of the Perceptron Model

Perceptrons suffered a loss of popularity at the end of the 1960's when the severity of their limitations became apparent. The counting arguments given above showed that they covered a relatively tiny fraction of the function space and the noncomputability arguments of Minsky and Papert [69] specifically enumerated classes of computations that they are unable to do. More recent research (Hopfield [86], McClelland et al. [86], Rumelhart et al. [86], Sejnowski et al. [86]), however, has shown that perceptrons can have extremely interesting properties when collected into networks and this section will discuss some of them.

One approach proposes that a large number of perceptrons be arranged in a grid as shown in Figure 7. In this case, each perceptron receives the output from every other member of the grid, and it sends its own output back to every other member of the grid.

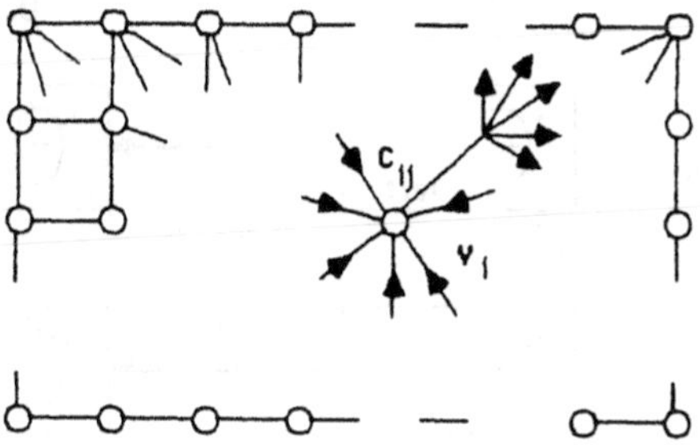

$$v_i = \begin{cases} 1 \text{ if } \sum_j c_{ij} v_j > c_{i0} \\ 0 \text{ otherwise} \end{cases}$$

Figure 7. An array of perceptrons.

This tightly bound and completely connected network has some surprising properties as will be explained here.

The target properties for the connectionist approach are illustrated in Figure 8. We assume in these discussions that visual patterns are to be processed although the approach is quite general and can be applied to any kind of signal processing. The first desired behavior is that of *rote learning.* We would like to be able to present an image to the grid of perceptrons and have that image stored. That is, suppose the individual perceptrons represent pixels on the grid and that black and white pixels are coded, respectively, as 1's and 0's on the perceptron outputs. Then the imposition on the grid of a pattern should be able to invoke learning such that the pattern will remain even after the input has been removed. The second target behavior is that of *content addressability.* If an image is stored in the memory, it should be possible to input the image to the grid and retrieve both the image and its associated information. If the image is presented in an incomplete form, the grid should be able to *automatically complete* the pattern, a third target property of the grid. If the grid is used to memorize several related patterns, it should have the property that it can *generalize* on the set to recognize common properties of the related patterns. Also, given an example from the pattern class, the grid should be able to use general properties to do *default assignment* of pattern details where a part of the pattern may not be complete. Finally, it is desired that the system capabilities should be distributed throughout the grid such that destruction of a portion of the grid would involve only *graceful degradation* of the total performance. It is desired that all of these behaviors be achieved by a distributed processing system in which local behavior involves only the most simple mechanism, in our case the perceptron, and yet global behavior achieves the above goals.

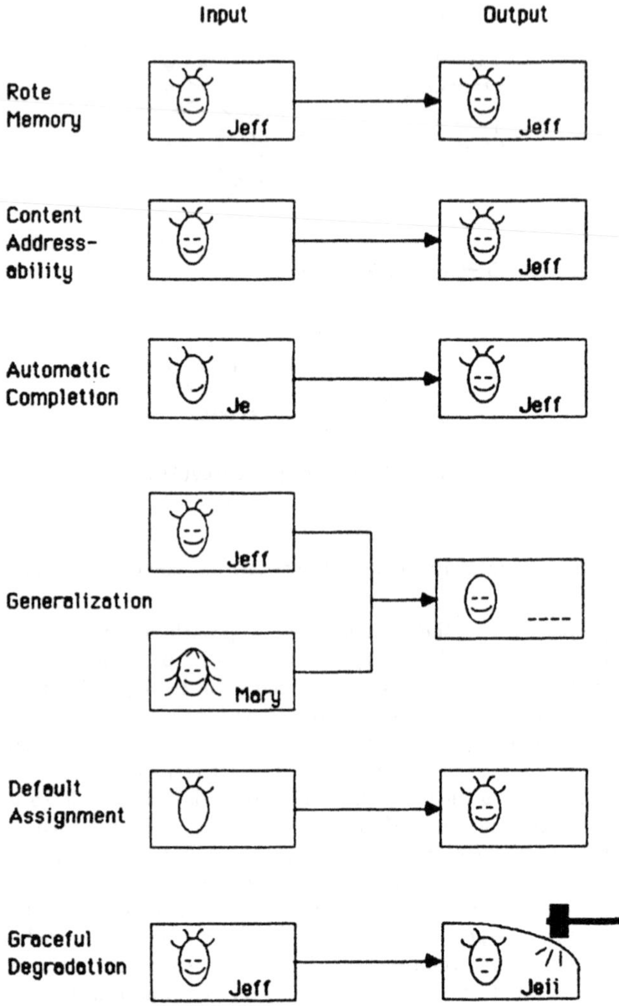

Figure 8. Desired properties for a connectionist system.

The learning machine has two modes of operation: *learning mode* and *normal processing*. In learning mode, the contants c_{ij} are being modified in the grid to achieve some new capability. Two learning methodologies will be described in later paragraphs. In normal operation, the contants c_{ij} are fixed and a computation proceeds as follows: Normal Processing

1. The external world imposes a signal on some part of the grid. Thus the output of certain units are fixed either at 0 or 1 without regard to their inputs.

2. The rest of the units have their outputs updated according to the perceptron rule.

$$v_i = \begin{cases} 1 & \text{if } \sum_{i \neq j} c_{ij} v_j > c_{i0} \\ 0 & otherwise \end{cases}$$

Given the new outputs for all units, they are repeatedly updated again and again until stability is achieved.

Of course, such a highly connected network with tight feedback is complex in its behavior. But its operation becomes more understandable if it is thought of in terms of the concept of *total energy*. Consider the cell update rule for individual units.

$$v_i = 1 \ \text{if} \sum_{i \neq j} c_{ij} v_j > c_{i0}$$

That is,

$$v_i = 1 \ \text{if} \sum_{i \neq j} c_{ij} v_j - c_{i0} > 0$$

The quantity $-(\sum_{i \neq j} c_{ij} v_j - c_{0j})$ is considered to be the *energy* of a particular cell if it is in the 1 state. The total energy of all the cells is the summation of the quantity for all cells in the 1 state.

Total energy $= - \sum_i \sum_{i \neq j} c_{ij} v_j v_i + \sum_i c_{i0} v_i$

The normal operation mode for the network thus involves the perceptron update rule at the local level but the minimization of total energy as defined here at the global level.

The concept of total energy is illustrated in Figure 9 where several sequential states (a), (b), (c), and (d) are shown with their respective energy levels. Suppose the designated cell in (a) is to be updated. Then its cell update rule computes whether $\sum_{i \neq j} c_{ij} v_j - c_{i0} > 0$, and if so then its output v_i will be changed to 1 and its contribution to total energy will be $-(\sum_{i \neq j} c_{ij} v_i - c_{i0})$. This will yield state (b) and the associated lower energy. However, in (b) another cell may be updated as shown and may not achieve a threshold to change state and result in no change of total energy (c). But an update of some other cell does achieve lowered energy as shown in (d).

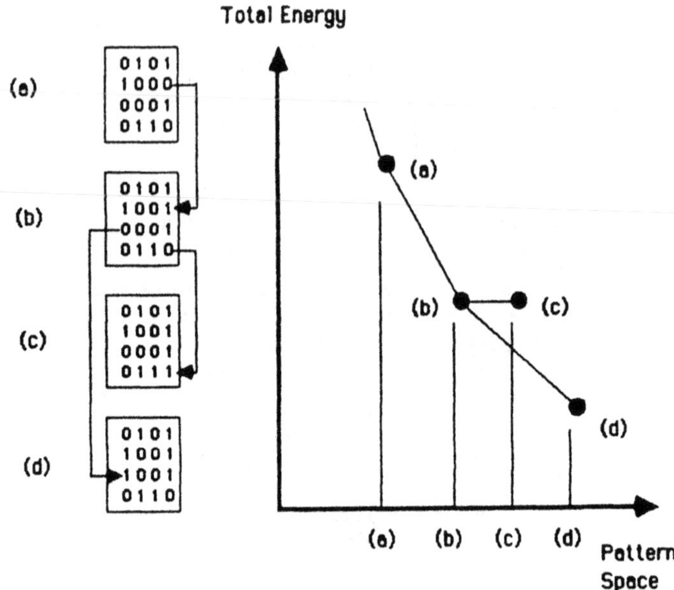

Figure 9. Seeking total energy during normal operation. (b) is preferred over (a) because it has lower energy. (c) is not preferred over (b), but (d) is.

Figure 10 thus shows the global view of total energy and the patterns associated with the energy minima. If the grid has been properly trained to recognize certain patterns, its energy minima will correspond to those patterns. If a new pattern is imposed on the grid that is an approximation to one of the given patterns, the energy minimization process should drive the rest of the grid to deform the new pattern into the shape corresponding to the nearest energy minimum. That is, the imposed pattern will tend to cause the system to move cell output in the direction of one of the memorized patterns. The process yields the various desirable properties described above, content addressability, completion of patterns, and so forth.

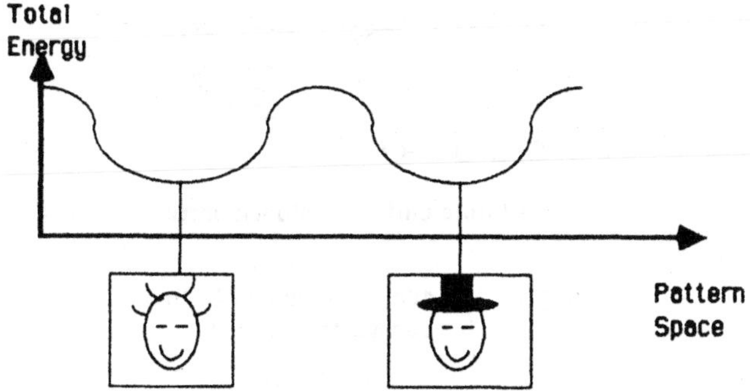

Figure 10. Total energy as function of pattern for a network trained to recognize two images. The minimum energy points correspond to the remembered images.

The above paragraphs show how the grid is to function in normal processing mode once the c_{ij}'s are known. We now turn to the question of the learning mode: How are these constants to be determined? Two learning methodologies will be given, one very simple method described by Hopfield et al. [86] and a more complex method developed by Hinton et al. [86].

The first method (Hopfield et al. [86]) is to simply let

$$c_{ij} = \sum_{q \in S} (2v_i^q - 1)(2v_j^q - 1)$$

where S is the set of patterns to be recognized and $v_i^q = 1$ if cell i in pattern q is black and $v_i^q = 0$ otherwise. Since the quantity $(2v_i^q - 1)(2v_j^q - 1)$ is 1 if cells i and j agree in q and -1 otherwise, c_{ij} simply counts how many times i and j agree less how many times they disagree on the patterns in the set S. This solution can be shown to work satisfactorily on some simple problems. But other strategies are needed on more realistic sized problems as will be described next.

Suppose, for example, there are so called *hidden units* in the grid as shown in Figure 11. These units do not receive inputs from the outside and their outputs are not visible from outside of the grid. These cells, however, are otherwise identical to the others in the grid, receiving inputs from every member, computing their local outputs, and sending them to every member of the grid. These cells perform the task of computing "intermediate results" which are needed by the computation but are not observable in the patterns to be recognized. Hinton and Sejnowski [86] have studied learning in this case and developed a learning methodology.

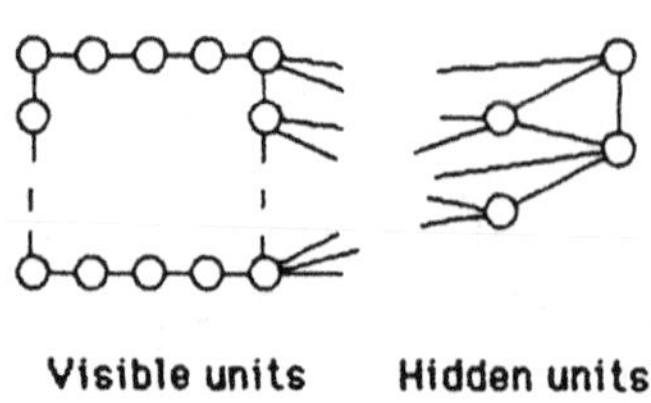

Figure 11. Adding hidden units to a connectionist grid.

The Hinton and Sejnowski strategy compute the c_{ij}'s iteratively using the formula

$$c_{ij}' = c_{ij} + K (p_{ij}^{+} - p_{ij}^{-})$$

where c_{ij}' is the newly computed value for the constant which previously had value c_{ij}, K is a constant (equal to 5 in their experiment), and p_{ij}^{+} and p_{ij}^{-} are values obtained as follows. The visible units of the grid were "clamped" with a pattern to be learned and the invisible units were allowed to stabilize at a minimum energy point using the perceptron update rule given above (in addition to simulated annealing described later). This was done for each pattern in the set S of target patterns to be learned. Then p_{ij}^{+} was computed to be the probability that both $v_i = 1$ and $v_j = 1$ for the set. (Thus if three patterns were to be learned and v_6 and v_8 stabilized at 1 on two of them and $v_6 = 0$, $v_8 = 1$ on the third, then $p_{68}^{+} = 2/3$.) Then the network was allowed to seek a minimum energy level with no units "clamped", that is with no inputs, and the values of the p_{ij}^{-} were again computed to be the probability that both $v_i = 1$ and $v_j = 1$.

This learning strategy follows the theory that if the system has no input and is left to seek minimum energy, it should naturally drift toward a learned pattern as indicated in Figure 10. If the learned patterns tend to have a higher probability p_{ij}^{+} that both $v_i = 1$ and $v_j = 1$ then the probability p_{ij}^{-} for the system running without input, then the constant c_{ij} should be increased by an amount proportional to the difference. That is, the learning algorithm attempts to change the c_{ij}'s in the direction of making the free running probabilities p_{ij}^{-} match the probabilities p_{ij}^{+} imposed by the target patterns.

An important part of the Hinton et al. methodology includes a sophisticated hill climbing strategy for finding energy minima. This methodology is designed to lift the system out of shallow local minimum positions which may falsely trap a system as shown in Figure 12. It is called *simulated annealing*.

Suppose that one randomly selects a pattern on the horizontal axis in Figure 12 and wishes the system to seek an energy minimum and find the learned pattern. However, because of the pecularities of the particular learned c_{ij}'s, suppose that a local minimum also exists as shown that has no associated meaning. Then the chance that the energy minimization will find the false minimum is quite high and the total system performance may be far from optimum. A mechanism is needed that will lift the search away from a false minimum and allow it to find the lowest available minimum.

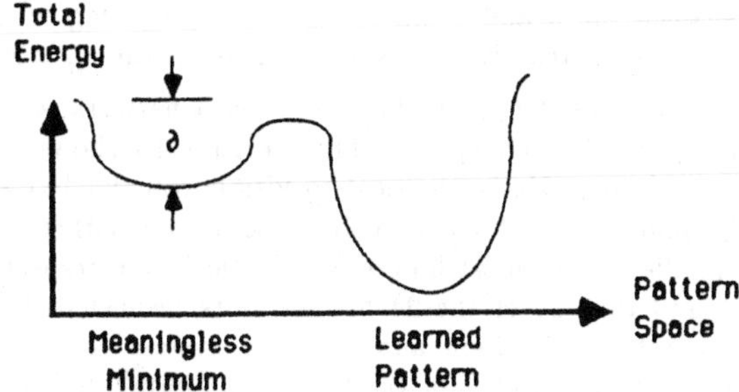

Figure 12. **Simulated annealing lifts the system out of its current minimum by ∂ units with the goal of finding a deeper minimum.**

The strategy for breaking away from a false minimum is to jump, occasionally during the minimization process, from the currently best known minimum to a randomly selected nearby pattern that has δ more energy than the current best. Then if one has found the false minimum of Figure 12, there is a reasonable probability that the continued search for a minimum will find the deeper minimum, the memorized pattern. If δ is large enough, it can lift the system over the barrier between the local and global valleys, and allow the search to settle into the lowest position. Lifting δ above the false minimum does not guarantee the discovery of the better solution and it may often fall back into the same local valley. But when it does achieve the better result, it will keep it. Additional δ leaps will not return the system to the previous false minimum.

But what value of δ should be used? If δ is too large, the search will be continuously kicked out of every minimum and may be returned to local valleys as often as it is to deeper ones. If δ is too small, the system will remain in whatever local low point it finds and the δ perturbations will not affect the quality of the result. The answer given by the simulated annealing method is to set δ at some obviously large value and then reduce it slowly to a value of zero. The early values of δ will be so large as to kick the search randomly all over the space regardless of where the minimum values are. But as δ is reduced it will eventually reach the very desirable level shown in Figure 12, and with good luck, settle into the global optimum. Continued lowering of δ will then lead to the discovery of this best value.

Simulated annealing can be used in both modes for the network, in normal operation when an energy minimum is sought as a response to an input and in learning mode when the p_{ij}^+ and p_{ij}^- values are computed by releasing the system to seek a minimum and then computing the correlations between the i and j cells. The Hinton and Sejnowski implementation of simulated annealing was to set cell v_i to 1 with probability

$$p_i = \frac{1}{1+e^{-\Delta E_i/T}}$$

where T is a parameter that acts like δ in the above discussion and ΔE_i is the change of energy of unit i between the 0 and 1 states. Then the learning schedule was repeated again and again with T decreasing steadily until stable values for the c_{ij} 's were found.

Hinton and Sejnowski used this strategy to train a network with 19 visible units and 24 hidden units to recognize the concept of shift. Figure 13 shows the units and the target behavior is that if visible row V_2 is identical to visible row V_1 but shifted left one, then the leftmost bit of V_3 should be on. If V_2 is identical to V_1 but either not shifted or shifted right one step, then the middle or rightmost bits of V_3 should be on, respectively. After 9000 "learning sweeps", they found that 19 of the 24 hidden units seemed to have learned patterns that contribute to the correct computation and that the system correctly recognized shifts 50%, 71%, 81%, 86%, 89%, 82%, and 66% of the time if the number of on units in V_1 was, respectively, 1,2,3,4,5,6, or 7.

V_3				1	0	0		
V_2	0	1	1	0	1	0	0	0
V_1	0	0	1	1	0	1	0	0

Figure 13. The 19 visible units on a learning problem. Since V_2 is equal to V_1 shifted left one, the leftmost bit of V_3 is on.

4. Conclusion

This paper gives a classification system for the kinds of learning machines based on several dimensions, whether learning is parametric or structural, the kinds of training information utilized, and so forth. Various machines have been categorized using this system and are discussed in Part I of this paper, here, or in other surveys.

The second portion of this paper discusses relationships between the sizes and distributions of the target and learnable classes of behaviors and the error levels and rates of learning. If the learnable class is large and well distributed with respect to the target class, the error rate for the learned behavior will be low but the time required to learn may be very long. If the learnable class is small, larger errors may occur but learning will be faster. The best performance is obtained if there is a close match between the size and distributions of the target and learnable classes.

Finally, a study of some connectionist learning machines has been included in the third section. These machines attempt to achieve a set of globally useful properties using an array of locally simple processors. The behaviors of the array can be understood in terms of the concept of total energy. Learning involves adapting the energy curve to place desired behaviors at minimum energy points, and normal system operation begins with an input pattern and uses hill climbing (possibly with simulated annealing) to find those points.

REFERENCES

Angluin, D. and C. Smith [83], "Inductive inference: theory and methods", ACM Computing Surveys .

Biermann, A. W. [72], "On the inference of Turing machines from sample computations", Artificial Intelligence, Vol. 3, pp. 181-198.

Biermann, A. W. [78], "The inference of regular LISP programs from examples", IEEE Trans. on Systems, Man, and Cybernetics , Vol. SMC-8, No. 8, pp. 585-600.

Biermann, A. W. [85], "Fundamental Mechanisms in Machine Learning and Inductive Inference", in Fundamentals of Artificial Intelligence, Eds. W. Bibel and Ph. Jorrand, Springer-Verlag.

Biermann, A. W., K. C. Gilbert, A. Fahmy, and B. Koster [86], "On the errors that learning machines will make", Tech. Report, Duke University.

Biermann, A., G. Guiho, and Y. Kodratoff [84], Automatic Program Construction Techniques, Macmillan Publishing Company.

Buchanan, B. and E. A. Feigenbaum [78], "DENDRAL and META-DENDRAL: their applications dimension", Artificial Intelligence, Vol. 11, pp. 5-24.

Carbonell, J. G., R. S. Michalski, and T. M. Mitchell [84], "An Overview of Machine Learning", in Machine Learning, Eds. R. Michalski, J. Carbonell, and T. Mitchell, Springer-Verlag, pp. 163-190.

Cohen, B. and C. Sammut [84], "Program synthesis through concept learning", in Automatic Program Construction Techniques, Eds. A. Biermann, G. Guiho, and Y. Kodratoff, Macmillan Publishing Company.

Gold, E. M. [67], "Language identification in the limit", Information and Control, Vol. 10, pp. 447-474.

Kodratoff, Y. and J.-P. Jouannaud [84], "Synthesizing LISP programs working on the list level of imbedding", in Automatic Program Construction Techniques, Eds. A. Biermann, G. Guiho, and Y. Kodratoff, Macmillan Publishing Company.

Langley, P., J. M. Zytkow, H. A. Simon, and G. L. Bradshaw [86], "The search for regularity: four aspects of scientific discovery", in Machine Learning, Volume II, Eds. R. S. Michalski, J. G. Carbonell, and T. M. Mitchell, Morgan Kaufmann.

Hinton, G. E. and Sejnowski, T. J. [86], "Learning and relearning in Boltzmann machines", in Parallel Distributed Processing, Vol. 1, Eds. D. Rumelhart and J. McClelland, M. I. T. Press.

Hopfield, J. and D. Tank [86], "Computing with neural nets: a model", Science, August, 1986.

Lenat, D. B. [77], "Automated theory formation in mathematics", Fifth International Joint Conference on Artificial Intelligence, pp. 833-842.

McClelland, J. and D. Rumelhart [86], Parallel Distributed Processing , Vol. 2, M. I. T. Press.

Michalski, R. S.[80], "Pattern recognition as rule-guided inductive inference", IEEE Trans. on Pattern Analysis and Machine Intelligence , Vol. PAMI-2, No. 2,3,4, pp. 349-361.

Michalski, R. S. [86], "Understanding the nature of learning", in Machine Learning, Volume II, Eds. R. S. Michalski, J. G. Carbonell, and T. M. Mitchell, Morgan Kaufmann.

Michalski, R., J. Carbonell, and T. Mitchell [84], Machine Learning, Springer-Verlag.

Michalski, R., J. Carbonell, and T. Mitchell [86], Machine Learning, Volume II, Morgan-Kaufmann.

Minsky, M., and S. Papert [69], Perceptrons , M. I. T. Press.

Mitchell, T.[82], "Generalization as search", Artificial Intelligence , Vol. 18, No. 2, pp. 203-226.

Mitchell, T., J. Carbonell, and R. Michalski [86], Machine Learning - A Guide to Current Research, Kluwer Academic Publishers.

Mitchell, T., R. Keller, S. Kedar- Cabelli[86], "Explanation-based generalization: a unifying view", in Machine Learning , Vol. 1.

Mitchell, T., P. Utgoff, and R. Banerji[84], "Learning by experimentation: acquiring and refining problem-solving heuristics", in Machine Learning, Eds. R. Michalski, J. Carbonell, and T. Mitchell, Springer-Verlag, pp. 163-190.

Muroga, S. [71], Threshold Logic and Its Applications, John Wiley and Sons, Inc.

Quinlan, J. R.[84], "Learning efficient classification procedures and their application to chess end games", in Machine Learning, Eds. R. Michalski, J. Carbonell, and T. Mitchell, Springer-Verlag, pp. 463-482.

Rumelhart, D. and J. McClelland [86], Parallel Distributed Processing , Vol. 1, M. I. T. Press.

Samuel, A. [67], "Some studies in machine learning using the game of checkers II - Recent progress", IBM Journal of Research and Development , Vol. 11, No. 6, pp 601-617.

Sejnowski, T., and C. Rosenberg [86], "NETtalk: a parallel network that learns to read aloud", Johns Hopkins University Tech. Report EECS 86/01.

Shapiro, E. Y.[83], Algorithmic Program Debugging, M. I. T. Press.

Shapiro, S. C. [87] (Editor), Encyclopedia of Artificial Intelligence, John Wiley and Sons, Inc.

Summers, P. [77], "A methodology for LISP program construction from examples", Journal of the ACM , Vol. 24, pp. 161-175.

Waterman, D. A. [75], "Adaptive production systems", Proc. of the Fourth International Joint Conference on Artificial Intelligence, pp. 296-303.

Wilkins, D. , W. Clancy, and B. Buchanan [86], "Overview of the Odysseus learning apprentice", in Machine Learning - A Guide to Current Research, Eds. T. Mitchell, J. Carbonell, R. Michalski, Kluwer Academic Publishers.

Winston, P. [75], "Learning structural descriptions from examples", in The Psychology of Computer Vision, Ed. P. Winston, McGraw-Hill.

Valiant, L. G.[84], "A theory of the learnable", Communications of the ACM , Vol. 27, No. 11, pp 1134-1142.

Topics in Planning

Sam Steel
Dept Computer Science, University of Essex
Colchester CO4 3SQ, United Kingdom

0. Preface

Planning is (after a period of disfavour) a large, popular and growing area of AI. What I have attempted to do is point out some of the choices that have to be made when one wants to reason about action, and to sketch some of the planning systems that have made those choices in different ways. Those sketches try to extract what seem to be the central ideas of a piece of work. That has meant a presentation sometimes rather different from the authors' own.

At the end are listed some good general introductions to planning. If you want to find out about the most recent work, I recommend (Georgeff & Lansky 86), (papers all of a high standard), (Brown 87) and IJCAI-87 (which had a gratifying number of planning papers in it.) The principal omissions are: the interaction of planning and knowledge (for which I have given some references); conditional planning; planning and language; distributed planning; plan recognition; execution monitoring.

1. Introduction

Any general term, such as "planning", is going to have soft edges and defy definition. Here are some generalities.

The central idea of planning is the stringing together of actions to transform the world from a given state to a desired state, without problems. So, by the time one comes to execute an action in the plan, one can be sure that that action will be possible.

It is worth contrasting that with something else that gets called "planning", as in "factory planning", but which might be called "scheduling". Scheduling takes a partially ordered set of actions as a given, and tries to give each action a precise time and a precise list of the objects and resources it is going to use. Clearly planning and scheduling fade into each other.

Planning can also be seen as a special case of "planning" as in "town planning" or "planning a kitchen", where what is happening is that some objects (cookers, sinks) are being laid out in some space (here, physical space), such that each object imposes constraints on other objects around it; and not just that; one object (a gas cooker, say) may not just constrain other objects (eg not to intrude into its space) but may actually demand the existence of other objects (as a gas cooker demands the existence of a gas supply pipe.) Planned action can be seen as the special case of planning of this general sort, where the objects arranged are actions, and the space they are arranged in is time. In fact, seeing this generalization does not making planning actions any easier. It does however show a difference between planning and pure constraint satisfaction problems. Actions can be like the gas cooker. Not only do they constrain other actions, but they actually demand the existence of other actions, usually to ensure the truth of their preconditions.

Within the parts of AI concerned with reasoning, problems usually have three aspects: representation; inference; and control. This is true within planning. The ideal presentation of planning would identify the axes of variation of representation, inference and control, and locate the various planners that people have devised in the space thereby defined. That cannot alas yet be done. The decisions about one aspect are too strongly linked to decisions about another. But since doing that would be very worthwhile, here are the axes as far as I can identify them. The main questions in each are:

** Representation

How shall we divide the continuous stream of the changing world? The main choice seems to be between taking as basic one of these two things:

* Some selection of temporal entities (instants, or intervals) with some structure imposed on them (Are instants dense? Do intervals meet? Do intervals overlap?). The focus is on when things happen, and the next problem is, how are facts about non-temporal parts of the world (chairs, blocks, colours) associated with such entities?

* Some selection of entities such as actions, states and events, with some structure imposed on them (If an action is executed, what is true after it?). The focus is on what changes in the world, and the next problem is, What are the possible temporal relations of such facts and changes?

** Inference

Given some divisions of the continuous world, what is the temporal relation between them? (Eg "Is A before, during or after B?") If some facts are associated with some of those divisions, what facts must be associated with the others? (Eg"If the cup was on the saucer before the door opened, is it still there after the door opened?")

** Control

In plan-making proper, what one has to control is search through the space of possible plans, which are going to be some sort of partial description of a possible future world. This has a sub-task: controlling the deduction about what facts are associated with particular divisions of the world, and what the relations between them are.

What approaches give one good control? Production systems? Strategies proposed to control deduction, as in mathematical reasoning? Constraint satisfaction? Self application of planning, leading to meta-planning?

2. The frame problem: what makes planning hard

2.1. The problem

Here is a review of the frame problem, followed by a discussion of some of the ways that it has been dealt with. Those ways show the difference between worrying about the correctness of one's representation and the efficiency of one's planning.

The most obvious way to divide the continuous world up is to divide it into states, or as they are often called in this context, "situations". History is sequence of states. Each state is associated with a set of facts. A change in that set of facts is the same as a change to a new state. Instead of representing the fact that the cat is on the mat as

```
on(cat11,mat34)
```

one has to say when this is true. One says

```
on(cat11,mat34,state616)
```

This is ordinary first order logic, talking about states. One can use the notational variant

```
on(cat11,mat34) @ state616
```

There can be functions from states to states. If F is such a function, then one can write

```
F(A1,A2,...An,State)
```

as the notational variant

```
F(A1,A2,...,An) # State
```

"Action # State" is the state the results from doing Action in State.

Though invented a long while ago (in AI terms) (McCarthy & Hayes 69) it is still a living and useful technique (Manna & Waldinger 86).

Now representing actions looks as if it should be easy. What is an action? Something that turns states into new states, as long as it is done in the right situation. For instance, if a monkey is under some bunch of bananas, he can reach up to grab them. (This example is derived from (Green 69)).

```
under(Place,Bananas) @ State &
at(Monkey,Place) @ State
->
has(Monkey,Bananas) @ (grabs(Monkey,Bananas) # State)
```

(Free variables are implicitly universally quantified.)

If these facts are true in state17

```
under(banana_place,bananas3) @ state17
at(monkey11,banana_place) @ state17
```

then monkey11 can easily prove

```
has(monkey11,bananas3) @ (grabs(monkey11,bananas3) # state17)
```

The state term allows one to read off a plan straight away. Can one continue this? Suppose there is an action

```
at(Monkey,Otherplace) @ State
->
at(Monkey,NewPlace) @ (go(Monkey,OldPlace,NewPlace) # State)
```

and the monkey starts planning in a state where he is not under the bananas:

```
under(banana_place,bananas3) @ state17
at(monkey11,non_banana_place) @ state17
```

It looks as if he ought to be able to argue

```
at(monkey11,non_banana_place) @ state17
->
at(monkey11,banana_place)
        @ (go(monkey11,non_banana_place,banana_place) # state17)

under(banana_place,bananas3)
        @ (go(monkey11,non_banana_place,banana_place) # state17)
at(monkey11,banana_place)
        @ (go(monkey11,non_banana_place,banana_place) # state17)
->
has(monkey11,bananas3)
        @ (grabs(monkey11,bananas3)
                # (go(monkey11,non_banana_place,banana_place)
                        # state17 ))
```

And again the state term exhibits the plan. But he can't. The problem is that he has the axiom

```
under(banana_place,bananas3) @ state17
```

but what he needs for the proof is

```
under(banana_place,bananas3)
        @ (go(monkey11,non_banana_place,banana_place) # state17)
```

In fact, of course ("of course" is always a bad sign in AI), the bananas have stayed in the same place. That has to be made explicit . How? One way is to add a rule to that effect - a frame axiom - to express the interaction of the predicate "under" and the action "go".

```
under(Place,Object) @ State
->
under(Place,Object) @ (Action # State)
```

But there are problems with this.

* One needs one frame axiom to say how each predicate survives each action. That is a lot of axioms.

* Frame axioms to be accurate must be complex. Eg: furniture stays in a room when I leave the room. But what if I am carrying the furniture? OK: stipulate "..unless it is being carried". But what if I am not carrying it, but it lies on something I am carrying? OK: stipulate "...or unless it lies on something being carried". But what if it is in fact tied to something in the room by a rope to short to let it leave the room? ... You see the point.

Now why does the frame problem matters so much? There are two reasons.

The minor one is this. Suppose one started with a complete description of the world, and then one executed a known plan in it. Ideally one would like to have a complete description of the world after the plan. Indeed, that is what one might expect to have. But if one can't always predict which facts have survived one's action and which haven't, then what one knows about the world must be incomplete.

The other, more important, reason is this. Suppose one has several goals. One wants to be able to tackle them more or less separately, because things are simpler like that. Suppose one achieves one goal, and then attacks the next. One has to know that the achieved goal will survive the achieving of the next, or one might as well not have bothered. For instance, suppose I want to have a clean frying pan and I want to have an omelette. I have to make the omelette first, because if I clean it first its cleanness won't survive the omelette making.

In fact, making that plan needs two things; first, that I can spot the interaction; and secondly, that I can do something about it.

What to do about spotting instances of the frame problem has been a crux in planning. There have been two sorts of response.

* Assume that facts survive actions unless you know they don't.

Examples of this are approach are non-linear planning and planning with time maps.

* Assume that facts don't survive actions unless you know they do.

Examples of this approach are goal regression and bigression and Hoare logic, (and deduction using situation calculus using frame axioms).

2.2. Assume facts survive actions unless you know they don't

2.2.1. Non-linear planning

Non-linear planning is important, both because a lot of practical planning can be done in it, and because it is the intellectual common stock of AI planning. But its dearest friend would not say it is perfect.

The central idea of non-linear planning is that plans are to be represented as partially-ordered nets of instantaneous actions. And because actions may disrupt goals already achieved, at least if one is unfortunate enough to order them in the wrong way (eg washing the frying pan before making the omelette), one should not order them until one has to. And when one has to, one must take care to order them the right way round. One makes the "least commitment" possible about the ordering of the actions.

(Though (if the agent executing the plan can only do one thing at a time) the order in which the actions are executed will be linear. It will consistent with, but more specific than, the partial order. If there are multiple agents, the lack of order can be realized as genuine parallelism.)

Adding order to non-linear plans is clearly something to do with how to deal with the frame problem and action interaction, rather than with how to detect it. The detection is made possible by the notion of "protection", described soon.

Actions have a name, preconditions and effects. For instance, the banana grabbing action would be

```
name:          grabs(Monkey,Bananas)
preconds:      under(Place,Bananas)
               at(Monkey,Place)
effects:       has(Monkey,Bananas)
```

This representation is known for historical reasons as the STRIPS operator representation (Nilsson 73). I will draw such an action as

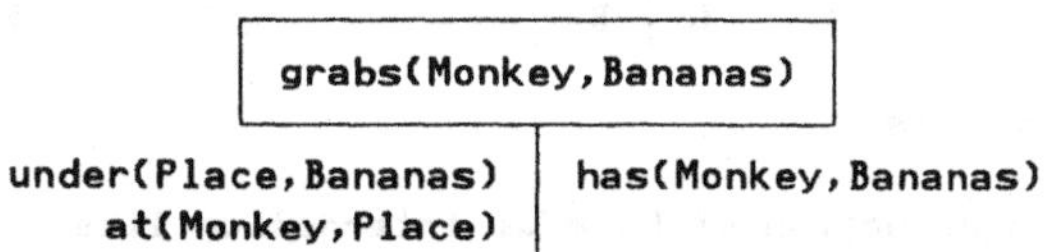

I also suppose two dummy actions, one, at the start of the plan, with only effects, to represent what is true in the initial state, one dummy effect for each initial fact; and another, at the end of the plan, with only preconds, to represent the overall goals of the plan.

For instance, if the overall goals are A and K, and the initial facts are K and C, then the embryonic plan can be drawn as

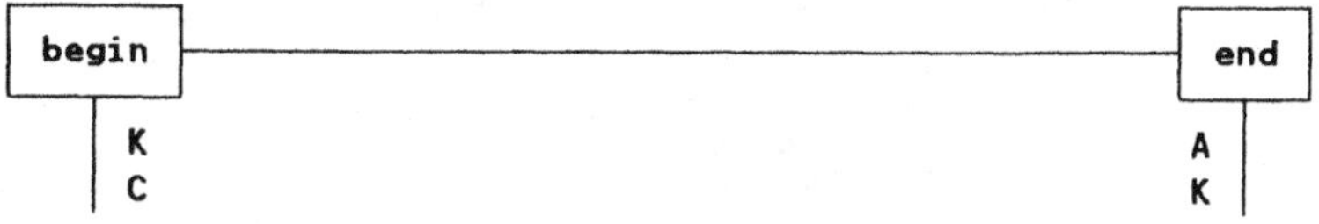

Now of course what happens is that each precond of any action in the plan has to be supported by the effect of some action earlier in the plan. This of course applies to the dummy nodes too. And when some effect of some earlier node is chosen as the support for some goal, one has to put something in the plan to indicate that from the moment of the effect's being brought about to the moment of its being relied on, it must not be disrupted by any intervening action. The something that does that is a "protection".

One can obtain support for a goal, either by relying on the effects of nodes already in the plan (continuing with the embryonic plan above)

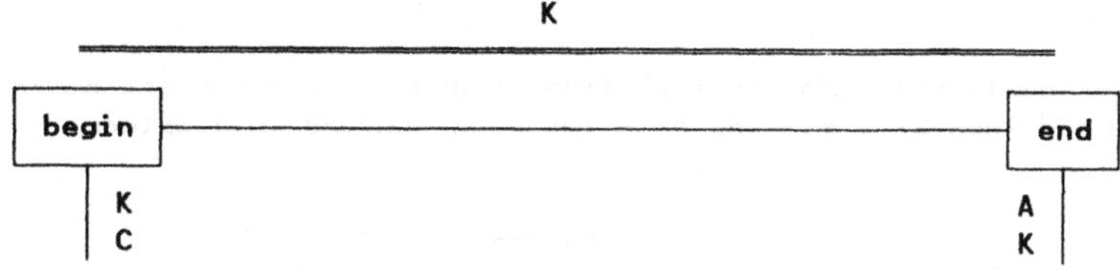

where single lines indicate temporal order, and double lines the extent of a protection; or by introducing new (instances of) actions into the plan, and relying on their effects:

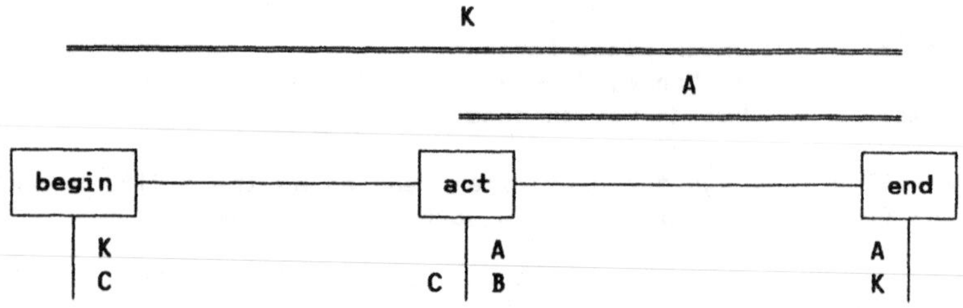

And now the plan is complete.

Protections assist with detection of harmful interaction like this. Because actions in a plan may be unordered relative to each other, there is the possibility of an action, one of whose effects is -X, ending up in parallel with a protection for X. Here is a fragment of a plan showing that.

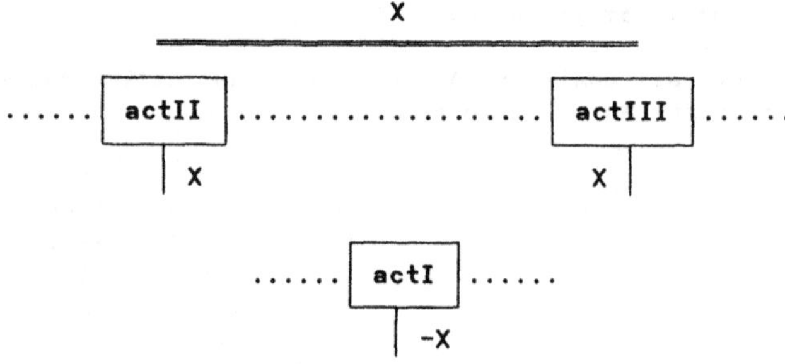

This does not mean that actI will definitely occur between actII and actIII, and thereby mess up the effect on which actIII is relying. But equally, nor does it rule the possibility out. It would be perfectly consistent with the ordering so far to linearize the plan into this defective shape.

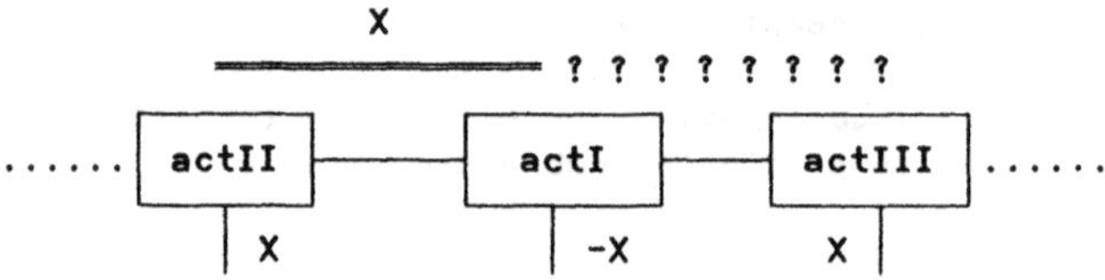

So the planner must spot such constellations - and protections are essential to doing that - and then it must linearize the plan instead into either

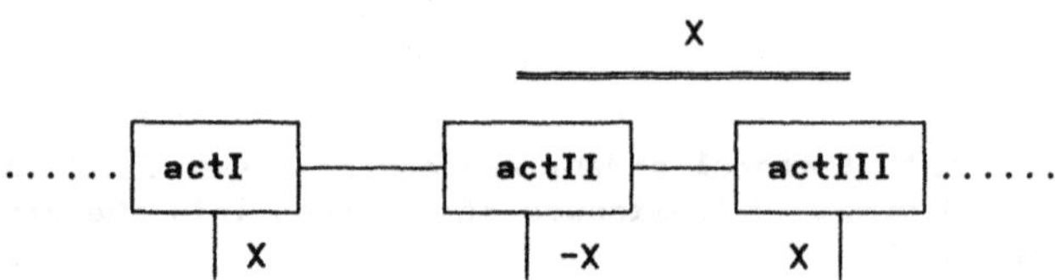

or

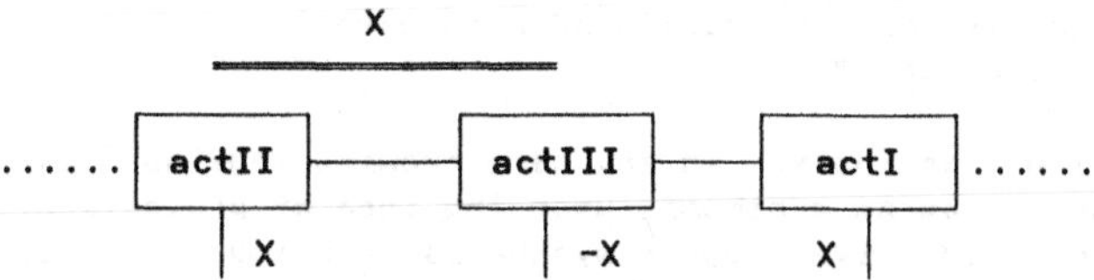

both of which are safe.

Observe how this is an answer to the frame problem. The problem in general is, how does one see whether facts survive actions? But one doesn't really want to do that in general; one wants to do it just for goals. One knows what those are; they are the labels of protections. Furthermore, a goal may be a goal only for part of the plan; so one only wants to check for interactions between protected goals and actions that might possibly occur at the right time to disrupt the protected goal. Again, protections and the partial temporal order together enable one to do that.

The reason the system is not perfect, even for instantaneous actions, is that an action may have effects that are not explicit. For instance, suppose that "in(cup,kitchen)" is protected somewhere in a plan, and the action "carry(saucer)from(kitchen)to(sitting_room)" , with effect "in(saucer,sitting_room)" occurs in parallel to it. Suppose further that at the time the action is done, the cup will be on the saucer. There will be no explicit conflict between the protected goal and the effect of the action, even though the cup will, disastrously, leave the kitchen. One might reply "Aha! Look for other changes that the explicit effect of an action entails.". But that is forward inference; and as always, the problem is that however far one infers forward, there is always the chance that the important consequence won't show up until the step just after the last one done.

So the protection approach is good for the problem about the number of frame axioms needed, but not about the problem about their complexity.

The deepest account of pure non-linear planning is (Chapman 87) which discusses Chapman's planner TWEAK and proves its completeness as a way of making a certain class of plans.

2.2.2. Time maps

Time maps allow a quite different planning process which also assumes that facts survive actions unless they are known not to. But time maps will only make sense once their representation of time and state is explained. That is done later. Consider them to have a virtual occurrence here too.

2.3. Assume that facts don't survive actions unless you know they do

Now let us look at a couple of methods that handle the frame problem and interaction by assuming no fact survives into the next state unless one can prove that it does.

These methods are much more familiar in reasoning about programs than in planning. That is partly historical accident and partly difference of emphasis. There is no point in reasoning about programs unless the reasoning is perfectly right. In planning, what you may want is a plan that works, reasonably quickly. But in fact (imperative) programming and planning are extremely similar. One can see a program as a plan of actions in the special domain where the objects are data items and variables, and the most-used predicate is "has_the_value(Variable,Item)".

Program synthesis and planning are in any case growing together. See for example (Dershowitz 85) where program synthesis uses the idea of protection; or (Manna & Waldinger 86) where a deductive program synthesis technique is applied to planning.

2.3.1. Bigression

The starting point of this approach is goal regression. That is the process of taking a goal and an action, and asking "What must be true before the performance of this action for the goal to be necessarily true after it?" The answer to that question is the regressed goal.

There are different ways of seeing goal regression, depending on how one sees actions. For instance, suppose there is the action

```
name:          carry(Bag)from(Place1)to(Place2)
preconds:      at(Bag,Place1)
effects:       at(Bag,Place2)
```

and suppose this rule is true

```
in(Object,Bag) &
at(Bag,Place)
->
at(Object,Place)
```

Then what is the result of regressing the goal

```
at(book,room1)
```

over that action? Here is a picture that suggests one way of answering the question.

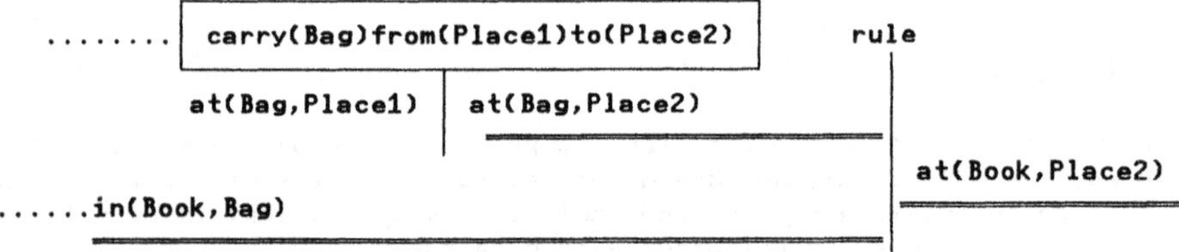

The rule reduces the goal to

```
in(book,Bag)&
at(Bag,room1)
```

and one conjunct is achieved by (an instance of) the action. The other conjunct, "in(book,Bag)" we know (from some suitable frame axiom) to survive the action unchanged. So if the other conjunct "in(book,Bag)" is true before the "carry" action, the goal is true after it, even though it is not an explicit effect of the action. So "in(book,Bag)" is the regressed goal.

There will be many facts which count as the regression of a goal. "The" regressed goal is the weakest regressed goal, often written "Act\Goal". That is, if R is a regressed goal, then R - > Act\Goal. "Act\Goal & H" is always another regression of Goal.

That says something about how goal regression helps reduce goals, but nothing about how it helps avoid goal interaction. Here is how that happens. Suppose that the goal had been the conjunct of two essentially independent goals

```
at(book,room1) &
on(parcel,table)
```

The "on(parcel,table)" goal will survive the action; so it can be part of the regressed goal

```
in(book,Bag) &
at(Bag,room1) &
on(parcel,table)
```

Nothing has been done towards "on(parcel,table)". Other actions will have to be inserted in the plan before the "carry" action to achieve it. But one can be sure that if they achieve "on(parcel,table)", then it will survive the subsequent action. This picture suggests what is happening.

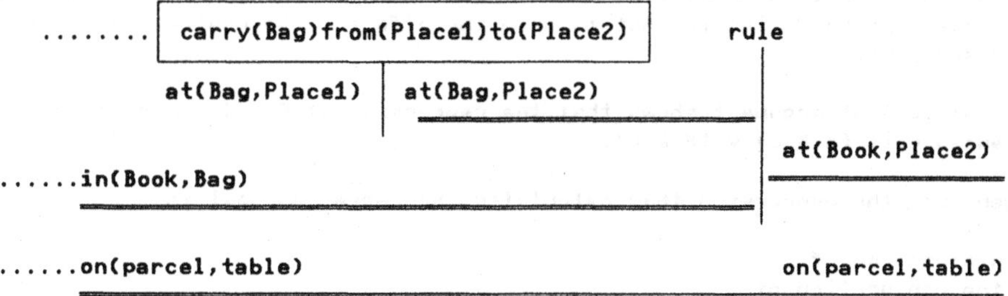

Now note that that approach depended on there being frame axioms to express what facts survive an action. But there is another possible approach: calculating the regressed goal from the action description. This could be done with situation calculus. But for variety and for historical reasons I shall do it with dynamic logic. What follows derives from (Rosenschein 81).

Dynamic logic is a modal logic concerned with action. The necessity operator [] takes an argument, the name of an action. It is then written as

```
[Action] Effect
```

with the intuitive meaning "Effect is true in all states occurring after the execution of Action". (There are refinements about what happens if Action does not terminate that I shall ignore.) Then, since the language of course has a conditional ("->"), one can also write

```
Precond -> [Action] Effect
```

with the intuitive meaning "If Precond is true in the current state, then Effect is true in all states occurring after the execution of Action". That is very like (bar issues of termination)

```
name:        Action
preconds:    Precond
effects:     Effect
```

What however it permits is actions with conditional effects. Suppose one has a bed-side light with a button switch. What happens when one presses the button depends on what is true when presses it; if the light is on, it goes off; if it is off, it comes on. That is impossible to represent with STRIPS operators. With dynamic logic it is expressible as

```
 on(Light) -> [push(Button)] -on(Light)
-on(Light) -> [push(Button)] on(Light)
```

Now suppose one has the following rules about an abstract action. (They involves only propositional logic. Predicate logic has been treated (Kautz 82) but introduces complexities that don't matter here.)

```
    A -> [Act] B v C
    G -> [Act] -B
F & E -> [Act] D
```

Suppose one's goal is C. Then one can ask: which combinations of effects of Act together entail C? The answer is: { B v C, -B }. The effect D doesn't help entail C, so it can be neglected. Now what must be true when one executed Act for both B v C and -B to be true afterwards? Obviously, A and G. So A & G is the weakest precondition for Act to have the effect C. So one has calculated the regressed goal.

The same sort of argument shows that the regression of C v D leads to the regressed goal (A & G) v (F & E).

In general, the expression that calculates the regressed goal is

```
the disjunction of
    the conjunction of
        the preconds of
            the rules about an action Act
                whose effects are collectively just sufficient
                to entail the goal.
```

or symbolically, if "Rules(Act)" are all the axioms about the effects of an Act,

```
DISJOIN { CONJOIN { Preconds | "Preconds -> [Act] Effects" e RR }
        |
          RR e Rules(Act) &
          { Effects | "Preconds -> [Act] Effects" e RR } |- Goal }
```

Notice though that the entailment relation occurs in this expression. This is not in general calculable. One has to use some sort of stand-in. A simple but useful stand-in is to say "A |- B" iff A and B are syntactically equal atomic formulae. But clearly that is not complete.

Just as one can regress a goal, one can progress a fact; that is, given that some fact Fact is true before Act, find what is the strongest claim that one can make about what will be true after Act. The strongest progressed fact is often written "Fact/Act". If the rules about Act are

```
       A -> [Act] J
       B -> [Act] K
     C v D [Act] L
```

then by a similar argument one can see that the progression of the fact (A v B) & D over Act is (J v K) & L. One can calculate progressions from

```
CONJOIN { DISJOIN { Effects | "Preconds -> [Act] Effects" e RR }
        |
          RR e Rules(Act) &
          Fact |- { Preconds | "Preconds -> [Act] Effects" e RR } }
```

If one has a goal regression mechanism, then one can go about planning like this:

```
Consider the plan so far constructed.
        (It will be a terminal fragment of the final plan, and have all its
        unachieved preconds at its start.)
Consider the plan fragment's unachieved preconds.
Choose an action.
        (Clearly heuristic guidance about which action to take is vitally
        important.)
Regress the plan fragment's preconds over the action.
Check that the regressed preconds are different from the given preconds.
        (Otherwise one has just introduced a redundant action. Ideally, the
        regressed preconds should be "simpler" than the given preconds. But that
        presupposes a metric for simplicity.)
If      the regressed preconds is implied by the given facts
then    Stop. (The plan is complete.)
else    Put the action onto the front of the plan fragment.
        Repeat the process with the extended plan fragment and the regressed
        preconds.
```

Here are pictures to suggest what is happening. One starts with a partial plan like this:

```
|                                                      |
| Facts                unachieved    | plan fragment   |
|                      preconds      |                 |
```

and then regresses the unachieved preconds over an action to produce this:

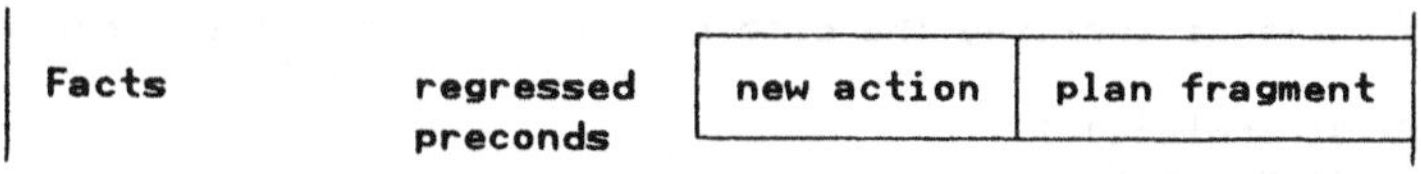

```
|                                                      |
| Facts         regressed  | new action | plan fragment |
|               preconds   |            |               |
```

And when eventually one finds Facts |- regressed preconds, one can stop.

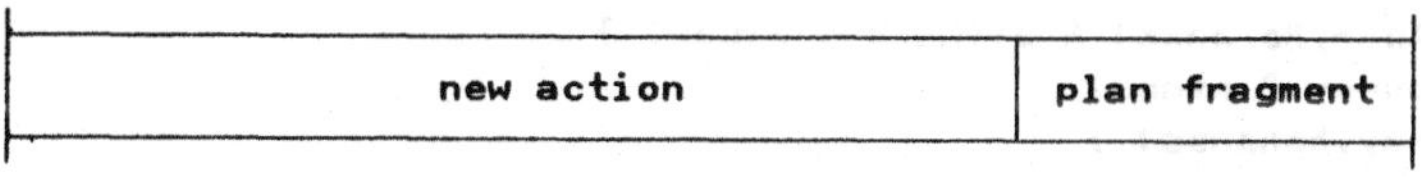

```
|                                                      |
|               new action             | plan fragment |
|                                                      |
```

But if one has a fact progression mechanism, one can work forward too. What one does is extend the algorithm given above so that it considers two plan fragments. The new fragment will be the start of the final plan. Instead of having unachieved preconds before it, it will have the strongest possible description of how the world would be after the its execution after it. Then, as an alternative to regressing a goal, one can progress a fact. When the facts produced by the initial fragment imply the goals of the final fragment, the plan is complete.

The formal modifications needed to do fact progression are obvious. I shall just give some illustrative pictures. One might start with

plan fragment	achieved effects	plan fragment

which, when a new action is added to the initial fragment, becomes

plan fragment	new action	progressed effects	plan fragment

And when progressed effects |- regressed goals, one gets the complete plan.

plan fragment	new action	plan fragment

To start the planning process, one would start with an empty plan, with the initial state as the achieved facts and the overall goals of the plan as the unachieved preconds.

initial state	overall goals

2.3.2. Hoare logic

Another way of representing action that is usually used to reason about programs, but need not be, is Hoare logic (Hoare 69). The central idea is to use expressions such as

```
{ Preconds } Act { Effects }
```

to represent the claim that, if Preconds are true before Act is performed, then Effects are true afterwards (as long as there is an afterwards - as long as Act terminates). For instance (writing the bits of such expressions one per line):

```
{ at(Monkey,Otherplace) }
  go(Monkey,OldPlace,NewPlace)
{ at(Monkey,NewPlace) }

{ under(Place,Bananas) & at(Monkey,Place) }
  grabs(Monkey,Bananas)
{ has(Monkey,Bananas) }
```

There are also rules about the composition of actions in various ways. The important one here is about sequences of actions.

```
{ P } Act1 { Q }      { Q } Act2 { R }
--------------------------------------
       { P } Act1 ; Act2 { R }
```

One can't immediately compose instances of the action rules above to make a banana-getting plan like this

```
go(monkey11,non_banana_place,banana_place); grabs(monkey11,bananas3)
```

because it is not true that

```
at(monkey11,banana_place)
```

entails

```
under(banana_place,bananas3) & at(monkey11,banana_place)
```

But frame axioms will cure that. Frame axioms will look like

```
{ SurvivingFact } Act {SurvivingFact }
```

and as one should have the rule

```
{ P } Act { Q }    { R } Act { R }
----------------------------------
    { P & R } Act { Q & R }
```

then one can take the frame axiom

```
{ under(Place,Bananas)
  go(Monkey,OldPlace,NewPlace)
{ under(Place,Bananas)
```

prove the survival of the fact about where the bananas are - a task previously done by goal regression -

```
{ at(monkey11,non_banana_place) & under(banana_place,bananas3) }
  go(monkey11,non_banana_place,banana_place)
{ at(monkey11,banana_place) & under(banana_place,bananas3) }
```

and then make a correct plan.

```
{ at(monkey11,non_banana_place) & under(banana_place,bananas3) }
  go(monkey11,non_banana_place,banana_place)
{ at(monkey11,banana_place) & under(banana_place,bananas3) }

{ under(banana_place,bananas3) & at(monkey11,banana_place) }
  grabs(monkey11,bananas3)
{ has(monkey11,bananas3) }
-----------------------------------------------------------------

{ at(monkey11,non_banana_place) & under(banana_place,bananas3) }
  go(monkey11,non_banana_place,banana_place) ;
  grabs(monkey11,bananas3)
{ has(monkey11,bananas3) }
```

Since the initial state proves the preconds of this complex action, and its effects prove the overall goal, it is a successful plan.

2.3.3. Contrast of situation calculus, dynamic logic and Hoare logic

A typical action will be expressed as

```
Preconds @ State -> Effects @ ( Action # State )

Preconds -> [Action] Effect

{ Preconds } Action { Effect }
```

The difference in these expressions is comparatively slight; the main difference is in how planning will be done with them.

States are not explicitly mentioned except in situation calculus. But that is not as big a difference as it might seem. The semantics of the other two is going to be something like "For all states S where Preconds are true, Effects will be true in any state T that arises when Action is done in S". States are being mentioned, but out of sight, in the meta-language.

A bigger difference is that situation calculus as so far presented supposes that there will always be exactly one state arising from the performance of an action in a given state S. That is because

```
Preconds @ State -> Effects @ ( Action # State )
```

is really something like

```
P(X,State) -> E(X,Action(State))
```

and because of what functions are. So there are problems for situation calculus in representing non-terminating action (with perhaps no successor state) or non-deterministic action (with perhaps many successor state). To overcome them, the functionalit of actions would have to be replaced with a relation such as

```
successor_state( OldState, Action, NewState )
```

The difference in use between them is this: situation calculus is just a theory, and can be used in any way the user likes. As usual, having such flexibility in theory is less use than the difficulty of controlling it in practice. Dynamic logic is naturally used to build a plan from the ends in. Partial plans like this

```
|[fragment]                                   [fragment]|
```

turn into partial plans like this

```
|[fragment][new action]           [new action][fragment]|
```

while Hoare logic would be used middle-out. Partial plans like this

```
|                  [fragment]                           |
```

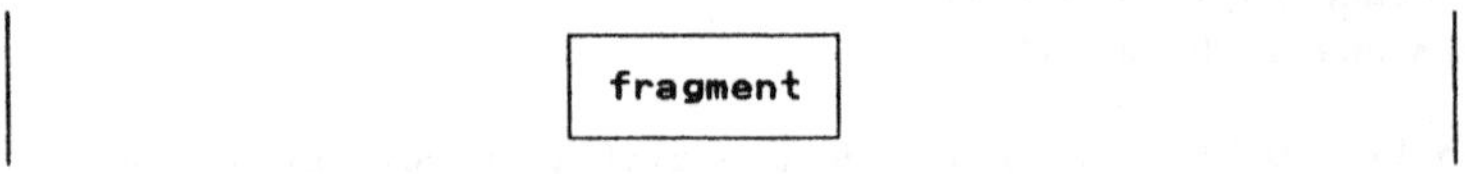

turn into partial plans like this

new action	fragment	new action

3. Actions that take time

Of course actions are not always instantaneous. Some of the issues of representation are

* What is the basic ontology for planning? Should one

    * Take actions states as basic, and associate time with them.

    * Take temporal entities as basic, and associate actions with them.

* Do actions overlap in time?

* Is time metric or merely relative?

What follows are accounts of three planners that give different answers to those questions, and which also have radically different approaches to inference and control.

3.1. Actions as basic, with associated time

This account follows DEVISER, created by Vere (Vere 83). Actions are taken as basic, in just the same the same way that they were in non-linear planning. Then metric time is added on, as a property of action instances. Though a plan may not insist on an ordering for two actions, an order will be imposed before execution. There is no idea of actions overlapping.

An instance of an action has a duration and a "window" - the earliest and latest times at which it may start. (This idea is well known in project planning and in operations research. What is novel here is its useful interaction with the idea of preconds and effects.)

If an action has duration, the questions arise, for how much of its duration does it need its preconditions to be true? and when in its execution do its effects become true? The most conservative answers possible are: the preconditions must be true throughout the action, and the effects are not achieved until the very end of the action.

Now suppose there is a constellation of actions in a plan like this, where the first achieves the preconds of the second.

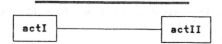

If actions have duration, one can look at this more closely, and see that the protection is essentially the useful part of the duration of the effect, and, assuming the ordering, should be drawn as

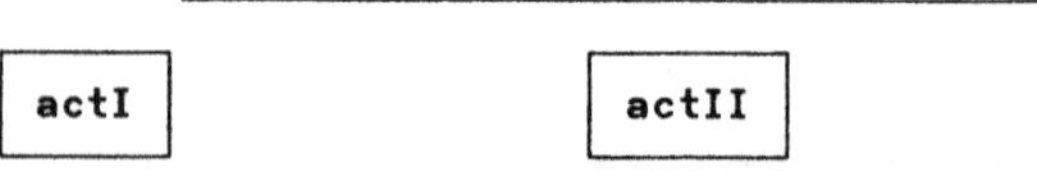

Since the effect must be true throughout actII, the earliest that actII can occur relative to actI is this

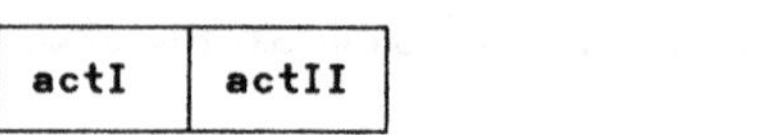

And since actI must start inside its window, the earliest that actI can start is as suggested here.

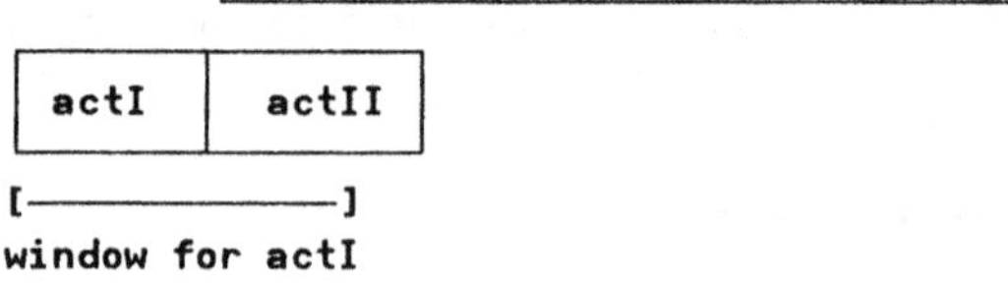

So

```
earliest start time for actII =
        earliest start time for actI +
        duration of actI
```

But actII will already have its own window. So the earliest start time for actII is constrained both as above, and by its own window. So its earliest start time must be the maximum of those two. The upshot is that if we take the example above, and put in numbers (the number in brackets is a duration),

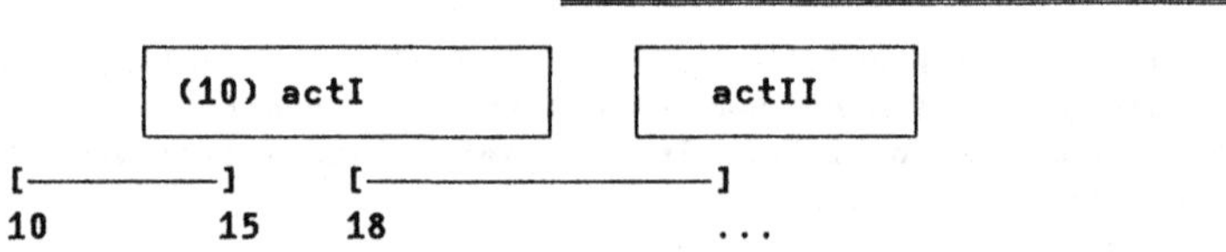

it turns out that the earliest start time of actII is not 18 but 20

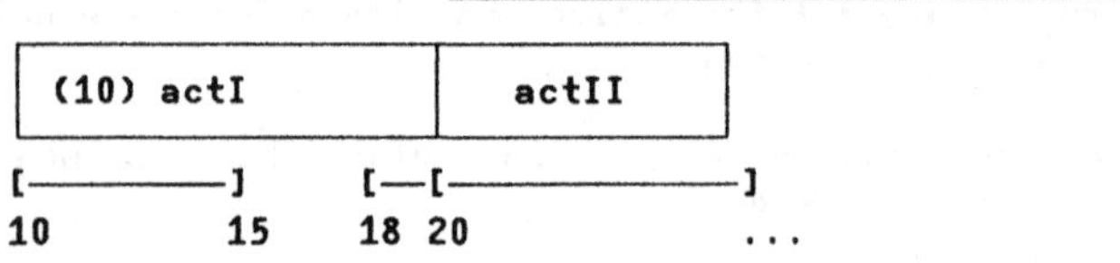

There is a similar argument about the latest start time of actII, leading to

```
latest start time for actII =
        latest start time for actI +
        duration of actI
```

These constraints only hold between ordered actions. As ordering is added, these constraints must be applied and the actions' windows perhaps narrowed. One of two things will happen. A window will have to have its latest start before its earliest start, which is impossible, so that one will have to backtrack to a choicepoint in the planning process; or planning will succeed, in which case the windows will be most precise statement possible of when the actions must be done. This may still leave some choice at execution time, unless the windows are really instants, of length 0.

3.2. Temporal entities as basic, with associated states and actions

These approaches start by choosing a theory of temporal entities, which may be point-like (in which case durations will have to be constructed out of them) or extended (in which case durations will be truly basic). Then facts and actions will be associated with those temporal entities. In particular, an action can be said to occur over some duration.

One approach is based on instants, the other on intervals. They also have radically different methods of control, but that is an orthogonal decision.

This account of temporal entities is crude. To be less crude would take a discussion of the semantics of the various representations mentioned, which would involve discussing the structure of suitable models. If you want to follow this area in planning, you will have to do that. For a profound account, see (Van Benthem 83). But it is not appropriate here.

3.2.1. Instants as basic

Suppose one takes time to be a dense linear order of instants. Let the ordering be "<". Then one could construct periods as pairs of instants. If i1 < i2, then <i1,i2> is a period. Then one can make claims about a fact being true throughout an interval.

    on(cat,mat) @ <i1,i2>

Similarly, one could claim that an action occurred over an interval.

    carried(fred,bag) @ <i5,i6>

(Note that this is a new use of "@"; its semantics are vague.)

Here is an approach that combines such a representation with non-monotonic reasoning. It follows (Dean & McDermott 87).

Intervals are constructed as <instant,instant> pairs, and sentences representing actions or states are associated with such intervals to construct things called "time tokens". Instants can be ordered, and so therefore can intervals. A history, or a predicted future, or a plan can be represented as a collection of time tokens and orderings. Such a collection can be seens as a database of facts about temporal relations of instants, and can be asked the question "Is instant1 before instant2?" The possible answers are "yes", "no", and, because not all instants need be ordered, "not known".

But consider what happens if you are told some fact; say, that block b becomes clear at some moment; and are then told a lot of other facts none of which actually involve something being put on Y. You are then asked whether Y is clear at some later time. You have not been explicitly told that it is, so you can't say categorically "yes". but the reply "yes, as far as I know" is reasonable. And a plan could be made on that assumption.

That is what the data base could do. An interval is held to persist up to an instant T unless its late endpoint is asserted to be before T. Such an assertion will arise

* either by explicit assertion by the user of the data base

* or if there are contradictory time tokens in the database, as in this constellation.

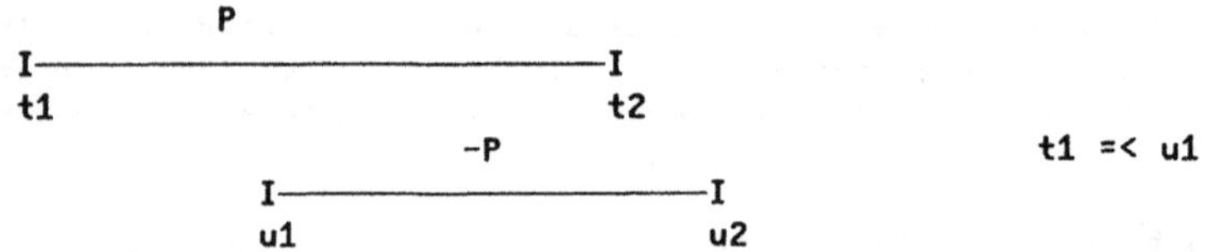

Then the time token for P is "clipped". It must stop when -P starts. Ordering assertions are automatically added, and the database becomes

```
          P
I---------I
t1        t2
               -P                       t1 =< u1
          I---------------I             t2 =< u1
          u1              u2
```

A database that handles time tokens in this way can be called a "time map". It implements the non-monotonic inference rule

```
if P ∂ <T1,T2> is provable
and T1 =< U1 is provable
and T2 =< U2 is not disprovable
then P ∂ <U1,U2>
```

Observe that this provides an answer to the frame problem. All facts persist unless they are explicitly terminated. That is why I mentioned this approach when discussing responses to the frame problem.

With such time maps, planning can be seen as a sort of deduction. (I give this account a more backward-chaining appearance than its inventors did.) Action schemata can be seen as rules about the existence of time tokens. For instance, the (simplified) action

```
name:          put_on(X,Y)
preconds:      clear(Y)
effects:       on(X,Y)
```

could appear as

```
∀ X Y t1 t2 u1 u2 v1 v2
        put_on(X,Y) ∂ <t1,t2> &
        clear(Y) ∂ <v1,v2> &
        v1 =< t1 & t2 =< v2
        ->
        ∃ t3 ( on(X,Y) ∂ <t2,t3> )
```

or in pictures, if the time-tokens drawn in single lines exist in this configuration, so does the time token drawn in double lines.

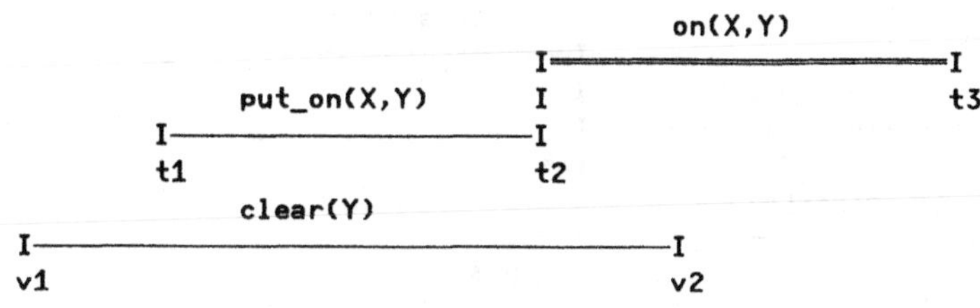

Consider planning for on(a,b) @ <t68,t69>
given the fact clear(b) @ <u57,u58>

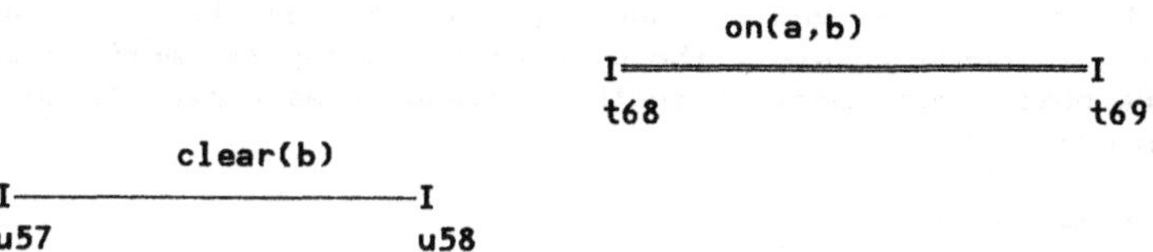

The planner will reduce "on(a,b)@<t68,t69>" using the rule about put_on above. That generates several subgoals. One is "put_on(a,b) @ <t67,t68>" (say), which is a hitherto uncontemplated interval, and which must be added to the time map. It should be asserted to start at a time after which one knows b is clear; that is, u57 =< t67.

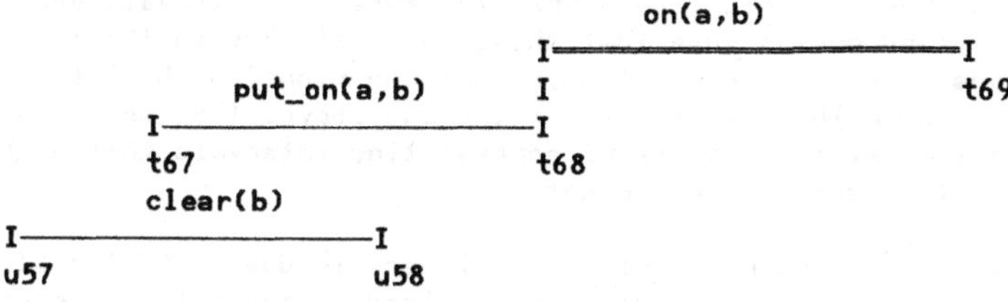

There are also the subgoals about b.

```
clear(b) @ <V1,V2> & V1 =< t67 & t68 =< V2
```

The database can prove

```
clear(b) @ <u57,u58> & u57 =< t67
```

because of how the "put_on" interval was ordered; but it cannot prove

```
t68 =< u58
```

But at least that isn't actually contradicted. So the planner applies the non-monotonic inference rule and assumes it. It concludes that b's being clear goes on long enough to act as precond for that action. The history envisaged is

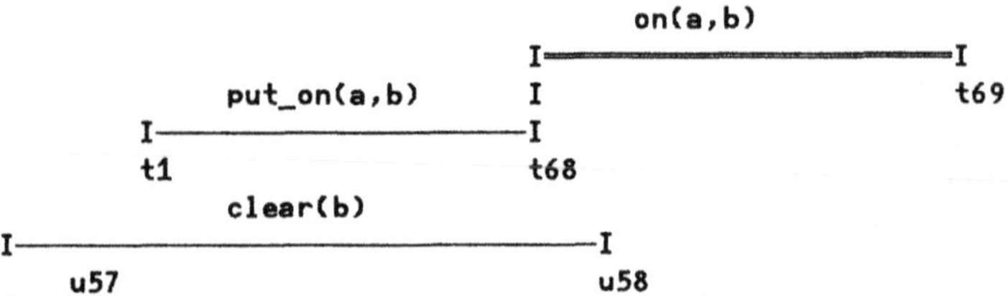

and the planner has succeeded in finding support for the goal interval.

There has been a trade-off. The effort of actually proving that facts persist long enough to be used is removed by assuming that they do. But that means that if it turns out they don't persist, the plan based on the assumption must be discarded and re-built. Some sort of truth maintenance machinery to do that is central to this approach.

3.2.2. Durations as basic

Suppose one takes time as a collection of intervals. Facts and actions can be associated with those intervals.

```
on(cat,mat) @ interval1
```

(Again, no semantics has been given for "@".) Then planning involves two things: ensuring that there are the right intervals to cause the intervals one wants actually to exist; and making sure that those intervals are in the right temporal relations. There are several ways that one might do that; for instance, doing theorem proving with assertions like the one above. That would be rather like situation calculus, but with terms representing intervals that might overlap, instead of states that could not.

Instead, here is a way of planning with such intervals due to (Allen 83), (Allen & Koomen 83) and (Tsang 87). Consider first reasoning about the intervals' temporal relations.

One needs to express the temporal relations between intervals. Since they are atomic, the relations must be primitive. There are 13 of them; those illustrated below, and their inverses. One is its own inverse.

relation	inverse
before	after
meets	inv-meets
overlaps	inv-overlaps
starts	inv-starts
equal	
during	inv-during
finishes	inv-finishes

If there is a choice of possible relations between interval1 and interval2, for instance like this that can be expressed by assertions of this form

interval1 { before, meets, overlaps } interval2

There are also transitivity laws about such relations. An obvious one is

Given such expressions, one can see the problem of finding a consistent ordering for a set of intervals as a constraint satisfaction problem. The variables being constrained are the (interval,interval) temporal relations. The possible values that such variables may take are the temporal relations listed above. For instance, if a set of intervals includes

int1 { before } int2, int2 { before } int3, int1 { before, after } int3

then the transitivity rules, and constraint propagation sharpen that to

int1 { before } int2, int2 { before } int3, int1 { before } int3

Machinery for this is described in (Tsang 87).

The constraints derive
* from the specification of the problem and the operators.
* from the transitivity rules.
* from the logical requirement that contradictory intervals be temporally disjoint.

The problem statement and operators have not yet been touched on, nor has anything been said about how the correct intervals are introduced into the plan. The main ideas are these. A plan and an action are the same sort of thing. They are collections of

- intervals
- assertions about what is true throughout each interval
- temporal relations between the intervals
- causal relation between the intervals

They must obey certain constraints.

- No contradictory intervals may overlap.
- Each interval must be "explained"
    - either by being caused by (a set of) other intervals
    - or by being initially declared to be explained
    - or by being an action

Clearly, intervals "causally explaining" intervals in this approach, and the existence of intervals and their ordering implying the existence of other intervals in the previous approach, are different ways of catching the same idea.

Here is an example about making an omelette and washing up the pan afterwards. The process of making such a plan starts with some very crude future history of the world. Some intervals are assumed to be given, to be explained. Those are marked with double lines. So it is known one starts with an egg, some water and a pan. It is not known when these intervals end. The other intervals are goal intervals, and need to be explained.

```
:::==== have(egg) ===========================:::

                          :::    have(omelette)            :::

                                   :::    clean(pan)        :::

:::======== have(water) ==================================:::

:::======== have(pan) ====================================:::
```

There will also be some action schemata, which are also possible histories, and which include their own temporal and causal relations. For example, this could be "fry".

```
:::   have(egg)      |== -have(egg) =========================:::
              |= fry =|=== have(omelette) ====================:::
:::          have(pan)                                        :::
```

There will be some sort of "cause" relation between the set { "have(pan)", have(egg)", "fry" } and each of "-clean(pan)", "have(pan)". There will also be temporal relations saying for instance that the "have(omelette)" interval is wholly after the "have(egg)" interval, and that the "have(pan)" interval includes the "fry" interval. Those relations do the work that declaring which sentences were effects and which preconds did in representations described earlier.

Planning progresses by merging such schema histories with the current plan. Intervals are equated, new causal relations are added, and the consistency of the combined temporal relations is checked. A new, more elaborated, but perhaps still imperfect history emerges.

```
:::== have(egg) =====|== -have(egg) =========================:::
              |= fry =|=== have(omelette) ====================:::
                                   :::    clean(pan)        :::
                     |=== -clean(pan) =======================:::

:::======== have(water) ==================================:::

:::======== have(pan) ====================================:::
```

That needs constraints added to prevent "clean(pan)" and "-clean(pan)" overlapping, and to explain "clean(pan)". If constraints to avoid "clean(pan)" and "-clean(pan)" overlapping are imposed and propagated, then the plan looks like this.

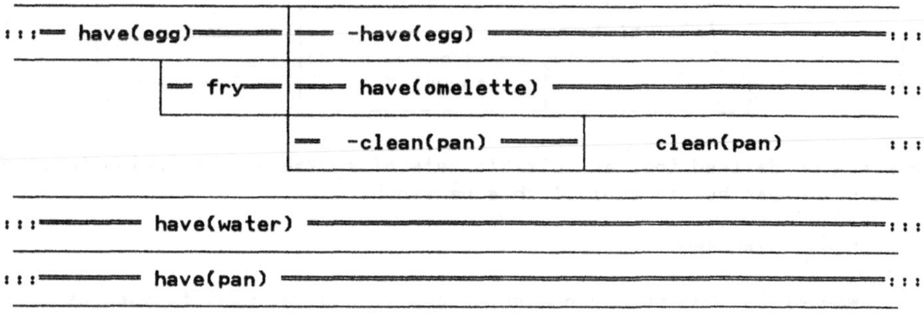

```
:::== have(egg)=======|=== -have(egg) ==============================:::
           |= fry=====|==== have(omelette) ==========================:::
                      |==  -clean(pan) =====|     clean(pan)         :::

:::========= have(water) ============================================:::
:::========= have(pan) ==============================================:::
```

Next the cleaning action

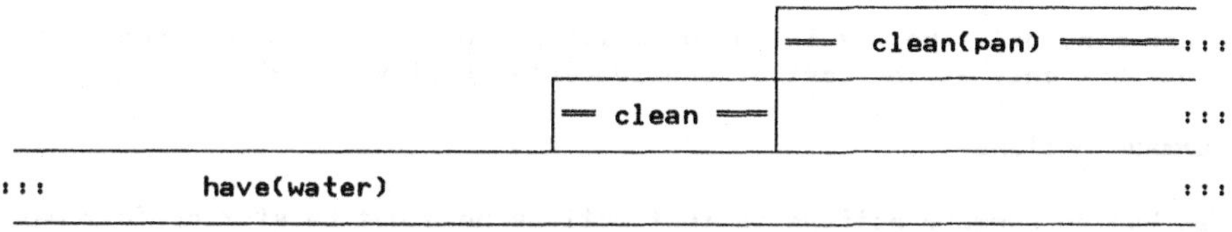

```
                                       |==  clean(pan) =========:::
                          |== clean ===|                        :::
:::         have(water)                                         :::
```

is merged, leading to the final plan.

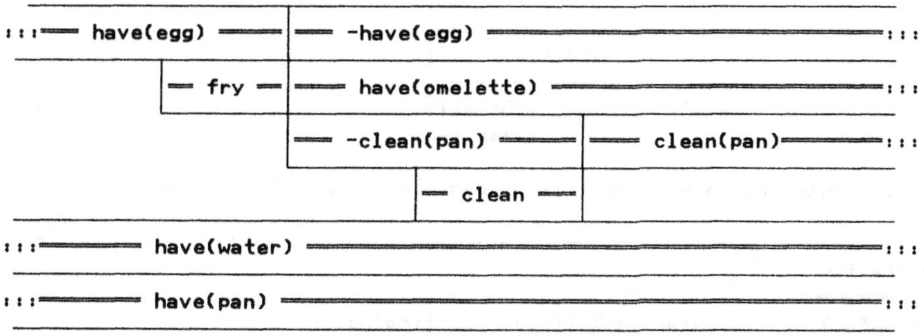

```
:::== have(egg) =====|=== -have(egg) ==============================:::
          |== fry ===|==== have(omelette) ==========================:::
                     |=== -clean(pan) =====|==== clean(pan)=========:::
                               |== clean ==|
:::========= have(water) ===========================================:::
:::========= have(pan) =============================================:::
```

It turns out (Allen & Hayes 85) that all the other relations can be defined in terms of "meet" and auxiliary intervals. "Meet(X,Y)" is intuitively this.

```
| interval X       |       interval Y          |
```

Eg this relation

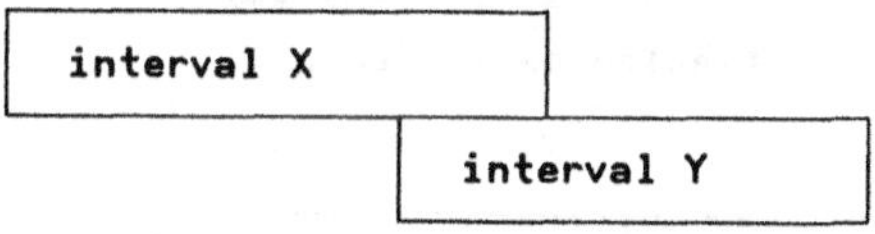

```
| interval X             |
                 |  interval Y        |
```

can be defined as suggested by this.

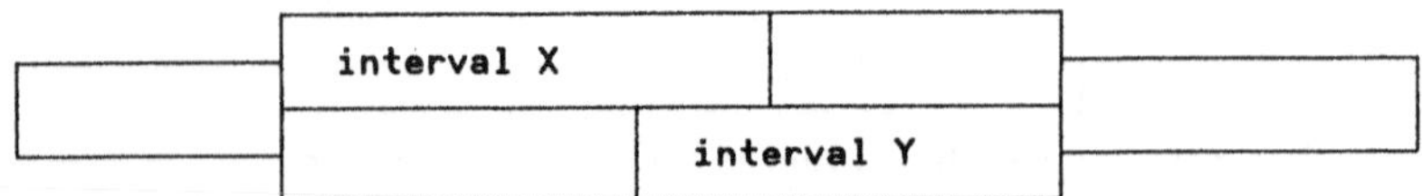

Instants can be defined too, as suitable sets of suitably overlapping intervals. But it is not clear how to exploit this parsimony.

4. Hierarchical planning

It is a commonplace that in any reasoning one will often want to suppress detail until it is appropriate. There are two ways of doing this in planning which are not always properly distinguished. They are the use of summary and abstract actions.

(There are many deficiencies in the examples in this section. They can easily be corrected, but only at the cost of considerable irrelevant detail.)

4.1. Summary actions

The idea behind summary actions is that actions need not be atomic. They may themselves have has the structure of a plan. That plan, the "body" of the action, is a more detailed account of what one has to do in order to count as performing that action. For instance, this action

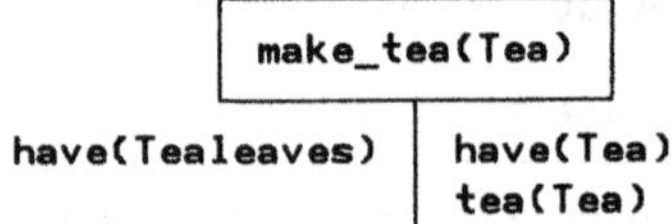

might, if looked at under a logical microscope, turn out to be this.

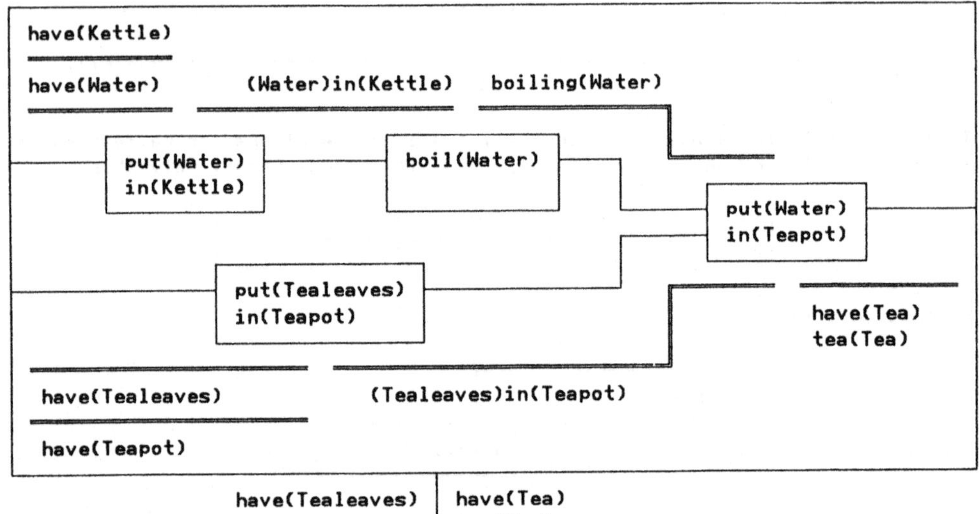

The picture suggests, as it is intended to, that the preconds and the effects of the summary action "make_tea(Tea)" are (subsets of) the preconds and effects of the entire plan that constitutes the action's body.

The standard reason for giving actions structure like this is to help control planning. One should start making a plan using only actions described at a summary level, suppressing most of the detail. Only if the plan can be completed at that level will one go out and work out the details. In the standard example, no-one plans how he will travel from Edinburgh to London by planning how he will walk to his front door. He will plan in terms of "go_to(Station)", "take(Train)", and only if that is not foiled by eg a known rail strike will he go on to plan how to get to the station. But before execution, every non-atomic action in the plan must be replaced by its body. (That process can be called action expansion). Then the resulting plan must be improved, and that process repeated until only atomic actions are left.

In order to package actions to assist that, only the odder, more likely-to-fail preconds should be mentioned in the summary. In "make_tea(Tea)", one is much more likely to have no tea-leaves than no teapot or kettle.

But there is another defence of hierarchical action description. Consider the actions "take_waltz_step", which I suppose (contrary to fact) to be

- slide left foot left
- bring right foot to it
- slide right foot right

It is not the preconds and effects of that action (where one's feet start and end) that define it, but what one's feet do on the way. That can only be described by letting "take_waltz_step" have that sequence of actions as its body. Summary actions actions are probably indispensable for representation even more than for control.

It is possible to devise a formalism that makes goal reduction and action expansion very similar. In essence, one can let a plan body be associated either with an action name (as described here), or with an action's effect. This happens in (Tate 76). But I shan't illustrate it.

4.2. Abstract actions

Abstract actions arise from applying the notion of an abstraction hierarchy to actions just as to any other sort of object. The action

make_edible_thing(X)

might have the specializations (or "refinements")

make_food(X) make_drink(X)

and make_drink might specialize to any of

make_tea(X) make_coffee(X) make_cocoa(X)

Such an approach goes very naturally with a plan representation that uses constraints. Specialization of one action may constrain the specialization of those around it. And specializations of actions and operands can interact. For instance, if the plan contained the action make_drink(X)

and X is specialized to "darjeeling"

make_drink(darjeeling)

then it is natural to suppose that the action should be specialized to

make_tea(darjeeling)

Though note that nothing has has been said about how that might be done, nor about the relationship of the preconds and effects of abstract and specialized forms of the same action.

A summary action may have more than one expansion. An abstract action may have more than one refinement. These choices introduce choicepoints into the planning process.

5. Control of planning

Making a plan almost always involves search in the space of partial plans. The operators in such a space are changes in plans; for instance: add and action; linearize an action; progress a fact. Which operators are needed or possible depends on the sort of plan being made. How does one control such search?

One way is to see the problem as nothing but search. The nodes of the search spaces are labelled with partial plans. These can be tested for being a solution. Then one can do some sort of blind search such as depth-first search. If one has a evaluation function, one can apply a standard heuristic search algorithm. I shall not discuss this, because there is nothing in it that belongs to planning rather than to search in general.

What might one do "instead"? There seem to be two current possibilities;

* Meta-level planning, in which meta-actions are considered and executed. A meta-action is an action that affects, not the domain in which the plan will be executed, but the plan itself.

(Meta-level planning can also be argued for as part of representation as well as of control. That is discussed below.)

* Constraint-based planning. Here a plan is seen as an object, containing sub-objects such as actions. The structure of that object must satisfy various constraints imposed on it. Planning is specialized constraint satisfaction.

(Though the approach described below to exemplify this turns constraints back into search operators.)

I put "instead" inside scare quotes because if an object (such as a plan) goes through a sequence of states as a result of operators being applied to it, then of course it is tracing a trajectory in the space of all possible states of that object. Any such trajectory is a search of that space. If the trajectory cannot at least in principle go through all points of the space, the search isn't complete. But the intuition behind sending the object down some particular trajectory may not be that of doing standard heuristic search.

5.1. Meta-level planning: for control

Plans are to achieve goals. Goals have to come from somewhere. If you are a computer program, they may be imposed on you by your user. If you are a slug they are an emergent property of your physiology. If you are a planning agent, then they (usually) come from from observing that the world is not, or soon will not be, as you would like it to be. A planner will have what one might call "themes" (after (Schank & Abelson 77)) such as "I am not hungry", which are things that one wants always to be true. It can also notice facts, such as "I am hungry". The fact contradicts the theme, and therefore the goal "I am not hungry" arises. Planning should then set to work to achieve that goal.

That is not offered as deep analysis of how all goals arise, but it is certainly true enough for what follows.

Now consider a system that performs actions but doesn't make plans. (Perhaps some animals are like this.) Nevertheless they respond to their environment and their (imputed) goals. How does this happen? It must be some sort of irreflective forward-driven system. One story one can tell goes like this. There are various actions that can achieve the goals. The actions are indexed to say what sort of goal they are useful for achieving. The system keeps an agenda of <goal, {suitable_action,suitable_action,...}> pairs. Each such entry on the agenda will be called a task. An agenda might look like this.

```
< -hungry, { eat_fruit, eat_meat } >
< -hot, { enter_shade, enter_water } >
< -thirsty, { drink_water } >
```

The system has some sort of executive for dealing with goals, themes, facts, tasks. For instance, it might obey the hard-wired rules

```
If you have theme T
and T is false
then create a task with goal T

If you have a task X with goal G
and there are no actions listed in the task X
then collect and record the actions suitable for G in task X
```

So far this is all forward-driven.

Now an agenda and a plan are not very different. The plan

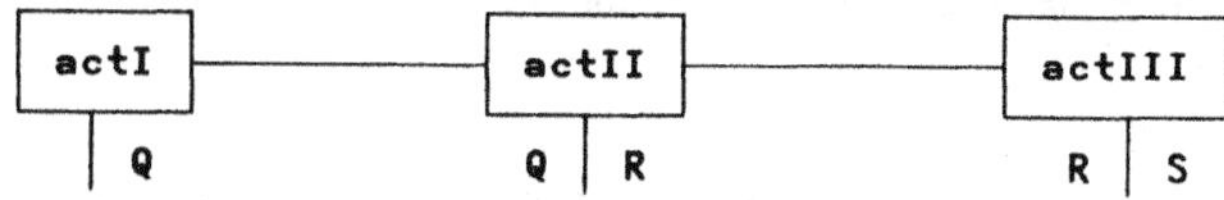

is very like the agenda

```
< S, {actIII} >
< R, {actII} >
< Q, {actI} >
```

though of course with added machinery indicating the teleological relations of the tasks; mainly, something to indicate which subgoals are protected, to avoid other actions in the plan destroying them. And because of this extra machinery the conditions on being a good plan can be much more detailed, and therefore more effective, than the conditions on being a good agenda could ever be.

The next step is to remark that, if one has themes about what makes a world state a good world state, then one can equally well have themes that say what makes a plan a good plan. And if a plan violates those themes, then goals of modifying the plan can be set up in just the same that goals of modifying the world were set up.

So one will have meta-themes, meta-goals and meta-actions. Just to give a concrete (though imaginary) example, a meta-agenda (for a non-linear planner) might look like this:

```
< protection violation between actIV and protection of S,
        { linearize actIV before protection of S,
          linearize actIV after protection of S } >
< unsupported precond P of actVII,
        { add instance of act IX to achieve P before actVII,
          add instance of act XII to achieve P before actVII } >
```

Now there will again need to be some forward-driven system that puts entries on this meta-agenda, or takes them off, or actually executes one of the meta-actions listed in one of the meta-tasks. When such a meta-action is executed, then the plan that will eventually actually be executed in the domain will be elaborated.

I could have gone straight from the idea of themes and agendas to the idea of meta-themes and meta-agendas, and have left out making the point that agendas are like plans. The reason I haven't is that it is worth stressing that the meta-agenda so far described is just that; an agenda, and not a plan. Talking of "meta-planning" is a little premature. Only when one has repeated the process, so that meta-agendas are replaced by meta-plans, and when the defects of meta-plans are listed as tasks on a meta-meta-agenda, will one be into meta-planning properly so called. As far as I know this has not yet been done.

Of course, however far one iterates this process, the top level is going to have to be forward-driven and irreflective.

Here are accounts of three meta-planners, in increasing order of complexity. For each of them, something is said about
* the sort of object plan being built.
* data structures that are used other than the plan itself.
* the repertoire of meta-actions that can be applied to the plan.
* the executive program that manages the meta-agenda.

5.1.1. TEAMWORK

This is a planner on which I worked with others at Essex. It was intended to test ideas, first about planning and communication, and later about dependency-directed backtracking and plan execution, that I shan't discuss here. But the rest of it makes a good first example.

The object plan is a non-linear precedence plan. The extra information about the plan is just the meta-agenda, which contains <meta-goal, meta-action*> pairs. Meta-goals are detected by pieces of code called "critics" that examine unexamined parts of a plan to see if there is anything wrong with it, such as a protection violation or an unreduced subgoal.

The meta-action repertoire includes
* linearize an action to avoid a protection violation.
* reduce a subgoal by
    * relying on the effect of an action already in the plan.
    * introducing a new action.

The meta-agenda is also used as the record of past decisions that may need to be undone on backtracking. The meta-actions in any meta-task can be divided into
* those previously tried but which led to failure later.
* the one (if any) most recently tried and not yet rejected.
* those not yet tried.
So if the agenda is seen as a stack, it is exactly a a stack of choice records as in the ordinary implementation of depth-first search.

The executive looks like this:

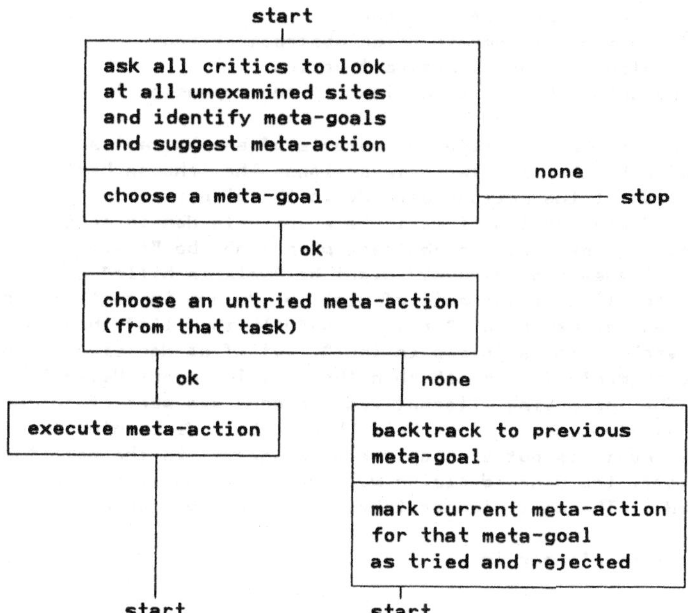

5.1.2. SPEX

This account derives from (Friedland & Iwasaki 85). (That paper in fact describes two planners. Both of them, and the next, emerged from the MOLGEN project at Stanford, and were intended to plan molecular genetics experiments. I am not clear what their intellectual family tree is.)

The object plan is a non-linear precedence plan, but abstract and summary actions are central. The main thing that one knows about domain level actions is what their refinements and abstractions are, and what sub-plans they summarize.

The extra information is the meta-agenda, and records of competing alternative refinements of an abstract action already in the plan. The meta-agenda is different from the prototype in that meta-tasks on it are just a single <meta-action> item. Meta-goals need not be recorded, since each meta-action does two things when executed: it alters the object plan; and it puts onto the meta-agenda any meta-actions that must follow it. Since the decision about what meta-action to execute has been made, knowing what it is for is pointless. This means that the meta-actions are more dependent on each other than previously. It also means that deciding whether some particular change to the object plan is made by one meta-action or its logical successor is not vital.

What the meta-agenda does allow is freedom to decide in which order meta-actions are executed. If the agenda is seen as a stack, one can use the usual FIFO/LIFO regime distinction to get depth-first or breadth-first plan elaboration; or one can assign meta-actions priorities, and execute them highest priority first.

The meta-action repertoire includes the following. (In fact I misrepresent all of them for simplicity. As indicated, the demarcation between meta-actions is not critical.)
* obtain the goal of the plan from the user, and put it on the meta-agenda.
* find a summary action to achieve a subgoal.
* collect the alternative refinements of an abstract action.
* choose the best refinement of an abstract action.
* replace a summary action by its expansion (if the expansion is unique).

The records of competing alternative refinements of an abstract action already in the plan are used by the last two meta-actions. The "choose best refinement" meta-action will look at the actions already in the plan in order to see if the context gives any advice about what would be a suitable domain action at that point in the plan. For instance, an abstract plan might be "travel, then sleep". The alternative refinements of "travel" might be "walk in hills" or "drive on motorway". The alternative refinements of might be "sleep in tent" or "stay in hotel" If the chosen refinement of "travel" is "walk in hills" then the best refinement of "sleep" would be "sleep in tent". But if no decision had been made about the best refinement of "travel" then the decision about "sleep" would have to be postponed. The "competing alternatives" records are part of the machinery for doing that. Nevertheless, as the choice has to be made eventually, the "choose best refinement" is put back on the meta-agenda, in the hope that next time it is taken off, the other decision will have been made, so permitting a decision to be made. (The next planner takes this strategy further.)

The executive for this planner is

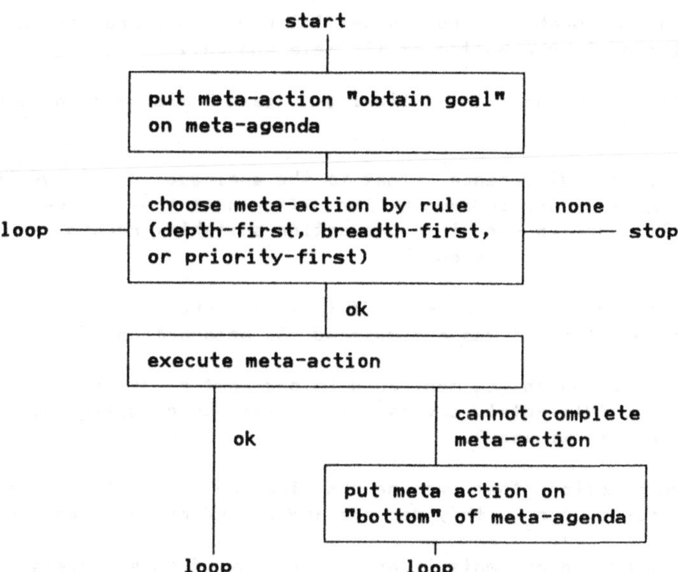

5.1.3. MOLGEN/Stefik

This account derives from (Stefik 81b).

The object plan is a non-linear precedence planner, again with an emphasis on abstract actions and their refinements.

The other important thing in plan representation is constraint propagation (Stefik 1981a) which I understand in this context as being like goal regression. Suppose the goal of a plan is that a gift be with a friend. An abstract plan "pack gift, then send gift" is discovered. Then "gift" is refined to "clock". But then the clock must satisfy the constraint "intact" when it arrives. This constraint can be propagated back (regressed) over "send", to impose the constraint "carefully packed" before "send". (That that is the appropriate constraint is a piece of domain knowledge.) To satisfy that constraint, "pack" must be refined to "pack in padded box" rather than say "pack in old envelope".

Quite a lot of information about the plan is extracted from the plan and kept outside it. There are meta-actions whose only effect is to gather and store such information. Among such information is

* tuples of objects in the plan whose refinements will influence the refinement of the others.
* notes of alternative refinements of objects.
* "differences" (in the sense of GPS) between what has achieved and what is till to be achieved.

The meta-agenda again mentions only meta-actions in the meta-tasks. But a distinction is made between "suspended" meta-tasks and the rest. Meta-actions are complex and their execution involves choices about precisely what should be done. There may be too little information to make such a choice confidently. A suspended meta-task is one which, because of lack of information about the plan on which it was acting, was unable to run to completion. (Those are the meta-actions that SPEX returned to the bottom of its meta-agenda.)

The meta-action repertoire includes the following. (Again I misrepresent some of them for simplicity.)

* Find an action to reduce a difference. (That is the analogue in this system of "achieve a subgoal".) Actions are indexed by the differences they reduce, as in GPS operator tables. If there is more than one action suitable, record the alternatives and suspend the meta-action.

* Replace a abstract action by its expansion If there is more than one expansion suitable, then record the alternatives and suspend the meta-action.

* Propagate a constraint on an object mentioned in one part of the plan to another part of the plan. (Ultimately several constraints congregating at one point may make a choice determinate.)

There are also some meta-actions that examine the plan and only alter the extra information about it; for instance, they may see and record differences.

The standard account of MOLGEN presents it as a hierarchy of three levels.
+ At the bottom, the object plan.
+ In the middle, a plan with abstract actions in it
+ At the top, a "meta-planning" level involving meta-actions called FOCUS, RESUME, GUESS, UNDO.

I think this is not the way to see it. The relation between the bottom and middle layers is one of abstraction; between the middle and top layers, it is one of meta-ness. So they do not form a hierarchy. (Let me emphasize that I am not therefore denigrating MOLGEN.)

The idea of the executive is as below. The parts of the flowchart are given names.

* Look at the plan. See what needs to be done. Put meta-tasks on the agenda.

* FOCUS: If there is a meta-task, and you are certain what to do about it (it is not suspended), then do it.

* RESUME: If there is a meta-task, and you previously were uncertain what to do about it (it is suspended) and the plan has changed, then then try it again. It may be possible to run to completion now.

* GUESS: If you are certain about nothing, but the plan is not finished (there are only suspended meta-tasks on the meta-agenda, and the plan has not changed, so there is no more evidence on which to base a decision), then guess what to do and do that.

* UNDO: If you find something wrong with the plan that cannot be cured by further elaborating it, you have earlier GUESSED wrong. You will have to backtrack to an earlier state and try applying a different meta-action to that state.

(Ideally one knows precisely which meta-actions led to any given part of the plan. So, given an incurable problem in the plan, one ought to be able to backtrack to a state just before the execution of one of the culprit meta-actions. In fact there are problems in doing this in general (Steel 1987) and (unsurprisingly) MOLGEN confesses to failure in this area.)

The flowchart of the executive is:

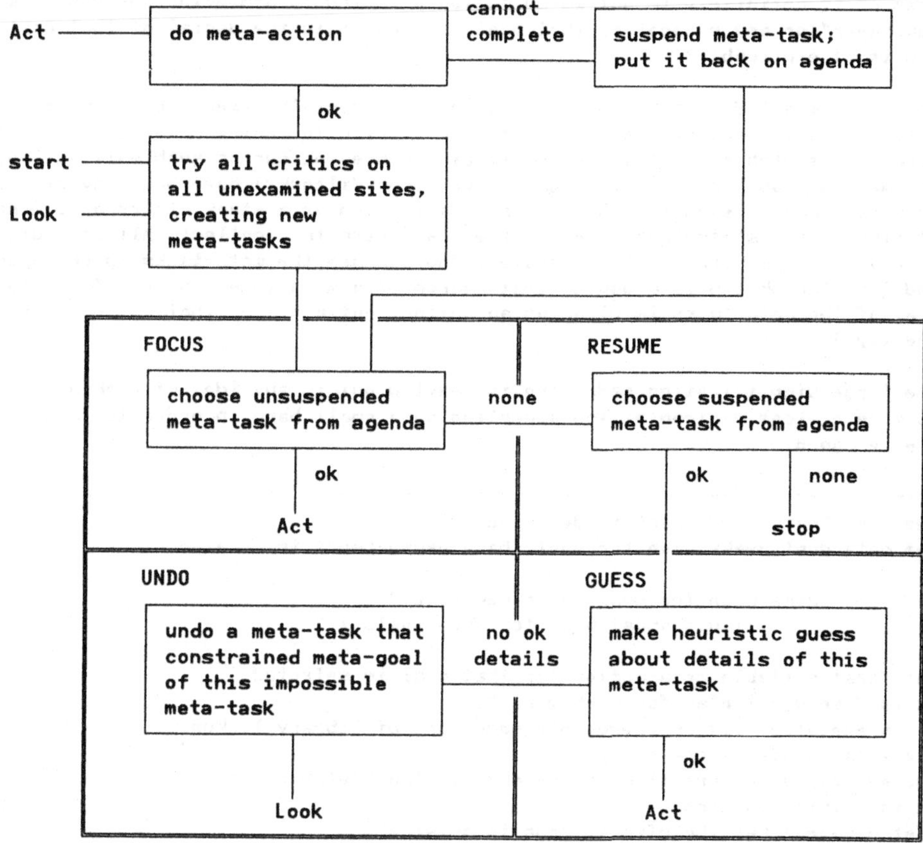

5.2. Meta-level planning: for representation

So far, meta-planning has been justified on grounds of efficiency in planning. It can be argued to be more important than that; there are some rational decisions that are inexpressible without it. Here are some examples.

5.2.1. Meta-actions are observed and reported

This example is due to (Wilensky 83). However, as he was concerned with representing plans for plan recognition rather than plan making, I have changed the machinery used to express it very considerably.

Consider this story.

> John wanted a paper.
> It was raining.

John didn't have a coat.
He decided not to get a paper.

The problem is that the last step is clearly a rationally explicable action, and it is part of what John decides to do when he thinks about getting a paper. What however it definitely is not is an action directed to achieving the goal "have newspaper" or any subgoal of that goal. Indeed it is the denial of that goal. So how is it explicable?

What is suggested is that that last step is in fact the execution of a meta-action that is part of the attempt to make a plan to achieve "have newspaper". Here is a sketch of what one might imagine happening during such meta-acting. The meta-actions involved (though derived from Wilensky) have been invented just so as to have an example. The meta-agenda is seen as a stack. There a pictures of its current state from time to time. Each meta-task collects all its suitable meta-actions as soon as it is created. One can see the meta-tasks as OR-nodes, and then the sketch is a depth-first search of a meta-level space. (The meta-goal of the meta-tasks is given as an action, not a state. That is just for brevity.)

One large simplification made here is leaving out is any idea of ranking goals as more or less desirable, and accepting some small harm in order to gain a greater good.

The goal "have newspaper" is detected.
The meta-goal "make plan for goal "have newspaper"" is created.

< make plan for goal "have newspaper",
{ use usual plan for such goals } >

The first suitable meta-action for that goal is selected.
It is "use usual plan for such goals".
It is executed. (It is presumably some sort of library lookup.)
The meta-agenda is now empty.
The effect is the creation of the object plan "fetch paper".
It is raining outside.
"Fetch paper" has the effect "John is outside".
So "fetch paper" has the side-effect "John is wet".
John has the theme "- John is wet".
So "fetch paper" creates a goal conflict.
(So far unmentioned.
It means a plan for some goal will violate another theme.)
The meta-goal "resolve goal conflict" is created.
(That is an automatic response to the presence of the goal conflict.)

< resolve goal conflict
{ prevent side-effect,
change plan that causes conflict,
abandon plan } >

The first suitable meta-action for that goal is selected.
It is "prevent side-effect".
It is executed.
The effect is the insertion of the action "put on coat" into the object plan,
(because via some bits of domain knowledge,
it is seen that its effect "John is wearing coat"
prevents the effect "John is wet".)

The action "put on coat" has the precond "John has a coat".
The meta-goal "make plan for "John has a coat"" is created.
(That is an automatic response to the presence of the precond.)

```
< make plan for "John has a coat",
        { use usual plan for such goals } >
< resolve goal conflict
        { prevent side-effect,
          change plan that causes conflict,
          abandon plan } >
```

The first suitable meta-action for that goal is selected.
It is "use usual plan for such goals".
It is executed.
It fails. (Since John does not have a coat, there is no such usual plan.)

```
< make plan for "John has a coat",
        { } >
< resolve goal conflict
        { prevent side-effect,
          change plan that causes conflict,
          abandon plan } >
```

An alternative suitable meta-action for that goal is sought.
None is found.
The meta-goal "make plan for "John has a coat"" is unachievable.
It arose because of the execution of the meta-action "prevent side-effect", which led to the insertion of the action "put on coat" into the object plan.
Undo that meta-action.

```
< resolve goal conflict
        { change plan that causes conflict,
          abandon plan } >
```

The meta-action "change plan that causes conflict" is selected.
.... Execution of this involves trying alternative actions
in the object plan. Assume they all fail ....

```
< resolve goal conflict
        { abandon plan } >
```

An alternative suitable meta-action
for the meta-goal "resolve goal conflict" is sought.
The meta-action "abandon plan" is selected.
It is executed.
The effect is that the whole object plan is deleted, and its goal dismissed.

The execution of last step is the decision itself (not the result of the decision, note) that was to be explained.

5.2.2. Cross-level planning

This is the other example. It is due to (Bartle 87).

John is looking out of his window, on the outskirts of town, wondering what birthday present to buy for a friend. He thinks:
I must buy a present for Fred.

I can do that in town.
What shall I get him?
Aha - the bus is about to leave.
I'll catch the bus,
decide what to do when I get to town,
and when I get there I'll do whatever I've decided.

What is odd here is the plan that John makes as he dashes for the bus. It mixes object actions (catching the bus) and meta-actions (making a plan, executing a plan) as if there were no difference. All the meta-planning approaches so far have assumed that the different levels of meta-ness are quite separate, each level containing actions that just mention the level below. But the example given shows that that assumption is, prima facie, wrong.

Furthermore, this seems to be quite a common event. Here are some very common sorts of plans of the form that all show plans that seem to involve actions of more than one level of meta-ness.

* I will find something out, then I will decide what to do, then I will do it.

* I'll ask someone else what they would do, and then I'll do that.

* I'll do this part of the task myself, and ask someone else to decide what to do about that other part, and to execute his own plan to. So the whole task will be achieved.

And here is a person apparently consciously reflecting on which of two meta-actions to perform.

* My child is not yet born, so I don't know its sex. Shall I choose a name for both a boy and a girl, or shall I wait till I know what it is, and then choose a name for the appropriate sex?

It is not yet clear what to do about representing and making such plans. But they can't be dismissed as marginal curiosities.

5.3. Planning with constraints

Here is a completely different approach to controlling search during planning. It follows Fox's factory scheduling system (Fox 83). The main ideas are that

* A plan should be described by the constraints on it.

* These constraints should be used, not as input to a constraint satisfaction algorithm, but to generate operators and heuristics for state-space search.

* Constraints should be divided into classes ("levels"). The search governed by one level of constraints should be completed. The schedule found should then be used as the start state of search controlled by the next level. The point of this is, as usual, decisions involve work and may be wrong. They should be postponed as long as possible.

This approach was invented to handle factory scheduling. It looks more like constraint satisfaction than like the planning so far described. It also looks as if it is applicable to many domains besides planning. And indeed, the strictly planning part of it, where suitable actions are found and ordered, is both small and simple. But outside the blocks world, a lot of planning is largely scheduling; planning aircraft flying orders, or oil rig maintenance, or manufacturing, or dozens of other activities are like that. Even in action-ordering planning, the proper binding of operands of actions may be best described by constraints.

Constraints in factory scheduling may be absolute (hard)

+ the operation of milling must be done on a milling machine

or just preferences (soft)

+ it is easier to make objects with lugs by milling than by forging
+ doing work in shift1 is preferred to doing work in shift2 or shift3

They may express a range of options

+ milling must be done on milling-machine-1 or milling-machine-2
+ a shift must be one of shift1, shift2 or shift3.

Constraints of a given level (assuming the level of a constraint is known) are collected, and at each level three things happen.

* Pre-search: the constraints are used to generate search operators and heuristics and an evaluation function. There is also a choice about the order in which operators are to be applied. Pre-search is a knowledge-based process. The knowledge is about scheduling, though, not about the domain scheduled.

* Search is performed: nodes are rated by an evaluation function, and only the N best nodes are retained. Search operators are applied to the highest-rated node. (This is beam search.)

* Post-search: if a solution is found, good. If no solution is found, go back and search more thoroughly; relax pruning to re-admit pruned spaces and/or create more operators to generate a larger space.

The constraints above might generate operators and heuristics like this:

constraint: a shift must be one of shift1, shift2 or shift3.
operators: refine a schedule with unfixed shift to one with shift fixed as shift1 (resp. shift2, shift3).

constraint: milling must be done on milling-machine-1 or milling-machine-2.
operators: refine a schedule with unfixed milling machine to one with milling machine fixed as milling-machine-1 (resp. milling-machine-2).

constraint: the operation of milling must be done on a milling machine.
heuristic: any schedule violating this is a failure node, and must be pruned.

constraint: doing work in shift1 is preferred to doing work in shift2 or shift3
heuristic: prune search below nodes labelled with a schedule shift fixed as shift2 or shift3.

(This is the sort of heuristic that might be abandoned at post-search after failure, in order to enlarge the search space)

constraint: it is easier to make objects with lugs by milling than by forging.
heuristic: rate schedules making objects with lugs by milling as better than those making them by forging.

(Clearly there is a choice between using a constraint to construct a pruning heuristic, and using it to construct an evaluation function. Pre-search would have to make such a choice.)

There are some parts of planning best done by processes that do not naturally fit this pattern. For instance, the earliest version of the schedule is developed like this.

* Accept the goal of the job.

* Look up a suitable sequences of actions for doing that job in a plan library.

* Given the current date and the due date and the durations of the actions, find the earliest and latest start times for the actions. (This can be slightly complicated by alternative possible action sequences, but it is mainly an application of standard OR techniques.)

But then the match improves. For instance, one can see the current factory schedule as being a set of constraints. Suppose a milling operation in the schedule being made is constrained to start between 8:00 and 16:00 and take 3 hours. One might already have

```
milling-machine-1 free from 9:00 till 13:00
milling-machine-2 free from 10:00 till 14:00.
```

It would be possible to turn those constraints into two search operators.

```
bind milling-machine to milling-machine-1
     start time of milling operation to 9:00-13:00

bind milling-machine to milling-machine-2
     start time of milling operation to 10:00-14:00
```

But equally, if it was decided that decisions about the time of an operation were more crucial than, and should be made before, decisions about which machine to perform an operation on, one might turn them into a generalized time constraint, talking about when there was at least one milling machine available (9:00-14:00).

```
bind start time of milling operation to 9:00-14:00
```

This is a weaker constraint on the time of the operation. It will then not force premature choices about the times of operations dependent on that milling operation. There will be less backtracking in the search for possible times for the whole schedule. Of course the decision about machines must be made eventually. It will appear as another couple of constraints to be used during search at the next level, when decisions about actual machines were to be made.

```
bind milling-machine to milling-machine-1
     start time of milling operation to 9:00-13:00

bind milling-machine to milling-machine-2
     start time of milling operation to 10:00-14:00
```

One of the most interesting future directions for this approach is to make the decision about when a constraint should be considered dynamically (####). Constraints that are likely to be hard to satisfy should be done early. For instance, when scheduling several jobs, the system might usually

+ satisfy all constraints for one job

+ then satisfy all constraints for the next job

But if it was spotted that some particular machines were a bottleneck, it would be wise to switch to the strategy

+ satisfy all constraints from any job about the use of the bottleneck resource

+ then satisfy all other constraints of any job

6. Further reading

6.1. Overviews

Cohen P, Feigenbaum E
chapter 15 vol 3, AI Handbook
Pitman (in UK)

A clear, though very selective, review of planning in historical order. Probably the best place for an absolute beginner to start.

Charniak E, McDermott D, 1985
chapter 9, Managing plans of action
in Introduction to Artificial Intelligence
Addison Wesley

A good and very modern review of planning, in anti-historical order. Reflects McDermott's work in NASL rather strongly. Next after AI Handbook for new reader?

Nilsson, Nils J: 1981
chapter 7 & 8, Principles of artificial intelligence
Spinger Verlag

Clear and detailed account of some of the earlier ideas in planning by someone who was there as they happened.

Tate A, 1985
A review of knowledge-based planning techniques
in Expert Systems '85, Cambridge Univ Press

A large bibliography, but the main thing about it is that it lays out very well the axes of variation of planning, and places different planners and techniques in that space. Helps one see how different work should be compared.

Grant T, 1986
Knowledge based planning and scheduling - a bibliography with abstracts
KBPG/TR/3, Dept Computer science, Brunel Univ.

Not everything, but the most comprehensive bibliography I know. Many entries have comments or abstracts.

Chapman D, 1987
Planning for conjunctive goals
Artificial Intelligence 32 (1987) 333:377

A theoretical putting-together of many parts of non-linear planning. Offers an account of a provably complete planner, if you accept sternly limited planning. Very good on relating different people's work.

6.2. Planning and knowledge

Moore, Robert: 1985
A formal theory of knowledge and action
in: Hobbs JR, Moore RC: 1985
Formal theories of the commonsense world
Ablex publishing corp.

The possible-world approach to reasoning about action and knowledge.

Konolige K, 1982
A first-order formalization of knowledge and belief for a multi-agent planning system
in Machine Intelligence 10, eds Hayes JE, Michie D, Pao Y-H
Ellis Horwood

A very elegant connection between a theory of belief that treats beliefs as sentences, and situation calculus.

Haas AR, 1986
A syntactic theory of belief and action
Artificial intelligence 28(1986) 245-292

On the importance of having descriptions of things of the right form before you can act on those things, as well as other ideas about what sort of actions can affect knowledge how.

Morgenstern, Leora: 1986
A first-order theory of planning, knowledge and action
99:114 in Halpern JY, ed
Reasoning about knowledge
Morgan Kauffmann

How to do the sort of thing Konolige proposes without having to have an infinite hierarchy of languages.

6.3. Planning with continuous quantities

Salter, Richard M: 1983
Planning in a continuous domain - an introduction
Robotica (1983) 85:93

A good but non-definitive account of how to plan with actions that change, not the world, but rules about how the world changes spontaneously.

References

Allen JF, 1983
Maintaining knowledge about temporal intervals
CACM 26:11

Allen JF, Koomen JA, 1983
Planning using a temporal world model
IJCAI 8

Allen JF, Hayes Pat: 1985
A common-sense theory of time
IJCAI-85 528:531

Bartle R, forthcoming
Cross-level planning
PhD thesis, Dept Computer Science, Essex University

Brown, Frank M (ed), 1987
The fram problem in artificial intelligence
Morgan Kaufman
Chapman D, 1987
Planning for conjunctive goals
Artificial Intelligence 32 (1987) 333:377
Dean, Thomas; McDermott, Drew: 1987
Temporal data base management
Artificial Intelligence 32 (1987) 1:55
Dershowitz, N, 1985
Synthetic programming
Artificial Intelligence 25(3) 323-373
Fox, Mark S: 1983
Constraint-directed search: a case study of job-shop scheduling
PhD thesis, Carnegie-Mellon University
University Microfilms 84-06442
Fox MS, Smith SF, 1984
ISIS - a knowledge-based system for factory scheduling
Expert Systems vol 1 # 1
Learned Information Inc
Friedland PE, Iwasaki Y, 1985
The concept and implementation of skeletal plans
Journal of automated reasoning vol 1 # 2
Georgeff, Michael; Lansky, Amy (eds):1987
Reasoning about actions and plans
Proceeding of 1986 conference
Morgan Kauffman
Green CC, 1969
Applications of theorem proving to problem solving
IJCAI-69
reprinted in Readings in AI, eds Nilsson N, Webber BN
Tioga
Hallam J, Mellish CS (eds): 1987
Advances in artificial intelligence
John Wiley
Hoare, CAR: 1969
An axiomatic basis for computer programming
CACM 12(10)
Kautz, Henry A: 1982
A first-order dynamic logic for programming
PhD thesis, University of Toronto
Computer systems research group technical report CSRG-144
McCarthy J, Hayes Pat J, 1969
Some philosophical problems from the standpoint of AI
in Machine Intelligence 4, eds Meltzer B, Michie D,
Edinburgh University Press
Manna, Zohar; Waldinger, Richard: 1986
A theory of plans
in (Georgeff & Lansky 86)
Nilsson Nils, 1973
Hieracrchical robot planning and execution system
SRI AI center technical note 76
Rosenschein, Stanley J: 1981
Plan synthesis: a logical perspective
IJCAI 1981 331:337
Sacerdoti ED, 1977
A structure for plans and behaviour
American Elsevier

Schank RC, Abelson RP, 1977
Scripts, plans, goals and understanding
Lawrence Erlbaum

Stefik MJ, 1981a
Planning with constraints - MOLGEN: Part 1
Artificial Intelligence 16(2) 111-139

Stefik MJ, 1981b
Planning and meta-planning - MOLGEN: Part 2
Artificial Intelligence 16(2) 141-169

Steel SWD, 1987
On trying to do dependency-directed backtracking...
in (Hallam & Mellish 87)

Tate A, 1976
Project planning using a hierarchical non-linear planner
Tech report 25, Dept Artificial Intelligence, Edinburgh Univ

Tsang EPK: 1987
Planning in a temporal frame; a partial world description approach
PhD thesis, Dept Computer Science, Essex University

Van Benthem, JFAK: 1983
The logic of time
D. Reidel publishing co.

Vere SA, 1983
Planning in time: windows and durations for activities and goals
IEEE PAMI vol 5

Wilensky R, 1983
Planning and understanding
Addison Wesley

Natural Language Systems

Jens Erik Fenstad
University of Oslo

A natural language system aims to provide an overall framework for relating the *linguistic form* of utterances and their *semantic interpretation.* And the relation between the two must be algorithmic.

The formal study of natural languages has always had an algorithmic flavor. This is part of our inheritance from the pioneering work of N. Chomsky. His *Syntactic Structures* from 1957 marked a theoretical renewal of linguistic science. And with this renewal a bond was soon forged with symbolic logic, a part of which is formal language theory. Chomsky himself was one of the active participants in this development. This theoretical development soon joined forces with the emerging computer science and a vigorous field of computational linguistics was established. This science does not only have important applications to the study of natural languages, it is also an integral part of computer science, e.g. in compiler design.

But this has been a computational linguistics with a main emphasis on morphology and syntactic processing. "Meaning" was always a recognized part of the total enterprise, but it never played a central role. Around 1967 R. Montague set up a model in which a technically adequate meaning component for the first time was added to the syntactic part. This work has had an important impact on recent theoretical work in linguistics. Montague's model is based on higher order intensional logic, which is not very algorithmic in spirit. But if linguistics is going to be an "applied" science, computational morphology and syntax need to be supplemented by a *computational semantics.*

Computational semantics, both theory and applications, is our main concern in these lectures. But semantics is part of a larger enterprise and cannot be seen in isolation from the other parts. After Chomsky there has been a number of important developments in syntactic theory. Some of them have had a primary linguistic motivation, e.g. the *Lexical-Functional Grammar* developed by J. Bresnan and R. M. Kaplan (see Bresnan 1982) and the *Generalized Phrase Structure Grammar* developed by G. Gazdar and a number of co-workers. Recently the GPSG has led to the development of a theory of *Head-Driven Phrase Structure Grammar* (see Pollard and Sag 1988), which in many of its techniques is similar to the work reported on in this series of lectures.

Other developments were primarily motivated from a computational point of view, e.g. the *Definite Clause Grammar* of F. C. N. Pereira and D. H. D. Warren, a formulation tailored for a PROLOG implementation (see Pereira and Warren 1982 and the recent book Pereira and Shieber 1987). We should also mention the *PATR-II* formalism developed at SRI International (see e.g. Shieber 1986). At the focal point of many of these developments stands the work of M. Kay on a unification-based approach to grammatical analysis. This work is again related to the "resolution" approach to logic and logic programming.

Remark. A good introduction to recent developments is the book *Lectures on Contemporary Syntactic Theories*, P. Sells 1985 and the survey paper *Computer Applications of Linguistic Theory*, P. K. Halvorsen 1987. The approach to computational semantics developed in these lectures is presented in full details in the book *Situations, Language and Logic*, Fenstad et al. 1987.

First Lecture: Background from Logic and Linguistics

In this first lecture we will present some background from logic and linguistics. We will do this by a (critical!) review of some basic features of Montague grammar and by an introduction to some elementary aspects of attribute-value systems.

Almost every system of grammar adopts the basic Aristotelian "subject-predicate" form, which is not surprising looking back to the history of grammar and logic from ancient to modern times. Thus we have the basic rule

$$\mathrm{S} \rightarrow \mathrm{NP}\ \mathrm{VP}$$

which states that a sentence is composed of a noun phrase joined with a verb phrase. Thus the structure of *John walks* is represented by

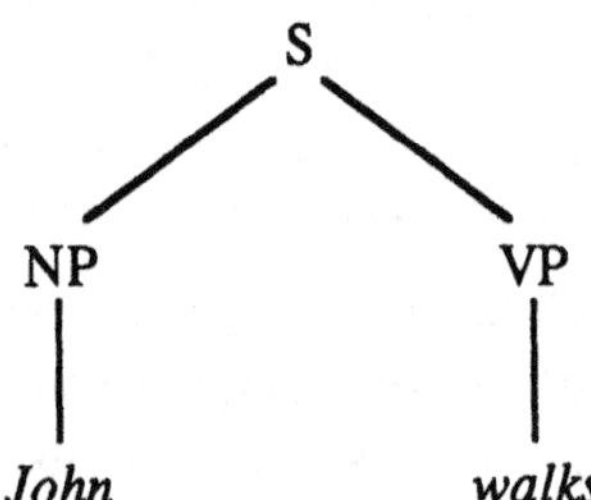

But the world consists of more than properties or intransitive verbs. People act together, i.e. we need relations or transitive verbs; thus the further rule

$$\mathrm{VP} \rightarrow \mathrm{V}\ \mathrm{NP}$$

which states that the verb phrase can be further analysed as composed of a verb and a noun phrase.

The structure of *John married Jane* is represented by

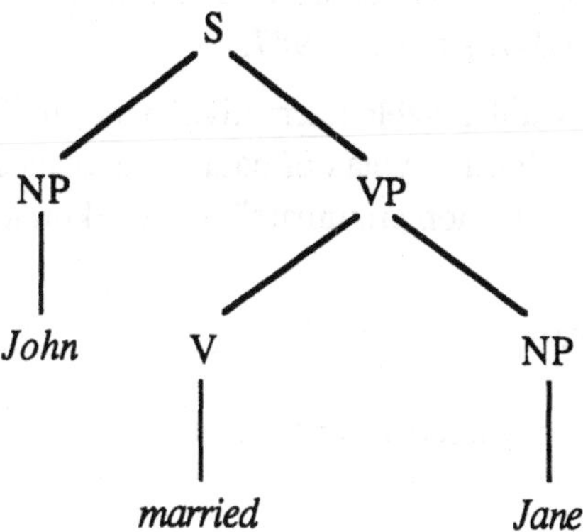

This is very simple and leaves almost all problems unresolved. Let us focus on two, one being syntactic in nature, the other a problem of logical structure.

Agreement: Nothing so far allows us to distinguish between the grammatically correct

John walks

and the grammatically incorrect

John walk

since both have the basic NP + VP form.

Logical form: One of the fundamental criticisms of B. Russel against the Aristotelian logic was that the basic logical form is *relational* and not of the "subject-predicate" form. But how to extract the correct relational form

marry(*John*, *Jane*)

from the syntax tree for the sentence *John married Jane*?

Montague Grammar

We shall in this section present the *extensional* part of Montague's model as given in his paper PTQ, *The Proper Treatment of Quantification in Ordinary English* (see Montague 1974). The full Montague model consists of two basic parts

A. *Extended Categorical Syntax*
B. *Translation into a System of Higher-Order Intensional Logic.*

By restricting ourselves to the extensional part we may drop the intensionality aspect and in B translate into extensional higher order logic.

We should also remark that Montague's work and also the work of J. Lambek on the formal theory of categorical grammar have stimulated much recent research, see e.g. the collection of papers W. Buszkowski et al. 1987.

Thus categorical grammar is still a viable alternative to the "unification-based" approaches mentioned above as a theory for the syntax of natural languages. There has even been recent work on "categorical unification grammars", see Uszkoreit 1987.

A. *Extended Categorical Syntax*

We first define a class CAT of category symbols

1. $e,t \in$ CAT
2. if A, B $\in$ CAT, then $^A/_B$, $^A//_B \in$ CAT

Thus from the "primitives" e,t we generate an infinity of category symbols by means of the operations / and //.

Next, to each A $\in$ CAT there is associated a class of words $\mathbf{B}_A$, the *lexical items* of category A. For all but finitely many A, $\mathbf{B}_A = \emptyset$. The lexicon $\mathbf{B}$ is given by the union

$$\mathbf{B} = \bigcup_{A \in CAT} \mathbf{B}_A$$

Finally, we have the *derived syntactic rules*: A finite list of functions F_i is given which generates a set **P** of (derived) phrases from the lexical base **B**. Typically a syntactic rule has the form

$$F_i(\alpha_{A/B},\beta_B) = \gamma_A,$$

i.e. F_i is a binary operator which acts on a phrase α of category A/B and a phrase β of category B and produces a phrase γ of category A.

We will illustrate this rather abstract description by a number of examples.

1. *Intransitive verbs*: IV = $^t/_e$

$$\mathbf{B}_{IV} = \{\textit{run, walk, } \ldots\}$$

2. *Terms*: T = $^t/_{IV}$

$$\mathbf{B}_T = \{\textit{John, Mary, } \ldots\}$$

There is a syntactic rule F_1 which acts on a term and an intransitive verb and produces a sentence, e.g.

$$F_1(\textit{John,run}) = \textit{John runs}$$

We note that *John* is of category $^{t}/_{IV}$, *run* is of category IV. The result of applying F_1 to *John* and *run* is not merely the concatenation of the arguments, the morpheme *s* has been introduced to mark third person singular in the verb.

The analysis can be written in tree form:

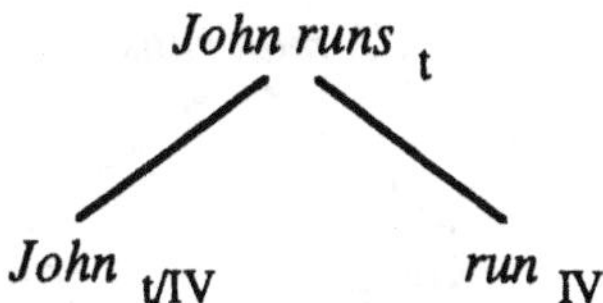

This corresponds to the basic S → NP VP rule.

3. *Transitive verbs*: TV = $^{IV}/_{T}$

$$\mathbf{B}_{TV} = \{marry, love, \ldots\}$$

We give a simple example:

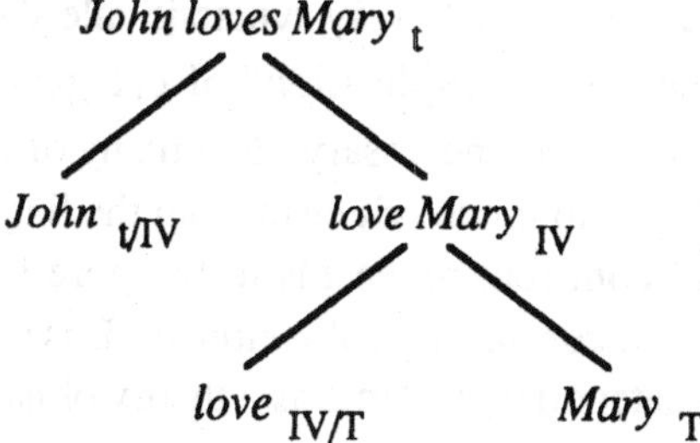

We have here a new syntactic rule F_2 which acts on a transitive verb and a term and produces an intransitive verb. This rule is purely categorical, i.e. a concatenation of the arguments.

4. *Adverbs modifying intransitive verbs*: IAV = $^{IV}/_{IV}$

$$\mathbf{B}_{IAV} = \{slowly, \ldots\}$$

A simple example:

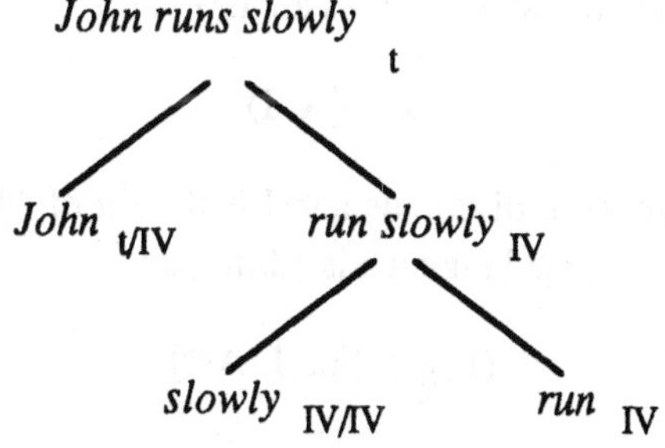

The new syntactic rule $F_3(slowly_{IV/IV}, run_{IV}) = run\ slowly_{IV}$ inverts the order of the arguments.

5. *Common noun*: $CN = {}^t/_e$

We give an example:

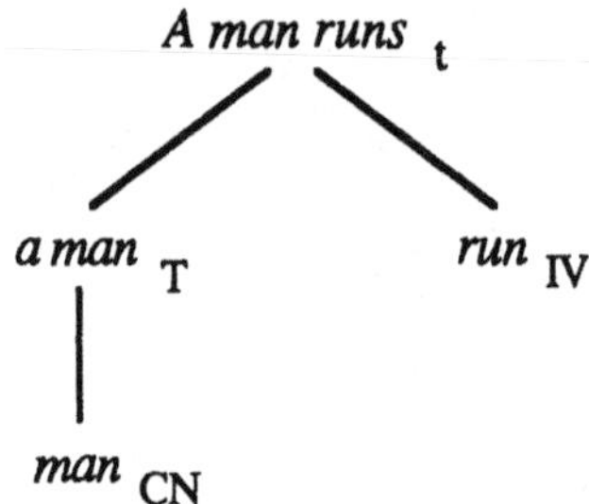

The new rule here acts on a single common noun and produces a term. The rule must specify which of *an, a* is to be chosen. Similar rules will produce: *the man, every man.*

This concludes our brief sample of the syntactic part of Montague's analysis. The leading idea of (pure) categorial grammar is that every syntactic rule should be a pure concatenation: $F(\alpha,\beta) = \alpha^\frown\beta$, and that the "multiplication" of category symbols, $A/B \times B = A$, should be the only consistency check necessary. Not many of Montague's rules measure up to this goal, and this has lead to much criticism from the linguistic side. However, the work inspired by Lambeks contribution seems to be more satisfactory as a syntactic analysis, and the reader should consult the collection W. Buszkowski et al. 1987 to form a more balanced opinion of categorial grammar as a theory of natural language syntax.

Before we turn to the second part of the Montague model we shall recall a few facts about logic. In *first order logic* we have model structures of the form

$$\mathcal{A} = \langle A, R_1, \ldots, R_i, \ldots \rangle$$

where A is a non-empty set of "individuals" and each R_i is a (set-theoretic) relation on A, i.e. $R_i \subseteq A^{n_i}$, where A^{n_i} is the n_i-fold cartesian product of A and n_i is the arity of the relation R_i. We assume that the reader is familiar with the standard first order languages and the proof theory where completeness is the fundamental property. Going beyond first order logic we have systems of higher order logic and various forms of intensional logics. In *intensional logic* the basic model structures are of the form

$$\mathcal{A} = \langle A, I \rangle$$

where A is a non-empty set of individuals and I is the set of "possible worlds". The interpretation of a predicate P of the language is a function

$$(P)_{\mathcal{A}} \in \mathrm{Fnc}[I, A^{n_P}]$$

from possible worlds to relations on A, n_P being the arity of the predicate P. We remind the reader that Fnc[X, Y] is the set of all functions from X to Y. The reader should note that intensionality on this account is a kind of "parametrized extensionality"; we shall return to this point below.

In *higher order logic* the basic domains are function spaces. A function space has a certain type and the system TYP of *types* is defined inductively by

1. $e, t \in TYP$
2. if $a, b \in TYP$, then $\langle a, b\rangle \in TYP$.

Domains are labeled by types in the following way

1. $D_e = A$
2. $D_t = \{0, 1\}$,

where A is a non-empty set of individuals and D_t is the set of truth-values,

3. $D_{\langle a,b\rangle} = Fnc[D_a, D_b]$.

To make the connection with first-order logic we see that $D_{\langle e,t\rangle} = Fnc[A, \{0,1\}]$ corresponds to the set of subsets of A, i.e. to the set of "properties" on A. Binary relations on A correspond to functions in $D_{\langle e,\langle e,t\rangle\rangle}$.

The language of higher-order logic is based on *application* and *abstraction*. We give a brief description: For each $a \in TYP$ we have a class ME_a of meaningful or well-formed expressions of type a.

1. For each $a \in TYP$ there is a set Var_a of *variables* of type a and a set of *constants* Con_a of type a; $Var_a \cup Con_a \subseteq ME_a$.
2. *Application*: If $\phi \in ME_{\langle a,b\rangle}$ and $\psi \in ME_a$, then $\phi(\psi) \in ME_b$.
3. *Abstraction*: If $\phi \in ME_b$ and $u \in Var_a$, then $\lambda u.\phi \in ME_{\langle a,b\rangle}$.
4. In addition we have the standard rules for propositional connectives and quantifiers.

Application and abstraction are connected through the important rule of *λ-conversion*:

$$(\lambda u.\phi)(\psi) = \phi[{}^{u}/_{\psi}]$$

where $\phi[{}^{u}/_{\psi}]$ comes from ϕ by replacing free occurrences of u in ϕ by ψ.

A *model* for the set ME of meaningful expressions is a pair

$$\mathcal{A} = \langle A, F\rangle$$

where A is a non-empty set and F is a map defined on the expressions of ME. Given A we generate the domains D_a, $a \in$ TYP; we require of the map F that if $\phi \in Con_a$ then $F(\phi) \in D_a$.

Further, if $F(\phi)$ and $F(\psi)$ are defined and ϕ and ψ are of the appropriate types, then

$$F(\phi(\psi)) = F(\phi)(F(\psi)),$$

where we on the right-hand side of the equality have ordinary functional application or evaluation. To interpret λ-abstraction we use a standard trick: Let $\mathcal{A} = \langle A, F \rangle$ be a model for ME. Extend ME to a language ME($\mathcal{A}$) by adding new constants c_h for each $h \in D_a$ and $a \in$ TYP. Extend F to ME($\mathcal{A}$) by setting $F(c_h) = h$. We then define

$$F(\lambda u.\phi)(h) = F(\phi[^u/_{c_h}]).$$

From this the rest of the semantics of ME is determined in the usual way.

We shall make another digression and add some words about *generalized quantifiers* before returning to the Montague model. The notion of generalized quantifiers will also be important in later parts of this lecture. The basic reference on this topic is Barwise and Cooper 1981; I pointed out in Fenstad 1979 that it was implicitly used by Montague in his PTQ paper to analyze general noun phrases.

Consider the following examples:

All men run	$\forall x[man(x) \rightarrow run(x)]$
A man runs	$\exists x[man(x) \wedge run(x)]$
John runs	$run(j)$

Let $\mathcal{A}$ be a first-order structure, $\mathcal{A} = \langle A, P_m, P_r, a_j \rangle$, where P_m interprets the predicate *man*, i.e. $(man)_{\mathcal{A}} = P_m$, P_r interprets *run*, and a_j interprets the constant j. We then have the following translations:

All men run	$P_m \subseteq P_r$
A man runs	$P_m \cap P_r \neq \emptyset$
John runs	$a_j \in P_r$

We see that in the model $\mathcal{A}$, *All* has an interpretation as a relation between subsets of A,

$$(All)_{\mathcal{A}}(P_m)(P_r) \text{ iff } P_m \subseteq P_r$$

Or, abstracting from the particular property of running, we can interpret the noun phrase *All men* in $\mathcal{A}$,

$$(All\ men)_{\mathcal{A}} = (All\ )_{\mathcal{A}}((men)_{\mathcal{A}}) = \{Y \subseteq A \mid (man)_{\mathcal{A}} \subseteq Y\}$$

If we also abstract from *men*, we get

$$(All\,)_{\mathcal{A}}(X) = \{Y \subseteq A \mid X \subseteq Y\}$$

In a similar way we get

$$(Some\,)_{\mathcal{A}}(X) = \{Y \subseteq A \mid X \cap Y \neq \emptyset\}$$

And, finally, we can interpret the proper noun *John* as

$$(John)_{\mathcal{A}} = \{Y \subseteq A \mid a_j \in Y\}$$

Thus relative to the model $\mathcal{A}$ *John* is nothing but the collection of properties that John has.

This may seem as an exercise in set-theoretic rewriting. But this change of perspective has proved to be very helpful. On the one side it has been useful in the analysis of general noun phrases, on the other side it has allowed us to study many non-logical quantifiers in simple extensions of first-order logic, see Barwise and Cooper 1981.

B. *Translation into a system of Higher-Order Logic.*

We shall now define the translation from **P** to ME. We first have a map f: CAT $\rightarrow$ TYP:

1. $f(e) = e$, $f(t) = t$
2. $f({}^{A}/_{B}) = f({}^{A}//_{B}) = \langle f(B), f(A)\rangle$.

Next a map g from a subset of the lexical base **B** to ME such that if $A \in$ CAT, $\alpha \in \mathbf{B}_A$ and $g(\alpha)$ is defined, then $g(\alpha) \in Con_{f(A)}$. The idea here is that g associates with elements of the *open* word classes suitable constants in ME.

Let us give a few examples:

(i) *run* $\in \mathbf{B}_{t/e}$: $f({}^{t}/_{e}) = \langle e, t\rangle$
$run' = g(run) \in Con_{\langle e,t\rangle}$

(ii) *man* $\in \mathbf{B}_{t//e}$: $f({}^{t}//_{e}) = \langle e, t\rangle$
$man' = g(man) \in Con_{\langle e,t\rangle}$

If $\mathcal{A} = \langle A, F\rangle$ is a model of ME we see that

$$(rrun'\,)_{\mathcal{A}} = F(run') \in \text{Fnc}[A, \{0,1\}]$$
$$(man'\,)_{\mathcal{A}} = F(man') \in \text{Fnc}[A, \{0,1\}]$$

i.e. both correspond to properties, i.e. subsets of the domain A.

Other items in **B** have special translations, e.g. *John* is translated as a generalized quantifier

$$John' = \lambda P.P(j),$$

where j is some suitable constant in Con_e. We should observe that the ME expression $\lambda P.P(j)$ in a model $\mathcal{A} = \langle A, F \rangle$ correspond to the set $\{Y \subseteq A \mid (j)_{\mathcal{A}} \in Y\}$.

Translation interacts with the syntactic rules according to the principle of compositionality, i.e. if F is either F_1, F_2 or F_3 then

$$(F(\alpha, \beta))' = \alpha'(\beta'),$$

where α and β are translated as α' and β', respectively.

Finally, if $\alpha \in \mathbf{P}_{CN}$ translates to α', then

$$(a/an\ \alpha)' = \lambda P.\exists x[\alpha'(x) \wedge P(x)]$$
$$(every\ \alpha)' = \lambda P.\forall x[\alpha'(x) \rightarrow P(x)]$$

We see once more that the generalized quantifier translation has been chosen.

This completes our presentation of the Montague model. Every piece has been brought together in a consistent whole. There is both a syntactic part and a semantic part and the two are connected in a precise and detailed manner. Let us look at two examples.

First consider the pair of sentences

John runs
A man runs

The generalized quantifier interpretation allows us at the same time to account for their syntactic similarity and their semantical differences.

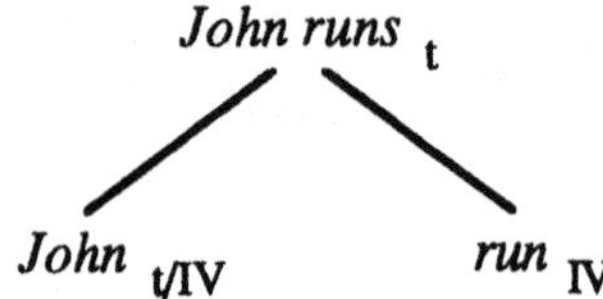

$$\begin{aligned}(John\ runs)' &= (John)'(run') \\ &= (\lambda P.P(j))(run') \\ &= run'(j)\end{aligned}$$

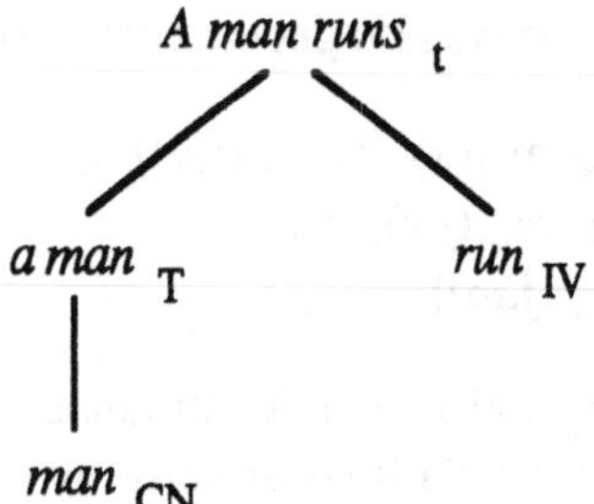

$$
\begin{aligned}
(\textit{A man runs})' &= (\textit{a man})'(\textit{run}') \\
&= (\lambda P.\exists x[\textit{man}'(x) \wedge P(x)])(\textit{run}') \\
&= \exists x[\textit{man}'(x) \wedge \textit{run}'(x)]
\end{aligned}
$$

The example is, of course, very simple. But it does come out right. Our next example is the sentence *John loves Mary.*

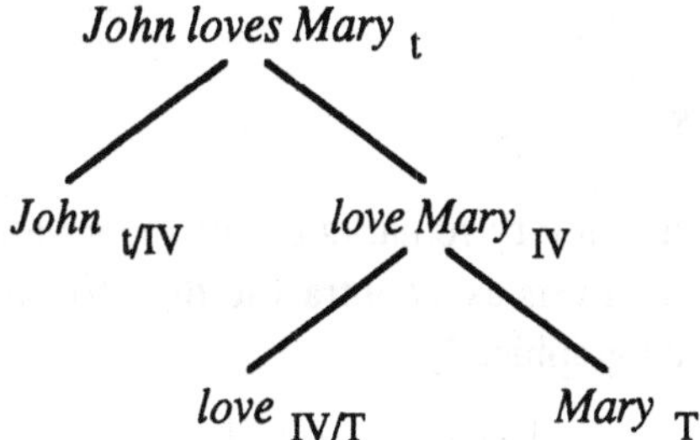

By our rules, the translation comes out as

$$(\textit{John loves Mary})' = \textit{love}'(\lambda Q.Q(m))(j)$$

We see that the translation of *love* is no longer a relation between individuals but a function of type <<e, t>, t>,<e, t>>. How does this square with our basic semantic intuitions?

There is an answer which some people have taken to be a success of the Montague theory. In ME we may have a primary relation $\textit{love}'_*$ of type <e, <e, t>>, i.e. a relation between individuals which is dictated by our intuition. Using abstraction we can in ME define a new constant *love′* by the equivalence

$$\textit{love}'(\mathcal{P})(x) \text{ iff } \mathcal{P}(\lambda y.\, \textit{love}'_*(x,y)),$$

where x and y are variables of type e and $\mathcal{P}$ a variable of type <<e, t>, t>. This lifted *love′* then has the correct type to match the syntactic analysis.

And evaluating the "lifted" relation we also get the correct semantics:

$$\begin{aligned} love'(\lambda Q.Q(m))(j) &= (\lambda Q.Q(m))(\lambda y.\, love'_*(j,y)) \\ &= (\lambda y.\, love'_*(j,y))(m) \\ &= love'_*(j,m)) \end{aligned}$$

But this is more a success of ingenuity than of substance. Higher order logic is based on a *constructionalism* where every object is constructed by abstraction from basic individuals. This is a severe limitation when we go beyond a knowledge world consisting of individuals and simple properties of individuals. To take one example, ***green*** is not abstracted from all things that are green; green is a *color* which belong to a separate *conceptual space.*

As remarked above the *intensionality* of the Montague system is nothing but a *parametrized extensionality*: Cancer is not a map from situations or or possible worlds to sets of individuals; this may give a correct *classification*, but it does not necessarily *explain*.

Attribute-value systems

We shall also add a few introductory remarks on attribute-value systems and present a simple example of an LFG-analysis as a contrast to the Montague model. An *attribute-value system* can be presented graphically as

$$\begin{bmatrix} ARG_1 & VAL_1 \\ \cdot & \cdot \\ \cdot & \cdot \\ \cdot & \cdot \\ ARG_n & VAL_n \end{bmatrix}$$

An attribute-value system is a finite function with domain $ARG_1, \ldots, ARG_n$ and with values $VAL_1, \ldots, VAL_n$. The values can either be atomic or themselves attribute-value systems.

The agreement problem *John walk / walks* was not treated very satisfactory by the Montague approach; the reader will recall that it was added verbally to the syntactic rule F_1. Let us see how this will be done using attribute-value systems and unification. With *John* we may have an associated attribute-value system:

(1) *John* $\quad \begin{bmatrix} \text{Agreement} & \begin{bmatrix} \text{Num} & \text{Sing} \\ \text{Pers} & \text{Third} \end{bmatrix} \end{bmatrix}$

Associated with *walks* and *walk* we have:

(2) *walks* $\quad \begin{bmatrix} \text{subj} & \begin{bmatrix} \text{Agreement} & \begin{bmatrix} \text{Num} & \text{Sing} \\ \text{Pers} & \text{Third} \end{bmatrix} \end{bmatrix} \end{bmatrix}$

(3) *walk* $\quad [\text{subj} \quad [\text{Agreement} \quad [\text{Num} \quad \text{Plural}\,]\;]\;]$

The interpretation of (2) says that *walks* looks for a subject with the agreement features Sing and Third. In a similar way *walk* looks for a subject with agreement feature Plural. We see that (1) and (2) are compatible, i.e. they "unify", whereas (1) and (3) fail to unify.

So far only motivation; we shall now describe a technique for turning this motivation into a precise technical theory. We shall adopt the formalism of LFG theory, see Bresnan and Kaplan 1982. A general introduction to unification-based approaches to grammar can be found in Shieber 1986. A more formal analysis of attribute-value systems can be found in the 1987 Stanford thesis by M. Johnson, *Attribute-Value Logic and the Theory of Grammar*.

Let us take as our example the sentence *John loves Mary*. This sentence can be generated by the following simple grammar:

S	→	NP	VP
		$(\uparrow \text{SUBJ}) = \downarrow$	$\uparrow = \downarrow$
VP	→	V	NP
			$(\uparrow \text{OBJ}) = \downarrow$

We have the following syntax tree:

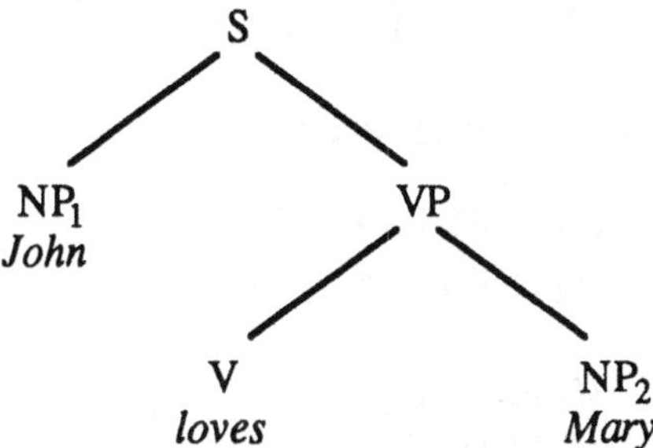

The idea is that we shall now be able to construct an attribute-value system from this syntax tree and from further information given in the lexicon. With the syntactic rules there are associated certain equations. They are of a general nature and contain "meta-variables", the arrows $\uparrow$ and $\downarrow$, which must be instantiated in each particular application. The procedure is as follows: Let f_1 be a function variable assigned to the top node S of the tree. With some of the other nodes of the tree there will be an associated equation derived from one of the syntactic rules, e.g. with the node NP_1 we have the equation $(\uparrow \text{SUBJ}) = \downarrow$. The $\uparrow$-arrow of this equation points to the mother of this node, i.e. the node S, and the $\downarrow$-arrow points to the node under consideration, i.e. the NP_1-node. We must then introduce a new variable f_2 to replace $\downarrow$, and we get the equation

NP_1: $\quad (f_1 \text{ SUBJ}) = f_2$

This equation means that f_1 is a function defined on a domain which at least includes the argument SUBJ.

In the same way we get the equations

VP: $f_1 = f_3$
NP$_2$: $(f_3 \text{ OBJ}) = f_4$

So far we have the following attribute-value system:

$$\begin{bmatrix} \text{SUBJ} & f_2 \\ \text{OBJ} & f_4 \end{bmatrix},$$

which tells us that the sentence expresses a relation with two arguments. What the relation and the arguments are will be read off the lexical information.

John	NP	$(\downarrow \text{PRED}) = John$ $(\downarrow \text{NUM}) = \text{SG}$
Mary	NP	$(\downarrow \text{PRED}) = Mary$ $(\downarrow \text{NUM}) = \text{SG}$
loves	V	$(\uparrow \text{PRED}) = love$ $(\uparrow \text{TENSE}) = \text{PRESENT}$ $(\uparrow \text{SUBJ NUM}) = \text{SG}$

The lexicon will contribute the following equations:

John:	$(f_2 \text{ PRED}) = John$ $(f_2 \text{ NUM}) = \text{SG}$
Mary:	$(f_4 \text{ PRED}) = Mary$ $(f_4 \text{ NUM}) = \text{SG}$
loves:	$(f_3 \text{ PRED}) = love$ $(f_3 \text{ TENSE}) = \text{PRESENT}$ $(f_3 \text{ SUBJ NUM}) = \text{SG}$

The $\uparrow$-arrow in the lexical equation $(\uparrow \text{PRED}) = John$ will be replaced by the function variable f_2 introduced at the node NP$_1$ to which the lexical item *John* is attached.

The combined set of equations imposes certain constraints on the "unknown" functions f_1, f_2 and f_3. When we seek a solution to this set of equations we shall always look for a minimal, consistent solution. *And this minimal, consistent solution is the attribute-value system associated with the given sentence.*

In our case we get:

$$\begin{bmatrix} \text{PRED} & \textit{love} \\ \text{SUBJ} & \begin{bmatrix} \text{PRED} & \textit{John} \\ \text{NUM} & \text{SG} \end{bmatrix} \\ \text{OBJ} & \begin{bmatrix} \text{PRED} & \textit{Mary} \\ \text{NUM} & \text{SG} \end{bmatrix} \\ \text{TENSE} & \text{PRESENT} \end{bmatrix}$$

In this case the various bits of information did unify, i.e. we had a consistent set of equations. The verb called for a subject with the agreement feature SG, i.e. (f_3 SUBJ NUM) = SG, which was precisely the agreement feature of the subject, (f_2 NUM) = SG.

Thus, through the system with constraint equations, we have a technique for implementing the "unification ideology". We also see that the attribute-value system has the "correct" relational form, but so far there is no explicit semantics.

Second Lecture: The Importance of Knowledge Representation

The world according to higher-order logic is constructed from a basic domain of individuals by λ-abstraction and function spaces techniques. This is not in itself ridiculous; the world of set-theory is constructed from the empty set by a similar kind of exercise. But applied to the "real" world it is an artificial exercise.

An alternative point of view would start from an array of many-sorted theories, from a "mixture" of different conceptual spaces. This is a point of view which has recently been forcefully argued by P. Gärdenfors, see his paper *Induction, Conceptual Spaces and AI* (Gärdenfors, 1987).

A *conceptual space* has a number of *quality dimensions*,

$$\mathcal{A} = \langle D_1, \ldots, D_n \rangle,$$

where each D_i is a separate quality, e.g. color, weight, space, time, temperature, mass, ... It is always assumed that each quality dimension D_i has some topological or metrical measure.

Take *color* as an example. We could either construct the color spaces as the standard "scientific theory", basing ourselves on properties such as wavelengths etc., or we could construct color as a three dimensional conceptual space; the three dimensions being

- *hue*
- *brightness*
- *saturation*,

where brightness and saturation are linear and hue circular (the color circle).

Taking topology seriously we also have a reasonable candidate for the notion of *natural kind*: A property P is a natural kind if it designates a *convex region* in a conceptual space; this would rule out the "grue" and "bleen" examples of N. Goodman. And associated with this notion of natural kind we have an obvious *induction principle*: Let P be a natural kind and let $a_1, \ldots, a_n$ be individuals observed to have the property P. Then every individual a in the convex hull of $\{a_1, \ldots, a_n\}$ also has the property P.

We shall not in these lectures elaborate further on the general theory of conceptual spaces. We would, however, like to take note of its relevance to the "naive physics" enterprise of AI (see Hayes 1984). We would also like to draw the readers attention to the renewed interest in many-sorted logic within AI, see A. Cohn 1987. Cohn's point of view is in many ways compatible with the approach taken here.

A theory of mass noun phrases

Color was one example of a conceptual space not constructed out of individuals, *mass* is another. The semantics of mass terms has been extensively studied in recent years, see Link 1983 and Lønning 1987. Here we give a very brief exposition of some themes from Lønning's approach.

His basic tool is a simple logic for the static theory of mass noun phrases.

LM: A language for mass noun phrases

The language has the usual propositional connectives: $\vee$, $\neg$. It has two operator symbols: - and $\cdot$ (to denote the boolean operations). And it has two logical determiners: *All* and *Some*.

In addition it has a non-empty set of constant symbols: a, b, c, ... And finally a (possibly empty) set of non-logical determiners: $D_1, D_2, \ldots$.

We have three kinds of expressions: *terms, quantifiers* and *formulas*.

1. Terms are defined inductively by the rules:
   i) Every constant symbol is a term
   ii) If s and t are terms, then so are (-t) and $(t\cdot s)$.

2. If D is a determiner and t a term, then D(t) is a quantifier.

3. Formulas are generated by the rules:
   i) If Q is a quantifier and t is a term, then Q(t) is a formula.
   ii) If p and q are formulas, then so are $(p \vee q)$ and $\neg p$.

The intended application is that constants should represent homogeneously referring nouns (*water, gold, coffee,...*), adjectives (*hot, blue, ...*), or verbs (*boiled, evaporated, disappeared, ...*). In addition to the logical determiners (*All, Some*) we could have a number of non-logical ones (*Much, Little, One kilo of, Less than two kilos of, ...*).

In this language we can represent the sentence *Much coffee disappeared* by the formula

$$Much(coffee)(disappeared)$$

where *Much*(*coffee*) is a generalized quantifier which combines with the term *disappeared* to produce the formula. A sentence such as *All hot water evaporated* would be represented by

$$All(hot \cdot water)(evaporated)$$

And a possible ambiguity in the sentence *Much coffee did not disappear* would be caught by the pair of formulas

$$\neg Much(coffee)(disappeared)$$
$$Much(coffee)(-disappeared)$$

Let us briefly indicate the semantics for this language. A *model*

$$\mathcal{A} = \langle \langle A, +, \times, ^{-}, 0, 1\rangle, [\cdot]\rangle$$

consists of a (not necessarily atomic) boolean algebra $\langle A, \ldots\rangle$ and an interpretation function $[\cdot]$ defined on the non-logical symbols such that

i) $[a] \in A$ for every constant a

ii) For each non-logical determiner D, [D] shall be a function which to every element $a \in A$ gives a subset $[D](a)$ of A. (For many purposes one may want to add the requirement that $b \in [D](a)$ iff $a \times b \in [D](a)$; the quantifier "lives on" $[D](a)$.)

We see that the interpretation in ii) is exactly the same type of interpretation – the generalized quantifier interpretation – that we discussed in connection with the Montague model. In the standard first-order case the model is based on a set of individuals, say I, and a property like *man* or *run* is interpreted as subsets of the domain I. Let $A = \wp(I)$ be the set of all subsets of I. Then A is an *atomic* boolean algebra. Now properties like *man* and *run* are elements of A, and the interpretation of the quantifier *All*(*man*), which we gave as

$$[All]([man]) = \{Y \subseteq I \mid [man] \subseteq Y\}$$

(using also in this case $[\cdot]$ to denote the interpretation), would now read as

$$[All]([man]) = \{b \in \wp(I) \mid [man] \leq b\},$$

where the inclusion relation $\subseteq$ on I is replaced by the less-than relation $\leq$ on $A = \wp(I)$.

We have been insisting on the technicalities of this point since the application of generalized quantifiers is by now almost as widespread as applications of standard first-order logic, see Barwise & Cooper 1981. The important thing to note in this example is that whereas in standard first-order logic everything is based on individuals, $A = \wp(I)$ is atomic, in the mass noun case A is not necessarily atomic, i.e. homogeneously referring mass nouns such as *water, gold, coffee*, have no *a priori* atomic parts. However, with a fixed language, with a fixed array of logical and non-logical determiners, there may be a limit to what we can describe, hence some interpretation of this particular language may have atomic parts. But that is a limitation of language, not of nature.

We return to the semantics of the logic LM. The model gives $[\cdot]$ on the non-logical symbols (satisfying i) and ii) above). We extend to all expressions of the language by the clauses:

iii) $[All](a) = \{b \in A \mid a \leq b\}$
$[Some](a) = \{b \in A \mid a \times b \neq 0\}$.

iv) $[-t] = \overline{[t]}$

v) $[D(t)] = [D]([t])$

vi) $[Q(t)] = \begin{cases} 1 & \text{if } [t] \in [Q] \\ 0 & \text{otherwise} \end{cases}$

vii) standard interpretation for $[\neg p]$ and $[p \vee q]$.

With this semantics the reader may verify the validity of the following assertions.

All water is water
All blue water is water
All blue water is blue

The reader may not be too impressed. But it is surprising to notice that several previous attempts to set up a logic for mass nouns have not been able to account for all of these examples in a "natural" way. Here they are reduced to the inclusions

$$[water] \leq [water]$$
$$[blue] \times [water] \leq [water]$$
$$[blue] \times [water] \leq [blue].$$

Can we account for the inference

Much(*water*)(*evaporated*)
All(*evaporated*)(*disappeared*)
∴ *Much*(*water*)(*disappeared*)

Here we have a non-logical quantifier Q = *Much*(*water*). Logic cannot in every case specify the meaning of the non-logical items, but logic can impose general constraints. A quantifier Q is said to be *monotone* with respect to a model $\mathcal{A}$ if for all a, b ∈ A the following holds: a ∈ [Q] and a ≤ b implies b ∈ [Q]. A determiner is called monotone if it always gives rise to monotone quantifiers. If we assume that *Much* is a monotone determiner, the inference above is valid. The premisses state that [*evaporated*] ∈ [*Much*(*water*)] and [*evaporated*] ≤ [*disappeared*] with respect to any model $\mathcal{A}$. Monotonicity of *Much* then gives the desired conclusion.

What we have presented is only a starting point for a more extensive analysis of mass noun phrases. We need a combined theory of *mass nouns*, *count nouns* and *amount terms*. We also need a theory which clearly shows the relationship between mass nouns and plurals, see again Lønning 1987. To complete the analysis one also needs a dynamic theory of mass terms.

We have presented this example here to show that logic is more than standard first-order logic. In fact, the primary *aim* of logic is the semantical analysis, the analysis of knowledge representations. The *tools* are the formal languages and the associated proof theories.

A logic of situations and partial information.

First-order logic, having a well-understood semantics and proof-theory, has been the paradigm for applications in AI. As argued above, the world view of first-order logic is too constrained for many "real" world applications; we may need a many-sorted structure where each sort is a conceptual space in its own right. In this section we shall add a further perspective. First-order logic is primarily a logic of complete and static information; after all it was developed as the logic of mathematical structures. But "real" world knowledge is seldom complete, e.g. in setting up a knowledge base we may at a given stage be able to record some "positive" facts and some "negative" facts, but in many cases our information is incomplete and we have to suspend judgement. Of course, at a later stage we may be in a position to decide further cases; in a sense knowledge "grows over time". But changes in the data base may force us to change logical inferences that we drew from the original one. We may thus be engaged in a complicated "updating" of information.

Standard first-order logic is not well suited to treat partial information. An atomic sentence $P(t_1, \ldots, t_n)$ is either true or false with respect to a model or data base. We shall in this section describe a semantics better suited to cope with problems concerning partiality.

Positive and negative facts. In standard model-theory we have a domain of *individuals* D and a set of *relations* over D. If r ∈ R is an n-ary relation we think of r as a set of ordered n-tuples over D, i.e. r is a subset of the cartesian product D^n. And the basic stipulation is that $a_1, \ldots, a_n \in D$ stand in the relation r iff $\langle a_1, \ldots, a_n \rangle \in r$, and that r does not hold of $a_1, \ldots, a_n$ iff $\langle a_1, \ldots, a_n \rangle \notin r$. Information is complete since either $\langle a_1, \ldots, a_n \rangle \in r$ or $\langle a_1, \ldots, a_n \rangle \notin r$.

In a situation of *partial information* we may not be able to assert either the *positive* fact that r holds of $a_1, \ldots, a_n$ or the *negative* fact that r does not hold of $a_1, \ldots, a_n$; the assertion may be undecided. It will prove convenient to change our basic format slightly and write

$$r, a_1, \ldots, a_n; 1$$

to assert that r holds of $a_1, \ldots, a_n$ and to write

$$r, a_1, \ldots, a_n; 0$$

to assert that r does not hold of $a_1, \ldots, a_n$. Since we may have neither $r, a_1, \ldots, a_n; 1$ nor $r, a_1, \ldots, a_n; 0$ in a given situation, *negation* may have either a weak or strong sense. The assertion

$$\text{not: } r, a_1, \ldots, a_n; 1$$

may mean that we have $r, a_1, \ldots, a_n; 0$ (*strong negation*) or it may mean that either the assertion is undefined, or if defined that $r, a_1, \ldots, a_n; 0$ (*weak negation*). In a situation of total information the distinction disappears.

Located facts: A fact may sometimes be *located* at a certain time and place. A medical examination takes place at a certain time and place and the resulting diagnosis makes sense only relative to that particular location. Some facts, e.g. mathematical statements, are better thought of as *unlocated.*

Thus in addition to individuals D and relations R we add the sort of *locations* L, and we think of an element $l \in L$ as a connected region of space-time. Thus we may locate our medical examination to the city of Oslo in the month of August 1987. The relation in this example may be the property of having some specified form of cancer, and the set of individuals may be some specific target group of the population, e.g. testing males between 50 - 55 of age for lung cancer. Note, that in this case it is not very intuitive to think of "lung cancer" as a subset of the male population between the age 50 - 55; compare our critical remarks against the "parametrized extensionality" of the standard systems.

Let r be an n-ary relation, l a location and $a_1, \ldots, a_n$ individuals. The format of a basic *located fact* is:

$$\text{at } l\text{: } r, a_1, \ldots, a_n; 1$$
$$\text{at } l\text{: } r, a_1, \ldots, a_n; 0$$

where the first expresses that at the location l the relation r holds of $a_1, \ldots, a_n$; the second expresses that it does not hold.

Situated facts: A knowledge base contains many facts, some located, some unlocated; some positive, some negative. We will use the word situation to describe this state of affairs. Thus a situation s determines a set of facts:

$$\text{in s: at l: r, } a_1, \ldots, a_n\text{; 1}$$
$$\text{in s: at l: r, } a_1, \ldots, a_n\text{; 0}$$

The first expresses that in the situation s at the location l, r holds of $a_1, \ldots, a_n$. We leave the reading of the second, as well as of the unlocated versions to the reader.

Situation semantics is grounded in a set of primitives

S	*situations*
L	*locations*
R	*relations*
D	*individuals*

We think of a situation as a kind of restricted, partial model which classify certain basic facts; beyond that we do not for our present purposes worry too much about "ontology", i.e. how situations are cut out of the phenomenological "wholeness" of the real world.

We assume that the primitives come with some structure. One minimal requirement is that each relation in R is provided with a specification of the number of argument slots or roles of that relation. For the purpose of these lectures we assume no structure on the set of situations and individuals, although we for both sorts could have had a relation of "being part of". The set L of locations is or represents connected regions of space-time and thus could be endowed with a rich geometric structure (e.g. if we would want to study shape and structure in connection with vision systems). To begin with, we shall be much more modest and assume that L comes endowed with two structural relations

$<$	*temporally precedes,*
$\circ$	*temporally overlaps,*

to account for a simple-minded analysis of past and present tenses.

Remark. Situation semantics was created by Barwise and Perry, see their book 1983. The theory has recently undergone many changes, we recommend the series of papers Barwise 1986 a, b, c for a more recent exposition. In these lectures we follow the approach of our book Fenstad et al. 1987.

The formal logic of situations

We shall give a brief introduction to some aspects of the *logic* of situations. The model theory of the logic is - as explained above - based on a multi-sorted structure

$$\mathcal{A} = \langle S, L, D, R, In \rangle$$

where In is the set of all tuples $\langle s, l, r, a_1, \ldots, a_n; i\rangle$ such that

$$\text{in } s: \text{at } l: r, a_1, \ldots, a_n; i,$$

$i = 0, 1$. In our book Fenstad et. al. 1987 we develop the mathematical study of this class of model structures; in particular, we prove several axiomatization theorems, thereby providing a complete inference mechanism for a multi-sorted logic based on a semantics of partial information.

The first step is to study *the logic of a fixed situation.* Let $s \in S$ and let

$$\mathcal{A}_s = \langle L, R, D; in_s\rangle,$$

where in_s consists of all tuples $<l, r, a_1, \ldots, a_n, i>$ such that $<s, l, r, a_1, \ldots, a_n, i> \in$ In.

The *language* L_3 of this model class is a two-sorted first-order language with atomic formulas

$$P(l, t_1, \ldots, t_n)$$
$$l_1 < l_2$$

where l, l_1 and l_2 are location variables or constants and $t_1, \ldots, t_n$ are individual variables or constants. The language L_3 will have both a *strong* negation $\neg$ and a *weak* negation $\sim$, as well as the standard propositional connectives $\wedge$, $\vee$ and quantifiers $\forall$, $\exists$.

Interpretation. Let ϕ be a formula of the language L_3 and let $\mathcal{A}$ be a full model structure. We shall use the notation

$$[\phi]^+_{\mathcal{A}}$$

to denote the set of all situations $s \in S$ which makes ϕ true, and

$$[\phi]^-_{\mathcal{A}}$$

to denote the set of all s which makes ϕ false.

Let us spell out some steps of the inductive definition of this satisfaction-relation. Let ϕ be an *atomic sentence*

$$P(l, t_1, \ldots, t_n)$$

of L_3. If $\mathcal{A}$ is a model of L_3, we have a map from constants of L_3 to the appropriate domains of the structure $\mathcal{A}$ which interprets these constants in $\mathcal{A}$. In particular, we have elements $P^{\mathcal{A}}, l^{\mathcal{A}}, a_1^{\mathcal{A}}, \ldots, a_n^{\mathcal{A}}$ of the appropriate sorts in $\mathcal{A}$ being the interpretations of P, l, a_1, …, a_n, respectively. Then for any $s \in S$

$$s \in [P(l, a_1, \ldots, a_n)]^+_{\mathcal{A}} \text{ iff } \langle s, l^{\mathcal{A}}, P^{\mathcal{A}}, a_1^{\mathcal{A}}, \ldots, a_n^{\mathcal{A}}, 1\rangle \in \text{In},$$
$$s \in [P(l, a_1, \ldots, a_n)]^-_{\mathcal{A}} \text{ iff } \langle s, l^{\mathcal{A}}, P^{\mathcal{A}}, a_1^{\mathcal{A}}, \ldots, a_1^{\mathcal{A}}, 0\rangle \in \text{In}.$$

For *atomic formulas* of the kind $l_1 \prec l_2$ we have

$$s \in [l_1 \prec l_2]^+_{\mathcal{A}} \text{ iff } l_1^{\mathcal{A}} \prec l_2^{\mathcal{A}},$$
$$s \in [l_1 \prec l_2]^-_{\mathcal{A}} \text{ iff not: } l_1^{\mathcal{A}} \prec l_2^{\mathcal{A}},$$

where the relation $\prec$ on the right hand side of the equivalence is the relation of temporal precedence on the set L of locations; note that there is no partiality involved with this relation.

For *strong negation* we have

$$s \in [\neg\phi]^+_{\mathcal{A}} \text{ iff } s \in [\phi]^-_{\mathcal{A}}$$
$$s \in [\neg\phi]^-_{\mathcal{A}} \text{ iff } s \in [\phi]^+_{\mathcal{A}},$$

and for weak negation we have

$$s \in [\sim\phi]^+_{\mathcal{A}} \text{ iff not: } s \in [\phi]^+_{\mathcal{A}}$$
$$s \in [\sim\phi]^-_{\mathcal{A}} \text{ iff } s \in [\phi]^+_{\mathcal{A}}.$$

The rest of the satisfaction relation (involving the propositional connectives $\wedge$, $\vee$ and the quantifiers $\forall$, $\exists$) is defined exactly as in standard first-order logic.

Let ϕ be a sentence of L_3 and $s \in S$:

$$\phi \text{ is } \textit{true} \text{ in } \mathcal{A}_s \text{ iff } s \in [\phi]^+_{\mathcal{A}}$$
$$\phi \text{ is } \textit{false} \text{ in } \mathcal{A}_s \text{ iff } s \in [\phi]^-_{\mathcal{A}}$$

A model $\mathcal{A}_s$ is called *consistent* if it satisfies the condition:

$$\langle l, r, a_1, \ldots, a_n, 1\rangle \in \text{in}_s \text{ implies } \langle l, r, a_1, \ldots, a_n, 0\rangle \notin \text{in}_s$$

If we drop this condition the model is called *generalized.*

There is nothing so far which excludes generalized models, but note that a generalized model $\mathcal{A}_s$ is consistent iff it satisfies the formula

$$\neg\phi \supset \sim\phi$$

for atomic ϕ, where $\phi \supset \psi$ stands for $\sim\phi \vee \psi$; This is easy to see:

$\neg P(l, a_1, \ldots, a_n) \supset \sim P(l, a_1, \ldots, a_n)$ is true in $\mathcal{A}_s$
iff $s \in [\sim\neg P(l, a_1, \ldots, a_n) \vee \sim P(l, a_1, \ldots, a_n)]^+_{\mathcal{A}}$
iff not: $s \in [P(l, a_1, \ldots, a_n)]^-_{\mathcal{A}}$ and $s \in [P(l, a_1, \ldots, a_n)]^+_{\mathcal{A}}$
iff not: $\langle l, P, a_1, \ldots, a_n, 0\rangle \in \text{in}_s$ and $\langle l, P, a_1, \ldots, a_n, 1\rangle \in \text{in}_s$.

We shall let L_3 also denote the logic of consistent models; due to partiality this is a three-valued logic. We shall let L_4 denote the logic of generalized models; because of the possibility of "inconsistent" situations this logic is four-valued. Note that an axiomatization of L_3 is obtained from an axiomatization of L_4 by adding the axiom

$$\neg\phi \supset {\sim}\phi, \quad \phi \text{ atomic.}$$

Finally, we let L_2 denote standard two-valued first-order logic.

The basic result about the logic L_3 is an *axiomatization* or *completeness theorem*. The proof follows from the standard pattern of constructing models for consistent sets of sentences. Since the logic of L_3 is obtained from the logic of L_4 by adding one new axiom scheme, it is trivial to construct consistent models for L_3 from generalized models of L_4. And models for L_4 are obtained by a L_4/L_2-reduction theorem, where we convert L_4-formulas to L_2-formulas by replacing strong negation pairs P, $\neg$P by new predicate symbols P^+, P^-. This will eliminate the strong negation symbol $\neg$ from formulas, since a normal form theorem for L_4 tells us that any formula ϕ can be replaced by a provably equivalent formula ψ in which $\neg$ occurs only with atomic parts (see Fenstad et al. 1987 for details).

Growth of knowledge

We mentioned above problems of non-monotonicity connected with partial information. When "knowledge grows", i.e. when more facts are decided, we may have to revise inferences drawn from a partial knowledge base. But we would like to know which inferences we may keep. We have the following characterization theorem.

A formula ϕ of L_3 is called 1-*persistent* if for any two models $\mathcal{A} = \langle L, R, D; in\rangle$ and $\mathcal{A}' = \langle L, R, D; in'\rangle$ where $in \subseteq in'$, if ϕ is true in $\mathcal{A}$ then ϕ is true in $\mathcal{A}'$. ϕ is called 0-*persistent* if $\neg\phi$ is 1-persistent, and it is called *persistent* if it is both 1- and 0-persistent.

Persistence is a model-theoretic notion. A formula ϕ of L_3 is called *pure* if it does not contain the weak negation symbol ~. Let $\phi \equiv \psi$ stand for $(\phi \supset \psi) \wedge (\psi \supset \phi)$, where $\phi \supset \psi$ abbreviates ${\sim}\phi \vee \psi$. Let $\phi \Leftrightarrow \psi$ stand for $(\phi \equiv \psi) \wedge (\neg\phi \equiv \neg\psi)$.

Theorem *ϕ is persistent iff there exists a pure ψ such that $\phi \Leftrightarrow \psi$ is provable in* L_3.

This result was proved by T. Langholm, who has later expanded on this theme in his Stanford thesis (1987), *Partiality, Truth and Persistence*. By standard interpolation techniques it is "easy" to find pure formulas ψ_1, ψ_2 such that both $\phi \equiv \psi_1$ and $\neg\phi \equiv \neg\psi_2$ are L_3-provable; the deep and difficult part is to find a common ψ.

Remark. *Non-monotonic reasoning* in a slightly different style has been a topic of broad interest in AI. The pioneering name her is J. McCarthy. A number of contributions can be found in a special issue of *Artificial Intelligence* vol. 13 (1980).

Other topics of relevance for our concerns is the renewed interest in *property theory* (see R. Turner 1987) and the use of *non-wellfounded set theory* to analyse so-called "circular" propositions, see Aczel 1988 and Barwise and Etchemendy 1987.

Third Lecture: Interpretations Versus Representations

How is the semantics of partial information to be connected to the analysis of natural languages? On intuitive grounds the sentence

John married Jane

as uttered at a location l_0 (the "discourse location") is true of a (described) situation s if there is some location l in s such that

in s: at l: *marry, John, Jane*; 1
$l < l_0$.

This is the idea; we shall analyse the *meaning* of a sentence ϕ as a relation between an utterance situation (which will determine l_0) and a described situation s.

But in order to implement this idea we must be able to compute some *representation* of ϕ which in some structured way exhibits the information "hidden" in the surface syntactic form.

In Montague grammar we used higher order intensional logic as a representational form. Here we will choose an attribute-value system which we will call a *situation schema* and which has a choice of primary attributes matching the primitives of situation semantics:

$$\begin{bmatrix} \text{REL} & — \\ \text{ARG.1} & — \\ \cdot & \cdot \\ \cdot & \cdot \\ \text{ARG.n} & — \\ \text{LOC} & — \\ \text{POL} & — \end{bmatrix}$$

Here the attributes REL, ARG.1, ..., ARG.n and LOC correspond to the primitives of *relations*, *individuals* and *locations*. POL, abbreviating *polarity*, takes either the value 1 or 0. The values in the schema can either be atomic or themselves complex attribute-value structures. The value of LOC is always complex.

Let us return to the sentence

John married Jane

We shall assign to this sentence the following situation schema, and we shall later give rules for how to compute the schema from syntactic form. Call the sentence ϕ_1, then SIT.ϕ_1, the situation schema associated to ϕ_1 will be:

$$\mathrm{SIT}.\phi_1 \qquad \begin{bmatrix} \mathrm{REL} & \textit{marry} \\ \mathrm{ARG.1} & [\mathrm{IND} \quad \textit{John}\ ] \\ \mathrm{ARG.2} & [\mathrm{IND} \quad \textit{Jane}\ ] \\ & \\ \mathrm{LOC} & \begin{bmatrix} \mathrm{IND} & \mathrm{IND.1} \\ & \\ \mathrm{COND}_{loc} & \begin{bmatrix} \mathrm{REL}_{loc} & \textit{precede} \\ \mathrm{ARG.1} & \mathrm{IND.1} \\ \mathrm{ARG.2} & \mathrm{IND.0} \end{bmatrix} \end{bmatrix} \\ & \\ \mathrm{POL} & 1 \end{bmatrix}$$

The interpretation of this schema is relative to an *utterance situation* u and a *described situation* s. The utterance situation decomposes into two parts

d	*discourse situation*
c	*the speakers connection*

The discourse situation contains information about who the speaker is, who the addressee is, the sentence uttered, the discourse location, and possibly further information. The speakers connection is used to determine the speakers meaning of lexical items.

A map g defined on the set of indeterminates of SIT.ϕ_1.LOC and with values in the set of locations L is called an *anchor* on SIT.ϕ_1.LOC relative to an utterance situation d,c if

$$g(\mathrm{IND.0}) = l_d$$
$$<, g(\mathrm{IND.1}), l_d; 1,$$

where l_d is the discourse location determined by d and $<$ is the relation of temporal precedence on L.

It is SIT.ϕ_1 that will be used to give the meaning of ϕ as a relation between the utterance situation d,c and the described situation s. We shall write this relation as

$$d,c[\mathrm{SIT}.\phi_1]s.$$

In the example this relation holds iff there exists an anchor g on SIT.ϕ_1.LOC relative to d,c such that

in s: at g(IND.1): c(*marry*), c(*John*), c(*Jane*); 1

Observe that the speaker's connection is a map defined on the (morphological) parts of the expression ϕ_1 and with values in the appropriate domains of the semantical model, i.e. c(*marry*) $\in$ R, c(*John*), c(*Jane*) $\in$ D. The latter means that we in this example have adopted a rather simple-minded treatment of names: The speaker's connection picks out a unique referent in the described situation.

Remark

In this simple case there is an obvious connection between the meaning relation d,c[SIT.ϕ_1]s and the satisfaction relation in the logic L_3.

Let (SIT.ϕ_1)* be the L_3-formula

$$\exists l(l < l_d \wedge \textit{marry}(l, \textit{John}, \textit{Jane})).$$

A model for L_3 is a structure $\mathcal{A}_s = \langle L, R, D; in_s \rangle$, for some $s \in S$. An utterance situation d,c can be used to give an interpretation of the non-logical symbols of the formula (SIT.ϕ_1)*: We let $d(l_d) = l_d$ be the discourse location in d and let c(*John*), c(*Jane*) $\in$ D, c(*marry*) $\in$ R be the interpretations of *John, Jane, marry*, respectively. Let us denote by $\langle \mathcal{A}_s, d, c \rangle$ the model $\mathcal{A}_s$ augmented by this interpretation. We then have the following equivalence:

$$d,c[\text{SIT}.\phi_1]s \ \text{ iff } \ \langle \mathcal{A}_s, d, c \rangle \models (\text{SIT}.\phi_1)^*.$$

This example can be turned into a systematic theory. However, we would not like to push this too far. This is a point of principle to which we will return below.

Complex roles

Roles can be described in more complex ways than by names with unique reference. Let ϕ_2 be the sentence

John married a girl

In this case our situation schema will be

$$\text{SIT}.\phi_2 \qquad \begin{bmatrix} \text{REL} & \textit{marry} \\ \text{ARG.1} & [\text{IND} \quad \textit{John}\,] \\ \text{ARG.2} & \begin{bmatrix} \text{IND} & \text{IND.1} \\ \text{SPEC} & \textit{A} \\ \text{COND} & \begin{bmatrix} \text{REL} & \textit{girl} \\ \text{ARG}'.1 & \text{IND.1} \\ \text{POL} & 1 \end{bmatrix} \end{bmatrix} \\ \text{LOC} & \text{---} \\ \text{POL} & 1 \end{bmatrix}$$

With the singular NP-reading we get

$$d,c[\text{SIT}.\phi_2]s$$

iff there exists an anchor g on SIT.ϕ_2.LOC relative to d,c and an extension $g' \supseteq g$ which anchors SIT.ϕ_2.ARG.2 in s, i.e.

in s: c(*girl*), g´(IND.1); 1

such that

in s: at g(IND.2): c(*marry*), c(*John*), g´(IND.1); 1

We have used an unlocated fact in the interpretation of ARG.2; this corresponds to the lack of tense marker in the subpart "a girl" of the sentence ϕ_2.

Let us look more closely at the format of ARG.2. The value of this attribute is really a notation for a generalized quantifier:

$\exists x\, [girl(x) \wedge \ldots]$
$\exists x \in girl\, [\ldots]$
Some(*girl*)(...),

where ARG.2.IND introduces the variable, ARG.2.SPEC introduces the determiner, and ARG.2.COND specifies the domain of variation of the quantifier.

It is possible, and for general theoretical purposes even desirable, to use the general quantifier reading for the interpretation. It works as follows:

From SIT.ϕ_2 we get two "fact schemata":

C_1: at IND.2: *marry*, *John*, IND.1; 1
C_2: *girl*, IND.1; 1

From fact schemata we introduce "abstracts" of the form

$\langle \text{IND.1} \mid C_1 \rangle$
$\langle \text{IND.1} \mid C_2 \rangle$.

In more complicated situations a fact schema may contain more indeterminates, hence determine different abstracts. Each abstract determines a "parametric set". We assume a referential reading of tense, hence we assume that there is an anchor g on SIT.ϕ_2.LOC relative to a discourse situation d,c. Then for each abstract and each specification d,c we have sets

$$_{d,c,s}X_{C_1} = \{a \mid d,c[C_1]s,a\} \quad \text{and} \quad _{d,c,s}X_{C_2} = \{a \mid d,c[C_2]s,a\}$$

with the natural reading of the defining conditions

d,c[C_1]s,a iff in s: at g(IND.2): c(*marry*), c(*John*), a; 1
and d,c[C_2]s,a iff in s: c(*girl*), a; 1.

From the SPEC of ARG.2 and the two abstracts we can form the "complex fact schema"

$$A(<\text{IND.1} \mid C_2>)(<\text{IND.1} \mid C_1>),$$

which is simply a notation for a generalized quantifier, and we have the interpretation

$$d,c[\text{SIT.}\phi_2]s$$

iff there exists an anchor g on SIT.ϕ_2.LOC relative to d,c such that

$$d,c[A(<\text{IND.1} \mid C_2>)(<\text{IND.1} \mid C_1>)]s,$$

i.e. iff

$${}_{d,c,s}X_{C_1} \cap {}_{d,c,s}X_{C_1} \neq \emptyset.$$

For complete details on this point, see Fenstad et al. 1987.

Resource situations and anaphoric reference

Let us make some brief remarks on the following pair of sentences:

ϕ_3: *The boy married Jane.*
ϕ_4: *The boy who married Jane loves her.*

For the first sentence we will compute the following schema:

$$\text{SIT.}\phi_3 \quad \begin{bmatrix} \text{REL} & \textit{marry} \\ \text{ARG.1} & \begin{bmatrix} \text{IND} & \text{IND.1} \\ \text{SPEC} & \textit{THE} \\ \text{COND} & \begin{bmatrix} \text{SIT} & \text{SIT.1} \\ \text{REL} & \textit{boy} \\ \text{ARG}'\text{.1} & \text{IND.1} \\ \text{POL} & 1 \end{bmatrix} \end{bmatrix} \\ \text{ARG.2} & [\text{IND} \quad \textit{Jane}\,] \\ \text{LOC} & — \\ \text{POL} & 1 \end{bmatrix}$$

We see that the COND of ARG.1 has been expanded with a new attribute SIT. In the interpretation of SIT.ϕ_3 the indeterminate SIT.1 will be anchored to some "resource situation", which may differ both from the discourse situation and the described situation, and which will be used to determine the domain of variation of the quantifier of ARG.1.

For ϕ_4 we will generate the following schema:

SIT.ϕ_4

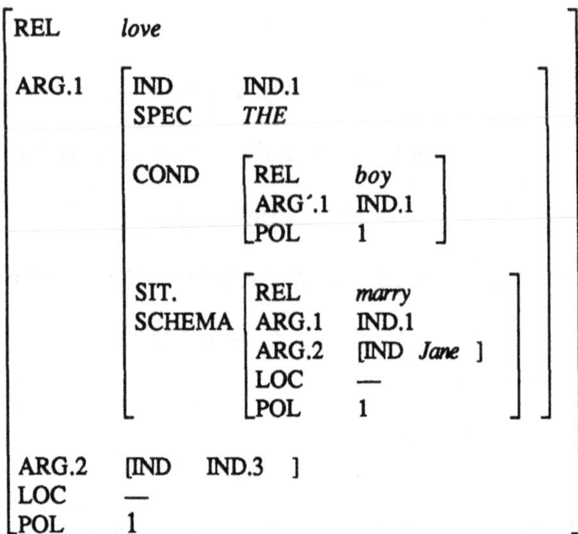

There are a number of comments to make. First we note that the value of ARG.1 has a new attribute SIT.SCHEMA to handle relative clauses.

Next we see that the schema has a "free indeterminate" IND.3 In many readings we would expect that *Jane* and *her* referred to the same individual. But how do we account for this sameness of reference? Indeterminates must be anchored, so we could have an anchor f on SIT.ϕ_4.ARG.2, and the sameness of reference would be recorded by the fact that f(IND.3) = c(*Jane*). But this is an added fact and would not count as a case of anaphoric linking. The latter case would require a further constraint equation

(ARG.1 SIT.SCHEMA ARG.2) = (ARG.2 IND)

It is not, however, obvious that we on syntactic grounds alone are justified in adding further constraints. It is not our purpose on this occasion to present a general theory of anaphoric reference. We would like to believe that the attribute-value formalism of situation schemata is flexible enough to accommodate various solutions.

On the formal theory of situation schemata

A situation schema is a complex attribute-value structure. The formal structure of such systems has recently been studied by M. Johnson in his Stanford thesis, *Attribute-Value Logic and the Theory of Grammar* (1987). He defines an attribute-value system as a triple $\mathcal{A} = \langle F, C, \delta \rangle$, where F is a set, C a subset of F, and δ a partial function from F×F → F such that δ is undefined on C×F; C is called the constant elements of $\mathcal{A}$. As a simple example let us take the following "truncated" version of SIT.ϕ_1:

REL	*marry*
ARG.1	[IND *John*]
ARG.2	[IND *Jane*]
POL	1

Here: $F = \{f_1, f_2, f_3, \text{REL}, \text{ARG.1}, \text{ARG.2}, \text{POL}, \text{IND}, 1, \textit{marry}, \textit{John}, \textit{Jane}\}$
$C = F - \{f_1, f_2, f_3\}$
$\delta(f_1, \text{REL}) = \textit{marry}$, $\delta(f_1, \text{ARG.1}) = f_2$, $\delta(f_1, \text{ARG.2}) = f_3$, $\delta(f_1, \text{POL}) = 1$,
$\delta(f_2, \text{IND}) = \textit{John}$,
$\delta(f_3, \text{IND}) = \textit{Jane}$.

We see that δ is to be thought of as functional application.

To study these structures he introduces a simple attribute-value language. This language has a set of variables *Var* and constants *Const* and in addition the truth-values *True*, *False*. *Terms* of the language are formed from the constants and variables by application $t_1(t_2)$.

If t_1 and t_2 are terms, then the equality $t_1 \approx t_2$ is a *wellformed formula*. Truth values are also wffs, and the class of wffs is closed under the propositional connectives $\sim A$, $A \vee B$, $A \wedge B$. If L(*Var*, *Const*) is an attribute-value language, we say that an attribute-value model $\mathcal{A} = \langle F, C, \delta \rangle$, augmented with a map $\phi: Var \rightarrow F$ and an injection $\chi: Const \rightarrow C$, is a model for L(*Var*, *Const*). A model provides *denotations* for terms of the language: $[c] = \chi(c)$, $c \in$ Const; $[x] = \phi(x)$, $x \in$ Var; and $[\![t_1(t_2)]\!] = \delta([t_1], [t_2])$ (the latter only if certain conditions of definability holds). Since we only have equality and propositional connectives, the definition of the *satisfaction relation* is entirely standard.

An axiomatization theorem is proved and the formal machinery is used to discuss various questions of decidability and undecidability in the theory of grammar; in particular, the algorithmic complexity of the parsing problem.

But perhaps the main interest in the formal language is that it can be used to formulate the constraint equations which allow us to generate the attribute-value structures from the syntax trees. Going back to the example *John married Jane*, it has a syntax tree

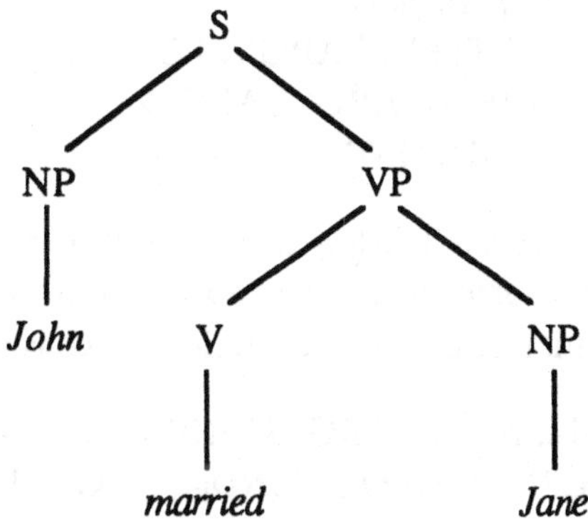

Here the basic syntax rules are

$$S \rightarrow \underset{(\uparrow \text{ARG.1}) = \downarrow}{NP} \quad \underset{\uparrow = \downarrow}{VP}$$

$$VP \rightarrow V \quad \underset{(\uparrow \text{ARG.2}) = \downarrow}{NP}$$

We can now quite simply formulate the constraint equations in our formal language, e.g. the equations associated with the S → NP VP rule are given by the formula: $x(\text{ARG.1}) \approx x_1 \wedge x \approx x_2$; the equation associated with the VP → V NP rule is given by the formula: $x(\text{ARG.2}) \approx x_1$. In the same way lexical constraint equations can be expressed by formulas of the language. And since these formulas are part of a well-understood logical system we have an efficient tool to study the formal theory of grammar, see Johnson 1987.

We shall not purse this general approach further in these lectures, but return to our specific kind of attribute-value structures, the *situation schemata*. In the class of all attribute-value structures the schemata so far discussed can be generated by the following set of rewriting rules:

SIT.SCHEMA → (SIT) REL^n ARG.1 … ARG.n LOC POL
SIT → *<situation indeterminate>*
REL^n → *<n-ary relation constant>*
ARG.i → {IND_e | IND (SPEC COND (SIT.SCHEMA)*)}
LOC → IND $COND_{loc}$
POL → {0 | 1}
IND_e → *<entity>*
IND → *<indeterminate>*
SPEC → *<quantifier>*
COND → (SIT) REL^1 ARG′.1 POL
$COND_{loc}$ → (REL_{loc} ARG′.1 ARG′.2
ARG′.i → {IND_e | IND}

In the examples discussed so far REL_{loc} will expand to one of the two relations of (temporally) overlapping and preceding. The "lexical expansions" are not included. To insure the correct identification of the roles, the following constraints are imposed

$$(\text{ARG.i.IND}) = (\text{ARG.i.COND.ARG}'\text{.1.IND})$$
$$(\text{LOC.IND}) = (\text{LOC.COND}_{loc}\text{.ARG}'\text{.1.IND})$$

From utterance to schema

To complete the picture we shall in one example describe how to compute the SIT.ϕ from an utterance ϕ. We shall use the LFG-formalism discussed above in connection with attribute-value systems. The general approach is explained in our book, Fenstad et al. 1987. We could also have used the more "logical approach" of Johnson 1987.

Let ϕ be the sentence *John married a girl*. The computation of SIT.ϕ from ϕ is arranged in two steps. First we assign a simple context-free phrase structure to ϕ, next we introduce a set of constraint equations which are partly associated with the nodes of the tree and partly with the lexical items. The *grammar* is as follows:

S	$\rightarrow$	NP $(\uparrow \text{ARG.1}) = \downarrow$	VP $\uparrow = \downarrow$
VP	$\rightarrow$	V	NP $(\uparrow \text{ARG.2}) = \downarrow$
NP	$\rightarrow$	DET	N
NP	$\rightarrow$	NPROP	

This gives the following constituent structure

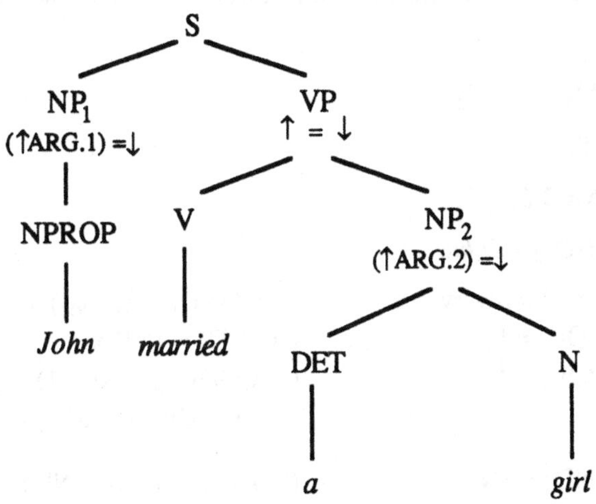

John	NPROP	$(\uparrow \mathrm{IND}_e) = \mathit{John}$
a	DET	$(\uparrow \mathrm{IND}) = \mathrm{IND.x}$ $(\uparrow \mathrm{COND}) = \downarrow$ $(\uparrow \mathrm{SPEC}) = A$ $(\downarrow \mathrm{ARG'.1}) = (\uparrow \mathrm{IND})$ $(\downarrow \mathrm{POL}) = 1$
girl	N	$(\uparrow \mathrm{COND\ REL}) = \mathit{girl}$
married	V	$(\uparrow \mathrm{REL}) = \mathit{marry}$ $(\uparrow \mathrm{LOC}) = \downarrow$ $(\uparrow \mathrm{POL}) = 1$ $(\downarrow \mathrm{IND}) = \mathrm{IND.x}$ $(\downarrow \mathrm{COND}_{loc}\ \mathrm{REL}_{loc}) = \mathit{precede}$ $(\downarrow \mathrm{COND}_{loc}\ \mathrm{ARG'.1}) = (\downarrow \mathrm{IND})$ $(\downarrow \mathrm{SUBJ\ NUM}) = \mathrm{IND.0}$

Using the techniques explained in the first lecture we get the following set of constraint equations:

NP_1:	$(f_1\ \mathrm{ARG.1}) = f_2$	
VP:	$f_1 = f_3$	
NP_2:	$(f_3\ \mathrm{ARG.2}) = f_4$	
John:	$(f_2\ \mathrm{IND}_e) = \mathit{John}$	
married:	$(f_3\ \mathrm{REL}) = \mathit{marry}$ $(f_3\ \mathrm{LOC}) = f_5$ $(f_3\ \mathrm{POL}) = 1$	$(f_5\ \mathrm{COND}_{loc}\ \mathrm{REL}_{loc}) = \mathit{precede}$ $(f_5\ \mathrm{IND}) = \mathrm{IND.x}$ $(f_5\ \mathrm{COND}_{loc}\ \mathrm{ARG'.1}) = (f_5\ \mathrm{IND})$ $(f_5\ \mathrm{COND}_{loc}\ \mathrm{ARG'.2}) = \mathrm{IND.0}$
a:	$(f_4\ \mathrm{IND}) = \mathrm{IND.1}$ $(f_4\ \mathrm{COND}) = f_6$ $(f_4\ \mathrm{SPEC}) = A$	$(f_6\ \mathrm{ARG'.1}) = (f_4\ \mathrm{IND})$ $(f_6\ \mathrm{POL}) = 1$
girl :	$(f_4\ \mathrm{COND\ REL}) = \mathit{girl}$	

We have a set of equations in the "unknown" functions $f_1, \ldots, f_6$. This set is consistent and *the minimal, consistent solution is precisely the situation schema* SIT.ϕ *associated with the sentence* ϕ.

Remark. We have in these lectures concentrated on theoretical issues. There have, however, been various pilot implementations. The grammar described in the book Fenstad et al. 1987 has been fully implemented at XEROX PARC using their LFG system. A fragment including prepositional phrases has been implemented at Oslo using the D-PATR format developed at SRI International, see Colban 1987. An analysis of direct questions has been implemented at Oslo in PROLOG using a Definite Clause Grammar to generate situation schemata, see Vestre 1987.

Toward an expanded formalism

The current format of a situation schema reflects what is computable from an utterance ϕ. However, more information may be necessary in order to spell out the meaning relation

$$u[SIT.\phi]s.$$

To evaluate a definite description one may need access to a "resource situation" in order to have the correct domain of interpretation of the quantifier. Questions of anaphoric reference may need further information from the utterance situation. And problems of quantifier scope cannot be decided from linguistic form alone.

One would like to expand the format of a situation schema to include this kind of information. This would give a schema more balanced between the utterance situation and the described situation. And it would be a prerequisite for a genuine theory of discourse.

Described situation	SIT.ϕ
Utterance situation, Background	[Quantifier scope, Resource situations, ...]

This is a format which we would like to have in a further extension of the theory. But it is not at all clear how the extra information, going beyond SIT.ϕ, is to be tamed and computed.

Remark. Ours is not the only – or first – analysis which stresses the importance of an intermediate representational form. Hans Kamp has over a number of years developed a *Discourse Representation Theory* (see e.g. Kamp 1981) which is closely related to our approach; see Sem 1987 for a comparative analysis.

Fourth Lecture: An Introduction to Some Applications

We shall in our last lecture touch on two large areas of application: *vision systems* and *question-answering systems*. Due to space and time limitations we shall only make some introductory remarks; full references will, however, be given.

Vision systems and natural language interfaces

A number of good reasons can be given for having a natural language access to vision systems.

(i) *A cognitive science perspective*: In this we aim for a computational theory of the interaction between natural language and vision.

(ii) *An artificial intelligence perspective*: Natural language as an efficient means to make the results of an image sequence analysis process accessible to humans.

These perspectives has guided the construction of the VITRA (Visual Translator) systems developed by W. Wahlster and coworkers at Saarbrücken; see Wahlster 1987 and André et al.1987. The system has two parts, VITRA CITYTOUR and VITRA SOCCER. We shall make a few brief remarks on the VITRA CITYTOUR.

The *discourse domain* of this system can either be a map of a part of a city which includes trajectories of all moving objects (synthetic scene) or a traffic scene at a street crossing (real scene).

The *conversational setting* of CITYTOUR provides answers to natural language queries about spatial relations and recognized events (e. g. during a fictitious sightseeing tour). It is assumed that both dialogue partners are located inside the scene.

Spatial concepts are obviously crucial for this implementation. We have *locative use of prepositions* (The school is *between* the theatre and the church); *directional use of prepositions* (She went *to the left of* the theatre); *path prepositions* (She went *along* the park); and verbs like *turn off/into*, *stop* and *start off.*

Locative prepositional phrases. An analysis of *locative* prepositional phrases within the framework of these lectures has been given by Erik Colban; see Colban 1987. Following this analysis we argue that in a sentence

John ran to the school

our intuition tells us that the location is a curve tracing a trajectory in space-time that ends at the (location of) the school.

A sample grammar for implementing this intuition is the following system :

$$S \rightarrow \underset{(\uparrow \text{ARG.1}) = \downarrow}{NP} \quad \underset{\uparrow = \downarrow}{VP}$$

$$NP \rightarrow \{\, \text{Det N} \mid \text{NPROP} \,\}$$

$$VP \rightarrow V \quad \underset{(\uparrow \text{ARG.2}) = \downarrow}{(NP)} \quad \underset{\substack{(\uparrow \text{LOC COND}) = \downarrow \\ (\uparrow \text{LOC IND}) = (\downarrow \text{ARG.1})}}{(PP)}$$

$$PP \rightarrow P \quad \underset{(\uparrow \text{ARG.2}) = \downarrow}{NP}$$

Remark. This grammar can easily be extended to handle *oblique objects* and *adjuncts*, e.g.

John handed the book to Ann,
John sent a letter from Norway to France,

where the oblique object is seen as a constraint on an (unexpressed) argument of the verb.

Let ϕ be our sample sentence (*John ran to the school*):

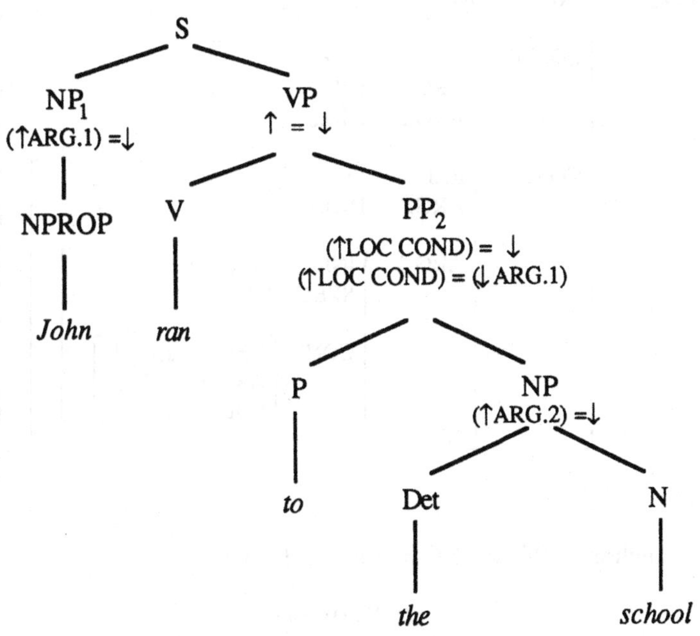

We have the following *lexical* information:

John	NPROP	(↑ IND) = *John*
the	Det	(↑ SPEC) = *THE*
school	N	(↑ IND) = IND.n (↑ COND REL) = *school* (↑ COND ARG.1) = (↑ IND) (↑ COND POL) = 1
ran	V	(↑ REL) = *run* (↑ LOC IND) = IND.n (↑ LOC CONDV REL) = *precede* (↑ LOC CONDV ARG.1) = (↑ LOC IND) (↑ LOC CONDV ARG.2) = IND.0 (↑ POL) = 1
to	P	(↑ REL) = *to* (↑ POL) = 1

Substituting for the meta-variables and solving in the standard way, we get the situation schema

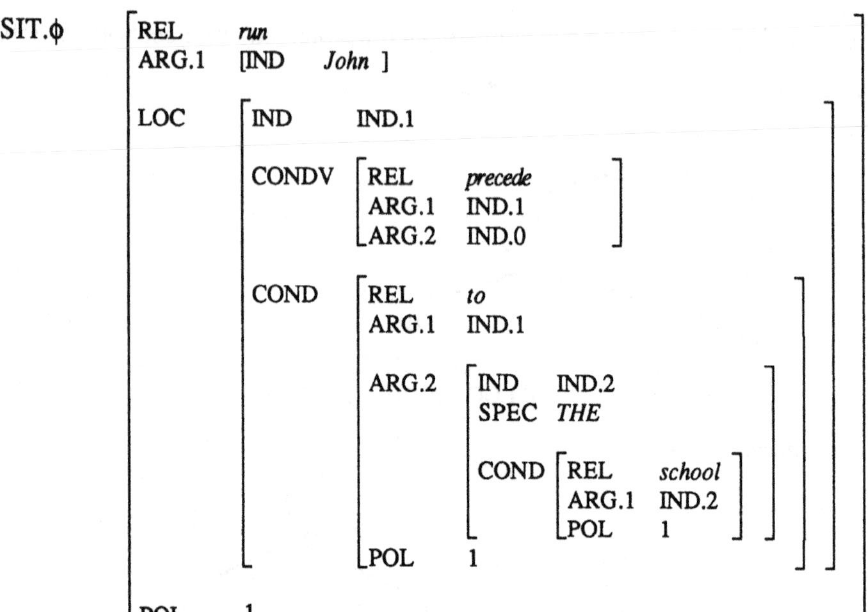

We let g be an anchor on SIT.ϕ.LOC relative to d,c, i.e.

$$g(\text{IND.0}) = l_d$$
$$<, g(\text{IND.1}), l_d; 1,$$

and let g´ be an anchor on SIT.ϕ.LOC.COND.ARG.2 in s, i.e. g´(IND.2) is the unique individual such that

in s: c(*school*), g´(IND.2); 1.

Then

d,c[SIT.ϕ]s

iff there is an anchor g on SIT.ϕ.LOC and an extension g´ ⊇ g which anchors SIT.ϕ.LOC and an extension g´ ⊇ g which anchors SIT.ϕ.LOC.COND.ARG.2 such that

in s: c(*to*), g(IND.1), g´(IND.2); 1
in s: at g(IND.1): c(*run*), c(*John*); 1

We think of g(IND.1) as a trajectory which stands in the *to*-relation (i.e. ends at) g´(IND.2), *the school*; this is specified by the interpretation c(*to*).

The aim now is to make the kind of linguistic analysis as exemplified above "available" to systems such as VITRA, and to use the logic developed for situational theory as an efficient inference mechanism for these systems.

Representations of direct questions

In the model-theoretic tradition the semantics of direct questions has always been an awkward topic. What is the *model-theoretic* meaning of a direct question? Various round-about answers have been tried; the semantics of a question is claimed to be the set of possible answers, each of which has a truth value. But one may "understand" a question and use it correctly in a communicative art without having to run through in ones mind the set of possible answers.

It seems more natural to suggest that a question is an *incomplete* situation schema which is to be treated as a query with respect to some intended knowledge base. This is an approach which has been pursued by E. Vestre in his Oslo thesis, Vestre 1987. I shall give a brief outline of his approach.

Remark. Some recent literature on questions within the linguistic and model-theoretic tradition is Engdahl 1986 and Groendijk and Stokhof 1984. From the AI perspective we mention the CHAT-80 system of Warren and Pereira 1980 and the TEAM system of Grosz et al. 1987. In a certain sense Vestre tries in his thesis to fuse the two traditions.

Situation schemata for direct questions

A situation schema for the (Norwegian) question

Hvem løp?

(*who is running*) could look as follows:

$$\begin{bmatrix} \text{REL} & \textit{l{\o}pe} \\ \text{ARG.1} & \begin{bmatrix} \text{IND} & x \\ \text{SPEC} & \textit{WH} \\ \text{COND} & \begin{bmatrix} \text{REL} & \textit{person} \\ \text{ARG.1} & x \\ \text{POL} & 1 \end{bmatrix} \end{bmatrix} \\ \text{LOC} & \begin{bmatrix} \text{IND} & l \\ \text{COND} & \begin{bmatrix} \text{REL} & \textit{overlap} \\ \text{ARG.1} & l \\ \text{ARG.2} & l_0 \end{bmatrix} \end{bmatrix} \\ \text{POL} & 1 \end{bmatrix}$$

We see that ARG.1.SPEC has a value WH which partly indicates that the schema could be treated as a query, but which also can be given an existential quantifier interpretation.

A schema for the question

Til hvilken skole løp Per?

(*to which school ran Per*) could be of the form:

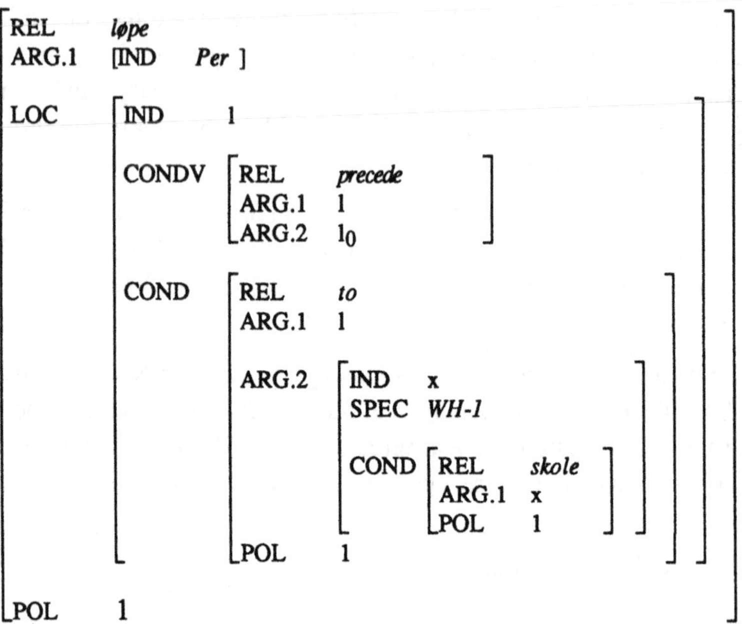

Here the LOC.COND.ARG.2.SPEC has the value WH-1 which indicates that we are asking a question about *the* school to which Per is running.

These schemata are an indication of the kind of representations that Vestre is discussing in his thesis (Vestre 1987). Challenging for the future is to discuss WHY-questions, but this will need a theory of conditional information.

The full system constructed by Vestre has a *main programme* for reading in and interpreting declarative sentences and direct questions. He uses a Definite Clause Grammar for the syntactic and morphological analysis. This is implemented in a reversible PROLOG-programme, i. e. we can generate the appropriate situation schema from a given sentence as well as generating a natural language sentence from a situation schema.

An important component of the system translates the situation schemata into a standard PROLOG-format. This is done by first translating SIT.ϕ into an L_3-formula (SIT.ϕ)*; see lecture two for some indications on this point. The final step in the translation builds upon the L_4/L_2-reduction theorem. To facilitate the further processing, questions are always reduced to a special *question normal form* and declarative sentences are translated to a special *quasi clausal form*. The upshot of these reduction procedures are that Vestre can use the standard PROLOG inference mechanisms to generate answers, i.e. to fill in the incomplete parts of the situation schema associated to the question. In an extended system one would aim for a direct implementation of a proof-procedure for the many-sorted partial logic.

What is a "good" answer?

This analysis of direct questions is part of our general approach to natural language systems. This means that we in the logic and model-theory associated to the representational form has *a tool for discussing general methodological issues*: What is a "good" answer; i.e. when is an answer *relevant*, when is it *informative*? These are questions Vestre 1987 starts to discuss using our general theoretical approach. Let us illustrate this discussion through a simple example.

Example. Let the "frame-situation" s be determined by the following facts:

in s:	*mann, Per*; 1	(*man*)
	mann, Kåre; 1	
	kvinne, Kari; 1	(*woman*)
	kvinne, Trine; 1	
	hund, Pluto; 1	(*dog*)
	politiker, Kari; 1	(*politician*)
	politiker, Per; 1	

We assume that there is given a discourse situation d, c such that l_d overlaps with l:

in s: at l:	*elske, Per, Kari*; 1	(*love*)
	elske, Per, Trine; 1	
	elske, Kåre, Trine; 1	
	elske, Trine, Kåre; 1	
	klappe, Per, Pluto; 1	(*pat*)

We also assume that a part $s_k \subseteq s$ is a "known situation":

in s_k:	*mann, Per*; 1	(*man*)
	kvinne, Trine; 1	
in s_k: at l:	*elske, Kåre, Trine*; 1	

Relevant answers. Let the question be

ϕ: *Hvilke menn elsker Trine?*

(*which men love Trine*). Notice that in the Norwegian version there is an ambiguity: Is Trine a "subject" or an "object"? One choice leads to the following

$$\text{SIT.}\phi \qquad \begin{bmatrix} \text{REL} & \textit{elske} \\ \text{ARG.1} & \begin{bmatrix} \text{IND} & y \\ \text{SPEC} & \textit{WH} \\ \text{COND} & \begin{bmatrix} \text{REL} & \textit{mann} \\ \text{ARG.1} & y \\ \text{POL} & 1 \end{bmatrix} \end{bmatrix} \\ \text{ARG.2} & [\text{IND} \quad \textit{Trine}\ ] \\ \text{LOC} & — \\ \text{POL} & 1 \end{bmatrix}$$

Let the following be offered as an answer:

ψ_1: *Per elsker Trine.*

This answer is *relevant*, because:

(a) it is true: d,c[SIT.ϕ]s;

(b) it is "about" the same relation as ϕ:
$$c(\text{SIT}.\psi_1.\text{REL}) = c(\text{SIT}.\phi.\text{REL})$$

(c) the "actors" in the answer are among the actors asked about:
$X_1 = [\text{WH}(\langle x \mid \text{in s: } \textit{mann}, x; 1\rangle)]$
$= \{M \subseteq D \mid \textit{Per} \in M \text{ or } \textit{Kåre} \in M\}$
$X_2 = [\textit{Trine}] = \{M \subseteq D \mid \textit{Trine} \in M\}$

We evaluate the NP's of the question, using the generalized quantifier approach and interpreting WH as existential quantifier.

For the answer we have:

$Y_1 = [\textit{Per}] = \{M \subseteq D \mid \textit{Per} \in M\}$
$Y_2 = [\textit{Trine}] = X_2$

We see that $Y_1 \subseteq X_1$ and $Y_2 \subseteq X_2$; i.e. the actors of the answer are among the actors asked about.

Let ψ_2 be the answer:

ψ_2: *Alle menn elsker Trine.*

(*all men love Trine*). This is also a relevant answer since (a) it is true in s; (b) it is about the same relation; and (c) $Y_1 \subseteq X_1$ and $Y_2 \subseteq X_2$ (in this case $Y_1 = \{M \subseteq D \mid \{\textit{Per}, \textit{Kåre}\} \subseteq M\}$). Also the answer

ψ_3: *En politiker elsker alle kvinner.*

(*a politician loves all women*) is relevant, as the reader may check by evaluating the appropriate NP's in s. Of course, in this case one may argue whether this should be counted as a relevant answer. However, if the answer is

ψ_4: *A dog loves Trine,*

this should not be counted as relevant, even if we assume that s is extended so as to make ψ_4 true, since

$$\begin{aligned} Y_1 &= [A(<x \mid \text{in s: } \mathit{mann}, x; 1 \wedge \text{ in s: } \mathit{hund}, x; 1>)] \\ &= \varnothing \end{aligned}$$

We should in addition to the inclusions $Y_i \subseteq X_i$ also require that each $Y_i \neq 0$.

We conclude with a brief remark on *informative answers*. Let the question once more be

ϕ: *Hvilke menn elsker Trine?*

And let SIT.ϕ be as above. A possible (and relevant) answer could be

ψ: *Per elsker Trine.*

This answer we would count as informative relative to the "known" situation s_k, since:

(a) Knowledge is added to s_k, i.e.: not: d,c[SIT.ϕ]s_k;

(b) Let C_1 and C_2 be the fact schemata

C_1: *mann*, x; 1

C_2: *elske*, x, *Trine*; 1

There is an $a \in D$, such that a = c(*Per*) and

d,c[C_1 and C_2]s, a

not: d,c[C_1 and C_2]s_k, a.

(Notice that in this simple example the interpretation of SIT.ϕ proceeds via the formula $WH(<x \mid C_1>)(<x \mid C_2>)$; in other and more complicated examples the description in (b) is only part of the "unraveling" of SIT.ϕ.

Our story is not complete. But we would like to believe that we have in Vestres thesis a felicitous beginning in the sense that we now have in our hands the necessary general and formal tools to carry the story on.

REFERENCES

Aczel P., 1988, *Non-Well-Founded Sets*, CSLI Lectures Notes no. 12, Stanford University.

André E., T. Rist and G. Herzog, 1987, *Generierung natürlichsprachlicher Äusserungen zur simultanen Beschreibung von zeitveränderlichen Systemen*, in Morik (ed.), *GWAI - 87, 11th German Workshop on Artificial Intelligence*, Springer, Berlin - Heidelberg.

Barwise J., 1986 a, *The Situation in Logic I*, in *Proceedings of the VII International Congress for Logic and Methodology*, Salzburg 1983, North - Holland, Amsterdam.

Barwise J., 1986 b, *The Situation in Logic II*, in Traugott, Ferguson, Reilly (eds.), *On Conditionals*, Cambridge University Press, Cambridge, UK.

Barwise J., 1986 c, *The Situation in Logic III*, in *Logic Colloquium '84*, North - Holland, Amsterdam.

Barwise and R. Cooper, 1981, *Generalized Quantifiers and Natural Languages*, Linguistics and Philosophy, vol. 4, 159 - 219.

Barwise J. and J. Etchemendy, 1987, *The Liar*, Basil Blackwell, Oxford.

Barwise J. and J. Perry, 1983, *Situations and Attitudes*, MIT Press, Cambridge, MA.

Bresnan J. (ed.), 1982, *The Mental Representation of Grammatical Relations*, MIT Press, Cambridge, MA.

Buszkowski W., W. Marciszewski and J. van Benthem, 1987, *Categorial Grammar*, J. Benjamins B. V., Amsterdam.

Chomsky N., 1957, *Syntactic Structures*, Mouton, Den Haag.

Cohn A. G., 1987, *A More Expressive Formulation of Many Sorted Logic*, J. Automated Reasoning, vol. 3, 113 - 200.

Colban E., 1987, *Prepositional Phrases in Situation Schemata*, Appendix A in Fenstad et al., 1987.

Colban E. and J. E. Fenstad, 1987, *Situations and Prepositional Phrases*, in *Proceedings of the European Chapter of the ACL*, Copenhagen.

Engdahl E., 1986, *Constituent Questions*, D. Reidel Publ. Comp., Dordrecht.

Fenstad J. E., 1979, *Models for Natural Languages*, in Hintikka et al. (eds.), *Essays on Mathematical and Philosophical Logic*, D. Reidel Publ. Comp., Dordrecht.

Fenstad J. E., P.-K. Halvorsen, T. Langholm and J. van Benthem, 1987, *Situations, Language and Logic*, D. Reidel Publ. Comp., Dordrecht.

Gazdar G., E. Klein, G. Pullum and I. Sag, 1985, *Generalized Phrase Structure Grammar*, Basil Blackwell, Oxford.

Groendijk J. and M. Stokhof, 1984, *On the Semantics of Questions and the Pragmatics of Answers*, Ph. D. thesis, University of Amsterdam.

Grosz B. J., D. E. Appelt, P.A. Martin and F. C. N. Pereira, 1987, *TEAM: An Experiment in the Design of Transportable Natural - Language Interfaces*, Artificial Intelligence, vol. 32, 173 - 243.

Gärdenfors P., 1987, *Induction, Conceptual Spaces and AI*, in *Proceedings of the Workshop on Inductive Reasoning*, Risø National Lab., Roskilde.

Halvorsen P.-K., 1987, *Computer Applications of Linguistic Theory*, in Newmeyer and Ubell (eds.), *Linguistics : The Cambridge Survey*, Cambridge University Press, Cambridge, UK.

Hayes P., 1985, *The Second Naive Physics Manifesto*, in Hobbs and Moore (eds.), *Formal Theories of the Commonsense World*, Ablex Publ. Comp.

Johnson M., 1987, *Atribute - Value Logic and the Theory of Grammar*, Ph. D. thesis, University of Stanford.

Kamp H., 1981, *A Theory of Truth and Semantic Representation*, in Groendijk et al. (eds.), *Formal Methods in the Study of Language*, Amsterdam.

Kay M., 1979, *Functional Grammar*, in *Proceedings of the Fifth Annual Meeting of the Berkely Linguistic Society*, University of California, Berkeley, CA.

Langholm T., 1987, *Partiality, Truth and Persistence*, Ph. D. thesis, University of Stanford.

Link G., 1983, *The Logical Analysis of Plurals and Mass Terms : A Lattice - Theoretical Approach*, in Bäuerle et al. (eds.), *Meaning, Use and Interpretation of Language*, W. de Gruyter, Berlin.

Lønning J. T., 1987, *Mass Terms and Quantification*, Linguistics and Philosophy, vol. 10, 1 - 52.

Montague R., 1974, *Formal Philosophy*, Yale University Press, New Haven, CT.

Pereira F.C.N. and S. M. Shieber, 1987, *Prolog and Natural - Language Analysis*, CSLI Lecture Notes no. 10, Stanford University.

Pereira F.C.N. and D.H.D. Warren, 1982, *An Efficient Easily Adaptable System for Interpreting Natural Language Queries*, Am.Journal of Computational Linguistics, vol.8.

Pollard C. and I. Sag, 1988, *An Information - Based Approach to Syntax and Semantics*, CSLI Lecture Notes no. 13, Stanford University.

Sells P., 1985, *Lectures on Contemporary Syntactic Theories*, CSLI Lecture Notes no. 3, Stanford University.

Sem H. F., 1988, *Discourse Representation Theory, Situation Schemata and Situation semantics : A Comparison*, in *Proceedings of the Nordic Linguistic Association*, Bergen.

Shieber S. M., 1986, *An Introduction to Unification - Based Approaches to Grammar*, CSLI Lecture Notes no. 4, Stanford University.

Turner R., 1987, *A Theory of Properties*, J.Symbolic Logic, vol. 52, 455 - 472.

Uszkoreit H., 1986, *Categorial Unification Grammar*, Report No. CSLI - 86 - 66, Stanford University.

Vestre E., 1987, *Representasjon av Direkte Spørsmål*, Cand. Scient. thesis, University of Oslo.

Wahlster W., 1987, *Ein Wort sagt mehr als 1000 Bilder*, Annales, Forchungsmagazin, vol. 1

Lecture Notes in Computer Science

Vol. 296: R. Janßen (Ed.), Trends in Computer Algebra. Proceedings, 1987. V, 197 pages. 1988.

Vol. 297: E.N. Houstis, T.S. Papatheodorou, C.D. Polychronopoulos (Eds.), Supercomputing. Proceedings, 1987. X, 1093 pages. 1988.

Vol. 298: M. Main, A. Melton, M. Mislove, D. Schmidt (Eds.), Mathematical Foundations of Programming Language Semantics. Proceedings, 1987. VIII, 637 pages. 1988.

Vol. 299: M. Dauchet, M. Nivat (Eds.), CAAP '88. Proceedings, 1988. VI, 304 pages. 1988.

Vol. 300: H. Ganzinger (Ed.), ESOP '88. Proceedings, 1988. VI, 381 pages. 1988.

Vol. 301: J. Kittler (Ed.), Pattern Recognition. Proceedings, 1988. VII, 668 pages. 1988.

Vol. 302: D.M. Yellin, Attribute Grammar Inversion and Source-to-source Translation. VIII, 176 pages. 1988.

Vol. 303: J.W. Schmidt, S. Ceri, M. Missikoff (Eds.), Advances in Database Technology – EDBT '88. X, 620 pages. 1988.

Vol. 304: W.L. Price, D. Chaum (Eds.), Advances in Cryptology – EUROCRYPT '87. Proceedings, 1987. VII, 314 pages. 1988.

Vol. 305: J. Biskup, J. Demetrovics, J. Paredaens, B. Thalheim (Eds.), MFDBS 87. Proceedings, 1987. V, 247 pages. 1988.

Vol. 306: M. Boscarol, L. Carlucci Aiello, G. Levi (Eds.), Foundations of Logic and Functional Programming. Proceedings, 1986. V, 218 pages. 1988.

Vol. 307: Th. Beth, M. Clausen (Eds.), Applicable Algebra, Error-Correcting Codes, Combinatorics and Computer Algebra. Proceedings, 1986. VI, 215 pages. 1988.

Vol. 308: S. Kaplan, J.-P. Jouannaud (Eds.), Conditional Term Rewriting Systems. Proceedings, 1987. VI, 278 pages. 1988.

Vol. 309: J. Nehmer (Ed.), Experiences with Distributed Systems. Proceedings, 1987. VI, 292 pages. 1988.

Vol. 310: E. Lusk, R. Overbeek (Eds.), 9th International Conference on Automated Deduction. Proceedings, 1988. X, 775 pages. 1988.

Vol. 311: G. Cohen, P. Godlewski (Eds.), Coding Theory and Applications 1986. Proceedings, 1986. XIV, 196 pages. 1988.

Vol. 312: J. van Leeuwen (Ed.), Distributed Algorithms 1987. Proceedings, 1987. VII, 430 pages. 1988.

Vol. 313: B. Bouchon, L. Saitta, R.R. Yager (Eds.), Uncertainty and Intelligent Systems. IPMU '88. Proceedings, 1988. VIII, 408 pages. 1988.

Vol. 314: H. Göttler, H.J. Schneider (Eds.), Graph-Theoretic Concepts in Computer Science. Proceedings, 1987. VI, 254 pages. 1988.

Vol. 315: K. Furukawa, H. Tanaka, T. Fujisaki (Eds.), Logic Programming '87. Proceedings, 1987. VI, 327 pages. 1988.

Vol. 316: C. Choffrut (Ed.), Automata Networks. Proceedings, 1986. VII, 125 pages. 1988.

Vol. 317: T. Lepistö, A. Salomaa (Eds.), Automata, Languages and Programming. Proceedings, 1988. XI, 741 pages. 1988.

Vol. 318: R. Karlsson, A. Lingas (Eds.), SWAT 88. Proceedings, 1988. VI, 262 pages. 1988.

Vol. 319: J.H. Reif (Ed.), VLSI Algorithms and Architectures – AWOC 88. Proceedings, 1988. X, 476 pages. 1988.

Vol. 320: A. Blaser (Ed.), Natural Language at the Computer. Proceedings, 1988. III, 176 pages. 1988.

Vol. 322: S. Gjessing, K. Nygaard (Eds.), ECOOP '88. European Conference on Object-Oriented Programming. Proceedings, 1988. VI, 410 pages. 1988.

Vol. 323: P. Deransart, M. Jourdan, B. Lorho, Attribute Grammars. IX, 232 pages. 1988.

Vol. 324: M.P. Chytil, L. Janiga, V. Koubek (Eds.), Mathematical Foundations of Computer Science 1988. Proceedings. IX, 562 pages. 1988.

Vol. 325: G. Brassard, Modern Cryptology. VI, 107 pages. 1988.

Vol. 326: M. Gyssens, J. Paredaens, D. Van Gucht (Eds.), ICDT '88. 2nd International Conference on Database Theory. Proceedings, 1988. VI, 409 pages. 1988.

Vol. 327: G.A. Ford (Ed.), Software Engineering Education. Proceedings, 1988. V, 207 pages. 1988.

Vol. 328: R. Bloomfield, L. Marshall, R. Jones (Eds.), VDM '88. VDM – The Way Ahead. Proceedings, 1988. IX, 499 pages. 1988.

Vol. 329: E. Börger, H. Kleine Büning, M.M. Richter (Eds.), CSL '87. 1st Workshop on Computer Science Logic. Proceedings, 1987. VI, 346 pages. 1988.

Vol. 330: C.G. Günther (Ed.), Advances in Cryptology – EUROCRYPT '88. Proceedings, 1988. XI, 473 pages. 1988.

Vol. 331: M. Joseph (Ed.), Formal Techniques in Real-Time and Fault-Tolerant Systems. Proceedings, 1988. VI, 229 pages. 1988.

Vol. 332: D. Sannella, A. Tarlecki (Eds.), Recent Trends in Data Type Specification. V, 259 pages. 1988.

Vol. 333: H. Noltemeier (Ed.), Computational Geometry and its Applications. Proceedings, 1988. VI, 252 pages. 1988.

Vol. 334: K.R. Dittrich (Ed.), Advances in Object-Oriented Database Systems. Proceedings, 1988. VII, 373 pages. 1988.

Vol. 335: F.A. Vogt (Ed.), CONCURRENCY 88. Proceedings, 1988. VI, 401 pages. 1988.

Vol. 337: O. Günther, Efficient Structures for Geometric Data Management. XI, 135 pages. 1988.

Vol. 338: K.V. Nori, S. Kumar (Eds.), Foundations of Software Technology and Theoretical Computer Science. Proceedings, 1988. IX, 520 pages. 1988.

Vol. 339: M. Rafanelli, J.C. Klensin, P. Svensson (Eds.), Statistical and Scientific Database Management. Proceedings, 1988. IX, 454 pages. 1988.

Vol. 340: G. Rozenberg (Ed.), Advances in Petri Nets 1988. VI, 439 pages. 1988.

Vol. 341: S. Bittanti (Ed.), Software Reliability Modelling and Identification. VII, 209 pages. 1988.

Vol. 342: G. Wolf, T. Legendi, U. Schendel (Eds.), Parcella '88. Proceedings, 1988. 380 pages. 1989.

Vol. 343: J. Grabowski, P. Lescanne, W. Wechler (Eds.), Algebraic and Logic Programming. Proceedings, 1988. 278 pages. 1988.

Vol. 344: J. van Leeuwen, Graph-Theoretic Concepts in Computer Science. Proceedings, 1988. VII, 459 pages. 1989.

Vol. 345: see inside front cover (LNAI).

Vol. 346: see inside front cover (LNAI).

Vol. 347: see inside front cover (LNAI).